Canada's Foreign & Security Policy

Soft and Hard Strategies of a Middle Power

Edited by

Nik Hynek & David Bosold

With a Foreword by

Stephen Clarkson

OXFORD

UNIVERSITY PRESS

OXFORD

UNIVERSITY PRESS

70 Wynford Drive, Don Mills, Ontario M3C 1J9

www.oupcanada.com

Oxford University Press is a department of the University of Oxford.
It furthers the University's objective of excellence in research, scholarship,
and education by publishing worldwide in

Oxford New York

Auckland Cape Town Dar es Salaam Hong Kong Karachi
Kuala Lumpur Madrid Melbourne Mexico City Nairobi
New Delhi Shanghai Taipei Toronto

With offices in

Argentina Austria Brazil Chile Czech Republic France Greece
Guatemala Hungary Italy Japan Poland Portugal Singapore
South Korea Switzerland Thailand Turkey Ukraine Vietnam

Oxford is a trade mark of Oxford University Press
in the UK and in certain other countries

Published in Canada by Oxford University Press

Copyright © Oxford University Press Canada 2010

The moral rights of the author have been asserted

Database right Oxford University Press (maker)

First Published 2010

Library and Archives Canada Cataloguing in Publication

Canada's foreign and security policy : soft and hard strategies of a middle power /
Nik Hynek, David Bosold, editors.

Includes bibliographical references and index.

ISBN 978-0-19-543169-8

1. Canada—Foreign relations—21st century. 2. National security—Canada. 3. Middle
powers. I. Hynek, Nikola II. Bosold, David

FC242.C368 2009   327.71009'0511   C2009-905490-6

Oxford University Press is committed to our environment. This book is printed on Forest
Stewardship Council certified paper, harvested from a responsibly managed forest.

Mixed Sources
Product group from well-managed
forests, and other controlled sources
www.fsc.org Cert no. SW-COC-002358
© 1996 Forest Stewardship Council

Printed and bound in Canada.

1 2 3 4 – 13 12 11 10

Contents

Foreword *Stephen Clarkson* v

Acknowledgements viii

Contributors x

Introduction: What Is Canadian Foreign and Security Policy? How Should We Study It? Why Does It Matter? *David Bosold and Nik Hynek* xii

Part I **Re-examining Middlepowerhood in Canada's Foreign and Security Policy** 1

Chapter 1 Whither the Middle-Power Identity? Transformations in the Canadian Foreign and Security Milieus *Tom Keating* 3

Chapter 2 'Middlepowerhood' and 'Middlepowermanship' in Canadian Foreign Policy *Kim Richard Nossal* 20

Chapter 3 Canada as a Middle, Model, or Civilian Power: What's in a Name? *David Bosold* 35

Part I: Questions for Critical Thought 56

Part II **Re-examining Canada's Soft Power** 59

Chapter 4 How 'Soft' Is Canada's Soft Power in the Field of Human Security? *Nik Hynek* 61

Chapter 5 The Transformation of Canada's Development Policy through the Security–Development Approach *Šárka Waisová* 81

Chapter 6 The Diplomacy of a Middle Power: Innovation and Its Limits *Jozef Bátora* 101

Chapter 7 Canadian Middle-Power Identity, Environmental Biopolitics, and Human Insecurity *Andrew Baldwin and Simon Dalby* 121

Chapter 8 Superpower, Middle Power, or Satellite? Canadian Energy and Environmental Policy *Gordon Laxer* 138

Part II: Questions for Critical Thought 162

Part III **Re-examining Canada's Hard Power** 167

Chapter 9 The Revolution in Military Affairs and the Dilemma of the Canadian Armed Forces *Wilfried von Bredow* 169

Chapter 10 A Security Community—'If You Can Keep It': Societal Security, Demography, and the North American Zone of Peace *David G. Haglund* 189

Chapter 11   Canada's Responses to Terrorism: Human Security at
Home?   *Kent Roach*   212

Chapter 12   Canada and the Atlantic Alliance in the Post-Cold War Era: More NATO
than NATO?   *Benjamin Zyla and Joel J. Sokolsky*   231

Chapter 13   Canada's Arctic Policy: Transcending the Middle-Power
Model?   *Petra Dolata-Kreutzkamp*   251

Part III: Questions for Critical Thought   276

Conclusion   *David Bosold and Nik Hynek*   280

Index   287

Foreword

Canadian foreign policy came of age in World War II when international relations were about solidarity with the Anglo-Saxon alliance in its apocalyptic battle against world domination by totalitarian enemies. It matured during the Cold War, which framed other great causes—the struggle against communism in the Sino–Soviet bloc; the construction of an international institutional architecture; the liberation and development of the ex-colonial world.

Within the comfort zone of fighting shoulder to shoulder with an over-whelmingly more powerful ally that happened to be the next-door neighbour to the south, the stellar foreign policy mandarins in Ottawa and the few international relations scholars across the country struggled to assert and define an identity for their profession's object. They knew Canada was not a great power—because its navy and air force, which had been the world's third and fourth largest after the destruction of the Axis forces, had been demobilized. But it was not an insignificant one, either. It played a noteworthy role in the foundation of the United Nations and the North Atlantic Treaty Organization, to which it contributed its armed forces, and was thought to punch above its weight in dozens of international institutions in which it was a willing and constructive participant.

When I was trying to come of age, these institutions were already in place. My college mates and I were excited by the much-hyped success of Canada's Secretary of State for External Affairs, Lester Pearson, in negotiating the first peacekeeping mission that brought an end to the catastrophic French/British invasion of Egypt in 1956. But by the mid-1960s, the gloss was coming off our idealism. Made-in-Canada napalm dropped by the US Air Force was incinerating women and children in Vietnamese villages, and the putatively anti-Communist war was generating social movements of protest both among black Americans, who were burning their ghettos, and in the ranks of middle-class America, whose young men were burning their draft cards. As a young academic, I found myself frequently milling around outside the

US consulate in Toronto, where vigils were held to protest the war in Vietnam while photographers took pictures of us for the CIA's files.

It was in this context that the former diplomat turned prolific analyst, John Holmes, coined the phrase that provides the unifying thread for this new collection. Still not at the top but certainly not at the bottom of the global power hierarchy, and still managing to maintain its membership in the most powerful states' best clubs, Canada, he wrote, was a 'middle' power that revelled in multilateralism, where it could bring its long experience in federal–provincial compromise to the world stage. Wet behind the ears though I was, I went into print to attack this concept for its fuzzy blandness, which took little account of Canada's satellitic relationship of weak-kneed servility to imperial America.

With the fall of the Berlin Wall in 1989 and the subsequent collapse of the Soviet bloc, with the triumphal entrenchment of neo-conservative economic rules in the World Trade Organization in 1995, with the new complexities arising from globalization's faster communications of information and capital, and with the economic rise of the Asian dragons, along with Brazil, India, and most of all China, Canadian foreign policy lost its bearings. As other countries rose, its relative standing in the world necessarily declined. Without their common enemy, its relationship with the United States became more competitive than collegial. Feeling unable to beat Washington's resurgent protectionism in the 1980s, the Progressive Conservative government of Prime Minister Brian Mulroney had joined the United States in a 'free trade' agreement that intensified its continental economic focus while abdicating significant federal and provincial policy levers.

Carrying the torch for the neo-conservative paradigm, the successor Liberal government of Prime Minister Jean Chrétien instituted radical budget cuts that added an endogenous pressure to Canada's foreign policy dilemma. Continuing reductions of both foreign aid funding and its diplomatic machinery wore down Ottawa's capacity for multilateral diplomacy. At the same time, analysts started bewailing Canada's global decline when they noted the consequences of these exogenous changes and endogenous retrenchments.

As Prime Minister Stephen Harper's minority government faces possible defeat and displacement by an internationalist Michael Ignatieff, it is an appropriate moment to revisit the long-standing debate about Canada's standing and role in the global community. This book's editors have focused their colleagues' contributions on contemporary Canada as a 'middle power', not in order to get into semantic hairsplitting over terminology but to provide interested readers in the classroom and the common room with 13 studies that are at once conservative and radical.

The book is conceptually conservative in the sense that it rejects the alternative labels (principal power? foremost power? model power? moral power?), considers efforts to 're-brand' Canadian foreign policy to be frivolous, and makes no new proposal for re-theorizing Canadian foreign policy. It challenges the declinist thesis by showing how significant Canadian contributions have been to NATO's military operations in the Balkans and Afghanistan since the end of the Cold War.

The thrust of these essays is also analytically conservative. Barring a few references to Canadian impotence vis-à-vis the United States, the authors consider foreign policy to be what Canada does overseas. Normatively speaking, they show how Canadian foreign policy has reflected a domestic bipartisan consensus in which Prime Minister Paul Martin continued in Jean Chrétien's footsteps and Stephen Harper trod past Martin's. Nor is there any visionary dreaming to be found in these pages. The analysts are professional and realistic, acknowledging also that an international consensus places Canada as increasingly an adjunct of Uncle Sam and, as a consequence, decreasingly relevant in multilateral matters.

At the same time, this book is radical, pointing out time and again the yawning gap between the rhetoric of Canada's politicians and Canadian citizens' self-image as unique, moral, model global citizens, on the one hand, and the disheartening reality of Canada's mediocre accomplishments in the recent past, on the other. Various chapters provide powerful critiques of Canada's international environmental irresponsibility by pushing the sale of asbestos on Third World countries, by sabotaging the Kyoto Accord on climate change, by failing to achieve a good stewardship of its energy riches. Chapters also document the institutional instability in Canada's foreign policy decision-making and the de-politicization of Canada's non-governmental organizations, which has turned NGOs into disciplined extensions of its foreign policy.

The role of the United States in determining Canadian foreign policy is not directly addressed, but Washington is the ghost haunting several of these chapters: the massive diversion of Canada's development aid from alleviating poverty to supporting a military operation in Afghanistan designed to curry favour in Washington; the use of immigration rather than criminal law to support the global war against terrorism and to mirror the US Patriot Act; and the shift of Canada's Arctic policy from multilateral circumpolar co-operation to a military-centred effort to buttress Ottawa's claim to sovereignty.

The editors have produced a collection of strong, easily absorbed chapters that reveal how Canada's standing in the global hierarchy remains in a state of middlepowerhood while its middlepowermanship leaves much to be desired in terms of its behaviour.

Stephen Clarkson
University of Toronto

Acknowledgements

This book had its origins in a series of formal and personal encounters in a number of places over the last four years. The editors met for the first time in Turku, Finland, in the summer of 2005. The Eighth Triennial Conference of the Nordic Association for Canadian Studies provided the perfect environment for a first exchange of their views on Canadian foreign and security policy and for discussions with leading academics in the field. During a Canadian Studies Seminar of the European Network for Canadian Studies held in Graz, Austria, a year later the idea for a broader research project was born. The Canada–Europe Award of the International Council for Canadian Studies (ICCS) eventually provided the financial support for research stays of several European contributors in Canada. In that respect, the help of David Haglund and Wilfried von Bredow in drafting the grant proposal and their continuous support in all stages of the project have been invaluable. The formal encounters of the editors during conferences and research stays were complemented by their equally important comradely meetings in Prague, Berlin, London, New York, and elsewhere.

During research stays in Canada in the spring and autumn of 2006 and autumn of 2007 we had the privilege to interview and talk to a number of people in DFAIT, DND, CIDA, and other governmental institutions. Notwithstanding their tight schedules, these officials granted us a considerable part of their time to share their insights with us. We cannot name all of them here but would like to express our sincere gratitude for their help and support. In addition, we would like to thank all the people from the non-governmental sector we met and who shared their views on governmental policies with us. Also in 2007, Charles Pentland generously invited us for a guest lecture to the Queen's University Centre for International Relations, where we had the chance to discuss various aspects of this book with some of the contributors. At Oxford University Press, Kate Skene and Kathryn West have been of tremendous help in supporting the project, pushing us to deliver the manuscript on time as well as in clarifying the overall structure of the volume. Phyllis Wilson was generous in her help in all matters related to the book contract and Richard Tallman, the copy editor, meticulously went through the entire manuscript. Five anonymous reviewers provided valuable comments on the structure and first outline of the book and three reviewers peer-reviewed all 13 chapters. We especially want to thank Dr Elizabeth Riddell-Dixon, University of Western Ontario, Dr Lasha Tchantouridzé, University of Manitoba, and Dr Reginald C. Stuart, Mount Saint Vincent University, for their work in reviewing the entire manuscript, which certainly improved the consistency of the whole volume and sharpened the arguments of the respective chapters. In general, we would like to thank all those who have made possible the publication of this book.

On a personal note, Nik would like to thank several scholars for sharpening his analytical skills, broadening and deepening his knowledge pool, and awakening his interest in Canada. Among those, the academic sponsorship of William Walters at Carleton University during Nik's research fellowship in 2006, made possible by winning the ICCS's Graduate Student Scholarship, was instrumental. The intellectual influence of Nikolas Rose of the London School of Economics and Political Science and Robert Jervis of Columbia University during Nik's visiting fellowships at these institutions has been tremendous. In addition, Mike Pugh of the University of Bradford and David Haglund of Queen's University have served as mentors and great sources of knowledge about peace studies and Canadian security, respectively. Last but certainly not least, Nik's father, Alois Hynek, Czech geographer and enthusiastic Canadianist, enkindled and further cultivated his son's interest in Canada as a country. The importance of their 1999 epic journey throughout Canada from Vancouver to Whitehorse to Halifax via countless universities, cities, towns, and villages will not be forgotten.

As for David, he would like to thank Alfred Pletsch for two years of excellent co-operation and crucial insights into the wider field of Canadian Studies during his time as a personal assistant when Pletsch was serving as the President of the Association for Canadian Studies in the German-speaking countries (GKS) from 2005 to 2007. Moreover, three former university teachers deserve to be mentioned here explicitly. The most crucial inspiration has been Wilfried von Bredow, whose seminars on Canada initiated an interest in the country's foreign policy when I was an undergraduate student in Germany. During studies at Université Laval in 2001 and 2002, the courses of Louis Bélanger and Gordon Mace were fundamental for a more profound grasp of the theoretical approaches to and issues in Canadian foreign policy. In addition, numerous research stays in Canada have been made possible by the International Council for Canadian Studies and by funding made available through DFAIT's Canadian Studies Program. The support of these institutions is hereby gratefully acknowledged.

Prague and Berlin, June 2009

Contributors

Jozef Bátora is Associate Professor at the Institute of European Studies and International Relations, Comenius University, Bratislava, Slovakia.

Andrew Baldwin is Lecturer in Human Geography, Departent of Geography, Durham University, United Kingdom.

David Bosold is Head of the International Forum on Strategic Thinking at the German Council on Foreign Relations, Berlin, Germany.

Wilfried von Bredow is Professor of International Relations, Institute of Political Science, University of Marburg, Germany.

Simon Dalby is Professor of Geography and Environmental Studies, Carleton University, Ottawa, Ontario, Canada.

Petra Dolata-Kreutzkamp is Lecturer at the Department of War Studies, King's College, London, United Kingdom.

David G. Haglund is Professor of Political Studies, Queen's University, Kingston, Ontario, Canada.

Nik Hynek is Research Fellow, Institute of International Relations, Prague, Czech Republic; Lecturer, Charles University and Metropolitan University, Prague; and Visiting Research Scholar, Saltzman Institute of War and Peace Studies, Columbia University, New York, USA.

Tom Keating is Professor in the Department of Political Science, University of Alberta, Edmonton, Alberta, Canada.

Gordon Laxer is Professor in the Department of Sociology, and Director of Parkland Institute, University of Alberta, Edmonton, Alberta, Canada.

Kim Richard Nossal is the Sir Edward Peacock Professor of International Relations, Queen's University, Kingston, Ontario, Canada.

Kent Roach holds the Prichard-Wilson Chair in Law and Public Policy at the Faculty of Law, University of Toronto, Toronto, Ontario, Canada, with cross-appointments in criminology and political science, and is Fellow of the Royal Society of Canada.

Joel J. Sokolsky is Principal of the Royal Military College, of Canada and Professor of Political Science, Kingston, Ontario, Canada.

Šárka Waisová is Head of the Department of International Relations and Political Science, University of West Bohemia, Pilsen, Czech Republic.

Ben Zyla is a Social Sciences and Humanities Research Council Canada post-doctoral research fellow at the Centre for International Relations, Queen's University, Kingston, Ontario, Canada.

What Is Canadian Foreign and Security Policy? How Should We Study It? Why Does It Matter?

David Bosold and Nik Hynek

In 2003, the London-based weekly *The Economist* wrote that 'a cautious case can be made that Canada is now rather cool.' The article went on to stress that 'Canadian writers and other cultural figures enjoy unprecedented international success' (*The Economist*, 2003: 15). The media echo in Canada was, unsurprisingly, positive and self-assured. The more or less subtle caveats—'cautious case', 'rather cool'—were easily brushed aside and left Canadian commentators gleaming with pride (CBC, 2003). This new mood of pride and self-confidence was also reflected in an advertisement campaign of a Canadian book retailer, which stated that 'the world needs more Canada'. Traces of Canada's sedimented societal and political discourses on the relative status of the country in the international system have, too, been present in the realm of Canadian foreign and security policy analysis (e.g., Granatstein, 2004; Kirton, 2007a; Cohen, 2003; James et al., 2006; von Bredow, 2003). This volume, however, attempts to prove neither whether Canada is, indeed, cool nor whether the world needs more Canada. Nor is it about rectifying the claim of the 2005 *International Policy Statement* that the essence of Canadian foreign and security policy (hereafter referred to as CanFSP[1]) is that of exerting a 'role of pride and influence in the world' (DFAIT, 2005). Yet, its content is strongly related to these claims since it scrutinizes in the following pages the ways in which Canadians have perceived themselves and their country's role in the world.

What Is Foreign and Security Policy?

The Link

Like any other book on Canada's international policies, this one is concerned with questions of foreign and security policy in general. The terms 'foreign policy' and 'security policy' are used in myriad ways and in combination. An American political theorist and philosopher, William Connolly (1993), following the work of Walter Gallie, has referred to such terms as 'essentially contested concepts'. In other words, considerable discrepancy exists in how various people think about these political terms. One conclusion we can draw from Connolly is that it would be a worthless endeavour to propose a single and appropriate definition for these terms. This does not mean, however, that we should not try our best to come as close to their delimitation as possible. In the context of this book, this means that our aim is to provide a conceptual analysis (rather than a denoting definition) of 'foreign and security policy' as well as understanding of the terms that can be considered key conceptual staples of the three sections that make up this book: middle power, soft power, and hard power.

In terms of the usage in this volume, 'foreign and security policy' highlights two crucial aspects. First, foreign policy refers to relations between and among states on the international level. They are formulated domestically (though often influenced by international dynamics) and subsequently pursued outside of a given country, as 'foreign' suggests. While a number of actors maintain relations worldwide, including non-governmental organizations (NGOs), multinational corporations (MNCs), and intergovernmental organizations like the United Nations (UN) and the North Atlantic Treaty Organization (NATO), none of these can conduct foreign policy in a strict sense. This is because the conduct of foreign policy proper falls into the domain of states (see Nossal, 1997: 4, 7–13). Until recently, this claim was repeatedly challenged. The argument put forward by critics of a narrow, state-centric understanding of foreign policy was that due to globalization and the growing complexity and plurality of international affairs, states lost power and influence to new actors in the global arena. It took the most severe economic downturn in over 70 years following the 2008 credit crunch to demonstrate that states have still retained considerable leverage to shape international affairs.

Foreign Policy

As a working definition, we can say that 'foreign policy' consists of those relations, strategies, and actions that a state authorizes, carries out directly, or outsources in its interactions with actors beyond its borders, mainly other states. A state's foreign policy is inevitably influenced by its internal (domestic) dimension, which features three factors:

1. A political community comprises a state's citizens, who form in some cases a single nation and in others a multi-national polity (the latter being the case of Canada as a consequence of Quebec and the French factor, and of Canada's many First Nations).

2. A territory demarcates the inside and outside of a state.

3. This territory has to be controlled effectively, i.e., through something Robert Jackson and Carl Rosberg (1982) call the presence of 'empirical sovereignty' beyond the terms of juridical sovereignty. As the second largest country in the world this represents more of a challenge for Canada than for small countries such as Luxembourg or Singapore. As Chapter 13 of this volume illustrates, this principle of effective control or governance is specifically crucial when it comes to Canada's territorial claims in the context of Arctic sovereignty.

States, characterized by the three features mentioned above, have been interacting with other actors, mostly states, for a period of more than three centuries. This so-called Westphalian state system was established in the wake of the peace treaties of 1648, signed in the Westphalian cities of Münster and Osnabrück (located in today's Germany) and has been in place ever since. What is important to note here is that the nature of this system of sovereign states has been conceived of as the main source of insecurity. Based on the image of an anarchic system, an idea held by the majority of international relations scholars, the realm of the international has been presented as a dangerous space that may eventually threaten the survival of a given state and its citizens.

Security Policy

International security policy, based in ambiguity and uncertainty about the intention of other states, can be defined as a complement to foreign policy that encompasses those strategies and actions aimed at protecting the territorial integrity of a state and the well-being of its citizens. At first glance, such a definition may appear too narrow. Contemporary definitions and theories of security do, however, include a more comprehensive understanding of the term. What is to be protected is not, according to these broader definitions, only the state, as suggested by the national security paradigm. Rather, a number of other referent points come into play. The last 10–15 years have seen a number of new referent objects, such as the global ecosystem (environmental security), the flow of hydrocarbon resources (energy security), and the individual in the face of daily violence and risk (human security). An analysis of Canada's security policy, therefore, covers aspects that have only recently become framed as security issues (Bosold and von Bredow, 2006). Environmental protection and efforts to protect Canadians against attacks from transnational terrorist networks are but two examples of such a broader security agenda. In addition, we need to consider the difference between security policy, which inevitably transcends borders in the twenty-first century, and defence policy. As the above discussion shows, the former does not necessarily depend on military capabilities, as is the case in defence policy. Our understanding of security policy in Canada's context thus differs from the commonly accepted delimitation offered by Dewitt and Leyton-Brown. While we agree that 'security policy [is] not simply foreign or defence policy', we simultaneously reject (mainly on empirical grounds) their view that security policy is merely 'a lens or filter through which foreign policy informs defence policy' (Dewitt and Leyton-Brown, 1995: 3).

Perception Matters

The reason for emphasizing the importance of perception is, indeed, a crucial one since approximately half of the contributors to the volume at hand—and both editors—are not Canadians. Theorizing about Canada's role in the world, assessing its record in terms of past diplomatic successes, and examining its current status and practices in global affairs has been very much a cross-cultural endeavour (see Haglund, 2009). That is mainly due to two reasons. First, for Canada as a country with a very specific collective identity (see Ruggie, 1993), the crucial aspect of its international involvement can be said to be defined by Ringmar's (1996: 64) dictum that you need to know who you are in order to know what you want. In other words, collective identities shape national interests rather than vice versa, though cases have defied this observation (perhaps most notably, the issue of the environment). Second, the foreign and security policy literature on Canada has been shaped almost exclusively by 'native' scholars who have studied the foreign and security policies of 'their' country. We do not believe—and have confirmed it again during our editorial work on this book— that an analyst's nationality or even his/her academic background ('national traditions') determines particular value judgements and research approaches, nor do such characteristics identify whose analysis is 'better', 'more precise', or simply 'right'. They do, however, highlight the importance of perception, specifically that of a collective identity formation and of a national self-image.

Most Canadians characterize their country as being a technologically advanced, liberal society that places a greater emphasis on social equality than its southern neighbour. While this characterization certainly holds water in terms of any potential comparative study of Canada and the United States along any of a number of dimensions (e.g., Adams 2003), the image of Canada *outside* the country is still significantly different. When people outside of Canada are asked about Canada, they will—most probably—not refer to the country's *golden era* in the 1950s, its peacekeeping tradition, or its image as a 'good international citizen'. Rather, they will rhapsodize about the splendid nature of its 'untouched' forests and lakes, especially in Canada's North,[2] or emphasize the reliance of Canada on the US for its decisions concerning CanFSP. That said, some of the contributions in this book will present a more international outlook on CanFSP. Even more importantly, regardless of contributors' origins and nationality, *all* chapters have called into question what we call the 'sedimented truths' of Canadian foreign and security policy that have been present in the existing literature, and a number of the contributors explore these assumed 'truths' through previously unknown or marginalized primary and secondary data.

Limits and Selectivity of the Presented Approach

Canada–US relations

Generally, we use the term 'Canadian foreign and security policy' to highlight both that security policy cannot be conceived of in the absence of foreign policy and that the former does not take precedence over the latter in the pages that follow. Nevertheless, a number of caveats are in order. These concern the limits of the book in comprehensively addressing three traditional topics of our subject: (1) Canada–US relations; (2) the policy-making process; and (3) classical peacekeeping. A preliminary assessment of Canada's security and related issues and concepts will allow us to briefly address these limits and simultaneously to present arguments as to why the above three topics are absent from the rest of the volume in the form of dedicated chapters. Predominantly, Canada has been considered a state whose security has not been seriously challenged by a potential attack, with the possible exception of the Soviet Union during the Cold War (see Keating, 2002) and, indeed, with the significant exception of a threat emanating from transnational terrorism (see Roach, Chapter 11, this volume). This assessment was nicely captured in Raoul Dandurand's bon mot, that Canada was 'a fire-proof house, far from inflammable materials'.

The relative absence of a threat has made Canada a country that is secure but simultaneously outward-looking and strongly engaged in global affairs. Its economic dependence on trade in general and exports in particular, as well as the proximity to the US, has had an enormous impact on the country and its domestic and external policies. While Canada–US foreign and security relations are undoubtedly important, they are not addressed in this book in a specific chapter; rather, elements of this relationship are dealt with under different issue areas. The principal reason is the thematic logic of the book, which focuses on Canada as a middle power and on its soft-power and hard-power capabilities and limitations. Geographical logic is subordinate to such a thematic approach. Thus, where Canada–US dynamics are important, such as within themes of societal security, economic security, terrorism, or environmental security, the bilateral relations are discussed.

The Foreign and Security Policy-Making Process

Similarly, Canada's foreign and security policy-making processes are not discussed in a specialized chapter. The policy-making process is indeed a crucial aspect of CanFSP. Notwithstanding its importance, an analysis of the foreign policy process that could be contained in a single chapter is more difficult today than it was in the past. A good illustration for this change is the size and complexity of organizational charts of the Department of Foreign Affairs (DFAIT) or the Department of National Defence (DND). For instance, comparing the *Annual Report* of the Department of External Affairs in 1977 with that of a more recent *Performance Report* by DFAIT indicates a remarkable increase in the density of communication, complexity of topics, and number of actors involved, as well as the new relations between previously discrete agendas. What is more, one needs to add the informal dimensions of policy-making that features meetings of policy-makers with representatives of think-tanks, businesses, non-governmental organizations (NGOs), and various pressure groups. Precisely because so many things have changed in the making of Canadian foreign and security policy, the strongest points we can therefore make are to highlight those aspects where policy-making has changed profoundly (Chapters 4, 5, and 6) and to emphasize that the rather crude and technocratic way of presenting the foreign policy process as a linear organizational chart, which has been the case in the past, is nowadays no longer appropriate.

As to the policy-making process in general, authoritative works address general trends in policy-making and offer a myriad of insights. Among those explicitly addressing issues of CanFSP, the works of Kim Richard Nossal et al., Brian Tomlin et al., and Roy Rempel, deserve special mention. The second part of Nossal, Roussel, and Paquin's *International Policy and Politics in Canada* (2010) remains the most accessible account of the Canadian foreign policy process. In addition, Tomlin, Hillmer, and Hampson's 2008 volume offers a detailed and up-to-date account of the foreign policy-making process by analyzing various policy fields with their policy streams model. Rempel has produced two instructive but less comprehensive accounts of the foreign policy-making process. In *Chatter Box* (2002) he nicely illustrates the changing role of the House of Commons and the decline in Parliament's influence on CanFSP in general. Although one does not need to share his conclusion, his more recent book, *Dreamland* (2006), takes issue with the impact the human security agenda and idealist posture have had on policy-making and offers good insights into the day-to-day politics of foreign policy-making. A more general overview on the changes in policy-making and the bureaucracy is further illuminating, especially in understanding the impact of administrative reform on policy-making. The results of the so-called New Public Management (NPM) or results-based management (RBM) have had a significant impact on the policy-making process and therefore on CanFSP (see Savoie, 1999, 2003, 2008; and for the area of CanFSP, Hynek, Chapter 4, this volume, and Hynek, 2008).

Peacekeeping

The issue of classical, or first-generation, peacekeeping also will not be addressed in a specific chapter in this volume. Although it can still be considered a beacon of Canadian collective identity, nicely captured by the portrayal of a peacekeeper with a blue beret on the back of the $10 bill, there are reasons for taking a different approach here. Unlike the case of Canada–US relations, which are not considered in isolation here due to the subordination of the geographical logic to the thematic one, an explanation of the omission of peacekeeping from the book has a different reason. Put plainly, the post-Cold War world has experienced a sharp drop in the significance of the first generation of peacekeeping as devised by Lester B. Pearson and Dag Hammarskjöld in light of the Suez crisis of 1956. The transformation of warfare and an associated major shift from heavily regulated interstate conflicts to intrastate (civil) conflicts, which accompanied the end of the Cold War, have limited the use of classical peacekeeping. UN-backed missions based on the notion of a neutral buffer with the aim of physically separating states in conflict have largely been superseded by new types of peace support operations. Post-Cold War peacekeeping is sometimes called the second generation of peacekeeping and included more ambitious peace-building activities. Among these, peace enforcement missions (sometimes—though problematically—dubbed as the third generation of peacekeeping) and peace-building missions have been the most important.

The decline of classical peacekeeping has been one of the systemic features of the post-Cold War period. Thus, criticisms of the lack of Canada's continued commitment to these missions have been misplaced as these studies do not take into account systemic transformations of the international security environment and thus of appropriate peace operations. Accounts of authors like Andrew Cohen (2003) and others who base their critique on a simple numeric count of peacekeepers under a UN mandate are deeply flawed because peacekeeping has been replaced by the above types of peace support missions. For instance, Canada's contribution to NATO's International Security Assistance Force (ISAF) mission and the US-led Operation Enduring Freedom in Afghanistan are not peacekeeping missions. While the former is a good example of a more benign peace-building project, the latter has been a so-called peace enforcement mission that entails heavy elements of military counterinsurgency. Crucial aspects of these new forms of complex peace-building and peace enforcement will be addressed in Chapters 5, 9, and 12. In doing so, the authors explicitly challenge two problematic arguments prevalent in the current Canadian discourse on peacekeeping. One is the 'declinist argument', according to which the decline in peacekeepers deployed to foreign theatres illustrates the growing irrelevance of Canada in the UN system and in NATO. The second point answers to those critics who continuously lament about the shape of the Canadian Forces (CF), and shows that an increase in military spending and the number of troops may eventually allow the Canadian government to avoid the slide to irrelevance.

Concepts in Foreign Policy Analysis

An analysis of Canadian foreign and security policy necessitates a conceptual framework. Quite ironically, despite the fact that foreign policy forms an important part of international relations (IR), theories of IR have tended to neglect foreign policy analysis as one its key approaches (Carlsnaes, 2002). For that reason, concepts and theoretical approaches for the study of foreign policy are still considerably more limited in numbers than theories of IR (Hudson, 2005). A nice illustration of this fact is the prominence of what has been referred to as the level-of-analysis problem in political science, an idea dating back to the 1960s.

Levels of Analysis

Foreign policy analysis has retained a focus on the classical distinction of three levels or images that make up the foreign policy playing field. Looking at the interplay of different levels, i.e., the national and international levels (Singer, 1961) or three 'images', i.e., the individual, the state, and the international system (Waltz, 1959), these scholars have tried to make sense of international relations by dissecting global affairs into horizontal analytic parts that can then be studied separately. While such studies can provide a number of crucial insights into foreign policy in general and into the politics of Canadian foreign policy in particular (Tomlin et al., 2008: 13–21; James et al., 2006: 7ff.), such an approach may also suffer from a practical explanatory potential as well as from a considerable bias in terms of its supposed objectivity. One of the indicators of the latter has been a quest for political causality, which has been deeply problematic at its best and completely flawed at its worst. In other words, a study of various levels will often—though not always—make the case that a specific foreign policy decision such as the Kosovo intervention has been *caused* by the structure of the international system (e.g., the collective security system of NATO, whose members, including Canada, had to act in the light of unacceptable human rights violations) and/or the nature of a political leader (e.g., the psychological makeup of a Canadian Prime Minister, which can be studied within the subfield of political psychology). Although we do not want to dismiss such arguments in their entirety, we argue that one needs to simultaneously consider conditions and assumptions under which such interpretations of historical events have come to be formulated. It is for these reasons that collectively (intersubjectively) held political ideas, dominant discourses, and political relationships based on constitutive relationships rather than causal ones need to be part of any meaningful foreign policy analysis.

National Interest

A further commonly used prism for the study of CanFSP has been the study of the national interest (Holloway, 2006; Rempel, 2006; Stairs et al., 2003).

Conceptually, the national interest, a key feature of the (neo)realist school of IR, is diametrically opposed to any idealist, liberal internationalist, and constructivist approaches to foreign policy. It is grounded in the belief that ethical considerations (idealism) or international expectations and factors (liberal internationalism and constructivism) play a minor role in foreign policy and that a policy favouring and securing the prosperity and integrity of the state is desirable and therefore represents the 'national interest'. Recent accounts of Canadian foreign policy such as Holloway's study of a 'national interest perspective' argue that there are limits to idealism and altruism. This does not mean, however, that the author deliberately questions all aspects of CanFSP associated with idealism, such as the projection of Canadian values and identity (Holloway, 2006: ch. 11). On the whole, disentangling national interest and idealism is difficult in the case of Canada. Unsurprisingly, a scholarly attempt to study CanFSP in light of idealism therefore proposes to include some elements of a Canadian national interest by referring to such a blend as 'pragmatic idealism', which is said to have shaped CanFSP since 1945 (Melakopides, 1998). To sum up, one can make the argument that the debate of realism versus idealism in a strict sense is rather to be found in more popular accounts of CanFSP, such as Michael Byers's *Intent for a Nation* (idealism) and Rempel's *Dreamland* (realism) (Byers, 2007; Rempel, 2006). As the chapters that follow clearly demonstrate, the relevance of this ideal-typical debate is significantly reduced once specific issues are examined.

Principal Power, Middle Power, or Satellite?

Yet another prominent avenue of research has been associated with the analysis of Canada's power and its status. Depending on one's preference, Canada has been characterized as a principal power (Dewitt and Kirton, 1983), foremost power (Eayrs, 1975), middle power (Holmes, 1970; Chapnick, 2005), or satellite (Cooper, 1997: 13–19; Kirton, 2007a: 59–70). Each of these approaches focuses on various aspects of CanFSP and/or issue areas and therefore inevitably comes to a different conclusion. Canada's military power, for example, is certainly less impressive than its economic power. Indeed, there are considerable problems with some of these approaches. How should one be able to judge the claim of the principal power perspective that G8 membership has been a means for the country to 'Canadianize the global order' (Kirton, 2007b: 299), let alone come to grips with what is meant by 'Canadianizing' in the first place? None of these approaches is in its classical form particularly suitable for most aspects that are addressed in this volume. Heuristically, it makes little sense to study topics tackled here through complex neo-realism (principal power), liberal internationalism (middle power), or peripheral dependence (satellite). Moreover, since the common understanding of these terms is one-dimensional by defining power as status or might (mainly done through looking at determinants and using different kinds of measurement approaches), the chapters in this volume will make the case for a revised conception of middle power.

A Revised Middle-Power Approach

Seen in this light, the middle-power category is a useful conceptual instrument to address the aforementioned issues because it has the capacity to contain three interrelated dimensions. First, a middle-power analysis highlights aspects that are measurable and therefore that facilitate a comparative analysis. This category includes data such as population size, territory, per capita income, military spending, size of the armed forces, etc. It makes possible, at least to a certain extent, an assessment of the rank and status of a country vis-à-vis other countries. Such an analysis appraises the first dimension of a middle power, that is, middlepowerhood. A second dimension refers to what is called middlepowermanship (see Nossal, Chapter 2, this volume). It does not include aspects that are static or change slowly over time but addresses the domain of international behaviour, diplomatic means, and relevant practices. Canadian middlepowermanship encompasses a wide spectrum ranging from a preference for multilateralism to consensus-building in international organizations and the support for innovative solutions to global problems in carved functional niches. Regarding diplomatic behaviour in general and the latter point in particular, it would be erroneous to assume, as some authors suggest, that middlepowermanship is simply about international practices (Neufeld and Whitworth, 1997: 203–4). All practices have domestic roots in terms of political preferences and broader political-economic settings (see Hynek, Chapter 4, this volume). If one adds identity as a third dimension to the middle-power approach by asking questions regarding Canada's foreign policy role and the perception of this role by citizens—both domestically and internationally—it becomes possible to investigate a number of issues in CanFSP without falling prey to the limitations of a classical middle-power approach—as well as the principal power and satellite approaches (Bratt and Kukucha, 2006: 5). Notwithstanding these recent criticisms of the middle-power category, this book therefore makes an effort to highlight its potential and the analytic value.

Outline of the Book

The book is organized in three parts. Part I provides a theoretical re-examination of middle power in CanFSP; Part II explores Canada's soft power and its link to the concept of middle power; and Part III considers Canada's employment of hard power, including how this has been linked to the concept of middle power. In total, the 13 chapters address the currently most relevant aspects of Canadian foreign and security policy. The overarching and updated middle-power framework allows for a critical perspective on Canada's historic diplomatic record. In addition, it makes possible an analysis of Canadian foreign policy instruments, the changed nature of the domestic foreign policy(-making) environment, and the perceptions of Canada's foreign and security policy inside and outside of Canada.

In Chapter 1, Tom Keating argues that CanFSP has been informed by a combination of a strong commitment to internationalism and a stark recognition and acceptance of limited power capabilities. Keating maintains that these elements have encouraged Canada to define a foreign and security policy rooted in an acceptance of a middle-power status and engaged through a multilateralist strategy that would enhance the country's attributes and influence while creating structures and processes to reinforce global order and a more stable security environment. In addition, the opening chapter explores the evolution of this orientation through a review and analysis of the discourse and practice of Canadian security policy in the 1940s when Canadian security policy for the post-war order was being established. Keating also examines the evolution of this policy since the 1990s, when the opportunity and the need appeared to reassess the sources of and priorities for Canadian foreign and security policy. Keating holds that in both the historical period and in recent years under the Liberal and Conservative governments, a combination of structural factors at the global, regional, and domestic levels, as well as principles and ideas in the domestic and external environments, have shaped the overall transformation of Canadian foreign and security policy.

Kim Richard Nossal, in Chapter 2, picks up on some of the points raised by Keating. Most importantly, the utility of the label 'middle power' in international politics is recognized as being in need of further operationalization. This is being pursued through analysis of the discourse—both political and academic—about Canadian foreign and security policy. Nossal shows that we need to distinguish between the notions of 'middlepowerhood' and 'middlepowermanship'. He specifically argues that the concept of 'middlepowerhood' does not tell the analyst much about what—and who—middle powers in global politics are. On the other hand, middlepowermanship suggests that middle powers can be identified by a particular and unique diplomatic style. Nossal arrives at the conclusion that the concept of 'middlepowermanship' has comparable problems as an analytical tool. To get beyond these pitfalls, he proposes a dual move. First, Hynek's conceptualization of a middle power as a pragmatic, empty container that can be—and has been—repeatedly refilled with different contents under different circumstances is embraced. Second, Nossal demonstrates that one needs to recover the original ironic meaning given to middlepowermanship by John W. Holmes, who coined the term in the 1960s.

Only then, Nossal contends, does the concept become useful for the case studies explored in this volume.

In Chapter 3, David Bosold addresses recent attempts to move away from the middle-power label by referring to Canada as a 'model power'. He begins with an overview of methodological problems of the existing middle power conceptualization. Three models of middle power are dealt: the hierarchical model, the normative model, and the behavioural model. Bosold argues that one needs to incorporate the process of collective identity formation and role theory into any productive middle-power conceptualization. He then shifts his attention to the fallacies of rebranding Canada's collective identity. The most discussed proponent of an image change has been the Canada25 initiative with its notion of 'model power'. There have already been several similar domestic endeavours to reconstitute Canada's collective identity (e.g., the Canada 21 Council). Efforts to diminish the importance of hard military capabilities in particular are identified as a common feature. Internationally, the attempt to replace 'middle power' with 'model power' has been influenced by similar discussions in Germany and the European Union as a whole. The centrepiece of these debates has been the notion of 'civilian power'. Here, too, the principal aim has been to portray the entities in question as benign, non-military actors. Consequently, Bosold applies previous insights concerning the role theory and investigates the differences between the domestic versus international perception of CanFSP and the country's role in the world. Finally, he maintains that the purely semantic 'rebranding' of CanFSP will actually not result in the desired outcomes and uses the findings to reclaim the middle-power role for Canada.

Part II explores Canada's soft power, including its link to the concept of middle power. Nik Hynek, in Chapter 4, poses a seemingly absurd question of how soft Canada's soft power has been. Hynek chooses the human security/development nexus (HSDN), i.e., the field with Canada's allegedly best soft-power record, to demonstrate that things are not at all as one is told by existing narratives. The chapter is divided into two parts: the first part looks into the mainstream accounts of Canada's soft power in HSDN and establishes its central arguments; the second part challenges this narrative and in an attempt to rectify its empirical flaws offers an alternative answer to the question posed. Two key arguments of the mainstream discourse are revealed as nodes around which the narrative has been produced. These are the assertion that Canada has undergone significant democratization of its foreign and security policy since the end of the Cold War due to its prominent international moral standing and close relation to the UN, and that the human security/development nexus has been at the forefront of the erosion of the government of Canada's power at the expense of civil society gaining more political clout. The alternative interpretation begins with a challenge to the causal arrow between the government and NGOs ('NGOs pressure the government and thus the change occurs'), arguing that in order to understand NGOs' involvement in human security and development, one needs to look at earlier government-initiated domestic transformations of the non-profit and voluntary sector and their subsequent extension to cover Canada's international development NGOs. In addition, the chapter shows how the realm of HSDN has not been increasingly democratized, but disciplined and depoliticized by the introduction of results-based management, the service delivery model, and new forms of contractualism.

The link between security and development is germane to the next chapter, too. In particular, Šárka Waisová in Chapter 5 examines the transformation of Canada's development policy through the governmental merger of security and development, and shows that this process has led, at least partially, to the militarization of development assistance. Waisová begins her analysis by looking at the context of the post-Cold War security environment, notably an increase in civil conflicts and humanitarian emergencies that brought with them new sources of insecurity and risks. In addition, a more prominent role for the state in the maintenance/restoration of security emerged. The author then argues that although the link between security and development has been central to the UN understanding since the early 1990s, it was not really until the terrorist attacks on the United States of 11 September 2001 and the ensuing global War on Terror that the new perspective found its way into Canada's development and security policies. Within the context of a more integrative approach focusing on security risks emanating from poor countries the interplay of poverty, insecurity, violent conflicts, and terrorism has been taken seriously. Waisová subsequently focuses on an assessment of the content and implementation of Canada's new strategies regarding development policy. Linkages among aid, security, and terrorism, as well as institutional and organizational consequences that have resulted from the penetration of the development sector by security ideas, are considered. Waisová looks at new trends and strategies associated with the shift to a Conservative government in Ottawa in 2006 and uses the case of Afghanistan to demonstrate just how things have changed in practice.

Chapter 6, by Jozef Bátora, analyzes the use of soft power in Canadian diplomacy. Bátora holds that in this core area of governmental activity, Canada has been highly innovative in recent decades in seeking to maintain its middle-power status through a diplomatic strategy based on an effective wielding of soft power. The chapter begins with an overview of the institutional context of Canadian diplomacy, namely its organizational structure, organizational culture, and relations with the domestic environment. Bátora then discusses two central elements in new diplomatic practices for wielding soft power— Canadian public diplomacy and reforms of the Canadian diplomatic apparatus supported by information technology (IT). The former includes a focus on branding Canada as an attractive country, co-operation with NGOs in foreign policy delivery, and new kinds of outreach activities where the Canadian public is being actively drawn into foreign policy-making through consultation processes. The latter element includes innovative uses of IT in support of diplomatic efforts, where the Canadian government has been a vanguard among the governments worldwide. Here, the focus is both on internal reforms at DFAIT and on broader use of the Internet in public consultations of foreign policy. The chapter then compares these features of Canada's soft-power strategy to the capabilities and practices of two other actors commonly perceived as effective wielders of soft power—the European Union and Norway. Overall, the chapter provides an assessment of the potential and limits of Canada's recent innovations in diplomatic practice.

The two following chapters examine the environment and energy, respectively. In Chapter 7, Andrew Baldwin and Simon Dalby study Canada's environmental foreign and security policy in order to argue that while Canada has taken a lead in international discussions of human security and played a high-profile role in facilitating the signing and eventual ratification of the Kyoto Accord, its environmental record is much less 'green' than its international image suggests. They show that environmental security, understood in terms of sustaining environments at home and abroad, has been a very low priority in CanFSP. Specifically, domestic environmental matters have been incorporated into a neo-liberal framework whereby managerial initiatives have cleaned up and regulated only some aspects of environmental affairs but not tackled the basic political economy of extraction and mass consumption. In addition, they indicate that with the accession of the Conservative federal government to power in 2006, climate change was simply denied. Simultaneously, the exploitation of the tar sands in Alberta and other fossil-fuel projects have moved ahead rapidly. While this has generated a backlash, these policies emphasize the continuing importance of the resource extraction sector (including asbestos, the mineral greatly harmful to human health) in the Canadian economy and the ambiguities in its political economy allowing progressive image-making to coincide with business-as-usual industrial production at the cost of policies that are genuinely green. The results of this Janus-like approach are, on the one hand, a particular vision of Canadians as progressive global citizens and a collection of policy statements that articulate virtuous identities in contrast to the supposedly worse American record, and, on the other, rapacious forms of economic life and modes of consumption supporting the Canadian polity.

Similarly, in Chapter 8, Gordon Laxer investigates the mismatch between grand rhetoric and deeds in the issue area of energy security. The chapter looks critically at Prime Minister Stephen Harper's claim that Canada is an 'emerging energy superpower' in light of the fact that Canada has no national energy strategy to replace high oil imports to eastern Canada from OPEC countries in times of international supply crises. As Laxer shows, Canada has no strategic petroleum reserves and is thus the only member of the International Energy Agency without such reserves. Laxer argues that Canadian policy has veered between two poles—the export of resources to the US for quick economic gain versus Canada-first policies emphasizing sovereignty and economic diversification. The first pole is also associated with a foreign policy based on short-term interest, while the second pole is usually associated with sentiment or long-term values as the basis of Canadian foreign policy. With the focus placed on security since 9/11, asserts Laxer, one would expect the playing field in Canada to tilt back to the second pole. But, while the US has proclaimed a national energy policy with goals of national security, energy independence, and self-sufficiency, Canadian governments have remained rooted to the strategy of export in the West/import in the East. This policy is evaluated in light of mounting climate disasters, peak oil, and the recent weakening of the US as an export market and an economic model. Laxer concludes by stating that energy crises highlight the need for Canadian governments to see energy through the lens of national security.

The chapters in Part III explore Canada's hard-power strategies and connect these strategies to the notion of a middle power. Chapter 9, by Wilfried von Bredow, analyzes the phenomenon of the revolution in military affairs against the background of the dilemma of the Canadian armed forces. Von Bredow begins by the assertion that armed forces are not only perceived as the 'backbone' of each country's security; they are also an indicator of the power a country can actually exert and under which conditions this power can be exerted. According to von Bredow, to understand the role of the Canadian Forces (CF) in Canadian foreign and security policy one needs to evaluate two factors. First, no serious analysis of recent military capabilities, of the structure of the military, and of training and strength within the CF can be conducted without paying attention to the transformation, or revolution, in military affairs. Second, it is imperative to consider the environment in which the military operates, that is, the need for preparing the CF for new types of missions. In addition, findings of military sociologists regarding the relationship of the CF and Canadian society are discussed. The chapter then examines the CF as being at a crossroads between a NATO framework emphasizing multilateral combat operations and the UN-led peacekeeping role strongly favoured by the Canadian society—a logistic and perceptual dilemma that has yet to be resolved.

Analysis of a continental security community is the focus of David Haglund in Chapter 10. Specifically, Haglund explores the notion of societal security, demographic change, and the taken-for-granted status of a North American zone of peace. Haglund begins with the argument that scholarly research on security communities usually focuses on the conditions and consequences of their formation; rare are the works that examine how and why these arrangements might decay, and perhaps even disappear altogether. This is hardly a surprise, holds Haglund, given that in certain fortunate parts of the world, publics and elites alike have come to accept that interstate conflict, at least in their neighbourhood, is a vestige of the past. No matter how haphazardly managed relations among them might be, the dominant expectation is that their security community is virtually indestructible—or, in the vernacular, is 'idiot-proof'. This chapter subsequently offers a critical perspective on the issue of a continental security community framed by the economic zone of the North American Free Trade Agreement (NAFTA) involving Canada, the US, and Mexico. The potential impact of ethnic and religious diasporas on continental security is considered from the point of view of the American debate, not only because that debate has so many implications for America's northern and southern neighbours, but also because in a real sense those two neighbours, for different reasons, are increasingly stylized in the US as the source of the problem.

The next issue, studied by Kent Roach in Chapter 11, concerns Canada's reactions to international terrorism. In concrete terms, he examines Canada's evolving responses to international terrorism with a focus on how concepts of human security used by Canada abroad have influenced its domestic security policy. As Roach demonstrates, human security was used immediately after 9/11 to justify the hard and coercive power of new anti-terrorism laws that limited the rights of terrorism suspects. Since 2004, however, human security has been used to justify a softer and smarter all-risk security policy that aims to limit the harms to Canadians posed not only by terrorism but also by natural disasters and pandemics. Canada's responses to 9/11 are also assessed through the themes of Canada's desire to be a 'good international citizen' and its desire to respond to American concerns that Canada, in particular Canada's growing multicultural population, constitutes a security threat. Canada's immediate post 9/11 willingness to follow the American lead, including the invasion of Afghanistan, has been moderated by concerns about Canadian complicity in human rights abuses such as the rendition of Maher Arar to torture in Syria, as well as Canada's decision not to participate in the invasion of Iraq. Roach suggests that the government's concerns about human rights, multiculturalism, international co-operation, and human security provide a basis for claiming that Canada has pursued domestic security policies that are consistent with some of its foreign policy aspirations.

Canada's military involvement in Afghanistan, in light of the country's role in the post-Cold War North Atlantic Treaty Organization, is the subject of Ben Zyla and Joel Sokolsky in Chapter 12. They begin by arguing that most discussions on the impact of the Afghanistan mission on the future of NATO focus on transatlantic relations between the United States and the European allies. But for Canada, which is one of the few NATO allies that voluntarily deployed into the south, facing heavy resistance and fighting from Taliban insurgents, the Afghanistan operations have become the most salient dimension of its continued involvement in the Atlantic alliance. While this may seem surprising, they argue that, given the cutbacks in Canadian defence spending in the 1990s and the withdrawal of Canada's standing forces from Germany, it should not be. As Zyla and Sokolsky show, for example, during the so-called 'dark decade' Canada continued to make major contributions to NATO and European security, especially in the Balkans where its forces have been continuously engaged in operations to secure and maintain the peace. This chapter maintains that Ottawa's multi-faceted military and political support of the 'new' NATO of the post-Cold War era continued when the Alliance undertook its involvement in Afghanistan. Indeed, in its efforts to support NATO's mission in Afghanistan, Canada has demonstrated a dedication to the Alliance that seems stronger than NATO's collective commitment to itself.

Finally, Chapter 13, by Petra Dolata-Kreutzkamp, examines Canada's Arctic policy as a case study showcasing several interrelated foreign policy issues of particular relevance to Canada as a North American, transatlantic, and Arctic country. Looking at the bilateral (US–Canada) and multilateral dimensions of Canada's foreign policy in the Arctic, Dolata-Kreutzkamp also addresses the relevance of both the international environment—especially climate change and energy, changing geopolitics, and competition in the Arctic—and the domestic level for the formulation of such policies. As becomes clear from the examination of the latter, a bureaucratic politics approach is most useful in disentangling the different interests that have to be accommodated through the policy-formation and political process. Arctic policy is a spatial and regional issue area characterized by a multitude of issues that are not always compatible in their specific goals and policy instruments: defence, development, human and environmental security. In addition, ideas and identities play an important explanatory role in the evolution of Canada's Arctic policies. Dolata-Kreutzkamp provides an overview of the instruments of foreign policy and investigates the shift from the approach of northern policy (1998) to the approach of northern strategy (2007) through which one can see the prioritization of hard over soft power in Canada's policy towards the Arctic.

Note

1.   We do not use the shorter acronym CFSP because it is widely used as the abbreviation for the Common Foreign and Security Policy of the European Union.

2. For example, a German charter airline has been offering direct flights to Yellowknife (NWT) and Whitehorse (Yukon) from Frankfurt during the summer season for the last five years. This is all the more surprising given that not a single Canadian airline offers a direct flight from Ottawa or Toronto to either of these destinations. Canada's North has long held a fascination for Europeans. A notable recent example is the German-produced coffee-table book, with extensive text, *Canada North of Sixty* (Boden and Boden, 1991). French President Jacques Chirac was among the first foreign dignitaries to visit Nunavut after it became a separate territory in 1999.

References

Adams, Michael. 2003. *Fire and Ice: The United States, Canada, and the Myth of Converging Values.* Toronto: Penguin.

Boden, Jürgen F., and Elke Boden, eds. 1991. *Canada North of Sixty.* Oststeinbek/Toronto: Alouette Verlag/McClelland & Stewart.

Bosold, David, and Wilfried von Bredow. 2006. 'Human Security: A Radical or Rhetorical Shift in Canada's Foreign Policy?', *International Journal* 61, 4: 829–44.

Bratt, Duane, and Christopher J. Kukucha. 2007. 'Studying Canadian Foreign Policy: Various Approaches', in Bratt and Kukucha, eds, *Readings in Canadian Foreign Policy: Classic Debates and New Ideas.* Toronto: Oxford University Press, 1–8.

Byers, Michael. 2007. *Intent for a Nation: What Is Canada For?* Vancouver: Douglas & McIntyre.

Carlsnaes, Walter. 2002. 'Foreign Policy', in Walter Carlsnaes, Thomas Risse-Kappen, and Beth A. Simmons, eds, *Handbook of International Relations.* London: Sage, 331–49.

CBC. 2003. 'Magazine Says Canada Is "Cool"', at: <www.cbc.ca/canada/story/2003/09/27/economist030927.html> (14 Feb. 2009).

Chapnick, Adam. 2005. *The Middle Power Project: Canada and the Founding of the United Nations.* Vancouver: University of British Columbia Press.

Cohen, Andrew. 2003. *While Canada Slept. How We Lost Our Place in the World.* Toronto: McClelland & Stewart.

Connolly, William E. 1993. *The Terms of Political Discourse*, 3rd edn. Princeton, NJ: Princeton University Press.

Cooper, Andrew F. 1997. *Canadian Foreign Policy: Old Habits and New Directions.* Scarborough, Ont.: Prentice-Hall.

———, Richard A. Higgott, and Kim Richard Nossal. 1993. *Relocating Middle Powers: Australia and Canada in a Changing World Order.* Vancouver: University of British Columbia Press.

Department of Foreign Affairs and International Trade (DFAIT). 2005. *Canada's International Policy Statement. A Role of Pride and Influence in the World: Overview.* Ottawa: DFAIT.

Dewitt, David B., and John Kirton, 1983. *Canada as a Principal Power.* Toronto: John Wiley.

Eayrs, James, 1975. 'From Middle Power to Foremost Power: Defining a New Place for Canada in the Hierarchy of World Power', *International Perspectives* (May/June).

The Economist. 2003. 'A New Spirit', 27 Sept., 15.

Granatstein, J.L. 2004. *Who Killed the Canadian Military?* Toronto: HarperCollins.

Haglund, David G. 2009. 'And the Beat Goes On: "Identity" and Canadian Foreign Policy', in Robert Bothwell and Jean Daudelin, eds, *Canada Among Nations 2008: 100 Years of Canadian Foreign Policy.* Montreal and Kingston: McGill-Queen's University Press, 343–67.

Holloway, Steven Kendall. 2006. *Canadian Foreign Policy: Defining the National Interest.* Peterborough, Ont.: Broadview Press.

Holmes, John W. 1970. *The Better Part of Valour: Essays on Canadian Diplomacy.* Toronto: McClelland & Stewart.

Hudson, Valerie M. 2005. 'Foreign Policy Analysis: Actor-Specific Theory and the Ground of International Relations', *Foreign Policy Analysis* 1, 1: 1–30.

Hynek, Nik. 2008. 'Conditions of Emergence and Their Effects: Political Rationalities,

Governmental Programs and Technologies of Power in the Landmine Case', *Journal of International Relations and Development* 11, 2: 93–120.

Jackson, Robert, and Carl Rosberg. 1982. 'Why Africa's Weak States Persist: The Empirical and Juridical in Statehood', *World Politics* 35, 1: 1–24.

James, Patrick, Nelson Michaud, and Marc J. O'Reilly, eds. 2006. *Handbook of Canadian Foreign Policy*. Lanham, Md: Lexington Books.

Keating, Tom. 2002. *Canada and World Order: The Multilateralist Tradition in Canadian Foreign Policy*, 2nd edn. Toronto: Oxford University Press.

Kirton, John. 2007a. *Canadian Foreign Policy in a Changing World*. Scarborough, Ont.: Nelson Education.

———. 2007b. 'Canada as a G8 Principal Power', in Duane Bratt and Christopher J. Kukucha, eds, *Readings in Canadian Foreign Policy: Classic Debates and New Ideas*. Toronto: Oxford University Press, 298–315.

Melakopides, Costas. 1998. *Pragmatic Idealism. Canadian Foreign Policy 1945–1995*. Montreal and Kingston: McGill-Queen's University Press.

Neufeld, Mark, and Sandra Whitworth. 1997. 'Imag(in)ing Canadian Foreign Policy', in Wallace Clement, ed., *Understanding Canada: Building on the New Canadian Political Economy*. Montreal and Kingston: McGill-Queen's University Press, 197–214.

Nossal, Kim Richard. 1997. *The Politics of Canadian Foreign Policy*, 3rd edn. Scarborough, Ont.: Prentice-Hall.

———, Stéphane Roussel, and Stéphane Paquin. 2010. *International Policy and Politics in Canada*. Toronto: Pearson Education.

Rempel, Roy. 2002. *The Chatter Box: An Insider's Account of the Increasing Irrelevance of Parliament in the Making of Foreign Policy*. Toronto: Dundurn.

———. 2006. *Dreamland: How Canada's Pretend Foreign Policy Has Undermined Sovereignty*. Montreal and Kingston: McGill-Queen's University Press.

Ringmar, Erik. 1996. *Identity, Interest and Action: A Cultural Explanation of Sweden's Intervention in the Thirty Years War*. Cambridge: Cambridge University Press.

Ruggie, John G. 1998. *Constructing the World Polity: Essays in International Institutionalization*. New York: Routledge.

Savoie, Donald J. 1999. *Governing from the Centre: The Concentration of Power in Canadian Politics*. Toronto: University of Toronto Press

———. 2003. *Breaking the Bargain: Public Servants, Ministers, and Parliament*. Toronto: University of Toronto Press.

———. 2008. *Court Government and the Collapse of Accountability in Canada and the United Kingdom*. Toronto: University of Toronto Press.

Singer, David J. 1961. 'The Level-of-Analysis Problem in International Relations', *World Politics* 14, 1: 77–92.

Stairs, Denis, et al. 2003. *In the National Interest: Canadian Foreign Policy in an Insecure World*. Calgary: CDFAI.

Tomlin, Brian W., Norman Hillmer, and Fen Osler Hampson. 2008. *Canada's International Policies: Agendas, Alternatives, and Politics*. Toronto: Oxford University Press.

von Bredow, Wilfried, ed. 2003. *Die Außenpolitik Kanadas*. Wiesbaden: Westdeutscher Verlag.

Waltz, Kenneth. 1959. *Man, the State, and War*. New York: Columbia University Press.

Part I

Re-examining Middlepowerhood in Canada's Foreign and Security Policy

Whither the Middle-Power Identity? Transformations in the Canadian Foreign and Security Milieus

Tom Keating

Introduction

The Inukshuk has become an iconic representation of Canada. An Inukshuk is a directional marker constructed out of rocks piled in shapes that for many represent human figures. Traditionally, they have been used in the Arctic where other kinds of natural markers are often unavailable. As markers that can provide guidance for travellers, by some accounts they also are symbols of safety, hope, and friendship. The Inukshuk represents a point of certainty in an often harsh, uncertain, and unchartered environment. The Inukshuk has become a popular image in Canada, including its use as an icon for the Vancouver 2010 Olympic Games. It has become so popular among outdoor enthusiasts that Canadian parks officials have been dismantling the many casually constructed Inukshuks that appear in their parks to prevent hikers from mistaking them for the permanent cairns that have been in place to guide hikers for generations.

Thinking about Canada as a middle power brings to mind the Inukshuk and its role as an aid to lost or confused travellers so they might understand where they are and where they are headed. Their popularity is a reminder of the care that should be taken in transforming a useful symbol into a misleading practice. The idea of middle power has played a useful function in locating Canadian foreign policy in the harsh environment of global politics. It has provided a point of orientation from which generations of policy-makers and publics have sought to chart Canada's course as the world around it tumbles seemingly out of control. Like the Inukshuk, the value of the middle power idea is only useful if it retains some connection to its origins, and if we are not to be beguiled by revisionist interpretations that will only lead astray.

Developments since the end of the Cold War suggest that Canadian foreign policy has lost its bearings. Perhaps this is not too surprising, for much has changed and continues to change around the globe. Indeed, it would not be an exaggeration to say that change has accelerated over the past 20–25 years. It is also less surprising, in light of the fact that much of the literature on Canada's place as a middle power was rooted in the Cold War years, a period that in retrospect might be considered unique. The Cold War provided a set of structural constraints on all states, but especially on Canada given its close alignment with the United States. Equally important, the prominence of a specific set of security concerns during the Cold War provided greater clarity about the country's position and its potential role in global politics. All of this was reinforced by a domestic constituency that provided a supportive consensus for policy-makers to engage in an active internationalist foreign policy that would both protect Canadian security within the American-led alliance system, while fostering an international order that was attentive (if not always responsive) to concerns for stability, peace, and justice. This middle-power foreign policy was not constrained by its relationship to the US, but was actively involved in a wide array of international activities, much of which revolved around the United Nations (UN) system of organizations.

The end of the Cold War and subsequent developments have thrown this structured external environment into disarray. The shifting international terrain has been accompanied by a variety of domestic phenomena that have upset the pattern of Canadian foreign policy. An aggressive approach to deficit reduction throughout much of the 1990s effectively decimated government resources devoted to international activity. A variety of different leaders have also contributed to the confusion as they seek to distinguish themselves from their predecessors and highlight different priorities for Canadian foreign policy. The domestic consensus that supported Canada's internationalist foreign policy has been fractured by debates over the importance of values as opposed to interests, over the extent of political and economic integration with the US, over the role of military force and support for more traditional forms of UN peacekeeping, and over the nature and proper response to new security threats. The mood is captured by Andrew Cooper:

> With the entire span of orthodox notions about Canadian foreign policy under stress, the temptation is simply to ditch what we have long taken to be the central narrative. Through one lens, a fragmented and contested mass of identity politics is taken to trump familiar assumptions about Canada's status in the world. Through another lens,

the test for Canada remains that of finding its way back to a condition where it can project an appropriate set of national ambitions. (Cooper, 2007: 987–8)

The result has been a foreign policy sorely in need of an Inukshuk to provide a bearing from which Canada can once again engage the international community. In this changed environment, is it worth retaining the idea of middle power to guide Canada's foreign policy in the twenty-first century? A variety of alternative proposals have been advanced by leaders and pundits, and policy priorities have shifted in response. Yet there remains a great deal of uncertainty about which direction Canadian foreign policy is, and should be, headed. Before considering the continued relevance of the middle-power idea, it is helpful to take a look at where we have been to see what guide history may provide.

Exploring the Past

The middle-power idea emerged in Canadian debates on Canada's involvement in the post-World War II international order:

> The evidence of Canada's new position in the world is unmistakable. Her relatively small population and lack of colonial possessions prevent her from being a major Super Power. But her natural wealth, the capacity of her people, the strength she has exerted and the potentialities she has displayed show that she is not a minor one. Henceforth in world politics she must figure as a Middle Power. (Gelber, 1946)

Canadian foreign policy-makers had long been concerned with their status in the international community. This was likely a result of the nature of their road to independence and their use of international forums like the League of Nations to define that independence from Britain. The concern for status continued after World War II and the idea of middle power was used to proclaim a place for Canada in the community of nations.

The idea of middle power was rooted in an assessment of the mix of capabilities and interests that Canada possessed. A middle power was concerned about international order, because the condition of that order had implications for the government's ability to pursue other objectives. Yet, as a middle power, Canada lacked the military and economic capacity to have a direct and substantial influence on other states, or to put it another way, to wield power. The idea of a middle power did not rest on rank alone, but, and especially in the context of the early years of the UN, also included a combination of capabilities and commitment. The arguments were that characteristics such as those attributed to Canada (a surplus of material resources, a diplomatic corps able and willing to get involved, interests and ideas about how problems should be addressed) should be recognized with enhanced opportunities for participation and responsibility within the newly formed institutions. For some, this was primarily a matter of recognition. For others it was a matter of influence over policy deliberations among the country's allies (see Chapnick, 2005). For yet others, a middle power with foreign policy objectives that differed from those of greater or lesser powers would be able to make a distinctive contribution to the world political scene.

While debates on the analytical utility of the middle-power concept had really yet to emerge, there was more agreement at the time on the policy objectives being pursued. Foremost among these was an interest in securing a more stable international order that would prevent the recurrence of a major war while supporting other Canadian interests. The policy objectives translated into support for institutions and a multilateral decision-making process. In the words of John Holmes: 'Lesser powers always feel the need of international institutions and international law and regulation more acutely than stronger powers' (Holmes, 1986: 13). These policy objectives also fostered a commitment to become an active, responsible participant in global politics. 'Canada had an overriding interest in the development of institutions and practices conducive to peace, tranquility and orderly adjustment in world politics' (Cox, 1989: 824). That these interests were accorded so much importance was not, however, surprising.

> There is nothing particularly high-minded or unselfish about a strongly internationalist policy on the part of a country that so obviously cannot protect its people and its interest except in collaboration with others. (Holmes, 1970: 2)

Clearly, not all states that could claim something approximating middle-power rank took the same approach to the world that Canadian policy-makers did. For Canada, however, its relative position in the global hierarchy of power informed the internationalist course of Canadian foreign policy for the last half of the twentieth century.

The persistence of a concern for international order through multilateralism on the part of Canadian policy-makers has resulted, in part, from Canada's position in the society of states. As a minor power, lacking aspirations to great power status yet possessing wide-ranging political and commercial interests in various corners of the globe, international peace and stability supported by a system of international law and institutions have been viewed as essential for the successful pursuit and protection of purely national interests. It is therefore not surprising that someone like Lester Pearson would link national interests to internationalism. As he wrote in his memoirs, 'nationalism and internationalism were two sides of the same coin. International co-operation for peace is the most important aspect of national policy' (Pearson, 1971: 283).

Don Munton and Don Page (1977: 602), in their review of the government's planning for the post-war period, identify a similar theme: 'Lesser power status led to a set of images which gave greater emphasis to systemic, as opposed to bipolar, conditions and which, though they highlighted the role of the two great powers, reflected a concern for the problems on both sides that might lead to another war.' In the view of Martin Wight (1995: 66) this internationalist orientation is characteristic of minor powers because 'the powers who by definition were without "general interests" were more capable than the great powers of pursuing consistently what might be regarded as the universal interest of upholding international law and order.'

The post-World War II international order was preserved in part by the balance of terror between the superpowers, in part by a network of international associations or regimes, in part by a system of international law, and in part by timely and effective diplomatic interventions by countries like Canada with an interest in preserving this order. In practice, this could be seen in the Canadian government's extensive support for the work of the UN, including, but not limited to, peacekeeping operations. It can also be seen in the active mediatory diplomacy undertaken by Canadian officials, much of it within institutions such as the UN, NATO, and the Commonwealth. It can be seen in Canada's significant material contributions to NATO for its first two decades. It was at the same time evident in efforts to use NATO as both an armed guard against and a diplomatic vanguard towards the Soviet Union. Canada's concern for global order could also be seen in efforts to bridge the growing North–South divide with some material assistance and much more diplomatic goodwill. Development assistance programs, for example, continued to expand into the 1980s.

Continuity in the practice of foreign policy was the defining characteristic of Canadian foreign policy throughout much of the Cold War era. There were variations and departures, but the deviations were few and largely confined within a rather broad set of parameters that kept Canadian foreign policy actively engaged in supporting global order. This was done in its formal alliance network of NATO and NORAD, as well as in its more internationalist commitments largely undertaken through the UN, with a supporting role for the Commonwealth. The internationalist orientation, combined with the interest in process and order, was articulated in Louis St Laurent's Gray Lecture, the foreign policy doctrine of Canada's post-war government. It continued to inform much of the practice of Canadian foreign policy for the ensuing four decades. The approach reflected a sense of responsibility on the part of successive governments to be actively engaged in a wide range of global affairs. This orientation also was evident in an ongoing interest in supporting multilateral institutional arrangements that would serve both national interests and global order considerations. The approach was generally supported with a significant commitment of materials, personnel, and ideas. Indeed, the contribution was widely recognized by others in the international community who turned to the Canadian government to contribute to international efforts in such areas as peacekeeping, diplomacy, and development.

For the government's part, much of this involvement reflected a desire to ensure continued access to the decision-making processes of close allies, especially the US, and to multilateral associations. In some sense, the spirit of functionalism elaborated during the negotiations establishing the United Nations in the mid-1940s continued to influence policy-makers well into the 1960s. While some have questioned the concern for process and denigrated the apparent unwillingness to pursue more substantive positions, it would seem that, especially in the context of the Cold War, a state willing to support and facilitate an ongoing dialogue among conflicting parties was of some use in bringing the two sides together. This internationalist policy also reflected the limits of a middle power through its emphasis on diplomacy and institutions, rather than military or economic power. Perhaps most importantly, it was evident in an effort to be inclusive and avoid the excessive dogmatism that often reared its head in the Cold War. The middle-power idea that supported this was a combination of position, capability, and commitment. It was also very much a part of the ideational fabric that supported Canadian foreign policy in the government and among the general Canadian population.

The commitment to internationalism would appear frequently in the foreign policy statements of the government. In his widely cited Gray Lecture on 'The Foundation of Canadian Policy in World Affairs', then Secretary of State Louis St Laurent stated that 'it has never been the opinion of any considerable number of people in Canada that this continent could live unto itself.' He went on to say that Canadians 'have seen our own interests in the wider context of the western world. We have realized also that regionalism of any kind would not provide the answers to problems of world security' (St Laurent, 1947). Even when policy-makers disavowed the middle-power label, their foreign policy practice continued to exhibit the internationalist practices of the past. As Kim Nossal has argued, 'for all the cavalier words [of the 1970 review papers], Pierre Trudeau's government did not abandon those fundamentals of postwar internationalism which it had criticized so ardently' (Nossal, 1985). This included contributions to peacekeeping operations in Vietnam and the Middle East and even support for the Commonwealth as a forum for dialogue between North and South.

In the 1980s, the Canadian government assumed the forefront in efforts to revitalize the UN and multilateralism, when these were being challenged by the US and others. Their efforts were designed not only to serve Canadian interests but also to support the institution's contribution to global order and stability while encouraging peaceful change. Brian Mulroney's appointment of Stephen

Lewis as Canada's ambassador to the UN 'to take to the defence of the UN' reflects this ongoing commitment to an institutionalized, rules-based international order, a role Lewis fulfilled with enthusiasm. He openly and candidly criticized Americans, such as those in the Heritage Foundation, as 'anti-internationalist' in their efforts to reduce American commitments to the organization (Lewis, 1985: 6). Instead of lamenting the failings of the organization as American government officials tended to do, he worked to establish the friends of the UN, an informal group of country representatives who met intermittently and informally to discuss avenues for reforming the organization. He also oversaw the UN Special Session on Africa. In these and other activities, Lewis was a manifest expression of the Mulroney government's commitment to the UN. Many also saw the Mulroney government's anti-apartheid policy as another indicator of its middle-power activism (Wood, 1990; Black, 1991). The theme was reiterated in the Prime Minister's speeches: 'History shows the solitary pursuit of self-interest outside the framework of broader international cooperation is never enough to increase our freedom, safeguard our security, or improve our standard of living' (Mulroney, 1985). As Stephen Lewis remarked in a speech to the UN Association in the United States, support for the United Nations may be 'a little easier for Canada—a middle power, quite non-threatening, utterly non-nuclear, and with a particular advantage in being bilingual so that we have special access to the francophone world'. But he also argued that Canadians 'have above all, a lasting and visceral commitment to multilateralism which is ingrained and endemic to the Canadian character' (Lewis, 1985: 6).

Peter Lawler (2005) has argued that internationalism requires the support of both governments and their publics. Canadian foreign policy has been supported by a strong popular and elite commitment to responsible involvement in international affairs through multilateral associations (Nossal, 1985). The posture that Canadian foreign policy-makers have consistently adopted clearly has been consistent with the prevailing attitudes of the Canadian public (Munton and Keating, 2001). Public support for much of Canada's post-war foreign policy activity has been consistent with many of the values that have guided Canadians in their domestic political affairs. This lends validity to Denis Stairs's thesis that Canadian foreign policy is a manifestation of Canada's national political character (Stairs, 1982: 667). This view is also supported by what Kim Nossal (1985) described as dominant ideas. The perennial concern of policy-makers with national unity has, in turn, conditioned them to the at times tenuous consensus that governs interstate relations in the international system. The domestic experience made them leery of dogmatism and willing, indeed committed, to work with and support diversity. It is perhaps for this reason that Canadian foreign policy is sometimes scorned by the right and the left. Dogmatism from either the right or the left, however, has commonly been seen as inimical to international order. A pluralist and inclusive international order that remains stable is especially important for a state, such as Canada, that does not possess the necessary resources to project its own dogma effectively on others (as, one could argue, no state can). For most Canadian policy-makers in the post-World War II period a practical and effective foreign policy meant an acceptance of a pluralistic society of states with all of its inconsistencies and imperfections, along with a clear recognition of the limited power to alter this. In adopting this approach Canadian foreign policy-makers commanded considerable popular support and achieved some success and recognition.

Whither the Middle Power?

As suggested above, Canada's internationalist foreign policy was rooted in a number of middle-power characteristics, a combination of material conditions (its rank in the international condominium of power, its material capabilities), the expressed ideas and commitments of policy officials, and the support of Canadian society. As we move into the twenty-first century the same conditions no longer apply in the same fashion. Changes in the transnational environment have called into question the appropriateness of the middle-power label. They also present challenges to the middle-power sensibilities and internationalist ideas that encouraged and defined an internationalist foreign policy. For some, like Arthur Andrew (1993), the signing of the bilateral free trade agreement with the US marked the end of Canada's middle-power status. The free trade agreement reinforced the extensive economic integration that existed between the two countries. The increased export dependence that has resulted has left policy-makers and many domestic interests even more concerned with the state of the bilateral relationship. Rather than free Canada from the need to worry about the bilateral economic relationship, as Peyton Lyon once suggested would be the case, it has served to heighten this obsession in many quarters. The terrorist threat of the last decade has only exacerbated these concerns, as pressing security concerns have been added to the continental trade issues. As has been the case for other countries in the international community, economic interests have assumed greater significance in our foreign policy, and on many economic issues the preoccupation with our southern neighbours looms large. Whether for this or other reasons, Canada has been less willing and able to engage with the Americans effectively in support of broader foreign policy objectives.

For Cranford Pratt the change in policy direction is tied to societal consider-ations. Pratt (1989) has noted the declining domestic support for the active internationalism of past decades. He maintains that domestic interests have been influenced by the growth and power of a new, more commercially oriented faction of Canadian society. Domestic business groups supported the neo-liberal policies of the Washington Consensus and turned away from some of the internationalist policies that had supported a growth in Canada's development assistance policies during the 1970s. This has resulted in a shift in public support for Canadian foreign policy. Such shifts were a reflection of a more highly polarized debate over many aspects of contemporary international politics and a breakdown in the post-war foreign policy consensus (see Pratt, 1983–4).

The internationalist strand of Canada's middle-power orientation also took a significant hit in the 1990s when the Liberal government addressed its deficit crisis by making substantial reductions in spending on Canada's international policy (see Cohen, 2003). This sharp decline in military, diplomatic, and financial capabilities devoted to foreign policy activities left Canada with a store of 'soft power', which, while deployed during the late 1990s, had limited reach and questionable staying power. Jean Francois Rioux and Robin Hay (1997: 6) argue that this was more than just deficit reduction. It also reflected the orientation of the Prime Minister: 'The Chrétien government has been, in practice, if not in word, the most isolationist government since Mackenzie King's in the 1930s, all the while touting the official line that internationalism is still the Canadian doctrine in world affairs.' Declining capabilities were matched by declining commitments. Finally, Robert Greenhill (2005: 35) notes how outsiders have observed that the Canadian government has seemingly abandoned many of the characteristics of its liberal internationalist policies, calling attention to a 'decline in our reputation and relevance with the United States, decline in our leadership role in development, and decline in the international significance of our peacekeeping and other international security activities'.

While the material support for an internationalist foreign policy has declined, the political rhetoric in support of an internationalist policy has remained high both in the White Paper of 1993 and in the International Policy Statement released a decade later. Policy-makers continued to invoke the themes of middle-power activism used in the past despite the changed circumstances. Former Prime Minister Jean Chrétien said:

There is a lot of talk these days about Canada's role in the world. Our government has been active in achieving an international land mines treaty. In establishing an international court of criminal justice. With a Canadian as Chief Justice. In promoting the Africa initiative. In the war against terrorism. Canada has earned a unique role in the world. Disproportionate to our population, or the size of our economy, or the size of our military. We have earned this place through an unwavering commitment to the values of democracy, human rights and the peaceful resolution of conflicts. We help our friends most when we are true to that role and the values that underpin it. We have a stake in continuing to strengthen multilateral institutions whether to combat climate change, war crimes, or to make decisions about war. (Chrétien, 2003)

Both Prime Ministers Paul Martin and Stephen Harper emphasized their desire to restore Canada to a place of pride in the international community. Their comments reflected the concern shared by others—that Canada had slipped from its middle-power status—and their intent to shore up Canada's credentials. Martin invoked the middle-power concept in arguing that Canada should become a 'moral middle power'. For Stephen Harper, it was a matter of emphasizing that middle powers, such as Canada, are 'willing to assume responsibilities, seek practical, doable solutions to problems and . . . have a voice and influence in global affairs because they lead, not by lecturing, but by example' (Harper, cited in Hurst, 2007).

Despite the caution against preaching in Stephen Harper's comments, the rhetoric still does not always match the practice. There has been a quite noticeable lack of leadership and direction in Canada's foreign policy for a number of years. This is perhaps best illustrated by the succession of individuals who have passed through senior cabinet positions in areas related to foreign policy. Under the past three prime ministers over the past 15 years there have been eight foreign ministers, nine ministers responsible for international co-operation (and development assistance as part of this portfolio), and eight defence ministers. The average time in office has been less than two years. Combined with the more recent pattern of minority governments, this has encouraged a more transient foreign policy directed more by the political whims of the day than by any clear course of interests, let alone by responsibilities to the broader international community. The practice has clearly not matched the public perception of what Canada's foreign policy is or should be.[1]

Over the past few decades a quite significant redistribution of global power has occurred, especially among those most likely labelled middle powers. Canada now shares the stage with a wider array of actors, and despite the arguments of John Kirton that Canada retains a principal position among these actors, the sheer number of participants has implications for the scope and influence of Canadian foreign policy. For example, the emergence of Brazil, India, and China as key players in the World Trade Organization has diminished Canada's influence in shaping global trade negotiations. Discussions of reforming the UN do not include adding Canada to the Security Council, so if these reforms are ever accomplished Canada will drift further from this institution's central decision-making body. The government's reduced commitment to UN-sponsored peacekeeping operations also makes it difficult to sustain Canadian influence in this arena. The expansion in NATO membership and the growth in the EU have marginalized Canada within European security negotiations. To the extent that the EU begins to replace NATO in this arena, Canada will be on the outside. Discussions on expanding the G8 and the emerging G20 group both reflect a need and desire to adapt institutional practices to changing global conditions. The result, however, will be a further diminution in Canada's privileged access to central decision-making bodies. The stage is increasingly crowded and institutional preferences are changing.

The United Nations no longer serves as the core of Canada's internationalist strategy. In the security arena, the country's bilateral relationship with the US and its involvement in NATO have taken on greater significance, not only in the more traditional areas of transatlantic and continental security, but also in terms of the global security concerns surrounding failed and fragile states. Canadian contributions to UN peacekeeping operations in the early 1990s were among the largest of all nations, with more than 2,000 personnel deployed to UN operations around the world; Canada was also instrumental in undertaking the lead in deployments to Bosnia and alongside the Americans to Somalia and Haiti under the UN umbrella. The Canadian government was also actively promoting the expansion of the UN's peace support role, promoting the Agenda for Peace proposals of then UN Secretary-General Boutros-Ghali and advocating for a UN rapid reaction capability. By the mid-1990s, in response to developments in Bosnia, attention began to drift to NATO and Canadian forces were redeployed to support NATO operations. This was a reflection of changes within the Atlantic alliance. Member governments and the NATO leaders looked upon these interventions as a role for the alliance after its principal raison d'être, the Soviet Union, had disappeared. NATO began to take on tasks for which the UN had previously assumed responsibility. The UN, in turn, had an interest in using NATO to enforce Security Council resolutions and to delegate increasingly problematic security missions to an organization with greater capabilities. It also reflected a policy shift within Canada as NATO deployments overtook UN commitments. This was partly a response to the limitations and problems experienced by the UN in Somalia, Rwanda, and Bosnia.

The shift from the UN to NATO also seems motivated, in part, to demonstrate Canada's military credentials in a changing environment where the use of military force was taking on more prominence as an instrument in support of humanitarian interventions. These interventions were becoming increasingly assertive and militarized. The use of military force also remained a critically important aspect of US foreign policy. An interest in demonstrating to the US government Canada's capacity to make a significant contribution was at least partly responsible for the shift to support the more militarized NATO missions. Beginning in Bosnia, continuing in Kosovo, and settling eventually in Afghanistan, the Canadian Forces operating under NATO command symbolized the Canadian government's contribution to global order. The military and NATO were being used in support of both the more valued-inspired responsibility to protect principle and the campaign against terrorism informed more by national interest. Either way, it reflected a shift to armed interventions and the early use of military force to enforce internationally designed solutions to intra-state conflicts. These deployments abandoned the neutrality of earlier UN operations in defence of human security, democracy, freedom, or other concerns. Importantly, many of these operations were also based on a more limited international consensus, working from the more exclusive Western institution of NATO. This has given rise to concerns over legitimacy and the degree of international support.

The shift to a more interventionist foreign policy including the use of armed force has been a marked departure in Canadian foreign policy. Intervention, if not always its more militarized form, has received considerable support in some circles. Michael Ignatieff (2004) emphasized such practices in his O.D. Skelton Lecture: 'The focus of our foreign policy should be to consolidate "peace, order and good government" as the sine qua non for stable states, enduring democracy and equitable development.' The emphasis on values such as human rights emerged in the 1980s. This led to the articulation of principles and the development of policies in areas such as good governance, human security, and responsibility to protect. The turn to a policy designed to project our values and practices onto other societies is also evident in discussions on the establishment of a government-sponsored agency for promoting democracy abroad. Such views and developments reflect a tendency to emphasize substantive policy objectives and a position that these principles should override competing concerns for state sovereignty and, arguably, a more pluralistic view of the international order.

Proponents, of course, would argue the conditions that led to these interventions are themselves a source of significant disorder in the contemporary global community. The arguments that have been developed around the existence of failed and fragile states suggest that such states pose a direct and immediate threat to global order because they contribute to regional instability, exacerbate the movement of displaced persons and refugees, fuel the international arms trade, and, perhaps most importantly, become a potential safe haven for terrorists who can wreak havoc around the globe, particularly in Western nations. Yet, as Rob Huebert (2006) points out, the connection is not as clear as some arguments suggest. Some have maintained that for Canada, as for other Western governments, these interventions represent a convergence of interests and values, yet if this is the case it suggests a shift in both interests and values from Canada's previous experience as a middle power. In adopting this more dogmatic posture in response to the emerging crises of recent years, the government has chosen a narrower view of consensus-building than that espoused in the past. It has also supported the early use of military force in response to international crises, whereas past practice tended to favour diplomatic methods.

While there may be, indeed undoubtedly are, some very good reasons for promoting peace, order, and good government given our own experiences, it is still questionable whether the best method for promoting these changes is through the forced implementation of international norms. Such a stance assumes that we have the answers to solve the problems that riddle divided societies in other parts of the world. Experience should remind us that answers are not always exportable. A foreign policy designed to remake other societies is of concern on other grounds as well. This is especially problematic when one does not possess the capacity, let alone the commitment, to complete the desired changes. Democratization may be a good long-term outcome for as many states as possible, but does it make sense as a foreign policy activity directed towards a state that seems unwilling to commit to such change, if indeed it possesses the resources necessary for the time it would take to complete reforms? Current debates over Afghanistan demonstrate clearly that there is little support either within or outside of the Canadian government for the long-term commitment that such enterprises would require, if they were to be effective. The current situation in Afghanistan also demonstrates the inherent problems in trying to impose solutions on troubled societies.

The assumption that you can move in and out of these crises with effective results and with little real costs in terms of resources is a gross exaggeration. It is also anathema to the sort of views that animated policy officials in earlier periods. Canadian commitments, in the past, were assessed with respect both to the amount of international support and to the realization that commitments needed to be open-ended in order to give every opportunity for a successful outcome. Moreover, earlier commitments were guided by a profound sense of the limits on what could be accomplished. The Canadian public seems enamoured with the country's traditional UN peacekeeping role because this role did not involve extensive or intensive armed combat. Another less frequently mentioned aspect of these activities was their limited objectives. Deployments to Suez and Cyprus, and to Vietnam through the International Control Commission, were undertaken without an exit strategy or the preset termination dates that mark many contemporary deployments. They also were tasked with more modest, though not inconsequential, mandates.

The problems brought on by developments in the area of intervention are not Canada's alone. They do, however, stretch the limits of what middle powers can aspire to, and raise questions about how a middle power should deal with such matters as intervention, coalitions with a limited number of members, and the use of armed force to reform other societies. As Lawler (2005: 448) writes, 'The principal challenge now for any resuscitated internationalist alternative to the dominant narrative of Western foreign and security policy is an investigation of what kinds of national context can generate an internationalist discourse sufficiently sensitive to the cultural complexities of the contemporary world or contemporary multi-ethnic states and to the dangers of a presumptive moral universalism.'

The government's response to failed states and its interests in intervention and democracy promotion have not been as fully supported in the wider international community. The early use of force has also been problematic and has perhaps contributed to the exacerbation of instability in the international society. In addition, it has created problems in maintaining domestic support (see, e.g., Dorn, 2008). These practices have created a disjuncture between the government's foreign policy and public perceptions of what that policy is or should be (University of Ottawa, 2005). To the extent that middle-power internationalism is a reflection of both material and ideational assets, the latter would still seem to be very much in place, despite the varying foreign policy practices. This is of particular importance for Canada, both as an active internationalist state and as a multi-ethnic society that seeks its own security along with its desire to define a foreign policy that commands the support of the body politic.

The middle-power idea remains popular among political leaders and pundits, yet today's world and Canada's place in it are very different from that of the 1940s. Canada is today more of a regional player, more focused on the US than it was in the immediate post-war period and with limited involvement beyond North America, yet it remains reliant on a stable global order for both peace and prosperity. The Canadian population, on the other hand, is more multicultural than it was in the early post-1945 years and is becoming more diverse with each passing year. The global connections of the peoples of Canada are increasing, yet their ideas on the role that Canada should play in the world seem strikingly similar to those of internationalist sentiments of earlier generations, thus reinforcing the need for the Canadian government to remain actively engaged in the pursuit of this order. With a population drawn from all corners of the world, with an economy directly or indirectly reliant on a stable and expansive global trading order, with a security environment defined by a relatively meagre capability and a geopolitical position between a melting Arctic and a formidable American power, Canadian foreign policy cannot afford an isolationist approach to global politics. Instead, it requires a state committed to the internationalist enterprise with the capacity to act in areas of diplomacy, defence, and development in a manner that can make a difference by promoting and then supporting useful practices, by winning the support of helpful governments, and by contributing to the welfare of populations in need.

Conclusion

Where, then, are we to find the Inukshuk for Canadian foreign policy in today's world? There may appear to be good reasons to jettison the middle-power label, given the number, variety, and rapidly changing capacities of relevant actors in the contemporary global system. Canada's middle-power status has been matched by emerging powers, such as India, Brazil, and South Africa, with potentially both the capacity and commitment to be more involved. In response, the Canadian government must be resigned to a more crowded stage and perhaps a less prominent role. Less prominent does not, however, mean insignificant. While the stage has clearly become more crowded, the opportunity and the need remain for Canada to define its place, a place that reflects our shifting material capabilities and, equally important, that reflects our ideas and our diplomatic ability to resolve differences and build support for a stable international order. The role requires leadership, focus, ongoing commitment, and a great deal more by way of investment in material capabilities than has been the case in recent years. It will also entail an effort to re-engage the US in this collaborative enterprise. A US government at odds with many parts of the global community is especially problematic for Canadian foreign policy, as it sets up competing, if not conflicting, objectives that are difficult to reconcile. A US government willing to engage with other states, however, provides an opportunity for Canada itself to recommit to an internationalist foreign policy to meet the challenges of the early part of the twenty-first century.

Jennifer Welsh (2004: 6) has argued that 'the middle power mantra is losing its punch, and the gap between the expectation of what Canada *should* do and the reality of what it *is* doing is growing wider and wider.' There is considerable truth in such a criticism. What is less clear is where exactly the problem lies. The expectation of what Canada should be doing has grown exponentially over the past 10–20 years. The idea that we should be actively engaged in reconstructing other societies, from Kosovo to Afghanistan and Darfur, has become a common and popular refrain. At the same time, the actual material contribution has been in decline or at best stagnant. The reality of what we are doing is not always evident. Contributions such as struggling to maintain limited security in a small region of Afghanistan at considerable human and economic cost or providing some outdated vehicles and a small training contingent to the African Union in Darfur are not inconsequential, but they are unlikely, on their own, to resolve either one of these conflicts. There is a considerable gap here between the 'should' and the 'is'. The two need to be reconciled, but both need to shift.

An effective internationalist policy requires more extensive resources. Yet these resources also need to be deployed more effectively in support of commitments that are more realistic. Canada built its foreign policy reputation on a middle-power idea that recognized an opportunity, a responsibility, and a capacity to make a contribution to the international community. The potential rewards for this type of contribution remain as significant as ever. So, too, do the imperatives for an internationalist foreign policy guided by a middle-power idea that reminds Canadians and their government of what is possible.

In this vein there may still be a place for this Inukshuk. It might, in the words of Reinhold Niebuhr (1952: 174), encourage 'a sense of modesty about the virtue, wisdom and power available to us for the resolution of [history's] perplexities' while sustaining the commitment to stay involved.

Note

1. For a sample of the views of Canadians, see, for example, The Canada's World Poll, January 2008, at: <www.canadasworld.ca/quizzesa/pollresu>.

References

Andrew, Arthur. 1993. *The Rise and Fall of a Middle Power: Canadian Diplomacy from King to Mulroney*. Toronto: James Lorimer.

Black, David. 1991. 'Australian, Canadian, and Swedish Policies towards Southern Africa: A Comparative Study of Middle Power Internationalism', Ph.D. dissertation, Dalhousie University.

Chapnick, Adam. 2005. *The Middle Power Project: Canada and the Founding of the United Nations*. Vancouver: University of British Columbia Press.

Chrétien, Jean. 2003. 'Address on the Occasion of the Calgary Leader's Dinner'.

Cohen, Andrew. 2003. *While Canada Slept*. Toronto: McClelland & Stewart.

Cooper, Andrew F. 2007. 'Review of John Kirton's *Canadian Foreign Policy in a Changing World*', *International Journal* (Autumn): 987–8.

Cox, Robert. 1989. 'Middlepowermanship, Japan, and the Future World Order', *International Journal* (Autumn): 823–62.

Dorn, A. Walter. 2008. 'Peacekeeping, Then, Now, and Always', *Canadian Military Journal*, Department of National Defence, Ottawa, July. At: <www.journal.dnd.ca/vo6/no4/views-vues-01-eng.asp>.

Gelber, Lionel. 1946. 'Canada's New Stature', *Foreign Affairs* (Jan.): 277–80.

Greenhill, Robert. 2005. 'The Decline of Canada's Influence in the World—What Is To Be Done with It?', *Policy Options* (Feb.): 34–9.

Holmes, John. 1970. *The Better Part of Valour*. Toronto: McClelland & Stewart.

———. 1986. 'The United Nations in Perspective', *Behind the Headlines* 44, 1 (Oct.): 1–24.

Huebert, Rob. 2006. 'Failed and Failing States: The Core Threat to Canadian Security', in David Bercuson and Denis Stairs, eds, *In the Canadian Interest: Assessing Canada's International Policy Statement*. Calgary: Canadian Defence and Foreign Affairs Institute, 69–73.

Hurst, Lynda. 2007. 'On World Stage, Best Supporting Actor', *Toronto Star*, 26 Sept. At: <www.thestar.com/comment/columnists/article/261324>.

Ignatieff, Michael. 2004. 'Peace, Order, and Good Government. A Foreign Policy Agenda for Canada', O.D. Skelton Memorial Lecture. At: <www.international.gc.ca/odskelton/ignatieff.aspx?lang=eng>.

Lawler, Peter. 2005. 'The Good State: In Praise of "Classical" Internationalism', *Review of International Studies* 31: 427–49.

Lewis, Stephen. 1985. 'The Defensible United Nations', *International Perspectives* (Sept.–Oct.): 3–6.

Mulroney, Brian. 1985. 'Principles of UN Charter Signposts to Peace', *Statements and Speeches*, 85/14.

Munton, Don, and Tom Keating. 2001. 'Internationalism and the Canadian Public', *Canadian*

Journal of Political Science 34, 3: 517–49.

———— and Don Page. 1977. 'Canadian Images of the Cold War', *International Journal* 32, 3: 577–604.

Niebuhr, Reinhold. 1952. *The Irony of American History.* Chicago: University of Chicago Press.

Nossal, Kim Richard. 1985. *The Politics of Canadian Foreign Policy.* Toronto: Prentice-Hall.

Pearson, Lester. 1971. *Mike, Volume I.* Toronto: University of Toronto Press.

Pratt, Cranford. 1983–4. 'Dominant Class Theory and Canadian Foreign Policy', *International Journal* 39: 1–24.

————. 1989. 'Canada: An Eroding and Limited Internationalism', in Pratt, ed., *Internationalism Under Strain: The North–South Policies of Canada, the Netherlands, Norway, and Sweden.* Toronto: University of Toronto Press, 49–63.

Rioux, Jean-François, and Robin Hay. 1997. *Canadian Foreign Policy: From Internationalism to Isolationism.* Ottawa: Norman Patterson School of International Affairs, Carleton University, Discussion Paper No. 16.

St Laurent, Louis. 1947. 'The Foundations of Canadian Policy on World Affairs', Gray Lecture, *Statements and Speeches*, 47/12.

Stairs, Denis. 1982. 'The Political Culture of Canadian Foreign Policy', *Canadian Journal of Political Science* 15, 4: 667–90.

University of Ottawa. 2005. 'Government "Out of Step" with Canadians on Foreign Policy Priorities: First uOttawa Ipsos-Reid Public Policy Poll', 11 Oct. At: <www.media.uottawa.ca/mediaroom/news-details_703.html>.

Welsh, Jennifer. 2004. 'Canada in the 21st Century: Beyond Dominion and Middle Power,' *Behind the Headlines* 61, 4 (Sept.): 1–15.

Wight, Martin. 1995 [1946]. *Power Politics*, 2nd edn, ed. Hedley Bull and Carsten Holbraad. Leicester: Leicester University Press.

Wood, Bernard. 1990. 'Canada and Southern Africa: A Return to Middle Power Activism', *Round Table* 315: 280–90.

Additional Readings

Bratt, Duane, and Christopher J. Kukucha. 2007. *Readings in Canadian Foreign Policy.* Toronto: Oxford University Press.

Cooper, Andrew F., Richard A. Higgott, and Kim Richard Nossal. 1993. *Relocating Middle Powers.* Vancouver: University of British Columbia Press.

Harder, Lois, and Steve Patten. 2006. *The Chrétien Legacy.* Montreal and Kingston: McGill-Queen's University Press.

Kymlicka, Will. 2007. *Multicultural Odysseys.* Oxford: Oxford University Press.

Keating, Tom. 2002. *Canada and World Order*, 2nd edn. Toronto: Oxford University Press.

Khanna, Parag. 2008. *The Second World.* New York: Random House.

Neufeld, Mark. 1995. 'Hegemony and Foreign Policy Analysis: The Case of Canada as Middle Power', *Studies in Political Economy* 48 (Autumn): 7–29.

Pratt, Cranford, ed. 1990. *Middle Power Internationalism.* Montreal and Kingston: McGill-Queen's University Press.

Rempel, Roy. 2006. *Dreamland.* Montreal and Kingston: McGill-Queen's University Press.

Welsh, Jennifer. 2004. *At Home in the World.* Toronto: HarperCollins.

Chapter 2

'Middlepowerhood' and 'Middlepowermanship' in Canadian Foreign Policy

Kim Richard Nossal

Introduction

The general themes explored in this volume—Canada's approaches to foreign and security policy in the contemporary era—owe much to a historical idea about Canada's place and role in global politics: as the other chapters in the introductory section by Tom Keating and David Bosold demonstrate clearly, the idea that Canada is a 'middle power' has enjoyed a long history in the way in which Canadians discuss foreign and security policy. Indeed, the 'middle power project', as Adam Chapnick (2005) has correctly called it, had its beginnings in the 1940s, when the government of Prime Minister William Lyon Mackenzie King sought a greater international role for Canada, commensurate with its considerable military and economic contributions during the World War II (Gelber, 1945–6; Glazebrook, 1947). But the idea was transformed as the Canadian government increasingly embraced a particular kind of diplomacy during the Cold War. By the 1960s, the term had become entrenched, cemented in place by its common use in academic, media, and political discourse (Holmes, 1966; Fox, 1977). Since then, it has been an enduring way of characterizing Canadian foreign policy, and has come to be very much part of Canada's emerging identity in contemporary global politics (see Wendt, 1992; Jepperson et al., 1996).

To be sure, as John Ravenhill (1998) reminds us, the idea of middle power has gone through distinct cycles of popularity. While the idea enjoyed a surge of popularity after Lester B. Pearson, Canada's Foreign Minister, was awarded the Nobel Peace Prize in 1957 for his diplomacy during the Suez crisis of 1956, its popularity declined in the late 1960s. In particular, Pierre Elliott Trudeau came to power in 1968 highly skeptical of the utility of the middle-power role and of the idea that Canada should try to be a 'helpful fixer' in the resolution of international conflict (Ichikawa, 1979). Indeed, the foreign policy review that Trudeau initiated in the late 1960s explicitly predicted that 'Canada's "traditional" middle-power role in the world seemed doomed to disappear.' The review, published in 1970, rejected the idea that there was a 'natural, immutable or permanent role for Canada in today's world. . . . To be liked and to be regarded as good fellows', *Foreign Policy for Canadians* asserted, with a barely suppressed sneer, 'are not ends in themselves; they are a reflection of but not a substitute for policy' (Canada, 1970: 6, 8).

But it is indicative of the longer-term entrenchment of the idea that Canada is a middle power that by the end of his long years in office, Trudeau had come full circle. His 'peace mission', undertaken in the winter of 1983–4 with the intention of reducing tensions between the United States and the Soviet Union, was not only an example of the 'helpful fixing' that he had so trenchantly criticized in the late 1960s—Trudeau cast his 'peace mission' in the language of middle power, arguing to Parliament that middle powers could play a 'constructive part' in defusing superpower tensions (Canada, 1983–4; see also Granatstein and Bothwell, 1990: 363–76).

Trudeau's full circle reflects the degree to which the idea of the middle power has enjoyed an enduring popularity in Canadian foreign policy. It is true that in the three official government statements on foreign policy issued by Trudeau's successors—Brian Mulroney in 1985, Jean Chrétien in 1995, and Paul Martin in 2005—the term tended to be avoided altogether or used in the same pejorative tone as Trudeau's 1970 foreign policy paper. Thus, for example, the words 'middle power' do not appear at all in either the 1985 discussion paper on foreign policy issued by the Mulroney government or the government statement issued by the Chrétien government in 1995 (Canada, 1985, 1995). And in Paul Martin's *International Policy Statement*, issued in April 2005, the term is only used in a disparaging way: the *IPS* declared that 'the traditional notion of Canada as a middle power' was 'outdated' and lamented that 'Our old middle power identity imposes an unnecessary ceiling on what we can do and be in the world' (Canada, 2005: 2, 5). And yet, despite the reticence in official discourse, Canadian leaders would continue to use the phrase in their speeches to describe Canada as a middle power, as Ravenhill (1998: 321) notes. In this sense, Stephen Harper, who assumed the prime ministership in February 2006 after the Conservative Party of Canada won a minority government in the January general election, was following a well-trod path when he argued in a speech to the Council on Foreign Relations in New York in September 2007 that Canada was a middle power (Canada, 2007).

It is perhaps not surprising that the middle-power idea developed certain mythologies over the years as it became increasingly entrenched in public discourse. For example, as the Cold War wore on, Canada's *geographic* location in the 'middle' between the two superpowers got turned into an *ideological/political* middle ground, with Canada cast as a country 'in the middle' between the United States and the Soviet Union, rather than as a country ideologically and militarily allied with the United States against the Soviet Union. Jennifer Welsh (2004a: 134) best exemplifies this particular revisionist perspective when she writes that 'During the frosty decades of the Cold War, the role of a middle power seeking to find a niche between the United States on the one hand and the Soviet Union on the other made a lot of sense for Canada.' To be sure, a number of Canadians saw Canada's political location in these terms, including some Canadian political leaders, such as Pierre Trudeau. For example, Allan Gotlieb (2006: 61), Canada's ambassador to Washington, noted in his diary that when Trudeau gave a speech on arms control in Chicago in May 1982, the Canadian Prime Minister painted the two superpowers as *equally* responsible for endangering world peace and that there was a moral equivalence between the two superpowers. As Granatstein and Bothwell (1990: 375) put it, 'Trudeau suffered from what his critics saw as an apparent unwillingness or inability to distinguish between the superpowers. Andropov's Russia was infinitely worse than the United States, even Reagan's United States, but Trudeau often seemed unable to make the distinction.'

Equally common was the mythology that Canada, the middle power, was selflessly dedicated to peace, conflict resolution, and international activism. And certainly over a period of six decades, historians, political scientists, former policy-makers, and others from a variety of political and epistemological perspectives, and from a number of different countries, kept adding to an ever-burgeoning literature on middle power in international politics, helping to develop and entrench thinking about the nature of middle power in world politics, creating what Adam Chapnick has termed a myth 'crafted to justify the attainment of disproportionate influence in international affairs' (Chapnick, 2000: 188; see also Molot, 1990).

However, despite the longevity of the term in both the scholarly literature and in political discourse, the concept of middle power remains, 60 years on, both ambiguous and elusive. Mark Neufeld (1995: 97) has rightly observed that the very ambiguity of perspectives on middle power allows the term to be used in a variety of ways—and thus for a variety of political purposes. Nikola Hynek (2007: 140) goes further, arguing that the emptiness of the middle-power concept is why it is so long-lived: 'The category of middle power is thus considered an *empty form* which needs to be—and has actually been—refilled again and again.'

The 'refilling', such as it has been, has taken very different forms over the past six decades. Thus, when Canadian politicians characterize Canada as a middle power, we have to remember that the meaning of the term, its political importance, and the policy implications of using the term to explain or justify policy behaviour all depend heavily on time and context.

For example, the embrace of the middle-power notion by Canadian policy-makers in the 1940s was driven by different factors, and had very different political objectives, than when the term was used in the 1960s, the 1990s, or at present. In the 1940s, the idea that Canada was a middle power was a useful way for the King government to press for international recognition of countries like Canada in the global order that was emerging after World War II. As a relatively new concept, it was used by Canadian policy-makers primarily for *external* purposes; as Denis Stairs (1998: 272) reminds us, when the 'middle powers' pushed the idea that they should be more privileged in the emerging world order than smaller states, 'this was "positional politics," and nothing more.'

By contrast, when Lloyd Axworthy, Canada's Minister of Foreign Affairs between 1996 and 2000, described Canada as a middle power in 1997, it was largely for *domestic purposes* (Axworthy, 1997). By the 1990s, 50 years after it had first been bruited by Canadian officials, the idea of middle power had become deeply associated in Canadian political culture with the innovative diplomacy of Lester Pearson. It can be argued that by using this term, Axworthy was trying to create in the minds of Canadians an alignment between his own brand of activism in global politics and Pearsonian diplomacy, even though they differed markedly in both purpose and style. Pearson's diplomacy in the 1950s had been quiet and generally conducted out of the glare of the media. As importantly, Pearson had always been concerned about ensuring that the United States government was on side and supportive of Canadian ideas. Finally, Canadian diplomacy in the 1950s had been driven by either highly selfish goals or, at the very minimum, enlightened self-interest.[1] By contrast, Axworthy's approach to international affairs was often bluntly undiplomatic. His diplomacy was often openly anti-American, and he clearly did not mind if the United States was not 'on side' on key Canadian initiatives. Finally, Axworthy's foreign policy tended to be driven by an idealism that was often disconnected from Canadian national interests. The best example of what Fen Osler Hampson and Dean F. Oliver (1998) called Axworthy's 'pulpit diplomacy' was his highly successful campaign to secure a global ban on anti-personnel landmines, even though his crucial contribution to the process was entirely (and inappropriately) overlooked by the Norwegian Nobel Committee when it awarded the 1997 Nobel Peace Prize to the International Campaign to Ban Landmines and its founder, Jody Williams.[2]

The fact that in Canadian politics 'middle power' has such ambiguous and changeable meanings suggests that in order to assess the 'soft' and 'hard' dimensions of Canada's middle power we have to make some careful distinctions about the terminology we use. In particular, we need to distinguish between 'middlepowerhood' and 'middlepowermanship'. How one analyzes the use by the Canadian government of soft and hard power in contemporary global politics will heavily depend on which conception we embrace.

'Middlepowerhood': Middle Power as Condition

In the literature on middle powers, there are two distinct ways of conceptualizing middle power. The first is the *positional*,[3] or, as Chapnick (1999: 76–9) would have it, the *hierarchical* approach. In this view, middle powers are those states in international politics whose size and power put them in the 'middle' between the great powers and smaller states. Such a hierarchical calculation was nicely characterized by Pearson in May 1944, while he was serving in the Canadian embassy in Washington. Canada, he wrote, is:

> among a group of states which are important enough to be necessary to the Big Four [the United States, the United Kingdom, the Soviet Union and France] but not important enough to be accepted as one of that quartet. As a matter of fact, the position of a 'big little Power' or 'little Big Power' is a very difficult one. . . . The big powers have power and responsibility, but they also have control. We 'in-between States' sometimes get, it seems to me, the worst of both worlds. (Quoted in Eayrs, 1975: 6)

This concern with locating one's country in the hierarchy of world powers was hardly new. As Carsten Holbraad reminds us, the idea of ranking powers hierarchically from 'large' to 'small', with 'medium' powers located, not surprisingly, in the 'middle', has been a persistent feature of descriptions of international relations dating back at least to Thomas Aquinas (Holbraad, 1984: 42). In the sixteenth century, Giovanni Botero praised the 'middle-sized state' (Welsh, 2004b: 3), and in the nineteenth century, German authors were interested in the idea of the *Mittelmächte*—those middle-sized powers located geographically in between the great powers (Holbraad, 1971; see also Nolte, 2006: 17ff.).

It is the desire to determine a country's *status* or *condition* as a middle power that gives rise to the idea of 'middlepowerhood'—a disagreeably ugly word but one that is nonetheless technically correct. In Old English, *hád*—rank or condition—was a noun that stood on its own, though often combined with others, as in *mægd-hád* (to be in the condition of a maid, i.e., a virgin). Although the modern English *-hood* only survives as a suffix, it conveys precisely *condition* or *status*: as in childhood, adulthood, priesthood, etc. In this usage, 'middlepowerhood', very simply, is the condition of being a middle power.

However, the problem with 'middlepowerhood' as an analytical category is that it very quickly becomes tautological unless the *condition* it purports to describe is carefully defined. If 'middlepowerhood' is to be meaningful, one needs to be able to determine what the criteria of the status and condition are going to be. Just as such oppositional notions as *childhood* and *adulthood* mean nothing without the specification of what constitutes the difference between a child and an adult, so, too, must 'middlepowerhood' come with some set of measures to distinguish the condition of being a middle power from 'smallstatehood' and 'greatpowerhood'. In essence, we need to know how to determine into which '-hood' a particular state falls.

And there is no agreement in the literature on the precise measures to be used for such a ranking exercise. For some, determining the 'middle' in global politics is little more than an intuitive and impressionistic assessment of which states are neither 'great powers' nor 'small states'. In this view, we just *know* that countries like Canada, Australia, and South Africa are middle powers simply because they are not states like the United States, the Russian Federation, or China, on the one hand, and, on the other, are not states like Costa Rica, Vanuatu, or Chad.

For others, by contrast, 'power ranking' can be determined in a positivist and empirical way by invoking such measurable characteristics as geographic size, size of population, size and nature of the economy, level of industrial and technological development, degree of economic dependence, size and sophistication of military capabilities. Thus, for example, Laura Neack (1992: 6–11) used cluster analysis with five national attribute indicators—gross national product per capita, military expenditures per capita, population, infant mortality rate, and adult literacy rate—in an effort to determine what precisely constituted a 'middle state', as she termed this category of states. Likewise, Jonathan H. Ping's 'hybridization theory' of middle powers depends heavily on a positivist and statistical exploration of some key attributes of middle powers, particularly those in the Asia-Pacific region (Ping, 2005: esp. ch. 3).

However, as a number of critics have noted, a definition of 'middlepowerhood' based on objective attributes is not really possible because the attributes themselves are, as Chapnick (1999: 77) reminds us, arbitrary, and thus lead to what in essence are arbitrary definitions. Thus, for example, Peyton Lyon and Brian Tomlin, using a series of indices of national power, argued in 1979 that 'Canada should now be regarded as a major power' (Lyon and Tomlin, 1979: 72). Likewise, according to Neack's empirical calculations, Canada is not a 'middle state' but a 'great power', a conclusion shared by those students of Canadian foreign policy who argued that Canada was a 'principal power' or a 'foremost power' (see Nossal et al., 2007: 127–30).

And if one looks for non-arbitrary ways of making the cut, other definitional problems emerge. For example, Chapnick argues that during the Cold War era the veto power on the United Nations Security Council could be used as a clear non-arbitrary way of distinguishing between those at the unambiguous 'top' of the international hierarchy of states—the Soviet Union and the United States, the world's superpowers—and all other states, the 'non-superpowers'. In his view, the veto gave three states that were not superpowers—the People's

Republic of China, France, and the United Kingdom—a privileged position that put them in the 'middle' between 'superpowerhood' and all other states in the international system. In the brief post-Cold War moment (1991–2001), when the United States emerged as the unipolar hyperpower, Chapnick suggests that the Russian Federation should be included in this 'middle' group. But Chapnick uses the example of the UN veto precisely to show the limitations of such attempts to define 'middlepowerhood' objectively: he recognizes that Britain, China, France, and the Russian Federation might have the veto on the Security Council, thus distinguishing them from all other states, but no one thinks of these countries as being middle powers (Chapnick, 1999: 78–9).

'Middlepowermanship': Middle Power as Diplomatic Behaviour

While some students are impelled towards the idea of 'middlepowerhood' by the definitional challenge posed by the simple question 'What is a middle power?', others have focused on the idea that middle power in international politics has less to do with *condition* than with *behaviour*. In this view, a state is a middle power not because of what it is, but rather because of what it *does*. In other words, middle powers pursued a particular kind of diplomacy in international affairs.

It is argued that three essential features of 'middle-power diplomacy' can be identified. First, middle-power diplomacy tends to seek compromise in global politics. Middle powers—in large part precisely because they are not great powers and because they tend to be so negatively affected by great-power conflict—recognize that conflict is an inevitable and unavoidable condition of global politics. While conflicts of interest between peoples organized into sovereign states can be resolved by a winner-take-all approach, middle-power diplomacy is animated by the idea that the conditions of peace in global politics are not advanced by attempts at zero-sum wins. Rather, compromise, in which parties to a dispute are able to secure some of their objectives and protect some of their interests, is seen as a more effective and durable means of conflict resolution. For that reason, middle-power diplomacy has traditionally been associated, as John W. Holmes (1966: 16) put it, with adopting 'a middle or mediatory position in conflicts'. Middle-power diplomacy was concerned with bringing two sides in a conflict together, putting an emphasis on negotiating peaceful resolution to the differences that will be an inevitable feature of global politics. In this sense, as Charles-Philippe David and Stéphane Roussel (1998: 134) argue, the mediatory inclination of middle-power diplomacy also fits with the essentially conservative nature of middle powers: they seek 'to preserve and strengthen the stability of the international system' rather than to seek change in global balances of power or privilege.

Second, middle-power diplomacy tends to seek multilateral solutions to global problems, issues, and conflicts of interest. While governments of middle powers may on occasion embrace unilateral or bilateral approaches to policy problems, these are seen as a distinctly second-best solution. The preferred approach is to entrench political solutions to global issues in multilateral agreements, embedding implementation of these agreements in international or multilateral institutions.[4] No matter what the issue—the introduction of new rules for the management of the world's oceans; atrocity crimes being committed in a country; the transnational spread of infectious disease; dealing with climate change; reconceptualizing the idea of national sovereignty; the rise of jihadist extremism; or accelerating global development—the preference of middle powers is for a multilateral response.

Finally, middle-power diplomacy is marked by what Australia's Minister of Foreign Affairs from 1988 to 1996, Gareth Evans, called 'acts of good international citizenship' (Evans, 1991: 322–6; Cooper et al., 1993: 19–20). Evans was referring to the tendency of some states to involve themselves in global politics in ways that might not be expected if a very narrow definition of self-interest were being used. Thus, for example, involvement in most of the international peacekeeping operations during the Cold War was rarely in the narrow self-interest of most of the governments that contributed to these operations. But the middle powers that contributed to peacekeeping operations were deemed to have a somewhat wider definition of self-interest at work, one that was usually more indirect and usually characterized as 'enlightened self-interest'. In other words, contributing to peacekeeping operations in a distant region was normatively good not only because it might bring stability and order to that region, which would be normatively good for the people there, but might also contribute to the creation and maintenance of a broader global peace, which was normatively good for the country contributing to the peacekeeping operation.

But the inclination of middle-power diplomacy to engage in acts of good international citizenship is also deemed to be animated by morality: the idea of doing the 'right thing', the unwillingness to look with indifference on injustice, and the willingness to infuse foreign policy behaviour with particular ethical values. Participating in military action to prevent atrocity crimes, engaging in democracy promotion, encouraging 'best practices' in running elections, co-operating in debt relief for heavily indebted poor countries—these are held to be the mark of middle-power diplomacy.

This range of foreign policy behaviours classically associated with middle powers has been called 'middlepowermanship'. It seeks to capture the propensity of some governments to try to find particular diplomatic niches (Cooper, 1993: 1–24), to exhibit entrepreneurial and technical leadership on selected issues on the global agenda (Cooper et al., 1993), and in particular to be 'norm entrepreneurs' in global affairs, seeking to introduce different ways of conceptualizing global issues and new, innovative, and creative ways of coping with them (Ingebritsen, 2002). For their part, many Canadian leaders have sought to articulate what constitutes middle power diplomacy. The most recent formulation was by the Conservative Prime Minister, Stephen Harper, who said in September 2007 that middle powers 'step up to the plate to do their part . . . willing to assume responsibilities, seek practical, do-able solutions to problems and who have a voice and influence in global affairs because they lead, not by lecturing, but by example' (Canada, 2007).

Now it is true, as a number of critics have argued, that the behavioural model of middle-power diplomacy brings us no closer to an objective definition of what a middle power is. Chapnick (1999: 76), for example, notes correctly that those who advocate a behavioural approach to the identification of middle powers in world politics inevitably 'work backwards' by 'examining the international activities of a state such as Canada and then defining middle power behaviour by these same actions'. In short, 'middlepowermanship' is how one defines middle powers, and those who engage in 'middlepowermanship' are middle powers—a classic tautology.

Moreover, as will be readily evident, numerous states in the international system, large and small, exhibit many of these attributes in their diplomacy. Stairs (1998: 281) notes that one cannot find a set of behaviours or 'facilitating conditions' that are *only* associated with 'middling power'. On the contrary: the vast majority of states in the contemporary global system are attached—to a greater or lesser extent—to multilateralism and multilateral institutions as a means of resolving global policy issues. The number of exceedingly small states, and even those states that are treated as pariahs and excluded from regular interstate intercourse, such as the Democratic People's Republic of Korea or the Union of Myanmar (also known as Union of Burma), are not true autarkies. Even the United States, which is often criticized as overly unilateral, remains deeply committed to multilateral institutions and, more often than not, to multilateral approaches to global issues.[5]

Likewise, compromise is hardly the unique preserve of a limited number of states in global politics. On the contrary, compromise is widely sought by the vast majority of states in their engagement with each other. Even those states that are not shy about being robustly aggressive in the pursuit of their own interests will at times seek compromise (most commonly when confronting another state equally aggressive in the pursuit of its own interests).

Finally, it is not clear that middle powers engage in the acts of 'good international citizenship' that are supposed to set them apart from other states. To be sure, it is true that Canadian leaders in particular have sought to portray their country as more selfless and moral than others in international politics, particularly the great powers, and these claims have led some American critics to sneer at Canadian pretensions to be a 'moral superpower' (e.g., Goldberg, 2002). While no Canadian leader ever used that term—on the contrary, Paul Martin, Prime Minister from December 2003 until February 2006, referred to Canada as a 'moral middle power' (CTV News, 2004)—there is little doubt that an essentially moralizing tone was often used by Canadian politicians in describing their country's foreign policy.[6] Certainly the apogee of this kind of Canadian self-flattery occurred during Martin's prime ministership. If there is one example that illustrates perfectly Martin's vastly inflated conception of Canada in the world, it was the unscripted 'victory speech' he delivered to the Liberal caucus on 19 May 2005 after his minority government narrowly avoided defeat on the budget by a single vote. Martin breathlessly assured the cheering Liberal MPs that they had not been voting just for a budget: 'What we voted for was a vision of a Canada dynamic and leading the world. We will set the standard by which other nations judge themselves' (Dawson et al., 2005).

It is also true that Canadians have tended to buy uncritically into what I have termed the 'ear candy' rhetoric of their governors about their magnificent contributions to world affairs (Nossal, 2005). As Denis Stairs (2003) put it bluntly: 'Canadians have grown alarmingly smug, complacent, and self-deluded in their approach to international affairs', thanks in large part to the 'active encouragement of their leaders'. But the empirical record suggests that the putative altruism of the middle powers relative to other states is largely mythical. Canadian governments may have embraced policy positions on some issues that *appear* disconnected from Canadian interests, such as the championing of the landmines ban or the regulation of small arms. But when Canadian interests are directly involved—for example, on matters of development assistance or trade—the record reveals that in their policies and programs towards the rest of the world, Canadians are no less selfish, stingy, or relentlessly parochial than any other people in the international system (Nossal, 1998–9; Cohen, 2003).

In short, when one looks carefully at 'middlepowermanship' in practice, particularly in the Canadian context, it is not clear that we have a distinct kind of global diplomacy pursued by middle powers. Instead, what we have is the persistent *assertion* of uniqueness that is supposed to be the preserve of middle powers—what Nikola Hynek (2007: 138) calls 'a self-constructed middle power'. The absence of an objective basis for these claims of uniqueness brings us to question whether 'middlepowermanship' remains a useful analytical concept.

Conclusion: Recovering 'Middlepowermanship'

In this chapter I have outlined why both 'middlepowerhood' and 'middle-powermanship' are fraught as theoretical concepts. 'Middlepowerhood' is particularly problematic in the absence of widely accepted objective characteristics that would allow us to distinguish 'middlepowerhood' from either 'greatpowerhood' or 'smallstatehood'. Given its definitional difficulties, there are good reasons to be skeptical about its utility—reasons that go well beyond its ugliness as a word. But 'middlepowermanship' is also a problematic term, since the characteristics of what is called middle-power diplomacy are also exhibited by other powers, great and small. But does that mean that 'middlepowermanship' cannot be useful in analyzing foreign policy? To find its utility, we must go back to John W. Holmes, a former senior official in the Canadian Department of External Affairs who in 1960 left government service to head the Canadian Institute of International Affairs and teach at the University of Toronto and York University.

Holmes first used the word 'middlepowermanship' in the mid-1960s at a conference on Canada as a middle power (Holmes, 1966; see also Holmes, 1970: 16). But we now tend to forget that Holmes coined the word not as analytical tool but as an ironic critique of Canadian foreign policy-makers. By the mid-1960s, with the celebration of Canadian middle-power diplomacy in full bloom, Holmes became increasingly worried about, as he put it, 'the glorification and formalization of a kind of diplomacy that was really just commonsensical and not as unique as we were hinting' (Holmes, 1984: 368). Hunting about for a way to criticize this glorification of Canadian diplomacy, Holmes chose 'middlepowermanship' as an ironic counter to a term that had commonly been used in the mid-1950s to criticize a particular style of diplomacy in the United States, 'brinkmanship'. 'Brinkmanship' had been coined by James Reston of the *New York Times* in the mid-1950s, and had been inspired by the writings of British humorist Stephen Potter, whose satirical books on 'one-upmanship' and 'lifemanship' had been published in the early 1950s. Reston had used 'brinkmanship' to criticize the diplomacy of John Foster Dulles, Secretary of State in the administration of Dwight D. Eisenhower, that had sought to bring the United States and the Soviet Union to the brink of war as a type of American diplomacy. So, if an appropriate way to critique American foreign policy was to call it 'brinkmanship', Holmes reckoned that 'middlepowermanship' was an equally good word to critique the tendency of Canadians to overglorify their foreign policy as though it was unique.

But, as Holmes later ruefully admitted, what had begun as a tongue-in-cheek jab at Canadian diplomacy got transmogrified into something far more serious than he had originally intended. Holmes admitted that he should have realized that what had happened to 'brinkmanship' might also happen to 'middlepowermanship'. In the case of 'brinkmanship', what had started as a critical journalistic characterization of a particular style of diplomacy was ironically embraced by the very officials it had been coined to criticize, and moreover, was used with considerable braggadocio to celebrate that aggressive style of diplomacy. As importantly, 'brinkmanship' was also appropriated by the academic community and turned into an analytical category to analyze international crises (e.g., Lebow, 1981: esp. ch. 4), in the process stripping it of its original critical and ironic connotation. Exactly the same thing happened to 'middlepowermanship': the word did indeed enter the discourse of Canadian foreign policy, but without its original irony or critical intent. Holmes (1984: 368) explains that when he first used the word:

> The mood in the land was earnest. A new breed of scholars was now adding greatly to our sophistication about foreign policy, but seeking somewhat too arduously to define the indefinable. The word 'middlepowermanship' began to buzz. Editors and politicians needed something to cling to, and . . . the illusion gained ground that the multifarious range of international involvements could be subsumed in a succinctly definable 'foreign policy.'

Given its critical and ironic origins, some might argue that 'middlepowermanship' should simply be discarded. But I would suggest that there is utility in continuing to use the word to describe and analyze Canadian foreign policy behaviour. However, to recover its utility as an analytical category, we need to return it to the way Holmes originally used it—in other words, we need to use it with some irony, in order to encourage us to think critically about how foreign policy-makers in Canada tend to use 'middlepowerhood' to justify and popularize their foreign policy decisions.

After all, what we have seen since Holmes first questioned Canadian 'middlepowermanship' in the 1960s is a continual revisiting of the middle-power theme by Canadian politicians who have sought to convince Canadians that there is a distinct and unique style of Canadian diplomacy in global affairs. This has been a recurring and generally unbroken process, from Pearson in the 1960s to Harper in 2007.[7] As such, it is a process reflected in all of the case studies examined in this book. Thinking about the strategies that the Canadian government has embraced in foreign and security policy, involving the use of both soft and hard power, as *middlepowermanship*—but in an ironic Holmesian way—allows us to expose more clearly the degree to which the stories that Canadians tell each other about their country's involvement in world affairs have not changed much in 40 years.

Notes

1. Though, as John W. Holmes (1984: 381) reminds us, the 'early successes of Canada as a middle power were attributable to our skill in producing sound ideas for the general rather than just the Canadian interest.'
2. The deeply symbiotic relationship between Williams and Axworthy was crucial to the achievement of a landmines ban. Without Williams and the ICBL, Axworthy would never

have been able to pull off his highly undiplomatic 'surprise challenge' to other governments that generated the impetus for a ban (for details, see Tomlin, 1998: 15–20). But without Axworthy and the diplomatic resources of the Canadian state, Williams and the ICBL would never have been able to achieve the global ban so quickly. By all accounts, US anger at being sandbagged by Axworthy's 'surprise challenge' sparked a sustained American effort to lobby the Norwegian Nobel Committee not to include Axworthy with Williams and the ICBL as equal winners of the 1997 Peace Prize even though Axworthy was as clearly deserving as Williams of recognition.

3. The variant of the 'positional' perspective—that middle powers are *ideologically* or *politically* positioned between great powers—was noted above.

4. The best contemporary statement is Keating (2002).

5. While some argue that the administration of George W. Bush from 2001 to 2009 was unusual in its unilateral approach to global politics, American unilateral impulses have historically been a persistent problem for both friends and enemies of the United States. For example, see Nossal (1997) for Canadian views of American unilateralism during the administration of Bill Clinton. However, for all the criticisms that can be levied at American unilateralism, in fact the US government, under even the most unilaterally minded president, remains a multilateral player in global politics.

6. There are a number of examples of such moral smugness in Lloyd Axworthy's memoirs: see Axworthy (2003).

7. Even if, as Hynek (2007: 138) reminds us, the meaning attached to the middle-power discourse of Canadian political leaders has not been entirely linear.

References

Axworthy, Lloyd. 1997. 'Canada and Human Security: The Need for Leadership', *International Journal* 52, 2 (Spring): 183–96.

———. 2003. *Navigating a New World: Canada's Global Future*. Toronto: Knopf.

Canada, Secretary of State for External Affairs. 1970. *Foreign Policy for Canadians*. Ottawa: Queen's Printer.

———, Secretary of State for External Affairs. 1985. *Competitiveness and Security: Directions for Canada's International Relations*. Ottawa: Supply and Services Canada.

———. 1995. *Canada in the World: Canadian Foreign Policy Review*. Ottawa: Government of Canada.

———. [2005]. *A Role of Pride and Influence in the World: Canada's International Policy Statement*. Ottawa: Government of Canada.

Chapnick, Adam. 1999. 'The Middle Power', *Canadian Foreign Policy* 7, 2 (Winter): 73–82.

———. 2000. 'The Canadian Middle Power Myth', *International Journal* 55 (Spring): 188–206.

———. 2005. *The Middle Power Project: Canada and the Founding of the United Nations*. Vancouver: University of British Columbia Press.

Cohen, Andrew. 2003. *While Canada Slept: How We Lost Our Place in the World*. Toronto: McClelland & Stewart.

Cooper, Andrew F. 1993. 'Niche Diplomacy: A Conceptual Overview', in Cooper, ed., *Niche Diplomacy: Middle Powers after the Cold War*. London: Macmillan, 1–24.

———, Richard A. Higgott, and Kim Richard Nossal. 1993. *Relocating Middle Powers: Australia and Canada in a Changing World Order*. Vancouver: University of British Columbia Press.

David, Charles-Philippe, and Stéphane Roussel. 1998. '"Middle Power Blues": Canadian Policy and International Security after the Cold War', *American Review of Canadian Studies* 28, 1 and 2 (Spring–Summer): 131–56.

Eayrs, James. 1975. 'Defining a New Place for Canada in the Hierarchy of World Power', *International Perspectives* (May–June): 15–24.

Evans, Gareth. 1991. *Australia's Foreign Relations in the World of the 1990s*. Melbourne: Melbourne

University Press.

Fox, Annette Baker. 1977. *The Politics of Attraction: Four Middle Powers and the United States.* New York: Columbia University Press.

Gelber, Lionel. 1945–6. 'Canada's New Stature', *Foreign Affairs* 24 (Oct.–June): 277–89.

Glazebrook, G.P. deT. 1947. 'The Middle Powers in the United Nations System', *International Organization* 1, 2 (June): 307–15.

Goldberg, Jonah. 2002. 'Bomb Canada: The Case for War', *National Review* 54, 22 (25 Nov.): 30–2.

Gotlieb, Allan. 2006. *The Washington Diaries, 1981–1989.* Toronto: McClelland & Stewart.

Granatstein, J.L., and Robert Bothwell. 1990. *Pirouette: Pierre Trudeau and Canadian Foreign Policy.* Toronto: University of Toronto Press.

Hampson, Fen Osler, and Dean F. Oliver. 1998. 'Pulpit Diplomacy: A Critical Assessment of the Axworthy Doctrine', *International Journal* 53, 3 (Summer): 379–406.

Holbraad, Carsten. 1971. 'The Role of Middle Powers', *Cooperation and Conflict* 6, 1: 77–90.

———. 1984. *Middle Powers in International Politics.* London: Macmillan.

Holmes, John W. 1966. 'Is There a Future for Middlepowermanship?', in J. King Gordon, ed., *Canada's Role as a Middle Power.* Toronto: Canadian Institute of International Affairs, 13–28.

———. 1984. 'Most Safely in the Middle', *International Journal* 39, 2: 366–88.

Hynek, Nikola. 2007. 'Humanitarian Arms Control, Symbiotic Functionalism, and the Concept of Middlepowerhood', *Central European Journal of International and Security Studies* 1, 2 (Nov.): 132–55.

Jepperson, Ronald L., Alexander Wendt, and Peter J. Katzenstein. 1996. 'Norms, Identity, and Culture in National Security', in Katzenstein, ed., *The Culture of National Security: Norms and Identity in World Politics.* New York: Columbia University Press, 33–75.

Ichikawa, Akira. 1979. 'The "Helpful Fixer": Canada's Persistent International Image', *Behind the Headlines* 37 (Mar.): 1–28.

Ingebritsen, Christine. 2002. 'Norm Entrepreneurs: Scandinavia's Role in World Politics', *Cooperation and Conflict* 37, 1: 11–23.

Keating, Tom. 2002. *Canada and World Order: The Multilateralist Tradition in Canadian Foreign Policy*, 2nd edn. Toronto: Oxford University Press.

Lebow, Richard Ned. 1981. *Between Peace and War: The Nature of International Crisis.* Baltimore: Johns Hopkins University Press.

Lyon, Peyton V., and Brian W. Tomlin. 1979. *Canada as an International Actor.* Toronto: Macmillan.

Molot, Maureen Appel. 1990. 'Where Do We, Should We, Or Can We Sit? A Review of Canadian Foreign Policy Literature', *International Journal of Canadian Studies* 1, 2: 77–96.

Neack, Laura. 1992. 'Empirical Observations on "Middle State" Behavior at the Start of a New International System', *Pacific Focus* 7, 1 (Mar.): 5–21.

Neufeld, Mark. 1995. 'Hegemony and Foreign Policy Analysis: The Case of Canada as a Middle Power', *Studies in Political Economy* 48: 7–29.

Nolte, Detlef. 2006. 'Macht und Machthierarchien in den internationalen Beziehungen: Ein Analysekonzept für die Forschung über regionale Führungsmächte', *GIGA Working Papers* 29, German Institute of Global and Regional Studies, Oct.

Nossal, Kim Richard. 1997. '"Without Regard for the Interests of Others": Canada and American Unilateralism in the Post-Cold War Era', *American Review of Canadian Studies* 27 (Summer): 179–97.

———. 1998–9. 'Pinchpenny Diplomacy: The Decline of "Good International Citizenship" in Canadian Foreign Policy', *International Journal* 54, 1 (Winter): 88–105.

———. 2005. 'Ear Candy: Canadian Policy toward Humanitarian Intervention and Atrocity Crimes in Darfur', *International Journal* 60, 4 (Autumn): 1017–32.

———, Stéphane Roussel, and Stéphane Paquin. 2007. *Politique internationale et défense au Canada et au Québec.* Montréal: Les Presses de l'Université de Montréal.

Ping, Jonathan H. 2005. *Middle Power Statecraft: Indonesia, Malaysia and the Asia-Pacific.* Aldershot: Ashgate.

Ravenhill, John. 1998. 'Cycles of Middle Power Activism: Constraint and Choice in Australian and Canadian Foreign Policies', *Australian Journal of International Affairs* 52, 3: 309–27.

Stairs, Denis. 1998. 'Of Medium Powers and Middling Roles', in Ken Booth, ed., *Statecraft and Security: The Cold War and Beyond*. Cambridge: Cambridge University Press, 270–86.

———. 2003. 'Myths, Morals, and Reality in Canadian Foreign Policy', *International Journal* 58, 2 (Spring): 239–56.

Tomlin, Brian W. 1998. 'On a Fast-Track to a Ban: The Canadian Policy Process', *Canadian Foreign Policy* 5, 3 (Spring): 3–23.

Trudeau, Pierre Elliott. 1987. *Lifting the Shadow of War*, ed. C. David Crenna. Edmonton: Hurtig.

Welsh, Jennifer. 2004a. *At Home in the World: Canada's Global Vision for the 21st Century*. Toronto: HarperCollins.

———. 2004b. 'Canada in the 21st Century: Beyond Dominion and Middle Power', *Behind the Headlines* 61, 4: 1–30.

Wendt, Alexander. 1992. 'Anarchy Is What States Make of It: The Social Construction of Power Politics', *International Organization* 46, 2 (Spring): 391–425.

Additional Readings

Cox, Robert W. 1989. 'Middlepowermanship, Japan, and the Future of World Order', *International Journal* 44 (Autumn): 823–62.

Hayes, Geoffrey. 1993–4. 'Middle Powers in the New World Order', *Behind the Headlines* 51: 1–25.

MacKay, R.A. 1969. 'The Canadian Doctrine of the Middle Powers', in Harvey L. Dyck and H. Peter Krosby, eds, *Empire and Nations: Essays in Honour of Frederic H. Soward*. Toronto: University of Toronto Press, 133–44.

Pratt, Cranford. 1990. 'Has Middle Power Internationalism a Future?', in Pratt, ed., *Middle Power Internationalism: The North–South Dimension*. Montreal and Kingston: McGill-Queen's University Press, 143–67.

Ungerer, Carl. 2007. 'The "Middle Power" Concept in Australian Foreign Policy', *Australian Journal of Politics and History* 53, 4: 538–51.

Wood, Bernard. 1988. *The Middle Powers and the General Interest*. Ottawa: North–South Institute.

Chapter 3

Canada as a Middle, Model, or Civilian Power: What's in a Name?

David Bosold

Introduction

The Canadian 'middle-power' image has come under some hefty criticism over the last decade, most notably by analysts such as Jennifer Welsh. This points to a serious identity crisis, at least in respect of the country's foreign policy. Tom Keating has reminded us in the first chapter that the middle-power image, like the Inukshuk, serves as a directional marker. It has also served as an instrument for foreign policy analysts to delineate Canada's place and role in the world or to define the areas where its efforts were measurable and visible. Recent years have seen attempts to 're-brand' the country by using other images, such as that of 'model power'. This, however, has neither put an end to the country's ongoing soul-searching nor made easier the work for those who intend to analyze Canada's foreign policy more thoroughly. By comparing the traditional Canadian image of 'middle power' to that of 'civilian power'—which has been used to characterize German foreign policy as well as the Common Foreign and Security Policy of the European Union (EU)—it will be demonstrated that a shift to 'model power' will not solve the problem of finding a more accurate category than the old middle-power label. The reason for this assessment lies in the peculiarity of the Canadian political and academic discussion regarding the problem of the demise of Canada's middle-power role. Politically speaking, one will not see increased international influence by simply switching to a new brand. Analytically speaking, we will see the same pitfalls and difficulties if we use a new term to replace 'middle power'. Basing this chapter on a more elaborate analysis of the Canadian 'autism' and placing it against the backdrop of the past debates on Canadian foreign policy will permit us to better understand the potential of the middle-power category as an overarching structure for analyzing soft and hard power. Moreover, using an identity-based definition of 'middle power' will allow for a clearer understanding of *alter* and *ego* in a role-theoretical conceptualization of middle power.

The Methodological Problems of Middle-Power Theory

As presented in greater detail in the two previous chapters, referring to Canada as a middle power has been advocated by scholars on the grounds of analyzing the country as a middle power in hierarchical, normative, and behavioural terms. All perspectives highlight important facets of Canada's foreign policy behaviour. They are, however, non-exhaustive and lack a more far-reaching analysis of identity. In addition, they have been challenged by other Canadian scholars due to inherent methodological weaknesses.

The Hierarchical Model

The *hierarchical model* focuses on a supposedly 'objective' and quantifiable criterion for measuring and assessing Canada's role in the world vis-à-vis other countries (Ravenhill, 1998: 310). Typical measures for establishing such a ranking of states include geographic size and position, per capita income, and military power (Chapnick, 1999: 76ff.).[1]

Ironically, the most powerful rejection of defining Canada as a middle power in hierarchical terms has been demonstrated by Canadian scholars intending to define Canada's rank in the world. At the core of this type of scholarship stands a debate on how to define and measure power, primarily assessing the power capabilities of states (military, economic output, economic structure, cultural independence) and determining which aspects matter. A number of texts have since been featuring the three images of Canada as a principal power, satellite, and middle power (Cooper, 1997b: 6–22; Nossal, 1997: 52ff., Kirton, 2007: 12–14). At the heart of this debate is the selection of the policy fields and capabilities considered to have an impact on Canada's power in the conduct of its foreign policy. If the economic and cultural dependence of the Canadian state is scrutinized, it is not surprising to find the conclusion that the United States has significantly decreased Canada's room for manoeuvre (Bosold, 2003). To theorize about Canada as a satellite of the US thus implies that, although Canada might chart its own course, the possibility remains marginal and the course will be constrained. Referring to Canada as a principal power necessitates the selection of other factors related to where and how power is wielded and how power can be aggregated (Dewitt and Kirton, 1983; Kirton, 2007: 14). It is based on a set of five criteria (Kirton, 2007: 83) out of which Canada's membership in a number of international organizations and clubs, as well as the size of its military and the responsibility it assumes to provide for international peace and stability, figure most prominently. The reasons for the different findings of these respective hierarchical approaches are thus less to be seen in the differences of their interpretations than in the selection of the aspects and policy fields they study. Yet, all three approaches are problematic on the grounds of devoting too much attention to global factors. Their explanatory power is focused too much on systemic factors and excludes non-quantifiable, intersubjective aspects.

The Normative Model

The *normative model* is based on the assumption that middle-power foreign policy has to be, and actually is, conducted on the grounds of higher normative principles (Welsh, 2004a: 158; Cooper et al., 1993: 18; Holbraad, 1971: 82; Jordaan, 2003; Pratt, 1990: 143ff.). That is, middle-power foreign policy is supposed to be guided by less selfish motives than the dominating schools of international relations theory assume.[2] Canada's self-understanding of a middle power acting as a 'helpful fixer' or 'good international citizen' is a case in point. It highlights the view that Canada's foreign policy preference for narrow national interests is supposed to take a back seat to the well-being of all nations and the stability of the global order. A field where such policies are said to be most visible is North–South relations (Holbraad, 1971: 80). With decreases in official development assistance (ODA) and the continuous refusal by the industrialized countries to open Western markets for the products of the developing world over the last 15 years, the accuracy of the normative middle-power approach has now been rightly called into question. Some scholars argue that the developments of the last decade, which saw a rise in humanitarian interventions and the adoption of the 'responsibility to protect' principle by the UN General Assembly in 2005, serve as proof that middle powers such as Canada continue to strive for a better and more just global order, but, this time, in other policy fields.

Yet, one will also have to take seriously the criticisms by others that even if middle powers attempt to change the international legal framework, they will do so only if their respective national interests are not endangered. Put more succinctly, normative middle-power diplomacy will always be limited in two ways. First, middle powers will only act in the name of a global common good if the new order will be at least as beneficial for them as the previous one. Second, their attempts to transform the global order will always be more oriented towards moderate improvement than radical transformation (Jordaan, 2003: 167). Since their own power and well-being depend on the status quo and the relative benefits of their relationship with the global power(s), they act as balancers and not as a revolutionary force. That said, one should not underestimate the self-interest of normative middle-power diplomacy to sustain the current global order as an important ingredient of their foreign policy. In addition, such an analysis always runs the risk of neglecting the double standards that usually arise in the conduct of such a 'normative', 'ethical', or 'moral' foreign policy (Rempel, 2006; Heins and Chandler, 2007; Nimijean, 2006: 75–8).

The Behavioural Model

Although normative considerations will ultimately influence behaviour, the reasoning of scholars proposing a *behavioural model* is straightforward and pragmatic. They argue that what is to be studied is what middle powers 'actually do' (Cooper et al., 1993: 7) as opposed to what they 'should do' (this, again, being the normative dimension). Recent studies have pointed to a defining set of features of middle-power foreign policy. They find a preference for multilateralist solutions to global politics, a willingness to forge compromise and to project progressive domestic values onto the global level (e.g., ibid., 19–22; Welsh, 2004b: 585; Jordaan, 2003: 174ff.; Michaud and Bélanger, 2000: 107). Like the preceding middle-power models, this one also suffers from a series of shortcomings. Generally speaking, any such study will not be able to overcome the methodological problem of the arbitrary nature in defining a middle power in the first place. All studies necessitate such an arbitrary a priori decision (Apel, 1984: 56). Put differently, there are no 'natural' middle-power traits that precede the analysts' selection of criteria that define a middle power. In the words of Chapnick (1999: 76): 'That middle powers are those that practice middle power internationalism, and that middle power internationalism describes the behaviour of middle powers is a tautology.' If deviation from a hitherto defined idealized middle-power behaviour over time actually falsifies the theoretical model depends on the rigidity of the analytical criteria.

An example: if multilateralism is a defining feature of middle-power behaviour, the falsification of my theoretical approach depends on my definition of multilateralism. If I, for instance, stick to the classic definition provided by Robert Keohane, that multilateralism 'refers to coordinating relations among three or more states' (quoted in Ruggie, 1993: 8), does that mean that Canada does not act multilaterally if it *also* co-ordinates its relations with non-state actors as in the Ottawa Process to ban landmines? The answer will ultimately depend on one's definition of multilateralism. It is the same problem encountered by Cooper, Higgott, and Nossal in their study of Canadian and Australian foreign policy. They analyze the foreign policy of the two countries by presenting idealized middle-power behaviour, and observe change over time. Instead of refuting the notion of middle power, they argue that systemic structures forced the nations to adapt, thereby 'relocating' them in the global order (Cooper et al., 1993: 172–3). According to the authors, the adaptation process was mostly visible in terms of the technical and entrepreneurial nature of the leadership exercised by these secondary powers. Critics demur that such a stance proves that there is no analytical value to 'middle power' as such. The important point here, then, is that one has to be aware that the theory idealizes and generalizes a certain foreign policy behaviour or technique at a specific moment in time. While the critics have a point, the more interesting aspect is how we should deal with behavioural change in analytic terms. We can and should still look for reasons beyond the one offered by Cooper et al. Foreign policy may change because of systemic shifts, but reasons for foreign policy change might also be found on a level other than that of the international sphere.

A Critique of Previous Middle-Power Analyses

What is hence problematic about the recent scholarship in more practical terms is the absence of identity as a crucial determinant of Canada as a middle power. Two reasons in particular can be identified for this failure. First, most of the widely held beliefs about or myths of Canadian foreign policy since World War II were articulated in a narrative of Canada as middle power (Keating, 2002: 9–10). The inventiveness and skills of Canadian diplomats, the nation's attempt to contribute to a more just global order, and the country's contribution to the United Nations in general and peacekeeping in particular are difficult to conceive of outside the framework of Canada as the middle-power par excellence (Holloway, 2006: 236–8). Second, the study of Canadian identity in a role-theoretical model is able to explain the ongoing disconnect between Canadians and non-Canadians in assessing the international contribution of Canada on the global stage. For that reason, the most crucial aspect of middle-power identity in the subsequent analysis is the process of identity formation.

Identity Formation and Role Theory

Ideally, identity is the simultaneous unfolding of two interrelated processes that are unified in the sociological category of 'role'. Quite simply, identity, here, is the result of an actor's perception of what he or she does, or should do, and the affirmation or rejection of that action by others. The first is what scholars refer to as 'role conception', the latter is termed 'role expectation' (Kirste and Maull, 1996; Harnisch and Maull, 2001: 138ff.; Aggestam, 1999). An example is the widely held belief among Canadians that their country is an important peacekeeper (Hayes, 1997). What transforms this collective identity into 'real' political action is an assessment under which circumstances the Canadian public and political decision-makers deem it necessary to 'act' as peacekeepers. The call for a Canadian peacekeeping role in Sudan's Darfur province put forward by Michael Byers (2007: 61ff.)

and others is a nice illustration of the power of collective identity and role conception as far as (Canadian) foreign policy is concerned (Blanchfield, 2007). When then US Secretary of State Condoleezza Rice distinguished the purpose of the US army from that of the Canadian Forces (CF) by holding that 'we don't need to have the 82nd Airborne escorting kids to kindergarten' she implicitly affirmed the Canadian belief of being a nation of peacekeepers, or, at least, of the CF being peacekeepers rather than fighters. Notwithstanding the counterfactual of Canadian battle deaths in Afghanistan (which proves that not *all* Canadian service personnel are necessarily peacekeepers), the crucial aspect brought into the equation is that the process of identity formation is a reciprocal one. The creation of a Canadian foreign policy role also depends on the expectations and beliefs held by others, here, the US Secretary of State.

In conclusion, a foreign policy role consists of an internalized belief of what Canada as a foreign policy actor deems appropriate in terms of its value system and world view, in short, the role conception, and, in addition, the external expectations by other states, that is, the role expectation.[3] Admittedly, an analysis of role expectation is a complex undertaking. It necessitates an in-depth study of how other countries (e.g., the US) assess the importance and capabilities of a specific country (e.g., Canada) to contribute to a common political outcome. Since the argument I want to make here is more modest, I will only refer to one aspect of role expectation, that is, whether the self-image of a country, its role conception or internal role perception, resonates with the perception of the country elsewhere. I will refer to the latter aspect as 'international role perception'.

Role Conception and Role Expectation as a Determinant of Ontological Security

Against the background of the conception of middle power as a foreign policy presented here, the Canadian uneasiness of being associated with its middle-power role today stems from a severe mismatch between role conception and international role perception. Jennifer Mitzen (2006: 342) has argued that the search for such a congruency is a deeply rooted 'individual-level need' that can also be 'scaled up' to the level of states. According to her, states seek 'ontological security', understood as 'the need to experience oneself as a whole, continuous person in time—as being rather than constantly changing—in order to realize a sense of agency'. The following section on attempts to 're-brand' the image of Canada in foreign affairs will show that domestic critiques of the middle-power category are rather a proof for Canada's ontological insecurity than a solution for the current impasse. It will also illustrate that it is difficult to uphold one's role if there is a growing disenchantment with that role by other states (Bischoff, 2003: 196).

The Fallacies of 'Re-branding'

The period since the 1990s saw a number of attempts to transform the image of Canada. They were either put forward in the period prior to the foreign policy statements of 1995 (Canada 21 Council, 1994; also see Stein, 1994) and 2005 (Canada25, 2004) or came out of the ministries of trade and industry in order to increase the economic competitiveness of Canada ('Brand Canada') (Grayson, 2001: 48). All initiatives were rooted in the belief that Canada had to be repositioned in the international system. The rationale of the 'Brand Canada' initiative has been rooted in the interest of augmenting the market share of Canadian products and services and to promote a more 'modern' image of Canada (Potter, 2002: 13). The argument of the model power proponents has been the need to put an end to Canada's old foreign policy image of middle power because it seemed not to reflect current realities and was out of touch with domestic perceptions of Canada's role in the world.

While the differences between the two re-branding endeavours may not seem evident at first glance, the conditions for their respective success are fundamentally different. The 'Brand Canada' approach will prove successful if non-Canadians can be convinced of the 'modern' and more authentic image of Canada. The brand's success is therefore exclusively determined by non-Canadians, which is why '[t]he creation and development of an international perception is important, even crucial' (Grayson, 2001: 48). In that sense, the whole strategy focuses on a change in role expectation, or international role perception. In the case of the proponents of model power, the reasoning is different. While the current foreign policy is also rejected on the grounds of not being successful enough, the overall success of this endeavour does not rest with international customers who buy Canadian products but with Canadian citizens themselves: 'Canada25 thus calls on Canadians to make the transition from Middle Power to Model Power—from a country whose influence is premised on its position within an outmoded global hierarchy to one that bases its influence on the capacity of its citizens to provide fresh perspectives, innovative ideas, and sustainable solutions' (Canada25, 2004: 66). Basically, the strategy calls for a new role conception.

Both re-branding strategies are hence unidirectional in the purest sense since they either 'reflect the way Canadians see themselves' or the way they want to be seen by others (Bátora 2005: 16). Yet, no efforts are taken to reconcile the existing perception of Canada at home—role conception—with that of Canada abroad—the international role perception, although Evan Potter noted as early as 2001 that there was 'a huge gap between how Canadians view themselves and how others perceive them' (quoted ibid., 6). As a closer look at the Canada25 report reveals, the plea for shifting from middle to model power is only a rhetorical move deeply rooted in the normative conception of middle-power theory. As we shall see later, this perception of the greatness of Canada is not shared outside its borders.

Canada as a Model Power?

The primary aims of the 'model power' report on a future Canadian diplomacy are a more efficient use of existing resources and the opening up of the foreign policy process to the citizenry. Fifteen years ago, the Canada 21 Council had been arguing along the same lines when it noted that 'fiscal restraints are real' and that the 'government must reach out to new strategic partners within society and use its economic, scientific and cultural resources, and its social, human, and intellectual capital . . . in protecting Canadian . . . security' (Stein, 1994: 11). Yet, the policy seems to have changed little in the meantime, according to the authors of Canada25:

> For much of the 20th century, three principles largely defined how Canadians engaged the world: a clear distinction existed between foreign and domestic issues; the federal government was the principal actor in addressing foreign issues; and international influence was linked to Canada's position within a recognized global hierarchy. . . . Today, these principles often contradict how Canada, and more specifically Canadians, engage the world. . . . As a result, the Middle Power framework—which once allowed us to effectively and successfully navigate a world dominated by superpowers—no longer serves its purpose. (Canada25, 2004: 4)

This one-sided interpretation of the hierarchical middle-power model reveals an analysis that is overtly simplistic in terms of cause and effect. It argues that the success of the 'old' middle-power model is no longer possible because the world has changed. While this mantra of 'change' is not new and has become a cliché—simply consult Mitchell Sharp's 1970 Foreign Policy Review or the 1985–6 one by Joe Clark for myriad examples of where and how the world had changed in previous years— the suggested solutions are not new either. Reconceptualizing Canada's foreign policy by making it a 'network node' (ibid., 10) in bringing to- gether Canadians living abroad, NGOs, corporations, and academics with their government counterparts, for example, is an idea that originated in the early 1990s. Earlier supporters of the idea, such as the Liberal Party in its 1993 'Red Book', argued in favour of such an approach on the basis of a 'democratization' of Canada's foreign policy (Ouellet, 1993) and the need to develop a 'niche diplomacy' (Cooper, 1997a) to cope with the fiscal problems at the time. In addition, the idea to 'transform' DFAIT from a ministry 'implementing' foreign policy into a bureaucratic actor 'coordinating' foreign policy (Canada25, 2004: 27–8) seems to be anachronistic because of the multitude of joint policy development and diplomatic initiatives that have been conducted since the mid-1990s.[4]

Model Power—Moral Power?

Not surprisingly, then, we see the (maybe not so) distinct contribution of Canada25 and, earlier, of the Canada 21 Council in the propagation of specific foreign policy niches that, in earlier stages, were also supported by Canadians who identified with the middle-power image: peacekeeping/post-conflict reconstruction, environmental protection, economic prosperity, and a more just global economic order (Stein, 1994: 11; Canada25, 2004: 34–60). Canadian governments not only had embraced these progressive ideas before the 1990s, they also made them an issue to demonstrate the benign and advanced nature of a liberal, internationalist Canadian society. The idea that Canada is still supposed to be at the forefront in these areas is nowhere better reflected than in the heading 'Lead by example' (Canada25 2004: 47). It is the widely held belief among Canadians that their country is a moral beacon, a view that perpetuates the diplomatic tradition of Canada's middle-power role as that of a moral, a normative power (Andrew, 1993: 29).

Civilian Power

The European Union and some of its member states, most notably Germany, have been holding similar convictions about the nature of their foreign policies. Originating in the early writings of François Duchêne, who (fore) saw the potential of the European Community in being a 'civilian group of countries long on economic power and relatively short on armed force' (Duchêne, 1973: 19–20), the idea of the pacifying role of the EU has since been taken up by a number of scholars (Orbie, 2006; Smith, 2004). For Hanns Maull, who has been propagating the 'civilian power' concept for the study of Germany's foreign policy (2007), six objectives define a civilian power, namely its efforts to: (1) constrain the use of force; (2) strengthen the rule of law; (3) promote participatory forms of decision-making and multilateralism; (4) promote conflict management and resolution; (5) promote social equity and sustainable development; and (6) promote an international division of labour (Harnisch and Maull, 2001: 4). Reading through the list of civilian power traits and juxtaposing them with Canada's historic record, it is not surprising that Canada's foreign policy is characterized by Europeans as one of a civilian power (Telò, 2006: 51). Who would be willing to seriously contest that the objectives put forward by the proponents of the civilian power concept were not congruent with the normative dimension of Canada as a middle power?

Model Power, Civilian Power, Middle Power

If the model power is not a radical departure from the more traditional middle power, the civilian power image makes no exception. All concepts broadly share the same objectives, means, and ends to foreign policy. Why, then, should it matter if we use a different term for the very same thing? In regard to the substance, the terminology matters not at all. There is continuous and widespread political and societal backing of a Canadian foreign and security policy that embraces soft- and hard-power capabilities, a policy that addresses global problems with a variety of political instruments. Among those, we will find the use of force but also multilateral diplomacy and attempts to strengthen international (humanitarian) law. Yet, the conduct of such a policy does not depend on a specific label, be it model or civilian power. There is thus a pragmatic case for sticking with the initial image of middle power. As Kim Richard Nossal rightly pointed out in the previous chapter by referring to the work of Nik Hynek (2007), a term such as 'middle power', 'model power', or 'civilian power' is simply an empty container that can be filled with new content. One should add that the most crucial point is that there is *some* content. Put differently, certain policies and issues will need to be associated with the semantic container. For the last 50 years, 'middle power' has been one of the key terms of the Canadian foreign policy discourse in order to define the foreign and security policy content. In the last decade, 'human security' has become a 'sub-container' of middle power.

If we continue to study—in the language of the hitherto used metaphor—how the content (read: the political issue and its related political process) is related to the container (read: the term 'middle power'), the following aspects are important. First, we need to be able to identify transnational but so far neglected problems that may be approached by a middle power or a group of like-minded secondary powers. Second, we must determine which facets of power need to be analyzed. Finally, it is crucial to evaluate the diplomatic activities by assessing not only how they were conducted but also how they were perceived domestically and by other states and actors.

Neglected Issues

In some policy areas we can observe demand for new and innovative solutions. Most of the policy issues are global in nature but simultaneously secondary issues on the agendas of the bigger powers such as the US or the EU. Examples of middle-power activism include the 1987 signing of the Montreal Protocol in order to stop the depletion of the ozone layer and the negotiation of the Ottawa Convention on Anti-Personnel Mines 10 years later. Regarding the prospects for success of middle-power diplomacy, Jennifer Welsh (2004a: 157) argues that in an era of the US as the 'dominant power', the traditional niches for middle powers have become smaller. Similarly, Cooper et al. (1993: 14, 16) suggest that the most promising time for such activities is a period of relative great power decline. Considering the fact that the US was seen as the world's sole superpower at the time of the Canada 21 Council's deliberations and even as the 'new Empire' at the time of the publication of the Canada25 report in 2004, the characterization of America has been put on its head recently. In the wake of the financial crisis that struck in the fall of 2008 and with its military capabilities overstretched due to simultaneous deployment in Iraq and Afghanistan, US power now seems dwarfed. If the prospects for successful middle-power diplomacy really depend on a decline of US power, one would be tempted to proclaim the dawn of a new golden era of Canadian foreign policy. Yet, we should perhaps look for a more sophisticated way to study power and the effects of power.

Measuring Power Capabilities

Instead of equating power with the size of a nation's military, its economic growth, the size of its stock market—facets of power that suggested the US was to remain the world's sole superpower for years to come—a middle-power analysis should rather look to both soft- and hard-power aspects of foreign policy, as well as to the global demand side. 'Power' is a complex and highly contested term. As the example of the US illustrates, assessing power capabilities requires our understanding of the means by which power is exercised. Moreover, the study of power is subject to an analytic framework stipulating that the result, e.g., a change in policy, has occurred because of the initial and deliberate exercise of power. Most Canadian foreign policy studies, including the ones in this volume, ascribe power capabilities to the institutional and individual actors of the Canadian state, such as the diplomatic corps, military forces, and trade officers.[5] Other Canadian actors, such as the North–South Institute from the non-governmental sector and Bombardier from the corporate sector, are usually left out of the equation. Therefore, Jennifer Welsh asks:

> Does it *matter* whether the Canadians making a difference in the global arena are positively identified as Canadian? My hunch is no. If we really believe in a networked world, and global citizenship, it shouldn't matter who is doing the work—only that the work gets done. (Welsh, 2005: 59)

Notwithstanding the call for a more comprehensive account of Canadian foreign policy, methodological problems and the fact that citizens and people abroad equate a state's foreign policy with the actions of its officials are simple but powerful arguments for sticking with the more traditional understanding.

Hard Power, Soft Power, Tacit Power

In contemporary international relations literature we find, *grosso modo*, three forms of power. The most classical form is hard power, which is closely related to military capabilities and other means to exert a repressive form of authority over another actor, most often another state. Current examples of the use of hard power include anti-terrorist counter-insurgency operations and robust peace enforcement missions (Holloway, 2006: 74–6; Rempel, 2006: 170–1). A second form of power analysis focuses on non-material forms of power, which are exerted by states acting as moral leaders and norm entrepreneurs. Such a form of soft power is wielded by states such as Canada, which seek to strengthen the international legal architecture through new regulatory frameworks, e.g., international treaties (Nye, 2002: 10; Tomlin et al., 2008: 222–3). Yet another example is the exercise of altruistic leadership, e.g., through the commitment of some states to contribute more than their fair share to a negotiated outcome (Bachmann and Sidaway, 2009).[6] In recent years, studies from a variety of other disciplines, including political economy, sociology, and geography, have analyzed more tacit forms of power, such as structural adjustment programs, which operate in transnational networks of multinational companies and international institutions or, at the domestic level, in supposedly apolitical sites such as public administration or schools (Larner and Walters, 2004; Dean, 1999). Such forms of power analysis are largely absent from this volume. However, some of the aspects are addressed in the chapters by Hynek (Chapter 4) and Bátora (Chapter 6), which focus on the domestic setting of Canadian foreign policy. By and large, subsequent chapters in this volume scrutinize the hard- and soft-power dimensions.

Evaluation of Foreign Policy

Besides the 'what' of middle-power diplomacy, that is, the concrete policy issues and processes that are being dealt with, some form of evaluation is important, too. The 'how' of an analysis—'how good', 'how successful'—is the key determinant of the ontological security of a middle power. As I pointed out above, the role of a middle power necessitates some sort of raison d'être, an inherent belief of the purpose of the state in its dealings with others. In the case of Canada, this belief has been shaped by its diplomatic history—the role in the Suez crisis and other international conflicts, its development policy, its human rights policy—and the subsequent formation of narratives that become part of the national identity (Thomsen and Hynek, 2006). Canadians have, in addition, always linked their diplomatic merits abroad with their economic and social successes at home. According to the unwritten truisms of Canadian collective identity, their society is also a more just, open-minded, and tolerant one than those of most other Western nations, most notably that of the United States. The result of such a glorification of one's cultural supremacy is the value-driven nature of a state's foreign policy. At least since its inception in the 1995 foreign policy review, *Canada in the World* (DFAIT, 1995: ch. 5), the projection of Canadian values has become an important pillar of Canadian foreign policy (DFAIT, 2005: 4). From the perspective of role theory, such a stance emphasizes the role conception (e.g., 'good international citizen', 'human security champion') and the role performance (e.g., Canadian efforts to negotiate the ban on anti-personnel mines) and neglects role perception by other actors. The result is a considerable variance between how Canadians measure their diplomatic success and influence and how the very same policies are assessed by others. From such a vantage point, the current crisis in Canadian diplomacy is foremost the result of an unawareness of what other countries expect Canada to do (role perception) and what policy-makers do on the behalf of Canada (role conception and its exercise). A closer look at the public opinion data of recent years will shed some light on the relationship between the two. It will also explain why the public euphoria about Canada's growing role in the world after the signing of the Ottawa Convention was short-lived and is nothing more than a modern myth (Hynek, 2008).

Internal Role Perception: How Canadians Perceive Their Country's Role in the World

Although Canadians are undecided as to whether an independent foreign policy should be favoured over a close(r) relationship with the US (Gravelle, 2007), most Canadians (71 per cent) believe that their country currently exerts some influence in the world. They actually think that the influence has risen over the past 20 years (63 per cent), not least because of Canada's peacekeeping role and its efforts in fighting terrorism (Simons Foundation et al., 2008: 29). Two-thirds of citizens are satisfied with the country's position in the world (Carlson, 2005) and an equal share are also content with the role the country plays on the world stage (Burkholder, 2003), in both cases overriding the respective assessments of their countries by Americans and Britons. Most interestingly, however, the evaluation of Canada's foreign policy by the citizens goes beyond issues of status and rank in world politics and also addresses issues of national identity, and hence role conception. Eighty-six per cent of the public believe that Canada can act as a 'role model to other countries' (Simons Foundation et al., 2008: 36) and three-quarters expect it to pursue an active foreign policy (IRG, 2004: 14). When being asked to identify with a set of six specific role conceptions in foreign policy, Canadians favour two by a wide margin. The first, supported by 75 per cent of respondents, is the self-interested position that trade concerns should figure as the top foreign policy priority. The second option, held by 69 per cent of interviewees, is that of a 'soft-power' diplomacy, summed up in the statement that 'Canada should focus its international efforts on working with non-governmental organizations to build support for specific solutions to key problems, like the ban on landmines' (ibid., 21).[7] Regarding international role perception, 88 per cent of Canadians think that their country is viewed favourably in the world (Carlson, 2005).

International Role Perception: How Others See Canada's Foreign Policy

Based on two annual surveys, Future Brand's *Country Brand Index* (2008) and Anholt-GfK Roper's *Nations Brand Index* (2008), Canada indeed enjoys one of the highest reputations globally, ranking among the top five nations worldwide. Yet, this reputation does not include the field of foreign policy. When foreign policy is brought into the equation, Canada still fares comparatively well: 57 per cent of respondents in a survey conducted in 20 countries in 2006 viewed Canada as a 'global leader in human rights and peace in the world'. The assessment of Canadian leadership was, however, simultaneously challenged on the grounds of the finding that 43 per cent of the interviewees thought the country was doing 'pretty much what the United States wants it to do' (Angus Reid, 2006). While there are no data available for earlier periods, one is tempted to assume that the view according to which Canada's global influence increased over the last 20 years is not shared on a global level. It is at least refuted by non-Canadian decision-makers. According to Robert Greenhill, the author of a 2005 study among selected global foreign policy experts, the 1990s saw a Canada on the verge of irrelevance. Most cannot name any diplomatic initiative apart from the Ottawa Process where the country has been important in recent years. In addition, Canada is seen as living off its former reputation and falling short of actually delivering, given the high-pitched rhetoric (Greenhill, 2005a: 14–15, 20). In sum, Greenhill finds that:

> Canada's performance since 1989 is nothing for a country of our wealth and history of international engagement to be proud of. Our performance appears to have been well below our exaggerated rhetoric, well below our historical performance, and well below global expectations. (Ibid., 22)

Instead of being more important than in previous years, Canada's global importance is actually declining, at least in the eyes of non-Canadians. The important question is whether that is a problem.

Does It Matter How Others See Canada's Foreign Policy?

As poll after poll indicates, the percentage of Canadians who think their country has been making a difference globally—whether because of the country's contribution to NATO's involvement in Afghanistan or its role in negotiating the Ottawa Convention—remains high. On the other hand, Canada is playing an even lesser role in the eyes of foreign policy-makers in Europe, the US, and other parts of the world (Greenhill, 2005b). We can therefore observe a growing disparity between what Canadians think their country is achieving globally and how the same efforts are evaluated by others. Such a divergence of internal and external role perception has still gone unnoticed by the broader public thus far. It has, however, found its way into the circles of academics and policy-makers. Probably the best illustration of this fact is the shift in the titles of the *Canada Among Nations* series: the past 10 years have seen the fall from Canadian *Leadership and Dialogue* (1998), *A Big League Player?* (1999), and even *The Axworthy Legacy* (2001) to *A Fading Power* (2002) and *Coping with the American Colossus* (2003). Scholars have recently classified such laments as the 'declinist school' of Canadian foreign policy.[8] Generally speaking, such a reality check should be considered as a healthy endeavour. Yet, an open question remains: Why did the actual decline go unnoticed in the 1990s and why did a majority of scholars buy into the governmental *trompe l'oeil* of Canada as big league player and moral leader?

Conclusion: Reclaiming the Middle-Power Role

For the time being, it is surely more interesting to focus on the proposals for remedying the situation of decline. By and large, proposals have been made on two grounds, by calling for more resources (Granatstein, 2004: 231ff.; Cohen, 2003: 200; Rempel, 2006: 182) or by articulating a new image of Canada, the 'model power' being the most prominent one (Welsh, 2004a: 187ff.; Canada25, 2004), the 'energy superpower' being the most recent one set forth by the Harper government (Hester, 2007). If spending more will really narrow the gap between role conception and internal role perception, on the one hand, and international role perception, on the other, remains to be seen. It is likely, however, that spending more resources will result in higher visibility. Yet, making choices, opting for niches, and increasing assets may only increase visibility and not raise influence and international expectations. Canada's contribution to the International Security Assistance Force in Afghanistan is proof of the present government's will to regain the old status. Still, this contribution is neither explicitly appreciated by its allies nor has it resulted in a bigger influence of the country on NATO's overall Afghanistan strategy. Successfully reclaiming its status as middle power will thus require Canadians to select carefully and opt for those international niches where a Canadian contribution will have a strategic impact. As the Afghanistan deployment reveals, committing more troops to operational theatres than in previous years does not automatically yield a better reputation or a greater say among allies.

Undoubtedly, simply changing the brand from middle to model power will not suffice, perhaps not least because being a role model means a permanent exposure to highest moral standards and requires an impeccable record in matching rhetoric with action. Therefore, congruency between role conception and international role perception becomes essential. Any other option would be desirable only if Canadian policy-makers were content to align the foreign policy agenda with the opinions of the Canadian public (see also Rempel, 2006: 35–6). Since the public remains badly informed about the current state of Canada's external relations and seems to locate potential influence in those areas where Canada's record comes close to a disgrace, such as the environment, development assistance, and even traditional peacekeeping,[9] decision-makers are left with two options. Either they continue to live with a foreign policy that is sufficient to persuade citizens that Canada still matters on the global stage although it is perceived as less influential by those outside Canada, or they seek to balance the domestic and external expectations about their foreign policy. Simply aiming to realize the aspirations of one side, as the model power approach does by giving a key role to public opinion, will make the foreign policy 'Inukshuk' a populist instrument. It will also increase the chances that Canada won't be able to overcome its identity crisis in its external relations. If one should have learned anything from the last decade it is that the key to a successful—middle–power—foreign policy lies in a substantial overlap of role conception, internal as well as international role perception, and role expectation. Future success will therefore depend less on what Canadians want their political leaders to do than on the efforts of those leaders to translate the expectations and perceptions of other states into viable strategies that touch a chord with the beliefs of average Canadians.

Notes

1. Referring to the different strands of middle-power scholarship, Cooper, Higgott, and Nossal (1993: 17) argue that the factors determining the 'position in the international hierarchy', such as economic output, should be distinguished from a 'state's geography'. Their argument is twofold: on the one hand, middle power here can be understood as a regional power; on the other hand, it may be understood as a state that is, literally speaking, 'in the middle' between two bigger states and therefore acts a kind of 'buffer state' (Holbraad, 1971: 79). Since Canada is a state without a region and hence no regional power, we can skip the first caveat. Also, the second aspect is irrelevant here since the categorization of Canada as a middle power was never based—at least not primarily—on Canada's position as a 'buffer state' between the Soviet Union and the US during the Cold War.

2. According to neo-realist and liberal institutionalist scholarship, states act in an anarchic environment. The primary motive of a state in such a 'self-help system' is thus to assure its survival, i.e., its territorial integrity and the well-being of its population. Any altruistic behaviour is thus difficult to explain.

3. Aggestam's landmark study (1999) also specifies role performance as a third aspect of the foreign policy role of states. She writes that '[r]ole performance encompasses the actual foreign policy behaviour in terms of decisions and actions undertaken—the outcome.' That is identical with Cooper, Higgott, and Nossal's behavioural analysis of middle power. Since the additional analysis of role conception and role expectation does offer further

insights, I focus on the latter two categories in the ensuing analysis.

4. The initiatives promoted in the mid-1990s are a good illustration for the earlier development of such a 'network diplomacy'. Policy development issues were managed through the Canadian Centre for Foreign Policy Development (1996–2001; after 2001 the CCFPD became the Canadian Centre for Foreign Policy Development Division, which brought together experts from all parts of Canadian society). A more recent but focused model is managed by DFAIT's International Security Research and Outreach Program (ISROP) with its 'Fast Talk' teams. Besides policy development, policy implementation also has undergone significant changes along the line of suggestions put forward by Canada25. Numerous activities by non-state actors, such as background policy briefings, fieldwork, and negotiation position papers, made possible the co-ordination and implementation of Canadian human security policies in the 1990s (e.g., the Ottawa Convention, the International Criminal Court statute, the Treaty on Child Soldiers, and the Kimberley Process to ensure that violence is not funded by the diamond trade).

5. Kim Richard Nossal (1997: 67) puts it this way: 'Power is the ability to change the behaviour of others in ways that are conducive to Canadian interests . . . .' It can be assessed by the degree 'to which the government in Ottawa is able to achieve its objectives and secure Canada's interests as they are defined by officials'.

6. A number of examples can be found in the European Union, either by single member states or the Union as a whole. A case in point is the EU's climate and energy package, which commits the Union to reduce carbon emissions by 20 per cent until 2020. The same document commits EU members to reduce emissions by an additional 10 per cent if other countries, e.g., Canada, were to follow the initial voluntary agreement of a 20 per cent reduction (European Commission, 2008).

7. The option of reviving the days of the 'Golden Era' seems to be out of touch with a huge majority of Canadians when being confronted with the need for cuts in other policy sectors. The survey here reads as follows: 'Four out of five (81%) of Canadians reject the idea "We should spend what it takes to be the international power we used to be, even if it means doing without things we would like in areas like health and education"' (IRG, 2004: 22).

8. The most prominent examples bemoaning the current shape of Canada's foreign policy capabilities and proposing new avenues for mitigating the decline include Andrew Cohen's *While Canada Slept* (2003), Jennifer Welsh's *At Home in the World* (2004a), J.L. Granatstein's *Who Killed the Canadian Military?* (2004), and Roy Rempel's *Dreamland* (2006). See also Chapter 12, by Zyla and Sokolsky, in this volume.

9. The Canada's World Poll of January 2008 asked in which area Canada was most likely to act as a role model for other countries. Surprisingly, at least for any informed European, environmental policies emerged as the top choice (17 per cent) in the poll (Simons Foundation et al., 2008: 36). The Canadian record of CO_2 emissions on a per capita basis shows a 33 per cent increase since 1990 (US, +6.7 per cent; Sweden, +1.7 per cent; United Kingdom, –2 per cent; France, –6.2 per cent; Germany, –20 per cent: <hdrstats.undp.org/indicators/237.html>), which makes the country an absolute laggard in climate change policies. In addition, tar sands oil production and the low percentage of renewable energy production are severely hampering the prospects of Canada becoming an environmental model power in the years to come (also see Chapters 7 and 8, by Baldwin and Dalby and by Laxer).

References

Aggestam, Lisbeth. 1999. 'Role Conceptions and the Politics of Identity in Foreign Policy', *ARENA Working Papers*, WP 99/8. At: <www.arena.uio.no/publications/wp99_8.htm>. (18 Dec. 2008)

Andrew, Arthur. 1993. *The Rise and Fall of a Middle Power: Canadian Diplomacy from King to*

Mulroney. Toronto: James Lorimer.

Angus Reid. 2006. 'Canada Seen as Global Leader in Foreign Affairs', *Angus Reid Global Monitor: Polls & Research*, 11 Nov. At: <www.angus-reid.com/polls/view/canada_seen_as_global_leader_in_foreign_affairs/>. (18 Dec. 2008)

Anholt-GfK Roper. 2008. Press Release on 2008 Anholt-GfK Roper *Nation Brands Index Ranking.* New York. At: <http://www.gfk.com/imperia/md/content/presse/pm_roper_nation_brands_index_efin.pdf>. (18 Dec. 2008)

Apel, Karl-Otto. 1984. *Understanding and Explanation: A Transcendental-Pragmatic Perspective.* Cambridge, Mass.: MIT Press.

Bachmann, Veit, and James D. Sidaway. 2009. '*Zivilmacht Europa*: A Critical Geopolitics of the European Union as a Global Power', *Transactions of the Institute of British Geographers* 34, 1: 94–109.

Bátora, Jozef. 2005. 'Multistakeholder Public Diplomacy of Small and Medium-Sized States: Norway and Canada Compared', paper presented at the International Conference on Multistakeholder Diplomacy, Mediterranean Diplomatic Academy, Malta, 11–13 Feb.

Bischoff, Paul-Henri. 2003. 'External and Domestic Sources of Foreign Policy Ambiguity: South African Foreign Policy and the Projection of Pluralist Middle Power', *Politikon: South African Journal of Political Studies* 30, 2: 183–201.

Blanchfield, Mike. 2007. 'Canadians Favour Role in Ending Darfur Violence, Poll Shows', *Ottawa Citizen*, 19 May. At: <www.pollara.ca/Library/News/end_darfur_violence.htm>. (7 Dec. 2008)

Bosold, David. 2003. 'Amerikanisch-kanadische Beziehungen', in Wilfried von Bredow, ed., *Die Außenpolitik Kanadas.* Wiesbaden: Westdeutscher Verlag, 91–104.

Burkholder, Richard. 2003. 'Proud Canadians Assess Global Role and Image', *Gallup Poll, Government & Public Affairs*, 11 Mar.

Byers, Michael. 2007. *Intent for a Nation: What Is Canada For?* Vancouver: Douglas & McIntyre.

Canada 21 Council. 1994. *Canada 21: Canada and Common Security in the Twenty-First Century.* Toronto: Centre for International Studies, University of Toronto.

Canada 25. 2004. *From Middle Power to Model Power: Recharging Canada's Role in the World.* Toronto. At: <www.canada25.com/collateral/canada25_from_middle_to_model_power_en.pdf>. (18 Dec. 2008)

Carlson, Darren K. 2005. 'How Do Canada, U.S., Britain Look Through a Global Lens?', *Gallup Poll News Service*, 30 Aug.

Chandler, David, and Volker Heins. 2007. 'Ethics and Foreign Policy: New Perspectives on an Old Problem', in Chandler and Heins, eds, *Rethinking Ethical Foreign Policy: Pitfalls, Possibilities and Paradoxes.* London: Routledge, 3–21.

Chapnick, Adam. 1999. 'The Middle Power', *Canadian Foreign Policy* 7, 2: 73–82.

———. 2005. *The Middle Power Project: Canada and the Founding of the United Nations.* Vancouver: University of British Columbia Press.

Cohen, Andrew. 2003. *While Canada Slept: How We Lost Our Place in the World.* Toronto: McClelland & Stewart.

Cooper, Andrew F., ed. 1997a. *Niche Diplomacy: Middle Powers after the Cold War.* New York: St Martin's Press.

———. 1997b. *Canadian Foreign Policy: Old Habits and New Directions.* Scarborough, Ont.: Prentice-Hall.

———, Richard A. Higgott, and Kim Richard Nossal. 1993. *Relocating Middle Powers: Australia and Canada in a Changing World Order.* Vancouver: University of British Columbia Press.

Dean, Mitchell. 1999. *Governmentality: Power and Rule in Modern Society.* London: Sage.

Department of Foreign Affairs and International Trade (DFAIT). 1995. *Canada in the World— Canadian Foreign Policy Review.* Ottawa: DFAIT.

———. 2005. *Canada's International Policy Statement. A Role of Pride and Influence in the World: Overview.* Ottawa: DFAIT.

Dewitt, David B., and John Kirton. 1983. 'Canada as a Principal Power: A Study in Foreign Policy and International Relations', reprinted as 'Three Theoretical Perspectives' in Duane Bratt and Christopher J. Kukucha, eds, *Readings in Canadian Foreign Policy: Classic Debates and*

New Ideas (Toronto: Oxford University Press, 2007), 27–45.

Duchêne, François. 1973. 'The European Community and the Uncertainties of Interdependence', in Max Kohnstamm and Wolfgang Hager, eds, *A Nation Writ Large? Foreign-Policy Problems before the European Community*. London: Macmillan, 1–21.

European Commission. 2008. 'Climate Change: Commission Welcomes Final Adoption of Europe's Climate and Energy Package', Brussels. At: <europa.eu/rapid/pressReleasesAction. do?reference=IP/08/1998&format=HTML&aged=0&language=EN&guiLanguage=en>. (18 Dec. 2008)

Future Brand. 2008. *Country Brand Index 2008 Report*. New York. At: <www.countrybrandindex. com/>. (18 Dec. 2008)

Granatstein, J.L. 2004. *Who Killed the Canadian Military?* Toronto: HarperCollins.

Gravelle, Timothy B. 2007. 'Public Opinion towards Canadian Foreign Policy in the 21st Century', paper presented at the Canadian Political Science Association annual meeting, Saskatoon, 30 May–June 1.

Grayson, Timothy. 2001. '"Brand Canada" or Branded Canadian?', *Policy Options/Options Politiques* 6 (June): 47–9.

Greenhill, Robert. 2005a. *Making a Difference? External Views on Canada's International Impact*. Toronto: CIIA. At: <www.igloo.org/ciia/download/Library/ciialibr/national/nation~1/ interimr>. (18 Dec. 2008)

———. 2005b. 'The Decline of Canada's Influence in the World—What Is To Be Done for It?', *Policy Options/Options Politiques* 2 (Feb.): 34–9.

Harnisch, Sebastian, and Hanns W. Maull, eds. 2001. *Germany as a Civilian Power? The Foreign Policy of the Berlin Republic*. Manchester: Manchester University Press.

Hayes, Geoffrey. 1997. 'Canada as a Middle Power: The Case of Peacekeeping', in Cooper (1997a: 73–89).

Hester, Annette. 2007. *Canada as the 'Emerging Energy Superpower': Testing the Case*. Calgary: Canadian Defence and Foreign Affairs Institute.

Holbraad, Carsten. 1971. 'The Role of Middle Powers', *Cooperation and Conflict* 6, 1: 77–90.

Holloway, Steven Kendall. 2006. *Canadian Foreign Policy: Defining the National Interest*. Peterborough, Ont.: Broadview Press.

Holmes, John W. 1970. *The Better Part of Valour: Essays on Canadian Diplomacy*. Toronto: McClelland & Stewart.

Hynek, Nikola. 2007. 'Humanitarian Arms Control, Symbiotic Functionalism and the Concept of Middlepowerhood', *Central European Journal of International and Security Studies* 1, 2: 132–55.

———. 2008. 'Conditions of Emergence and Their Effects: Political Rationalities, Governmental Programs and Technologies of Power in the Landmine Case', *Journal of International Relations and Development* 11, 2: 93–120.

Innovative Research Group (IRG). 2004. *Visions of Canadian Foreign Policy*. Toronto: IRG, 4 Nov. At: <www.cdfai.org/PDF/Visions%20of%20Canadian%20Foreign%20Policy.pdf>. (18 Dec. 2008)

Jordaan, Eduard. 2003. 'The Concept of a Middle Power in International Relations: Distinguishing between Emerging and Traditional Middle Powers', *Politikon: South African Journal of Political Studies* 30, 2: 165–81.

Keating, Tom. 2002. *Canada and World Order: The Multilateralist Tradition in Canadian Foreign Policy*, 2nd edn. Toronto: Oxford University Press.

Kirste, Knut, and Hanns W. Maull. 1996. 'Zivilmacht und Rollentheorie', *Zeitschrift für Internationale Beziegungen* 3, 2: 283–312.

Kirton, John. 2007. *Canadian Foreign Policy in a Changing World*. Scarborough, Ont.: Nelson Education.

Larner, Wendy, and William Walters, eds. 2004. *Global Governmentality: Governing International Spaces*. London: Routledge.

Maull, Hanns W. 2007. 'Deutschland als Zivilmacht', in Siegmar Schmidt, Gunther Hellmann, and Reinhard Wolf, eds, *Handwörterbuch zur deutschen Außenpolitik*. Wiesbaden: VS Verlag,

73–84.

Michaud, Nelson, and Louis Bélanger. 2000. 'Canadian Institutional Strategies: New Orientations for a Middle Power Foreign Policy?', *Australian Journal of International Affairs* 54, 1: 97–110.

Mitzen, Jennifer. 2006. 'Ontological Security in World Politics: State Identity and the Security Dilemma', *European Journal of International Relations* 12, 3: 341–70.

Neufeld, Mark. 1995. 'Hegemony and Foreign Policy Analysis: The Case of Canada as a Middle Power', *Studies in Political Economy* 48: 7–29, reprinted in Duane Bratt and Christopher J. Kukucha, eds, *Readings in Canadian Foreign Policy: Classic Debates and New Ideas* (Toronto: Oxford University Press, 2007), 94–107.

Nimijean, Richard. 2006. 'The Politics of Branding Canada: The International–Domestic Nexus and the Rethinking of Canada's Place in the World', *Revista Mexicana de Estudios Canadienses (nueva época)* 11: 67–85.

Nossal, Kim Richard. 1997. *The Politics of Canadian Foreign Policy*, 3rd edn. Scarborough, Ont.: Prentice-Hall.

Nye, Joseph S. 2002. *The Paradox of American Power*. New York: Oxford University Press.

Orbie, Jan. 2006. 'Civilian Power Europe: Review of the Original and Current Debates', *Cooperation and Conflict* 41, 1: 123–8.

Ouellet, André. 1993. 'The Commitments of a Liberal Foreign Policy Agenda', *Canadian Foreign Policy* 1, 3: 1–6.

Potter, Evan. 2002. *Canada and the New Public Diplomacy*. Clingendael Discussion Paper in Diplomacy 81. The Hague: Netherlands Institute of International Relations 'Clingendael'.

———. 2004. 'Branding Canada: The Renaissance of Canada's Commercial Diplomacy', *International Studies Perspectives* 5, 1: 55–60.

Pratt, Cranford. 1990. 'Has Middle Power Internationalism a Future?', in Pratt, ed., *Middle Power Internationalism: The North–South Dimension*. Montreal and Kingston: McGill-Queen's University Press, 143–67.

Ravenhill, John. 1998. 'Cycles of Middle Power Activism: Constraint and Choice in Australian and Canadian Foreign Policies', *Australian Journal of International Affairs* 52, 3: 309–27.

Rempel, Roy. 2006. *Dreamland: How Canada's Pretend Foreign Policy Has Undermined Sovereignty*. Montreal and Kingston: McGill-Queen's University Press.

Simons Foundation et al. 2008. The Canada's World Poll, Jan. At: <thesimonsfoundation.ca/projects/canadas-world-poll/>. (18 Dec. 2008)

Smith, Karen E. 2004. 'Still "Civilian Power EU"?', paper presented at the Citizenship and Democratic Legitimacy in the EU Workshop, 'From Civilian to Military Power: The European Union at a Crossroads?', Oslo, 22–3 Oct. 2004. At: <www.arena.uio.no/cidel/WorkshopOsloSecurity/Smith.pdf>. (18 Dec. 2008)

Stein, Janice Gross. 1994. 'Canada 21: A Moment and a Model', *Canadian Foreign Policy* 2, 1: 9–14.

Telò, Mario. 2006. *Europe: A Civilian Power?* Houndmills, Basingstoke: Palgrave Macmillan.

Thomsen, Robert C., and Nikola Hynek. 2006. 'Keeping the Peace and National Unity: Canada's National and International Identity Nexus', *International Journal* 61, 4: 845–58.

Tomlin, Brian W., Norman Hillmer, and Fen Osler Hampson. 2008. *Canada's International Policies: Agendas, Alternatives, and Politics*. Toronto: Oxford University Press.

Welsh, Jennifer M. 2004a. *At Home in the World: Canada's Global Vision for the 21st Century*. Toronto: HarperCollins.

———. 2004b. 'Canada in the 21st Century: Beyond Dominion and Middle Power', *The Round Table* 93, 376: 583–93.

———. 2005. 'Fulfilling Canada's Global Promise', *Policy Options/Options Politiques* 2 (Feb.): 56–9.

Additional Readings

Baldwin, David A. 2002. 'Power and International Relations', in Walter Carlsnaes, Thomas Risse, and Beth A. Simmons, eds, *Handbook of International Relations*. London: Sage.

Black, David R., and Heather A. Smith. 1993. 'Notable Exceptions? New and Arrested Directions in Canadian Foreign Policy Literature', *Canadian Journal of Political Science* 26, 4: 745–74.

Bow, Brian, and Patrick Lennox, eds. 2008. *An Independent Foreign Policy for Canada? Challenges and Choices for the Future*. Toronto: University of Toronto Press.

Campbell, David. 1998. *Writing Security*, 2nd edn. Manchester: University of Manchester Press.

Canada Among Nations. Montreal and Kingston: McGill-Queen's University Press, 1989–97 and 2004–today; Toronto: Oxford University Press, 1998–2003; Toronto: James Lorimer 1984–8).

Dewitt, David B., and David Leyton-Brown, eds. 1995. *Canada's International Security Policy*. Scarborough, Ont.: Prentice-Hall.

English, John, and Norman Hillmer, eds. 1992. *Making a Difference? Canada's Foreign Policy in a Changing World Order*. Toronto: Lester.

Hart, Michael. 2008. *From Pride to Influence: Towards a New Canadian Foreign Policy*. Vancouver: University of British Columbia Press.

Hey, Jeanne A.K. 2003. *Small States in World Politics: Explaining Foreign Policy Behavior*. Boulder, Colo.: Lynne Rienner.

Irwin, Rosaline, ed. 2001. *Ethics and Security in Canadian Foreign Policy*. Vancouver: University of British Columbia Press.

James, Patrick, Nelson Michaud, and Marc J. O'Reilly, eds. 2006. *Handbook of Canadian Foreign Policy*. Lanham, Md: Lexington Books.

Little, Richard. 2007. *The Balance of Power in International Relations: Metaphors, Myths and Models*. Cambridge: Cambridge University Press.

Melakopides, Costas. 1998. *Pragmatic Idealism: Canadian Foreign Policy 1945–1995*. Montreal and Kingston: McGill-Queen's University Press.

McBride, Stephen M. 2005. *Paradigm Shift: Globalization and the Canadian State*, 2nd edn. Halifax: Fernwood.

Morrison, David R. 1998. *Aid and Ebb Tide: A History of CIDA and Canadian Development Assistance*. Waterloo, Ont.: Wilfrid Laurier University Press.

Pratt, Cranford, ed. 1996. *Canadian International Development Assistance Policies: An Appraisal*, 2nd edn. Montreal and Kingston: McGill-Queen's University Press.

Rempel, Roy. 2002. *The Chatter Box: An Insider's Account of the Irrelevance of Parliament in the Making of Canadian Foreign and Defence Policy*. Toronto: Breakout.

Urmetzer, Peter. 2005. *Globalization Unplugged: Sovereignty and the Canadian State in the Twenty-First Century*. Toronto: University of Toronto Press.

Part I: Questions for Critical Thought

Chapter 1

1. Has Canada's foreign policy experienced some turbulence since the end of the Cold War?
2. Would Canadians rather support spending additional tax dollars on development assistance, on the military, or on foreign service officers?
3. Critically discuss the government's decision to provide more support to NATO-led peace support operations rather than UN-led operations.
4. What effects have the emergence of China, India, and Brazil had on Canada's role in multilateral institutions?
5. Do you think Canadian foreign policy has been too preoccupied with economic issues or not preoccupied enough with these issues? Explain.
6. What effect have changes in United States foreign policy had on Canadian foreign policy?
7. What effect has Canada's bilateral relationship with the United States, and especially its trade relationship under NAFTA, had on Canadian foreign policy?
8. Critically examine the argument that there has been a lack of leadership on Canadian foreign policy.
9. What are the central priorities that should guide Canadian foreign policy?
10. To what extent has the Canadian public had a realistic image of what Canada can do in the international realm?

Chapter 2

1. According to Nossal, how can one subdivide the literature on Canada as a middle power?
2. What have been distinct cycles of popularity in regard to the use of the discourse on middle power?
3. Is the middle-power concept a convincing theoretical framework for the study of CanFSP?
4. What specific mythologies have developed around the notion of middle power?
5. What are the defining characteristics of 'middlepowermanship'?
6. What are the defining characteristics of 'middlepowerhood'?
7. What is the relationship between the notions of 'middlepowermanship' and 'middlepowerhood'?
8. How can we assess the usefulness of middle power today?

9. What are the historical roots of the middle-power idea and which aspects of 'middlepowermanship' and 'middlepowerhood' have been reflected in that?
10. How can one recover the meaning and analytical utility of 'middlepowermanship'?

Chapter 3

1. What are the arguments of the critics of the middle-power approach?
2. Why do some analysts argue that 'model power' is a more appropriate characterization of Canada's foreign policy role/image?
3. What is the supposed difference between 'middle power' and 'model power'?
4. How can we conceptualize and study national identity in foreign policy analysis?
5. What are the key factors that have influenced Canada's foreign policy?
6. Which factors are not usually addressed by the middle-power approach?
7. How can we explain the difference in how Canadians perceive of their foreign policy as opposed to how non-Canadians perceive CanFSP? Does it matter? If yes, why?
8. If Canada, Japan, Germany, Australia, and Sweden are all seen to be middle powers, what does that tell us about the nature of middle powers? What are the common features that make those countries middle powers?
9. What is the value-added of role theory to Canada's middle-power status?
10. How far has the understanding of middle power changed over time? In case there has been a change, what might be the reason for that?

Part II

Re-examining Canada's Soft Power

Chapter 4

How 'Soft' Is Canada's Soft Power in the Field of Human Security?

Nik Hynek

Introduction

To some observers of Canada's involvement in international affairs, the question posed in the title will almost certainly seem redundant at best and absurd at worst. How could soft power be anything other than what it claims to mean? People's confusion in regard to this issue, at first sight, can be of two kinds: *conceptual* and *empirical*. In respect to the conceptual confusion, it is difficult to imagine that the notion of soft power could possibly be 'tainted' by its alleged opposite, hard power. Not only would such a move ruin the conceptual appeal of soft power as such (and its implicit normative desirability), as some could argue, but it would, first and foremost, threaten its analytical existence by making its relationship to hard power a matter of degree (i.e., real soft power would always be tainted by hard power to some degree) rather than of binaries (i.e., hard power and soft power as opposites of each other). Indeed, in any introduction of a new concept, some degree of simplification and mutual exclusivity is needed. The case of Joseph Nye Jr, who introduced the notion of soft power, is no exception: he stated that soft power is as much defined by what it is as by what it is not (hard power). In Nye's own words, soft power is:

> the ability to achieve desired outcomes in international affairs through *attraction rather than coercion*. It works by convincing others to follow, or getting them to agree to, norms and institutions that produce the desired behaviour. Soft power can rest on the appeal of one's ideas or the ability to set the agenda in ways that shape the preferences of others. If a state can make its power legitimate in the perceptions of others and establish international institutions that encourage them to channel or limit their activities, it may

not need to expend as many of its costly traditional economic or military resources . . .
hard power . . . threats and rewards. (Nye, 1990: 15–16)

Nevertheless, as the present chapter shows, full conceptual appreciation
of the notion of soft power is only possible after the original emphasis on
its contrast with hard power is replaced by an examination of the practical
means of achieving soft power. In concrete terms, the chapter demonstrates
that Nye is wrong in assuming that soft power always goes hand in glove with
attraction, as opposed to hard power always being linked to coercion. I will
show that such a generalization is both naive and deeply problematic, as soft
power can be exerted through subtle, sophisticated coercing and disciplinary
techniques. In other words, there is no intrinsic exclusive connection between
hard power and coercion, as the latter can be used as easily in the name of soft
power. This point leads directly to the supposed empirical absurdity regarding
the discussion of the 'softness' of soft power.

There is hardly any country as interesting as Canada in this context: it is the
country in which the government has appropriated the notion of soft power
for its own purposes and made it the central discursive staple of its foreign
and security policy in general and its human security agenda in particular. The
idea to link certain processes and trends already underway with the discursive
banner of soft power had its origin in the period when Lloyd Axworthy
served as Canada's Foreign Minister (1996–2000). In fact, Axworthy used this
discursive vehicle to suggest that Canada's foreign and security policy, with
its human security agenda, was inherently unique. He politically embraced
a powerful discursive series of (1) soft power, (2) democratization of foreign
policy, and (3) human security. He called it the basis of the so-called 'new
diplomacy of Canada': a two-way communication that was supposed to be
wise, horizontally stretched, non-secretive, and inclusive—a diplomacy that
was to push Canada's traditional image as a principled middle power to an
even higher level (see Bosold, Chapter 3, and Bátora, Chapter 6, this volume;
Bátora, 2006, 2008; Hynek, 2007). Judging by the number and prominence
of supportive accounts, this image of soft power has been well accepted,
and its attraction has been reproduced and recited again and again. It is
precisely against this backdrop that this chapter sets its own agenda, aims,
and priorities.

The chapter examines the notion of 'soft power' within Canada's human
security/international development agenda. The chapter is divided into two
parts: the first looks into the mainstream account of Canada's soft power and
establishes the central arguments; the second part challenges this narrative and,
in an attempt to correct its flaws, offers an alternative answer to the question
posed in the title. Two key arguments can be identified as the discursive
nodes around which the mainstream narrative has been produced: (1) the

assertion that Canada as a soft-power country has undergone a significant democratization of its foreign and security policy after the end of the Cold War; and (2) that the human security/international development agenda has been central to the erosion of the government of Canada's power at the expense of civil society gaining more political clout.

The alternative interpretation begins with a rebuttal of the usually 'stressed' causal arrow between NGOs and the government (i.e., the pressure of NGOs leads to changes of governmental preferences). This explanation argues that in order to understand NGOs' involvement in human security and international development and their role in creating an agenda, one needs to look at earlier government-initiated domestic transformations of the non-profit and voluntary sector and their subsequent extension to include Canada-based international development NGOs. Importantly, the chapter demonstrates that the realm of human security and development has not been increasingly democratized, but, on the contrary, it has been disciplined, constrained, and depoliticized by the governmental introduction of neo-liberal techniques, especially results-based management. What is more, the argument that the agenda has been less the result of international processes and middle-power identity politics than of a set of interlinked domestic processes is justified. Finally, the popular belief that the inclusion of NGOs is only on the liberal agenda is corrected.

The Mainstream Discourse on Canada's Soft Power

Democratization of Canadian Foreign and Security Policy

The democratization of Canadian foreign and security policy (CanFSP[1]) has been seen as one of the cornerstones of Canada's post-Cold War soft power (Axworthy, 1997; Axworthy and Taylor, 1998; and, for critical assessments, Nossal, 1995; Neufeld, 1999; Hampson and Oliver, 1998). The idea to expand the foreign and security policy-making process and make it more accountable to citizens dates back to 1993, with its first manifestations already discernible as early as 1985. During the 1993 federal election campaign, the Liberal Party introduced its vision of a radical change in the procedure and substance of CanFSP. The Liberals' agenda of election promises, *Creating Opportunities* (also known as the 'Red Book'), made it clear by stating that 'Canadians are asking for a commitment from government to listen to their views, and to respect their needs by ensuring that no false distinction is made between domestic and foreign policy' (Liberal Party of Canada, 1993a: 104–6). After their victory, the Liberals set up the National Forum on International Relations in March 1994 and established two parliamentary committees in charge of the CanFSP review process: the Special Joint Committee of the Senate and the House of Commons to review Canada's defence policy in

February 1994 and the Special Joint Committee of the Senate and the House of Commons to review Canada's foreign policy in March 1994. The then Minister of National Defence, David Collenette, summarized the work of the committee he was in charge of as follows: '[The committee] travelled across the country listening to the views of ordinary citizens, defence experts, disarmament advocates and non-governmental organizations. It sought the advice of our allies' (Canada, 1994).

The link between the domestic side of the democratization of CanFSP (the citizens' involvement in its formulation) and the actual conduct of CanFSP can be found in the Liberals' pre-election *Foreign Policy Handbook*. In this document, Axworthy and Christine Stewart argued that '[t]here must be more involvement by our NGOs in defining our role in the globe' (Liberal Party of Canada, 1993b).[2] According to the mainstream understanding, this argument reflects Canada's deep liberal internationalist commitment: citizens express their political preferences regarding CanFSP, the government translates them into a set of coherent policies, and it implements them internationally together with NGOs. According to Axworthy (1997), the entire democratization life cycle of CanFSP, including the use of NGOs as carriers of certain aspects of it, can be considered a way to project Canada's soft power. Axworthy does not forget to emphasize that an application of the inside-out logic of soft-power projection was only made possible by the implosion of the Soviet Union and by an escape from the 'grip of superpower rivalry' (ibid., 183). It is here that the reference to the notion of middle power is being made: in Axworthy's opinion, one can speak about middle-power diplomacy. The soft-power projection of Canadian influence is seen as the latest manifestation of Canada's well-recognized middle-power status, and a call for Canada to assume her golden internationalist past is renewed. The key role in solidifying a discursive connection between Mike Pearson's golden era middlepowerism and Axworthy's softpowerism has been played by the Canadian mass media (e.g., Gwyn, 2000).

The Landmine Case and the Victory of Civil Society

The principal case for demonstrating the empirical possibilities of Canada's soft power has almost invariably been the campaign to ban anti-personnel (AP) landmines. Eventually codified by the so-called Ottawa Convention, the campaign successfully resulted in their complete ban in 1997. Instead of recycling the mainstream discourse on the projection of soft power by both the Canadian government and Canada-based NGOs, a discursive analysis of the literature on the landmine case is in order. Accounts of the landmine case can be found at three levels of discourse: (1) accounts by direct participants/observers; (2) academic reflections on the landmine case; and (3) accounts linking the landmine case to the literature on global civil society. In regard to the first level, these narratives originate predominantly from NGO personnel and, to a lesser extent, from governmental officials and scholars. These accounts acquired a Bible-like status largely due to an anthology entitled *To Walk Without Fear: The Global Movement to Ban Landmines* (1998), edited by Maxwell A. Cameron, Robert J. Lawson, and Brian W. Tomlin. In their chapter, Stephen Goose and Jody Williams, formerly the Co-ordinator of the International Campaign to Ban Landmines (ICBL, a transnational advocacy network composed of hundreds of NGOs) and Nobel Laureate for Peace, argue that the landmine case is said to represent 'the compelling story behind the global humanitarian crisis and the "David vs Goliath" nature of NGOs taking on governments and militaries to ban a weapon used by armies for decades' (Williams and Goose, 1998: 23). When we look outside the volume, other existing narratives from participants/observers confirm this understanding (Goose and Williams, 2004; Williams, 2000; Clegg, 1999). In addition, this was the context in which Williams portrayed the ICBL as a 'new kind of superpower' in her Nobel Prize speech (Williams, 1997), as it makes use of soft-power strategies such as information technology and partnerships with middle powers, most notably Canada.

Academic reflections on the landmine case and its lessons are numerous, with the studies by Price (1999) and Matthew and Rutherford (2003) being the most intellectually sophisticated. Price begins his analysis by highlighting his interest in showing what role transnational non-state actors play in security-related issues. These actors produce international norms that shape and redefine state interests. Soft-power characteristics are placed high on the list of the factors that helped the ICBL to change the behaviour of states. In concrete terms, Price stresses the role of technological change. He explains that the use of the Internet allowed pressure to be exercised steadily by the ICBL network, eventually leading to its gaining access to the policy-making process (Price, 1999: 626). Matthew and Rutherford's analysis also examines the global nature of the movement to ban AP mines. They use Rosenau's *Turbulence in World Politics* as the theoretical plane upon which to unfold their argument. In this study, Rosenau (1990: 5) makes the distinction between 'the two worlds of politics', i.e., the world of transnational politics and the world of states, which were separated by macro global structures. Matthew and Rutherford (2003: 32) use this conceptualization as their point of departure and argue that the landmine case 'could be read as an example of the increasing dominance of the nonstate realm.' They add that '[eventually] the nonstate realm would emerge victorious' (ibid., 40–52). In this light, assertions made by other academics, such as Brem and Rutherford (2001: 171), who maintain that NGOs played a 'critical role . . . in instigating and facilitating the landmine ban', or by Warkentin and Mingst (2000: 246), who depict the landmine case as a 'victory' of global civil society, are not surprising.

The above two levels of accounts are closely linked to the global civil society literature. Besides Rosenau, one of the most influential global civil society-oriented scholars for the landmine discourse has been Paul Wapner, who maintains that global civil society 'is constituted by . . . transnational social movements . . . [and] such organizations clearly transcend the self-regarding character of states. . . . [F]or this reason, normative thinkers consider many of them promising agents of progressive social change' (Wapner, 2000: 14). It is no surprise, then, that Wapner imposes ideas from his global civil society scholarship on the landmine case to substantiate his abstract claims and back them up empirically. He uses already existing participant accounts to reaffirm that the Ottawa Convention 'would never have been considered, let alone signed, if it had not been for the ICBL and other active NGOs', and that the landmine issue is 'a paradigmatic case for studying the role and effectiveness' of global civil society (Wapner, 2004: 252).

Towards a More Ambitious Human Security

The use of soft power by the Canadian government in the Ottawa Process is usually connected with a broader paradigm of human security. The reasons are obvious: people-centred security dovetailed well with the concept of anti-personnel landmines as a humanitarian issue in which the suffering individual assumed the central position. Indeed, the early formulation of human security, both in the UN context and in the Canadian context, meant that issues traditionally viewed as military problems could be successfully reframed as humanitarian problems (UNDP, 1994; DFAIT, 1995). What is more, the fact that the human security agenda was used in Canadian decision-making circles as an important facet of Canada's foreign and security policy identity showed how closely the notions of soft power, middle power, and human security have been interlinked. According to Roland Paris:

> the idea of human security is the glue that holds together a jumbled coalition of 'middle power' states, development agencies, and NGOs—all of which seek to shift attention and resources from conventional security issues and toward goals that have traditionally fallen under the rubric of international development. (Paris, 2001: 88)

The distinction between middle powers as *followers* during the Cold War and middle powers as *leaders* after it has been used to explain why the Canadian government embarked on more ambitious foreign and human security policy initiatives only after the end of the Cold War (Cooper et al., 1991). The use of human security as a diplomatic and political agenda, within which the Canadian government has forged partnerships with both like-minded states and NGOs, can therefore be considered an ostensible example of what Andrew Cooper (1997) calls niche diplomacy. Indeed, Cooper's theoretical analysis of niche diplomacy and Axworthy's practical conduct of soft-power diplomacy are connected precisely by the niche of human security.

While the importance of the Canadian government's early articulation of human security for the success of the landmine ban has been widely discussed, comparatively little has been said about the reverse dynamics, that is, about the impact of the Ottawa Process on the rearticulation of the human security paradigm. As was already suggested, the human security agenda played the role of a structural condition for the landmine problem to become a political issue. In this process, landmines got reframed: the idea of landmines as a military problem was replaced by the idea of landmines as a humanitarian issue. A careful analysis, however, reveals that as much as the landmine case required human security for its success, human security simultaneously needed the landmines issue for its own political life. This is particularly evident when the period immediately following the successful legal codification of the landmine ban in 1997 is scrutinized. One specific effect of this success on the nature of Canada's human security has been the narrowing of a hitherto quite broad paradigm (Bosold and von Bredow, 2006). The result, known as Canada's approach to human security or as the Canadian school of human security, bears clear signs of the landmine case: 'Human security means freedom from pervasive threats to people's ... safety or lives ... [H]uman security encompasses a spectrum of approaches to ... protect civilians ... and to ensure security for ... populations' (DFAIT, 2000: 2). In addition, the issue of small arms and light weapons, the very topic chosen by Lloyd Axworthy and subsequently embraced by the Canadian government to build on the success of the landmine ban, further narrowed the Canadian approach.

It would be an unsubstantiated mistake, nevertheless, to consider the government-initiated process of narrowing the human security agenda as a weakening of the agenda. On the contrary, the narrowing was accompanied by a simultaneous increase in governmental ambition as far as the future plans for human security were concerned. This was manifested through two closely interconnected processes. In the first process, a far more systematic approach was introduced that made a number of previously marginalized and insulated issues the central part of the country's newly delimited official human security agenda, expanding it in the process. Aside from the issue of landmines, these issues were especially the regulation of small arms and light weapons, stopping the use of children in armed conflicts, attempts to reinforce the application of international humanitarian and human rights law, a plan to establish the International Criminal Court, the campaign to stop exploitation of children, activities related to processes of conflict prevention, and, finally, the fight against transnational crime (Human Security Network, 1999). The one common feature of all the listed topics is their intimate relationship to the protection of the physical security of individuals, i.e., the freedom-from-fear side of the human security paradigm.

In the second process, the successful codification of the landmine ban also led to the institutional consolidation of human security. This institutionalization began in 1998, when Canada signed the Lysøen Declaration with Norway, in which they pledged to work together on issues related to freedom from fear. A year later, the bilateral Declaration was broadened to include other like-minded countries, with the effect of establishing the Human Security Network. The link between the two processes and the notion of morally directed soft power can be seen in a speech delivered by the then assistant deputy minister of DFAIT, Paul Heinbecker:

> In *Foreign Policy* in the Fall of 1990, Joseph Nye defined 'soft power' as getting other countries to want what you want. It is 'co-optive power' in contrast to 'command power.' Just as human security complements national security, soft power complements hard or military power. In Nye's analysis, ideals matter, as does success. . . . If we want to promote tolerance and reconciliation, it helps to be a democratic, bilingual, multicultural country. If we want to co-opt other governments to our norm-setting humanitarian agenda, it helps to have a solid record of multilateralism. . . . We need to work with other countries and maximize each others' resources. In this regard, we are currently testing a couple of strategies. The first is to establish close working partnerships with a few other countries that share our outlook. . . . We also plan to work cooperatively with NGOs. The validity of a human security agenda and the credibility of a government–NGO coalition were boosted by the success of the Ottawa process to ban landmines. (Heinbecker, 1998)

It was seen as common sense in the landmine case to suggest that the issue has revived the fortunes of and the prospects for Canada's human security. As a part of this narrative, the Ottawa Process to ban landmines has played the role of a bridge between the discourse on Canada's human security and the discourse on human/NGO empowerment. In respect to the latter, the key claim was that as the power of global civil society has significantly increased due to the combination of the reconceptualization of security (national security → human security) and the successful campaign to ban landmines, citizens concerned about and involved in humanitarian issues have become politically empowered. Accordingly, the power of states was said to have eroded unless they realized the potential of their co-operation with NGOs (e.g., Canada as a middle power). A different story remains to be told, however, and other lessons can be drawn from the landmine case. In concrete terms, the production of a heroic discourse derived from the campaign to ban landmines has detached both the human security agenda itself and its academic reflections from reality. Indeed, some of the aspects of the alleged 'soft power', namely processes of closer co-ordination between NGOs and the government, actually began during the Conservative era of Brian Mulroney, thereby rendering problematic the usual claim about human security being a Liberal agenda.

An Alternative Interpretation: Soft-Power Simulation and Neo-Liberal Discipline

From Hyperreal Discourse to Existing Practices

In order to find out what kind of power has been at play between the government of Canada and Canada-based NGOs within the field of human security and international development, one needs to shift from the analysis of political discourses to an analysis of *political practices*. This is not to say, however, that the discourses are unimportant. To the contrary, the relationship between discourses and practices is always a mutually constitutive one. In other words, both discourses and practices are sites of political and semiotic power. The advantage of a practice-oriented investigation is that it allows one to cut through a thick and hardly penetrable layer of celebratory discourses that have significantly hindered the process of shedding new light on the issue at hand. Following the French sociologist and philosopher Jean Baudrillard, we can say that soft power can be conceived of as an example of a simulacrum in the sense that a simulacrum is not a copy of the real (i.e., it is hyperreal—a fantasy becoming the real) but still becomes an established truth (Baudrillard, 1988: 166–84). In fact, a wide gap has appeared between what has been said about the Canadian experience (the discourse on soft power) and what can be said about this field, both theoretically and empirically.

The alternative interpretation begins with two sets of challenges. First, the argument is being made that one needs to focus on micro-level processes rather than on globally framed discourses about the increasing power of global civil society. Second, a rebuttal of the usually stressed causal arrow flowing from the NGOs towards the government (i.e., the idea that the pressure of NGOs leads to changes of governmental preferences) is substantiated. As will become clear, the human security and international development agenda has not been increasingly democratized, as the mainstream discourse has it, but disciplined, constrained, and depoliticized by the governmental introduction of neo-liberal approaches, especially results-based management. In addition, the examination suggests that the key characteristics of the agenda have been less the result of international processes and middle-power identity politics than of a set of interlinked domestic processes.

Government-Initiated Transformations of the Third Sector

We first need to look at earlier government-initiated domestic transformations of the non-profit and voluntary sector and their subsequent extension to include Canada-based international development NGOs (see Hynek, 2008a). In transforming the Canadian non-profit and voluntary sector, the government played an important role in preparing the structural terrain for launching both the human security paradigm and specific humanitarian campaigns, especially the campaign to ban anti-personnel mines. The argument is straightforward: had it not been for the Canadian government re-examining and re-imagining its role in the maintenance of the socio-political order (more specifically, in the provision of public goods in the late 1960s and the 1970s), it would hardly be conceivable that the number of NGOs would have grown as it did, including the dramatic expansion of their role in society. Beginning in the 1960s, Canada's political elite began to recognize the potential of the third sector. Specifically to deal with international development NGOs, the Canadian International Development Agency (CIDA) established the non-governmental division within its Partnership Branch in 1968. As Katherine Scott (2003: 58) puts it, '[d]uring these early days of CIDA involvement, funding for NGOs was provided on a "responsive basis".' Government efforts to reconstitute the role of the third sector and the government's subsequent reliance on the third sector in many policy areas are evident in the significant growth of funding channelled to the third sector (Gidron et al., 1992). One thing that made the Canadian government unique was the extent of its funding for highly political advocacy organizations (Scott, 2003: 14).

In the wake of the second crisis of welfare liberalism in Canada, in the early 1990s the Canadian government resumed the dialogue with the country's third sector. The paramount objective was to shake up the status quo by engaging the third sector more, and for less money, as the country's budget was in deficit and severe funding cutbacks were imposed (Hall and Reed, 1998). Subsequently, the Department of Finance under Paul Martin reviewed the system of funding for the third sector in 1994, cutting funds by $300 million within a year (Miller, 1999: 76). What followed was a major review of the third sector, with input from both NGOs and the government. The NGOs, represented by 13 national umbrella organizations, established the Voluntary Sector Roundtable in 1995; its Panel on Accountability and Governance for the Voluntary Sector (PAGVS) produced a report in 1999. Importantly, the government did not respond directly to these efforts. Instead, it invited representatives of the third sector to participate in building a new type of government/third sector relationship within its newly established Voluntary Sector Task Force, supervised by the Privy Council Office (Brock and Banting, 2003: 8). These interactions also resulted in a report (Government of Canada/ Voluntary Sector Initiative, 1999). A comparison of the focus and agenda of the two reports is summarized in Table 4.1.

Subsequently, the government and the third sector jointly introduced the five-year, $94.6 million Voluntary Sector Initiative in 2000. The objective was

Table 4.1   The Third Sector and the Government's Priorities: Comparing and Contrasting the Two Reports

Third Sector: PAGVS Report, 1999	Government: Joint Tables Report, 1999
Democracy promotion	The establishment of a working plan
Building social trust and social capital	A road map to restructure the relationship
The government needs to recognize the sector's diversity	Strengthening the third sector's capacity-building
The government needs to respect the sector's desire for autonomy	Improvement of the regulatory framework
The government needs to provide the third sector with a voice within the cabinet	Better administrative relationships and training opportunities
Different reporting standards for smaller and larger organizations	Clearer guidelines regarding financial matters and funding and accountability enhancement
More flexible requirements for advocacy	The improvement of skills and technology management in the third sector

to translate the recommendations of the two reports into legislation. By 2007, *An Accord between the Government and the Voluntary Sector* and two codes of good practice, respectively focusing on policy dialogue and funding, had been approved (Government of Canada/Voluntary Sector Initiative, 2001; Joint Accord Table, 2002a, 2002b). When the mandate of the Voluntary Sector Initiative expired in 2005, the government set up the Task Force on Community Investment, which issued a report in 2006 that clearly embraced and further elaborated the agenda and language of the previous *Report of the Joint Tables* of 1999 (Task Force on Community Investment, 2006). The recommendations proposed in the third sector's PAGVS report were marginalized.

Desecuritization, Service Delivery, and New Contractualism

When human security was introduced as a foreign policy objective, it replaced an earlier emphasis on national security as a part of a wider attempt to make defence policy subordinate to foreign policy (Hynek and Bosold, 2009). It was no surprise, then, that the 1995 White Paper on foreign policy argued that '[m]ore and more, the concept of security is focussing on the economic, social and political needs of the individual . . . [i.e.] human security' (DFAIT, 1995). Human security can be seen, especially from the international level, as a result of a combination of the successful securitization of the traditional development agenda and the deepening of the previously dominant national security.

Nevertheless, an alternative perspective that focuses on domestic factors and conditions brings less expected findings. Specifically, Canada's human security can be understood as *desecuritization and domestication-at-a-distance of the international development agenda*. The landmine case, which has usually been seen as the most important issue within the human security agenda, and which has been hailed as a great victory for global civil society, serves as an important example for understanding this process. The successful conclusion of the Ottawa Convention banning anti-personnel landmines in 1997 was, in fact, the beginning of an era that would connect two hitherto separated realms: service delivery and international security/development. Oft-neglected post-1997 developments suggest that the landmines issue has been reframed from a security/development issue to one modelled on (previously domestic) public goods provision.

The result of the above process was a shift from involvement/citizenship to a new contractualism, whereby government would pay NGOs on a contract basis for the delivery of services. The aim of the former was to involve actors in consultations and negotiations, to give them a voice. With the conclusion of the Ottawa Convention, contractualism emerged as the dominant modus operandi, and this shift in emphasis challenges the victorious discourse regarding the ability of the human security agenda to empower people and the rise of a politically aware global civil society. Contractualism, after all, generally brings about a de-politicization of NGOs: they are essentially transformed from participating political stakeholders into responsible service delivery agents, or arms of the state. This has become possible by the government's detachment of human security policy-making from service delivery, in which the main aim is to ensure an equal opportunity for NGOs to compete for funding. The most important feature has been the move from core funding to project funding. This phenomenon has been clearly demonstrated by the ongoing abandonment of transfer payments in the form of grants, which are not subject to audit, and their replacement by conditioned and audited contributions. One of the consequences has been the homogenization of the Canadian NGOs that are involved in the implementation of human security. This trend has been visible through an emergence of two cleavages: small vs large organizations; and advocacy vs service delivery organizations. The result has been that larger service delivery organizations have been heavily favoured and advantaged over the smaller advocacy-oriented NGOs—in brief, it is the difference, for example, between an NGO advocating for the victims of AP mines by showing the human face of this issue and a defence-related industry involved in the lucrative though risky business of demining.

The link between the logic of domestic service delivery and its subsequent extension to the field of international security/development is crucial for one more reason: it allows one to explain why Canada's human security has been defined in very narrow terms as the freedom-from-fear doctrine. Such a reconstitution of the individual's role in the society is manifested by the transfer of responsibilities to Canada's NGOs, which are now active in international security/development. Specifically, an intimate relationship can be discerned between the image of an active subject/citizen in the society and the emergence of the individual in need of protection as the point of reference in the security discourse. This is clear from the government document in which the human security doctrine is outlined: 'Human security means freedom from pervasive threats to people's . . . safety or lives' (DFAIT, 2000: 2). This understanding of human security has stood in direct opposition to a conceptually much wider Asian human security approach (e.g., that of Japan) which has emphasized the importance of human empowerment and socio-economic development (Hynek, 2008b; Bosold and Werthes, 2005). Unlike Canada, Asian countries with a focus on human security have not gone through a similar transformation of political rationalities with a large transfer of responsibility to subjects/NGOs. Therefore, they have not focused on the protection of physical lives in their human security.

Results-Based Management and Risk Assessment of NGOs

The key instrument for the government to ensure the effective spending of its payments in the area of human security has become its reliance on risk assessment and results-based management (RBM). RBM was officially introduced for the first time in the CIDA *Policy Statement* of 1996, which stated that 'the RBM approach will assist CIDA in its efforts towards continuous improvement in results-orientation, focus, efficiency and accountability' (CIDA, 1996). In an updated guide to the concepts and principles, CIDA defines RBM as:

a means to improve management effectiveness and accountability by involving key stakeholders in defining realistic expected results, assessing risk, monitoring progress toward the achievement of expected results, integrating lessons learned into management decisions and reporting on performance. . . . A result is a describable or measurable change in state that is derived from a cause and effect relationship. There are two key elements of this definition: 1) the importance of measuring change; and 2) the importance of causality as the logical basis for managing change. . . . For example: 'if' the developmental outputs are achieved as expected, 'then' we should achieve the outcomes; and, 'if' the outcomes are achieved as expected, 'then' we should achieve the impact. (CIDA, 2006a)

As a result of the above definition, a number of notions have been reduced from their relatively wide common-sense meanings to more specific meanings. The notion of accountability was thus delimited to accountability for results (CIDA, 2006b), and the reasons for the inclusion of stakeholders in the project plan were subsequently limited to the need to expand the information base, to establish clear roles and responsibilities, and to create an environment where individuals accept that their accountability is about delivering results (CIDA, 1996).

Canadian results-based management has had *risk assessment* as its centre of gravity. As existing comparative studies suggest, the central issues of risk assessment and management of fiduciary risk in monitoring the use of government contributions (two tasks that were performed by government officials) have been unique to Canada (Lavergne and Alba, 2003). The effectiveness of projects carried out by NGOs has thus been measured strictly in terms of 'risk' and 'benefit' and the balance between the two. Available information suggests that DFAIT officials spend around 80 per cent of their time on financial risk management-related activities; the remaining 20 per cent of their time is devoted to everything else, such as the assessment of applications, managing and monitoring ongoing projects (non-financial risks), and developing new strategies (CCSD, 2006: 33).

Two interesting issues have usually been overlooked: (1) the selective application of risk assessment strategies; and (2) the distinction made between internal, or operational, risks and external risks. Regarding selective application, the CIDA *Business Process Road Map Overview* of 2008 makes risk assessment mandatory for 'a Canadian firm, NGO, foreign organization or INGO' entering into an *agreement* (either a contribution or a grant) with CIDA and for projects with a budget over $200,000 carried out by the specialized Financial Risk Assessment Unit within CIDA. However, *arrangements* (either contributions or grants) with 'an international governmental organization' such as the UN or the World Bank are not subjected to risk assessment at all (CIDA, 2008: 44). Why the NGOs are lumped together with companies that seek to make a profit and why the NGOs are implicitly seen as problematic in terms of their possible misspending of governmental funding, as opposed to the risk assessment 'amnesty' for the UN or the World Bank, is not explained anywhere. In regard to the second question, one would expect that different types of risks would be treated differently according to their specific features and nature. Nevertheless, the only difference between internal and external risks is made on the basis of their possible manageability:

> [Although] internal factors . . . could jeopardise the success of an initiative, e.g., program/ project complexity, ineffective technical advisors, poor communication among delivery partners . . . [and] they should also be monitored, they pose less of a threat than the external factors, since they are more easily brought within the manageable control. (CIDA, 1996)

Finally, CIDA has placed indirect pressure on the 'Southern' non-governmental partners of Canadian NGOs. This was seen, in certain regards, in the process of structuring and assessing joint NGO proposals for funding. In general, CIDA has highly favoured this type of partnership over individual applications. As well, the actual application form has arguably had a constitutive effect on Southern NGOs in such partnerships since it requires 'Western-standard' details about these NGOs and at the same time actively involves them in advanced liberal procedures. Risk identification and assessment have played an important role in this exercise, as can be deduced from one of the application questions: 'For each challenge or risk identified, please describe the strategies (if any) that you and your developing-country partner organization will use to overcome or mitigate these challenges and risks' (CIDA, 2006a: 19). Surprisingly, this practice has not been modified even after the audit of CIDA's Financial Risk Assessment Function of 2005 revealed the gap between CIDA expectations and the Southern NGOs' difficulty in complying with risk assessment procedures in operational environments.

Conclusion

This chapter has demonstrated that soft power in the area of human security is not at all what it has been said to be, either conceptually or empirically. Also, a seriously under-researched area exists in regard to the interactions between the Canadian government and Canada-based international development NGOs. A disconnect can be found between the mainstream hyperreality of the soft-power narrative in human security and the reality of existing practices in the same field. With regard to the former, two specific narratives were identified as central nodes for the successful production and acceptance of this recent discursive myth of soft power: the narrative on the democratization of CanFSP and the narrative on the victory and empowerment of civil society in the campaign to ban landmines. The principal factor running through both of these narratives, which in effect contributes to the semblance of coherence in the production of the overarching image of soft power, has been the discourse on Canada as a normatively based middle power. The landmine case is also important for another reason: it helped to establish the entire ambitious agenda of human security. While the Ottawa Process that led to the Convention banning anti-personnel mines was not a product of human security, this landmark achievement and the broader human security agenda were mutually constituted and reinforced in a series of cyclical developments.

The second part of the chapter sought to correct the flawed yet already sedimented knowledge of soft power in the field of human security and international development by refuting the commonly held belief that the landmine case and human security in general were the effect of the enormous, heroic pressure of NGOs on the government of Canada. Certain assumptions must be set aside, and a more productive set of questions needs to be considered. How was it possible to create such NGOs in the first place? What were the processes through which humanitarian-oriented NGOs were established? Who played a central role in this process, and what were the characteristics of these newly created NGOs? For these reasons, earlier government-initiated domestic transformations of the third sector and the subsequent extension of the third sector to include Canada-based international development NGOs were investigated. The analysis showed that the field of human security and international development has not been increasingly democratized but, on the contrary, disciplined, constrained, and depoliticized. The emergence of human security as a goal of foreign policy ought to be conceived of from a practice-centred perspective (i.e., the emergence of human security is less a result of international processes and middle-power identity politics than a powerful example of desecuritization). As was suggested, the process of desecuritization was made possible by the extension of the domestic service delivery model to this field as well as by the introduction of new disciplinary mechanisms. Among those, the approach of results-based management and its chief technique of risk assessment by CIDA were critically analyzed.

Notes

The financial support of the Academy of Sciences of the Czech Republic (grant identification number KJB708140803) is gratefully acknowledged.

1. I refrain from using the shorter acronym CFSP because it is the widely accepted abbreviation for the European Union's Common Foreign and Security Policy.
2. Following the Liberal victory in the 1993 election, Christine Stewart, who prior to entering politics had worked in the NGO field in Central America, was appointed Secretary of State (Latin America and Africa) and in 1997 she became Environment Minister. Axworthy first served in Chrétien's cabinet as Human Resources Development Minister, though he had been touted to receive the Foreign Affairs portfolio. At Human Resources, he was tasked with overseeing a major overhaul of Canada's social security, job retraining, and employment insurance programs. He replaced André Ouellet as Foreign Affairs Minister in 1996.

References

Axworthy, Lloyd. 1997. 'Canada and Human Security: The Need for Leadership', *International Journal* 52, 2: 183–96.
———— and Sarah Taylor. 1998. 'A Ban for All Seasons: The Landmines Convention and Its Implications for Canadian Diplomacy', *International Journal* 53, 2: 189–203.

Bátora, Jozef. 2006. 'Public Diplomacy between Home and Abroad: Norway and Canada', *The Hague Journal of Diplomacy* 1, 1: 53–80.

———. 2008. *Foreign Ministries and the Information Revolution: Going Virtual?* Leiden and Boston: Martinus Nijhoff.

Baudrillard, Jean. 1988. *Selected Writings*. Stanford, Calif.: Stanford University Press.

Bosold, David, and Wilfried von Bredow. 2006. 'Human Security: A Radical or Rhetorical Shift in Canada's Foreign Policy?', *International Journal* 61, 4 (2006): 829–44.

——— and Sascha Werthes. 2005. 'Human Security in Practice: Canadian and Japanese Experiences', *Internationale Politik und Gesellschaft* 1: 84–102.

Brem, Stefan, and Kenneth R. Rutherford. 2001. 'Walking Together or Divided Agenda? Comparing Landmines and Small-Arms Campaigns', *Security Dialogue* 32, 2: 169–86.

Brock, Kathy L., and Keith G. Banting. 2003. 'The Nonprofit Sector and Government in a New Century: An Introduction', in Brock and Banting, eds, The Nonprofit Sector in Interesting Times: Case Studies in a Changing Sector. Montreal and Kingston: McGill-Queen's University Press, 1–20.

Cameron, Maxwell A., Robert J. Lawson, and Brian W. Tomlin, eds. 1998. *To Walk Without Fear: The Global Movement to Ban Landmines*. Toronto: Oxford University Press.

Canada. 1994. *White Paper on Defence*. Ottawa: Department of National Defence.

Canadian Council on Social Development (CCSD). 2006. *Voluntary Sector Fund Application, Pan-Canadian Funding Practice in Communities: Challenges and Opportunities for the Government of Canada*. Ottawa: CCSD.

Canadian International Development Agency (CIDA). 1996. *Policy Statement: Results-Based Management in CIDA*. Gatineau, Que.: Government of Canada. At: <www.acdi-cida.gc.ca/cidaweb/acdicida.nsf/En/EMA-218132613-PP9#6>.

———. 2006a. *Voluntary Sector Fund Application Guidelines and Application Form for Joint Proposals, Version June 2006*. Gatineau, Que.: Government of Canada. At: <www.acdi-cida.gc.ca/inet/images.nsf/vLUImages/CanPartnership4/$file/Joint-applications.pdf>.

———. 2006b. *The Agency Accountability Framework*. Gatineau, Que.: Government of Canada. At: <www.acdi-cida.gc.ca/INET/IMAGES.NSF/vLUImages/Performancereview6/$file/AccFrmk.pdf>.

———. 2008. *CIDA's Business Process Road Map Overview*. Gatineau, Que.: Government of Canada. At: <www.acdi-cida.gc.ca/INET/IMAGES.NSF/vLUImages/RoadMap%202008/$file/RoadMap%20Overview%20January%202008.pdf>.

Clegg, Liz. 1999. 'NGOs Take Aim', *Bulletin of the Atomic Scientists* 55, 1: 49–51.

Cooper, Andrew F., ed. 1997. *Niche Diplomacy: Middle Powers after the Cold War*. London: Macmillan.

———, Richard Higgott, and Kim R. Nossal. 1991. 'Bound to Follow? Leadership and Followership in the Gulf Conflict', *Political Science Quarterly* 106, 3: 391–410.

Department of Foreign Affairs and International Trade (DFAIT). 1995. *Canada in the World*. Ottawa: Government of Canada. At: <www.international.gc.ca/foreign_policy/cnd-world/chap4-en.asp>.

———. 2000. *Freedom from Fear: Canada's Foreign Policy for Human Security*. Ottawa: Government of Canada.

Gidron, Benjamin, Ralph M. Kramer, and Lester M. Salamon. 1992. 'Government and the Third Sector in Comparative Perspective: Allies or Adversaries?', in Gidron, Kramer, and Salamon, eds, *Government and the Third Sector: Emerging Relationships in Welfare States*. San Francisco: Jossey-Bass, 1–31.

Goose, Stephen, and Jody Williams. 2004. 'The Campaign to Ban Antipersonnel Landmines: Potential Lessons', in Richard A. Matthew, Bryan McDonald, and Kenneth Rutherford, eds, *Landmines and Human Security: International Politics and War's Hidden Legacy*. New York: State University of New York Press, 239–50.

Government of Canada/Voluntary Sector Initiative. 1999. *Report of the Joint Tables*. At: <www.voluntary-sector.ca/eng/publications/1999/working_together.pdf>.

———. 2001. *An Accord between the Government and the Voluntary Sector*. Ottawa: Government of Canada. At: <dsp-psd.pwgsc.gc.ca/Collection/CP32-75-2001E.pdf>.

Gwyn, Richard. 2000. 'Axworthy Made a Difference', *Toronto Star*, 29 Sept.

Hall, Michael H., and Paul B. Reed. 1998. 'Shifting the Burden: How Much Can Government Download to the Non-Profit Sector?', *Canadian Public Administration* 41, 1: 1–20.

Hampson, Fen O., and Dean Oliver. 1998. 'Pulpit Diplomacy: A Critical Assessment of the Axworthy Doctrine', *International Journal* 53 (Summer): 379–406.

Heinbecker, Paul. 1998. 'Human Security, Remarks for an Address Given to a Canada–US Conference in Ottawa on Global Reach: Influencing the World in Different Ways', Organized by the Canadian Institute for International Affairs, 17 Oct.

Human Security Network. 1999. 'Ministerial Meetings: A Perspective on Human Security, Chairman's Summary', Lysøen, Norway, 20 May. At: <www.humansecuritynetwork.org/docs/Chairman_summaryMay99-e.php>.

Hynek, Nik. 2007. 'Humanitarian Arms Control, Symbiotic Functionalism and the Concept of Middlepowerhood', *Central European Journal of International and Security Studies* 1, 2: 132–55.

———. 2008a. 'Conditions of Emergence and Their Effects: Political Rationalities, Governmental Programs and Technologies of Power in the Landmine Case', *Journal of International Relations and Development* 11, 2: 93–120.

———. 2008b. 'Japanese Human Security: A Conceptual and Institutional Analysis', *Ritsumeikan Annual Review of International Studies* 7: 1–20.

——— and David Bosold. 2009. 'A History and Genealogy of the Freedom-from-Fear Doctrine', *International Journal* 64, 3 (Summer): 143–58.

Joint Accord Table of the Voluntary Sector Initiative. 2002a. *A Code of Good Practice on Policy Dialogue*. Ottawa: Voluntary Sector Initiative.

———. 2002b. *A Code of Good Practice on Funding*. Ottawa: Voluntary Sector Initiative.

Lavergne, Réal, and Anneli Alba. 2003. *CIDA Primer on Program-Based Approaches*. Gatineau, Que.: CIDA.

Liberal Party of Canada. 1993a. *Creating Opportunity: The Liberal Plan for Canada*. Ottawa: Liberal Party of Canada.

———. 1993b. *Foreign Policy Handbook*. Ottawa: Liberal Party of Canada.

Matthew, Richard A., and Kenneth R. Rutherford. 2003. 'The Evolutionary Dynamics of the Movement to Ban Landmines', *Alternatives* 28, 1: 29–56.

Miller, Christopher. 1999. 'Tough Questions Avoided: The Broadbent Report on the Voluntary Sector', *Policy Options* (Oct.): 75–9.

Neufeld, Mark. 1999. 'Democratization in/of Canadian Foreign Policy: Critical Reflections', *Studies in Political Economy* 58 (Spring): 97–119.

Nossal, Kim Richard. 1995. 'The Democratization of Canadian Foreign Policy', in Maxwell A. Cameron and Maureen Appel Molot, eds, *Canada Among Nations 1995: Democracy and Foreign Policy*. Ottawa: Carleton University Press, 29–43.

Nye, Joseph, Jr. 1990. *Bound to Lead: The Changing Nature of American Power*. New York: Basic Books.

Panel on Accountability and Governance in the Voluntary Sector (PAGVS, the 'Broadbent Panel'). 1999. *Final Report: Building on Strength: Improving Governance and Accountability in Canada's Voluntary Sector*. At: <www.voluntary-sector.ca/eng/publications/1999/building_strength.pdf>.

Paris, Roland. 2001. 'Human Security: Paradigm Shift or Hot Air?', *International Security* 26, 2: 87–102.

Price, Richard. 1999. 'Reversing the Gun Sights: Transnational Civil Society Targets Land Mines', *International Organization* 52, 3: 613–44.

Rosenau, James N. 1990. *Turbulence in World Politics: A Theory of Change and Continuity*. Princeton, NJ: Princeton University Press.

Scott, Katherine. 2003. *Funding Matters: The Impact of Canada's New Funding Regime on Voluntary Organizations*. Ottawa: Canadian Council on Social Development.

Task Force on Community Investment. 2006. *Achieving Coherence in Government of Canada*

Funding Practice in Communities. Ottawa: Human Resources and Social Development Canada.

United Nations Development Programme (UNDP). 1994. Human Development Report. Oxford: Oxford University Press.

Wapner, Paul. 2000. 'The Resurgence and Metamorphosis of Normative International Relations: Principled Commitment and Scholarship in a New Millennium', in Wapner and Lester Edwin J. Ruiz, eds, Principled World Politics: The Challenge of Normative International Relations. Lanham, Md: Rowman & Littlefield, 1–22.

————. 2004. 'The Campaign to Ban Antipersonnel Landmines and Global Civil Society', in Richard A. Matthew, Bryan McDonald, and Kenneth Rutherford, eds, Landmines and Human Security: International Politics and War's Hidden Legacy. New York: State University of New York Press, 251–68.

Warkentin, Craig, and Karen Mingst. 2000. 'International Institutions, the State, and Global Civil Society in the Age of the World Wide Web', Global Governance 6, 2: 237–57.

Williams, Jody. 1997. 'Nobel Peace Prize Lecture', 10 Dec. At: <gos.sbc.edu/w/williams.html>.

————. 2000. 'David with Goliath: International Cooperation and the Campaign to Ban Landmines', Harvard International Review (Fall): 87–8.

———— and Stephen Goose. 1998. 'The International Campaign to Ban Landmines', in Cameron et al. (1998: 20–47).

Additional Readings

Beier, J. Marshall. 2003. '"Emailed Applications Are Preferred": Ethical Practices in Mine Action and the Idea of Global Civil Society', Third World Quarterly 24, 5: 795–808.

Bland, Douglas M., and Sean M. Maloney. 2004. Campaigns for International Security: Canada's Defence Policy at the Turn of the Century. Montreal and Kingston: McGill-Queen's University Press.

Brinkert, Kerry. 2003. 'The Convention Banning Anti-Personnel Mines: Applying the Lessons of Ottawa's Past in Order to Meet the Challenges of Ottawa's Future', Third World Quarterly 24, 5: 781–93.

Chapnick, Adam. 2003. 'The Ottawa Process Revisited: Aggressive Unilateralism in the Post-Cold War World', International Journal 58, 3: 281–94.

Cruikshank, Barbara. 1993. 'Revolutions Within: Self-Government and Self-Esteem', Economy and Society 22, 3: 327–44.

Dean, Mitchell M. 1999. Governmentality: Power and Rule in Modern Society. London: Sage.

Dillon, Michael. 1995. 'Sovereignty and Governmentality: From the Problematics of the "New World Order" to the Ethical Problematic of the World Order', Alternatives 20, 3: 325–63.

Duffield, Mark. 2007. Development, Security and Unending War: Governing the World of Peoples. London: Polity.

Foucault, Michel. 2008. The Birth of Biopolitics: Lectures at the College de France, 1978–1979. Houndmills: Palgrave Macmillan.

Gordon, Colin. 1991. 'Governmental Rationality: An Introduction', in Gordon, Graham Burchell, and Peter Miller, eds, The Foucault Effect: Studies in Governmentality. Chicago: University of Chicago Press, 1–51.

Hall, John, et al. 2005. The Canadian Non-profit and Voluntary Sector in Comparative Perspective. Toronto: Imagine Canada, Johns Hopkins Comparative Nonprofit Sector Project.

LENPA Synthesis Report. 2005. Capacity Development under Program Based Approaches. Washington, DC. At: <www.dgroups.org/groups/CoOL/docs/CB-PBA-LENPA_Conference-Rpt_0405.pdf>.

Osborne, Stephen. 2001. Public Management: Critical Perspectives. London and New York: Routledge.

Page, Don. 1994. 'Populism in Canadian Foreign Policy: The 1986 Review Revisited', Canadian

Public Administration 37, 4: 573–97.

Stairs, Denis. 1995. 'The Public Politics of the Canadian Defence and Foreign Policy Reviews', *Canadian Foreign Policy* 3 (Spring): 91–116.

Thomsen, Robert, and Nik Hynek. 2006. 'Keeping the Peace and Unity: Canada's National and International Identity Nexus', *International Journal* 61, 4: 845–58.

Yeatman, Anna. 1998. 'Interpreting Contemporary Contractualism', in Mitchell M. Dean and Barry Hindess, eds, *Governing Australia: Studies in Contemporary Rationalities of Government*. Melbourne: Cambridge University Press, 227–41.

The Transformation of Canada's Development Policy through the Security–Development Approach

Šárka Waisová

Introduction

Preceding chapters have explored the Canadian image of 'middle power' and have asked what actually makes Canada a middle power. The authors question the validity and content of the middle-power model, showing that the concept became ambiguous and elusive—in short, a continued effort in Canadian soul-searching.[1] The aim of the present chapter is not to analyze the middle-power concept on the grounds of its methodological premises. Rather, it will highlight the changing nature of one of the attributes that are inseparable from Canada's middlepowerhood: the delivery of foreign aid and its underlying moral vision. The weakening of this moral dimension has been made possible by recent changes in policies that have led to the linkage of two formerly separated spheres: the so-called security–development nexus.[2] Development assistance policies have been increasingly penetrated by national security concerns and strategic interests that have led to a militarization of development aid programs. Although it seems that Canadian development assistance policy changed notably after the onset of Conservative government in 2006, the transformation of Canada's foreign aid policy started much earlier. The first government to abandon the moral dimension of development aid as the driving force behind such a policy was actually the Liberal government in the wake of the terrorist attacks on the United States of 11 September 2001. Many of the changes that occurred, however, were couched in a more benign rhetoric. The Tories brought further changes in the system of official development assistance (ODA) organization, delivery, and volume. Yet, these changes only followed up on the course set by former Liberal governments. Therefore, the Harper government has simply resumed the outreach efforts that had already been in place.

Development assistance has been recognized as playing a key role in Canada's overall foreign policy since the 1950s. After World War II, Canada became a leading peacekeeper and ODA donor, with the provision of foreign aid enjoying strong support from the public and Parliament for a period of more than 40 years (Pratt, 1994: 334). Ethical considerations gradually displaced economic and geopolitical factors as the principal determinant of Canadian aid policy, and Canadians and their governments accepted—that the country had an ethical responsibility towards those people beyond their borders who were suffering severely and were living in abject poverty—what Cranford Pratt refers to as 'humane internationalism' (ibid., 334–65; Pratt, 1990: 5). Foreign policy motivations focused on national security and national interest were therefore absent at least since the mid-1960s. A moral vision had become a powerful component of the political values of Canadian society (Lumsdain, 1993; Pratt, 2001), and a foreign policy with a 'human face' became hence a defining part of Canadian identity (Grayson, 2004; Hammerstand, 2000; Nossal, 1988; Suhrke, 1999).

Since the early 1990s, international assistance has continued to be seen as a vital instrument of Canadian foreign policy. What has changed, however, has been its moral motivation. Since 9/11, humane internationalism as a driving force for ODA has weakened and national security concerns, as well as a more narrow national interest, have become the central motivation of Canadian foreign development policies. The prerequisite of this conceptual shift in Canadian foreign aid has been the prominence of the security–development nexus. It initially helped to give birth to the Canadian version of the human security concept, but eventually it enabled the infiltration of national security concerns and related strategic interests into development policies.

It is important for several reasons to analyze and understand the change in Canadian development policy that has occurred since 9/11:

1. One of the important characteristics of Canadian middlepowerhood—the moral dimension of development assistance—has weakened at least since the fall of 2001.
2. A gap exists between what Liberals, in government until 2006, actually did and the rhetoric they used.
3. Liberal governments pretended[3] that their development policy was based on moral motivations to gather support for their decisions and to mask a foreign policy of ad-hocism.

The present chapter will not explore the overall change of Canadian development co-operation policies. Rather, attention will be devoted to the weakening of the moral motivations and humanitarian aspects of ODA and the penetration of that policy by national security concerns and other strategic interests. It will then address the impact and nature of the structural, institutional and policy transformations of Canadian development assistance. In the first part, we consider how the re-conceptualization of development aid and the incorporation of security issues into official development assistance were made possible by the securitization[4] of poverty, underdevelopment, and state failure. This shift towards a focus on security resulted in the security–development nexus. Notably, where poverty, underdevelopment, and state failure were considered threats to human security in the 1990s,[5] they came to be interpreted as threats to state security after 9/11. In the second part I analyze foreign policy documents and official government statements to demonstrate how the policies associated with the security–development nexus fundamentally altered Canadian development aid. Then, changes in political practice are highlighted, and we see how the conceptual change of the security–development approach is reflected organizationally. Finally, the conceptual change of development assistance is illustrated by looking at the implementation of policy on the ground in Canada's current engagement in Afghanistan.

The Emergence of the Security–Development Nexus and the Militarization of Development Aid

The idea about the mutual relationship between insecurity and underdevelopment emerged in the early 1990s but did not figure prominently on mainstream development or security agendas. Conceptually, the security–development nexus was not a wholly new thing; linkages between disarmament and development and the resulting impacts on the concept of security had been articulated within the UN system since the early 1980s. Whereas previous articulations, such as the Brandt and Palme Reports, did not find any expression in terms of policy change, this has changed since the 1990s. The first steps allowing the security–development nexus to become more than a normative posture were taken in the second half of the 1990s. The design of new integrated policies and the mushrooming of peace and state-building missions from Kosovo to East Timor and from the Solomon Islands to Haiti have led to a political 'locking in' effect. For most experts, it is now inconceivable to treat state security and the development of a market economy as two separate domains. This tendency has been reinforced after 9/11 in the context of the so-called global War on Terror. The security–development approach expanded first within the UN system (e.g., Boutros-Ghali, 1992; UNDP, 1994) as a result of the shift to the concept of human security and later became part of the development agendas of various countries (Canada, Ireland, Norway, and the Netherlands) and international organizations (mainly the Organization for Economic Co-operation and Development, the European Union, the World Bank, and the International Monetary Fund).

To structurally embed the security–development nexus into the development policies of industrialized countries, including Canada, it was therefore important to implement the concept within the Donor Assistance Committee (DAC) of the Organization for Economic Co-operation and Development. The DAC is responsible for co-ordinating aid policies among the biggest donors and thus significantly shapes the rules of foreign assistance. During the 1990s, the linkages between peace, security, and development effectively created a new developmental mantra. Donor countries expanded their aid projects to support security sector reform, demining, or demilitarization of former combatants, to name but a few (OECD, 1997, 2001). In the early 1990s, the security–development approach was based on ideas of economic development, which regarded poverty and underdevelopment as serious threats to human beings and development aid as a possibility not only for poverty eradication but for improving the state of human security in general.

This approach changed after 9/11, and consequently, so, too, did the attitude of many states in terms of their national development agendas. In the context of the War on Terror, poverty, underdevelopment, and state failure were newly and successfully securitized, this time from a threat to the dignity of human beings to a (potential) threat to national security. Because concerns for state security enable governments to use extraordinary measures (Buzan et al., 1998: 25), the securitization of development issues was used to legitimize the subordination of development aid to security interests. This, in turn, led to the use of development money for security purposes. Development aid since then has not been exclusively perceived as an instrument of poverty eradication but, moreover, as a way to eliminate terrorist threats (UNDP, 2006; OECD/DAC, 2004). One of the most evident consequences of the securitization of poverty, underdevelopment, and state fragility has been the militarization of aid, i.e., a shift in aid delivery by replacing civilian personnel with armed forces. Using aid delivery for strategic military purposes has resulted in degrading development aid from a political end to a militarized means. One of the practical results of this development has been the model of 'three-block war,'[6] which has been realized in the framework of Provincial Reconstruction Teams operating in Afghanistan.[7]

Conceptual Change of the Security–Development Approach in Canadian Development Policy

The security–development approach in CanFSP, which gradually evolved since the early 1990s, is based on a long tradition of Canadian ODA policies and participation in UN peacekeeping missions. As mentioned above, the approach has been internationally constituted in the context of the human security debate. Human security has been defined as 'freedom from fear and from want'. This conceptualization of security combined the physical and the material well-being of individuals and was based on the assumption that security is a precondition for development, and that a society, once developed, is less prone to violence and conflict. Canada took up the concept in the second half of the 1990s and became one of its biggest advocates. In the late 1990s Canada was a textbook example of a moral middle power and norm entrepreneur that assumed responsibility for those beyond its borders who are suffering severely and who live in poverty.

The radical change of the security environment after 9/11 and the ensuing global War on Terror did, of course, influence Canadian foreign and security policy. Canada felt threatened by the terrorist attacks on the US, and also supported US anti-terrorist action as a neighbour and NATO ally. Although Canada refused to join President George W. Bush's 'coalition of the willing', which invaded Iraq in March 2003, it has been engaged in the International Security and Assistance Force (ISAF) mission in Afghanistan since 2002. Besides its robust post-conflict reconstruction mandate there, it has also been engaged in the G8 Global Partnership Programs aiming to prevent state fragility and failure in Africa. The terrorist threat initiated a process of re-evaluation and consequently led to a transformation of national security and defence policies. Whereas the Canadian security–development approach drew on a more benign and developmental form of the human security paradigm in the 1990s, this approach changed in the context of the War on Terror. Ultimately, security concerns shifted from the protection of *any* human individual to the protection of the Canadian state and its citizens. Since 2001, development aid has been perceived as a potential instrument to contribute to Canada's security. In other words, what inspires Canadian assistance in underdeveloped areas and failed states is no longer a humanitarian or ethical motive but the perceived need of strengthening Canada's security. The change of Canada's security–development approach is demonstrated best by an analysis of the basic programmatic governmental and ministerial documents.

The first foreign policy document crafted within the security–development nexus was the Liberal foreign policy white paper, *Canada in the World* (1995). The document determined key foreign policy objectives—the promotion of prosperity and employment, the protection of Canada's security, and the projection of Canadian values and culture—and set mandates for Canada's ODA program. Arrangement and protection of basic human needs, gender equality, infrastructure services, human rights, democracy, good governance, private-sector development, and the environment were declared development assistance priorities (OECD, 2002). Official development assistance was understood not only as an instrument of poverty reduction but also as a way to contribute to a more secure and prosperous life for individual Canadians as well as people all over the world. The basic idea behind *Canada in the World* was a domestic issue, that is, what kind of Canada did Canadians want. The document itself represented, once more, the declaration of Canadian moral middlepowermanship and Canada's responsibility for what happened beyond its borders. It was based on the idea that Canada could do more than an average middle power. In fact, this document opened the door for implementing human security in foreign policy and strengthening the people-centred approach in all governmental policies. In the second half of 1990s Canada became the pioneer and strong advocate of human security-centred activities. The country strongly supported issues such as the Ottawa Process to ban landmines, the establishment of an International Criminal Court, the Kimberley Process to ban the use of the international trade in diamonds to finance conflict, and the negotiation of an international treaty on child soldiers. *Canada in the World* determined Canadian foreign policy for almost six years and its validity was reconfirmed by various Liberal representatives.

Canada's posture was not officially adjusted by a new white paper after 9/11,[8] but the 1995 document lacked those dimensions that were needed to grasp the new security environment and define Canada's participation in the global War on Terror. The Canadian government had to cope not only with new threats and risks but also had to take responsibility as a NATO member country. The Canadian situation was further complicated because of the proximity to the US and the special economic and trade relations with Washington. In reaction to the terrorist attacks and in quest of increasing national security, the Department of Foreign Affairs and Trade (DFAIT) started to increase the integration of foreign policy on trade and international aid, supported involvement in the international campaign against terrorism, and promoted an agreement among G8 leaders on measures to combat terrorism and stimulate economic growth in Africa (DFAIT, 2003a: ch. 4.4). This clear effort to increase national security represented a qualitatively different approach in comparison to the human security agenda of previous years. The change in the Canadian situation was reflected step by step in various government and ministerial documents and finally led to the country's first integrated foreign policy review, *Canada's International Policy Statement: A Role of Pride and Influence in the World*, which appeared in 2005. Over the period from autumn 2001 to autumn 2005 a large gap existed between government rhetoric in public and the policies on the ground. One could refer to this period as a time of Canada's identity crisis: the government was not willing to abandon the programmatic focus of the recent past but at the same time was aware that more needed to be done to ensure the security of the country and its citizens while simultaneously being a loyal NATO member.[9] The separation from previous policies was more complicated and difficult because the generosity and the moral motivation of development aid were deeply embedded in Canadian political culture and correlated to ethically responsive domestic welfare programs (Alain and Thérien, 1995).

In the period between late 2001 and 2005, the Canadian government was trapped in what could be referred to as 'somewhat in between'—in between what Canada *should* do and the reality of what it was actually doing. What Canada should do had been declared in *Canada in the World* and backed up by government statements. What Canada was actually doing was less mirrored in ministerial documents and more reflected by Canada's activities in Afghanistan. To illustrate the change that had occurred, it is necessary to explore the *Performance Report 2003* from the Canadian International Development Agency (CIDA) and the new national security policy based on *Securing an Open Society: Canada's National Security Policy* (2004) and its 2005 revision, subtitled *One Year Later: Progress Report on the Implementation of Canada's National Security Policy*.

CIDA's *Performance Report 2003* was the first document indicating the infiltration of national security concerns into the development agenda and the programmatic change of the security–development approach. The report declares security and stability as important conditions and prerequisites for poverty reduction and sustainable development, noting that security and stability abroad strengthens the security of Canada and its citizens (CIDA, 2003: Section III). According to CIDA, the country's development agenda includes the promotion of security sector reform, good governance, peace and order in fragile and failed states, and the creation of counter-terrorism capacities within national security policy. Thus, using development money for national security purposes and anti-terrorist activities was legitimized. A further step in replacing human security with national security within development co-operation policy was enshrined in the new national security policy. *Securing an Open Society*, released in 2004 and re-evaluated in 2005, set out the country's strategic interests—protecting Canada and the safety and security of Canadians; ensuring that Canada is not a base for threats to her allies; and contributing to international security—and thereby subordinated development co-operation policy to Canada's security targets. According to these policy statements, the national security concerns determine the types of assistance Canada provides to failing and failed states. Canada's international development co-operation aims to help states avoid slipping into conflict by re-establishing security. Resources intended for development aid are allocated to provide counter-terrorism assistance to failed and failing states as well as post-conflict stabilization and recovery (Canada, 2004b: 47–52; Canada, 2005: 50). The government anticipated close relations between the Canadian Forces and development institutions and placed the development instruments into the hand of Canadian Ministry of Defence and the military. Both the 2004 and

2005 policy statements confirmed the transformation of the Canadian Forces and its military strategy. The government championed the model of three-block war, having tested it in Afghanistan since 2003, where it was claimed to be effective after Canada became the lead nation for a Provincial Reconstruction Team in Kandahar in the southern part of the country.

The period between the autumn 2001 and late 2005 could be described as a time when the practical steps of the government and its ministries were ahead of the preparation of basic programmatic documents on which some policy procedures and practical steps should be based. The various policy documents from this period were created after the fact and reflected the reality that already had emerged, or at least the reality as it was perceived by the military.[10]

The document marking the end of this period was *Canada's International Policy Statement—Role of Pride and Influence in the World*, which established an entirely new approach to Canada's international development assistance as opposed to that expressed in 1995 in *Canada in the World*. In the *International Policy Statement* (IPS) Canada's commitment to a people-centred approach remains in the shade of a state-centred perspective, and the aid program becomes an instrument to promote national security and trade objectives. The *IPS* introduced Canada's first integrated approach to foreign policy, bringing together defence, diplomacy, and development (the so-called '3D approach'). The three 'Ds' are first of all supposed to promote the values of and bring security to Canadians and Canada. Development formally became the instrument for supporting defence and diplomacy. The *IPS* furthermore concentrated on revitalizing Canada's North American partnership, counter-terrorism operations, stabilizing failed and fragile states,[11] combatting weapons of mass destruction, enhancing international commercial engagement and promoting good governance, and, last but not least, crafting a new flexible diplomacy. The *IPS* confirmed the securitization of terrorism, poverty, underdevelopment, and state failure, and aimed to reduce such insecurities (priorities being Afghanistan, Haiti, and Sudan). Failed states thus were seen as a national security problem endangering Canadian strategic interests and threatening the welfare and security of Canadian citizens (see, e.g., North–South Institute, 2007). The *IPS* and the three 'Ds' opened space for the reorganization of DFAIT and CIDA, for a different rationale behind development assistance, and for reorganization of the Department of National Defence (DND) and the Canadian Forces. These changes had already begun before the publication of the *IPS*, but the *IPS* created a clear starting point for reorganization and officially confirmed the dominance of security interests.

To sum up, autumn 2001 to late 2005 represents an interim period when Canada's development co-operation policy abandoned the moral dimension and shifted its focus to the country's security and national interests. This period was rounded off by the *IPS*, which reflected Canada's identity crises. It used the earlier foreign policy rhetoric, including the moral imperative to help those beyond Canada's borders, but in fact it subordinated the development assistance to Canadian security and national interests. The *IPS* thus confirmed the change of the security–development approach.

Institutional and Organizational Consequences

The transformation of the security–development approach and the approximation of official development assistance to security policy required subsequently greater collaboration among the development, foreign policy, and defence policy camps. The conceptual change of the Canadian security–development approach and the penetration of national security issues into the development agenda were accompanied by wide institutional and organizational changes in development policy and foreign aid delivery. The main result of the transformation was the change in relationships between ministries and agencies, a modification of their mandates, budgets, and goals, and the establishment of new bodies reflecting the infiltration of national security concerns into development co-operation policies. Or, put differently, development co-operation becoming a national security instrument, highlighted by the appointment of new staff in senior policy and military positions.[12] Some of these institutional and organizational changes were explicitly announced in policy documents, but for the most part the transformation occurred spontaneously in the quest to resolve day-to-day dilemmas.[13]

The biggest shift occurred less on the ground than in the mutual relationships of Canadian International Development Agency, the Department of Foreign Affairs and International Trade, and the Department of National Defence.[14] The transformation included increasing the number of joint actions and also changes in ministerial responsibilities in planning and organization. To ensure the comprehensiveness of the three 'Ds', DFAIT and CIDA officials, together with officials from other federal departments, have been meeting biannually in an interdepartmental group to address security–development issues. In 2002, CIDA's mandate was extended 'to support international efforts to reduce threats to Canadian security' (OECD, 2007: 64) and CIDA's activities and programs were harmonized with DFAIT and DND in areas such as humanitarian assistance, conflict prevention, peace-building, and post-conflict reconstruction (CIDA, 2003). Subsequently, a significant portion of CIDA's funding was earmarked for the Royal Canadian Mounted Police and the Canadian Forces. The Canadian military has been administering dozens of aid projects together with CIDA since 2002, which has furthered the decade-long transition of the Canadian Forces from the earlier Cold War thinking to post-9/11 realities—that the serious threat to national security can come not only from state but also from non-state actors such as terrorist groups and from the failure of states that can lead to the spread of instability. The Canadian military, faced with whether and how to adapt to the new security environment, eventually accepted the US model of three-block war. Keeping with the model, the military started to provide humanitarian assistance. Furthermore, the deployment of the Canadian Forces Disaster Assistance Response Team (DART), a rapid-response unit of the Canadian Forces established in 1996 that provides humanitarian aid and gains time for deployment of long-term humanitarian aid and recovery resources, rests with the Canadian government, based on advice from DFAIT, DND, and CIDA (www.forces.gc.ca/site/Newsroom/view_news_e.asp?id=301).

Institutional and organizational changes took place as a result of the *IPS* and increasing Canadian engagement in Afghanistan since August 2005.[15] In October 2005, in need of further enhancing consistency and synergies between various parts of development assistance and security policy, DFAIT established a Global Peace and Security Fund (GPSF), its component programs being the Global Peace and Security Program, the Global Peace Operations Program, and the Human Security Program. The fund is financed from the development assistance budget. The aim of the GPSF is to provide a timely response to countries in crisis, mainly failing and collapsed states, that do not fall under the responsibility of the Department of National Defence and that are outside the core purposes of Canada's development aid.[16] The GPSF is managed by the Stabilization and Reconstruction Task Force (START), established in September 2005 and located in the International Security Branch of DFAIT. In addition to the management of the GPSF, START's mission is to enhance the government's capacity for international crisis response and to plan and deliver coherent conflict prevention, crisis response, peace-building, and stabilization initiatives in fragile and failed states (DFAIT, 2006).

After the change in government in January 2006, CIDA transformed the Canada Corps, originally launched in 2004 to contribute to good governance, human rights, and democracy in developing countries and fragile states, into an Office for Democratic Governance. The change was in response to the new focus on democracy and democratic governance, human rights, and the rule of law in developing countries. The Office established framework agreements with other governmental institutions to effectively fulfill the security–development approach.

The infiltration of the security–development approach by national security concerns has also been reflected by a structural transformation of the development aid budget, referred to as the international assistance envelope (IAE).[17] The IAE represents a co-ordinated effort, jointly funded and administered by the Minister for International Co-operation (a cabinet position created in 1996) in consultation with other ministries involved, particularly DFAIT and DND.[18] The IAE demonstrates the will to ensure an all-encompassing approach to reconstruction, including security, economics, social development, counter-terrorism, and peace-building.

Aid Programming under the Conservative Government

In light of the above, the government change since 2006 does not constitute a fundamental shift in the development assistance and the security-development approach. The Tories did bring further changes into the system of ODA organization, delivery, and volume. These changes, however, only followed the previous course of former Liberal governments.[19] Canada's present assistance to Afghanistan, perceived as helping to combat poverty and extremism and ultimately contributing to Canada's national security, is in line with the *IPS* and the *National Security Policy*, two key documents originating with Liberal governments. The Harper government has not initiated a general move towards greater emphasis on security issues; rather, it has resumed the outreach efforts that had already been in place.

The Harper government's continuation of the former Liberal security–development approach is reflected by the fact that the structure of the IAE and the level of expenditures within its component programs have remained at approximately the same level (Treasury Board, 2007), and that the organizational style and orientation of development co-operation—perhaps with the exception of prioritizing Latin America over Africa[20]—did not change much over the last two years. Indeed, some commentators noted that foreign policy issues were hardly mentioned during the 2005–6 election campaign and that it was therefore doubtful whether big changes in foreign policy were to be expected. Foreign missions such as in Afghanistan, Haiti, Iraq, and Sudan had been launched before the Tories assumed office and the extension of the Afghanistan mission until 2011 was rubber-stamped by the Conservative government and the Liberal opposition (CBC, 2008c).

The most significant difference has been the Tories' rhetoric regarding development policy and the importance and value being attributed to international assistance. While Liberal governments perceived development and humanitarian aid as a key element of Canada's international role and a way to restore Canada's influence in the world (Canada, 2004a), the Conservatives' focus was different. Stressing the need for development co-operation to be coherent with foreign policy and strategic interest, development aid has now been regarded as primarily contributing to Canada's security. Thus, the main change that can be attributed to the Conservative government has been their removal of the dichotomy that existed between the morally laden governmental rhetoric concerning development policy and its more security-oriented practice.

The Transformation of the Security–Development Approach in Practice: The Case of Afghanistan

Canada's engagement in Afghanistan serves as a good illustration of the conceptual change of the security–development approach, the discrepancy between Liberal rhetoric and operations on the ground, as well as the very different approach taken by the Conservatives. Due to the Liberal government's decision to put the three 'Ds' approach into practice in Afghanistan as early as 2003 (DFAIT, 2003b), the Afghanistan case makes it possible to demonstrate the interplay between development and security policies as these policies played out under the Liberals and the Conservatives.

Prior to 9/11, Afghanistan was one of the few places in the world that lacked any sort of connection to Canada, with the exception of a relatively limited $10 million annual Canadian contribution of humanitarian aid (CBC, 2008a). One of the reasons can be seen in the rather loose bilateral relations of the two countries. Canada first established diplomatic relations with Afghanistan in 1968. However, these diplomatic ties were severed when the Soviet Union invaded the country in 1979 and they were never fully re-established after the withdrawal of Soviet troops in 1989 until late 2001. This means that all Afghan regimes in the 22 years before 2001, including the one of the Taliban, were never formally recognized by Canada.

In February 2002, the Canadian Forces entered Afghanistan as part of the US-led Operation Enduring Freedom. To analyze and evaluate Canada's engagement in Afghanistan, it is necessary to understand that Canada became engaged there for various reasons. The 9/11 attacks were seen as an attack on the Western world, and therefore on Canada, too. Almost 30 Canadians died on that day, and the safety of Canadians and the security of Canada as a whole were considered to be seriously threatened. The subsequent invasion was seen by Foreign Affairs Minister John Manley as an opportunity for Canada to demonstrate international leadership (DFAIT, 2002).

Soon enough, the country's presence in Afghanistan became a controversial foreign policy issue. In total, Canadian governments made five major decisions regarding the mission in Afghanistan, all of which received parliamentary approval. The first decision was taken in 2001, when the Chrétien government granted direct military support for conducting the global campaign on terrorism by contributing troops to the US-led international coalition. It was not a peacekeeping mission, but a combat operation. The second decision occurred in February 2003 when the Chrétien government decided that the Canadian contribution to NATO's ISAF mission would be sending troops to Kabul. This mandate was adjusted in May 2005 when the Martin government announced a new and expanded course for the Afghanistan mission. The plan, representing the third decision by the government, included the redeployment of Canadian

Forces from Kabul to Kandahar. The next decision was taken in April 2006 when Parliament voted to extend Canada's military presence in Kandahar until 2009 and Prime Minister Harper announced an increase in development funding, thereby sustaining the flow of bilateral aid until 2011 (Chung, 2007). Following the recommendations of the Manley report in the spring of 2008, the House of Commons voted in favour of an extension of Canada's mandate in Kandahar province until 2011—the fifth major decision.

Since 2003, Canada's increasing engagement in Afghanistan has been necessary to achieve the government's security policy objectives in that country. Canadian policy advisers have argued that security in and the reconstruction of Afghanistan could only be achieved through the comprehensive 3D approach. Liberal governments referred to Afghanistan as a country belonging to the failed and fragile states category (Black, 2007: 325–6) and, on the basis of the *IPS*, made Afghanistan the largest recipient of assistance programs. Labelling Afghanistan a failed state serving as an operating base for terrorists threatening the safety of Canada and Canadians allowed Liberals to justify the participation of the Canadian Forces in combat operations. In August 2005, when the Canadian military presence shifted from Kabul, Canada assumed responsibility for the Kandahar Provincial Reconstruction Team (PRT), which brought together Canadian Forces with civilian police, diplomats, civil development experts, and officers of the Afghan government. The Canadian PRT also executed Canadian development assistance to Afghanistan, and since 2005 huge sums of development money have been spent on security-related issues such as security sector reform, the training of Afghan police and military forces, and other forms of state-building and humanitarian assistance. Afghanistan also gained money from the international assistance envelope for counter-terrorism capacity-building (CTCB). CTCB projects were supervised by PRTs and aimed at increasing border security, strengthening the capacity of the Afghan army and police, and formulating and applying new legal mechanisms. The fusion of security and development projects under the PRT agenda led to changes at the bureaucratic level within Canadian institutions.

When Stephen Harper and his government came into office, Afghanistan was already Canada's biggest recipient of bilateral assistance and the key changes in the relationship between the governmental branches and their responsibilities were in place. The worsening security situation in Afghanistan and the increasing number of casualties among the Canadian Forces led to a further prioritization of Afghanistan as a foreign policy issue but was not a reason for any further fundamental change. The Conservatives appointed a senior diplomat to co-ordinate military and development efforts as Canada's ambassador in Afghanistan, and transformed the head-of-mission position in Kabul into one of Canada's most senior diplomatic assignments; however, these changes corresponded to the changes made by Liberals. The fact that the

Harper government kept with prior Liberal steps was confirmed by the panel led by former Liberal cabinet minister John Manley. The panel rejected an option to allow troops to adopt a traditional peacekeeping role in Kandahar (which is what many Liberals called for after they left the government), saying that there was not yet peace to keep in Afghanistan (CBC, 2008b). Consequently, the Tory government, supported by some Liberals, extended the mission in Kandahar until 2011, shifting the emphasis of the mission's mandate to reconstruction and development in the region.

Policies on Afghanistan since 2001 therefore highlight that the differences between Liberals and Tories at the policy level are negligible—it has been a seamless mission of remarkable continuity from the outset. The Harper government did not re-conceptualize the overall security–development approach put forward by earlier Liberal governments. Rather, the Conservatives adjusted policies that had already been put in place by the Liberal government. The main difference is in the rhetoric used for explaining Canadian presence in Afghanistan to the public and the overall value attributed to development or defence policy, respectively.

Liberals justified the intervention on humanitarian grounds, stressing the 'moral imperative' of intervening to protect the vulnerable (Travers, 2006) and to defend Canadian values. Prime Ministers Chrétien and Martin subsequently argued that Canadian troops were responsible for the promotion of values such as freedom, democracy, equality, justice, and development (e.g., White House, 2002; Canada, 2004a). Liberals stressed that the Canadian Forces needed to work more closely with development workers to make any tangible progress in Afghanistan: 'When Canada deploys its forces in Kandahar, they will be assisted by aid officers and by diplomats in building confidence with the local population' (Martin, 2005).

Stephen Harper, on the contrary, has continuously stressed the linkage between Afghan domestic security and Canadian security by declaring that 'global security hinges on success in Afghanistan [and that] we [Canada] must build a successful alternative there in order to defeat extremism and terrorism everywhere' (*Winnipeg Free Press*, 2007) since 'rebuilding a shattered society and providing a stable security environment go hand in glove' (CBC, 2006).

Conclusion

Security issues found their way into international assistance policies since the early 1990s in the context of the human security agenda. Being a human security pioneer and advocate, Canada was among the first countries to implement a foreign policy based on a comprehensive view that linked individual security concerns with developmental aspects. The aim of Canadian development co-operation was to free people from fear and from want, in other words, to strengthen what has been referred to as human security. The driving force of development assistance at the outset was the feeling of responsibility for people beyond Canada's borders. Canadian policy was labelled as humane internationalism and Canada's international role became defined as that of a moral middle power. Thereby, moral motivations in development policy became part of Canadian political culture and of the country's international identity.

The global War on Terror and the subsequent securitization of poverty, underdevelopment, and state failure produced a change in the Canadian security–development approach. Ottawa recognized that it would no longer be possible to conduct development and security policy in the same manner as before 9/11 and adapted its development policy to the post-9/11 environment. Development assistance programs were penetrated by national security concerns and, subsequently, development policy was put in the service of security and defence policy. Since 9/11, development policy has been seen as an instrument of foreign and security policy rather than as a reflection of a commitment to humanitarian ideals. Subsequently, the institutional and organizational structure of Canadian development policies underwent deep transformation with the establishment of additional consultation mechanisms between line departments such as CIDA, DFAIT, and DND. Notwithstanding this procedural change, Liberal governments still used the humanitarian foreign affairs rhetoric. Beginning in the autumn of 2001, one could observe an increasing discrepancy between governmental humanitarian foreign policy rhetoric and practical policy steps. The absence of moral motivation in development policies, the reluctance to acknowledge this change, and the discrepancy between rhetoric and operation on the ground contributed to a foreign policy identity crisis in which the concept of Canada as a moral middle power was continuously challenged.

When the Conservative government of Stephen Harper declared development aid an instrument of Canada's foreign and security policy by ensuring the security of the Canadian federation and its citizens, no real revolutionary change of the Canadian development agenda on the ground occurred. What changed significantly was the government rhetoric. The Conservatives declared a clear link between underdevelopment, poverty, and failing states on one side and Canadian security on the other, and abandoned the rhetoric based on the 'defence of values, freedom, democracy, and liberty'. The Harper government hence harmonized its rhetoric with its actions and consolidated mechanisms codified by the Liberal government in the period from 2001 to 2005. One can argue, therefore, that the current foreign policy is more pragmatic and consistent in that respect. This is not to say, however, that Canada overcame the crisis of what its development and security policies actually stand for. To overcome this disconnect, Canada needs to redefine its international role. The contemporary middle-power role of Canada thus far remains 'an *empty form* which needs to be refilled' (Hynek, 2007: 140).

Notes

The financial support of the Academy of Sciences of the Czech Republic (grant identification number KJB708140803 and IAA708060701) is gratefully acknowledged.

1. For earlier discussions of the concept of middle power, see Cooper et al. (1993).
2. I use the terms 'security–development nexus' and 'security–development approach' in this chapter. While the first is commonly understood as a doctrinal shift in development aid and security policies throughout the West since the end of the 1990s, the second is what I consider to be the Canadian version of it.
3. I use the term 'pretend' here because the Liberals, when in power, deliberately used the rhetoric based on humane internationalism for decisions aimed at increasing national security. Party officials and bureaucrats knew that such rhetoric allowed them to reach many decisions more easily by reducing the probability of public protests. (Personal interviews with governmental officials at the Canadian International Development Agency in Ottawa during the last week of November 2007.)
4. The 'securitization' approach of the so-called Copenhagen School argues that security is less about a historically fixed understanding and quality of security than about the political processes that shape the understanding of security at a given time. In that sense, securitization is a more extreme version of the politicization of an issue considered crucial for the survival or well-being of the referent object, i.e., the state (national security), the environment (environmental security), etc. In the words of Buzan et al. (1998: 23–5), to securitize an issue means that the issue is 'presented as an existential threat, requiring emergency measures and justifying actions outside the normal bounds of political procedure. . . . The issue is not necessarily a threat because real existential threat exists but because the issue is presented as such a threat. . . . A discourse that takes the form of presenting something as an existential threat to a referent object does not by itself create securitization—this is a *securitization move*, but the issue is securitized only if and when the audience accepts it as such.'
5. The human security approach expanded the notion of security to include human individuals as referent objects and the violation of human rights, environmental scarcity and degradation, food insecurity, and economic insecurity as main threats. Interview with Lloyd Axworthy in *Canada World View*, special edn (Fall 1999), at: <www.dfait-maeci. gc.ca/canada-magazine/special/se1t3-en.asp>. (29 Feb. 2008)
6. This model is based on the idea that, before engaging in a high-intensity fight, it is appropriate that military forces first deliver humanitarian and development aid or assist others in doing so, and second, that they contribute to the stabilization of peace support operations. If these two steps do not prevent the outbreak of violence, then it is necessary to use military force. The model of 'three-block war' supposes that after the opening of military operations, the distribution of aid continues to help stabilize the situation. For additional information on the concept, see Farhoumand-Sims (2007).
7. Provincial Reconstruction Teams are responsible for post-conflict reconstruction and reconciliation and focus on the restoration of security, governance, and development in Afghanistan. They include military as well as civilian personnel (for example, officers from national development agencies) and are mainly under the responsibility of ministers of defence. For additional details, see Dzedzic and Seidl (2005).

8. Its validity was rhetorically confirmed by various leading Liberal personalities such as Paul Martin. See CBC (2004).

9. Personal interviews with DFAIT officials, Ottawa, 22–3 Nov. 2007.

10. Personal interview with Senior Defence Analyst, Conference of Defence Associations, Ottawa, 23 Nov. 2007.

11. The Canadian government uses the terms 'countries in transition', 'countries in conflict', and 'countries in crisis' for weak, failing, and failing states, depending on the context, although there are no precise definitions for these terms. For example, in 2002 Afghanistan was a 'country in conflict'; today it is a 'country in transition'.

12. In February 2005 General Rick Hillier was appointed Canada's Chief of the Defence Staff, symbolizing the nomination of a 'soldier's soldier' who, according to commentators, 'broke the bureaucratic mould that seemed to dictate many appointments [in Canadian military] since the Cold War'. *Toronto Star*, 16 July 2005, A19.

13. Personal interviews with government officials at DFAIT and DND, Ottawa, 22–3 Nov. 2007.

14. Other important players in Canada's international development co-operation include the Department of Finance, the Privy Council Office, the Treasury Board Secretariat, and the International Development Research Centre.

15. In August 2005 Canada assumed responsibility for the Kandahar Provincial Reconstruction Team and in February 2006 it obtained nine-month command of ISAF operations in southern Afghanistan.

16. These activities include measures such as eradicating anti-personnel mines, supporting peace processes, addressing small arms and light weapons (SALW) proliferation, supporting transitional justice and reconciliation, and improving peace enforcement and peace support.

17. The IAE—as a single expenditure grouping—was created in 1991 and was controlled by DFAIT (at that time, External Affairs). It has been seen by many as threatening CIDA and its autonomy in ODA delivery and programming. See Pratt (1994: 359).

18. Other issues in the international assistance envelope are managed in consultation with the Privy Council Office, the Department of Finance, and the Treasury Board Secretariat.

19. This is not to say that the Tories did not change the foreign policy at all; the Conservative government sought to improve the relationship with the US, and the first years of the government were indicative of this attempt. The Harper government barely changed the terms of Canada's development policy, however. See CBC (2007).

20. Harper's government has been shifting its focus to regions closer to Canada—most notably the Americas. This is understandable given the orientation on national security issues. A weakened interest in Africa was made public in a series of speeches by Prime Minister Harper (e.g., Freeman, 2007).

References

Alain, Noël, and Jean-Phillipe Thérien. 1995. 'From Domestic to International Justice: The Welfare State and Foreign Aid', *International Organization* 43, 2: 523–53.

Black, David. 2007. 'Canadian Aid to Africa: Assessing "Reform"', in G. Bruce Doern, ed., *How Ottawa Spends, 2007–2008: The Harper Conservatives—Climate of Change*. Montreal and Kingston: McGill-Queen's University Press, 319–38.

Boutros-Ghali, Boutros. 1992. *Agenda for Peace*. New York: United Nations. At: <www.un.org/docs/SG/agpeace.html>. (11 Feb. 2009)

Buzan, Barry, Ole Waever, and Jaap de Wilde. 1998. *Security: A New Framework for Analysis*. Boulder, Colo.: Lynne Rienner.

Canada. 2004a. Speech from the Throne to open Third Session of Thirty-Seventh Parliament of Canada, 2 Feb. At: <www2.parl.gc.ca/Parlinfo/Documents/ThroneSpeech/37-3-e.html> (22 Nov. 2008)

————. 2004b. *Securing an Open Society: Canada's National Security Policy*. Ottawa: Government of Canada, Apr.

————. 2005. *Securing an Open Society: One Year Later. Progress Report on the Implementation of Canada's National Security Policy*. Ottawa: Government of Canada, Apr.

Canadian Broadcasting Corporation (CBC). 2004. At: <www.cbc.ca/canadavotes2004/pdfplatforms/Liberal_platform_en.pdf>. (12 Feb. 2009)

————. 2006. 'Harper's Speech to the United Nations', 21 Sept. At: <www.cbc.ca/news/background/un/harper-un-speech.html>. (12 Nov. 2007)

————. 2007. 'Is the Harper Government Changing the Aid Game?', 21 Mar. At: <www.cbc.ca/news/background/cdngovernment/harper-aid.html>. (26 Oct. 2007)

————. 2008a. 'Canada in Afghanistan: What the Mission Is, and Where It Might Go Next', 22 Jan. At: <www.cbc.ca/news/background/afghanistan/canada.tml>. (26 Nov. 2008)

————. 2008b. 'Extend Afghan Mission If NATO Sends More Troops: Panel', 22 Jan. At: <www.cbc.ca/canada/story/2008/01/22/afghan-manley.html>. (26 Nov. 2008)

————. 2008c. Interview with John Manley, 15 Oct. At: <www.cbc.ca/canada/story/2008/10/15/f-manley-invu.html>. (21 Nov. 2008)

Canadian International Development Agency (CIDA). 2003. *Performance Report for the Period Ending March 31, 2003*. At: <www.tbs-sct.gc.ca/rma/dpr/02-03/CIDA-ACDI/CIDA-ACDI03D_e.asp>.

Chung, Talia. 2007. *Afghanistan: Chronology of Canadian Parliamentary Events*. Ottawa: Library of Parliament Infoservice, publication PRB 07-24E, 20 Nov. At: <www.parl.gc.ca/information/library/PRBpubs/prb0724-e.htm>. (28 Nov. 2008)

Cooper, Andrew F., Richard A. Higgott, and Kim Richard Nossal. 1993. *Relocating Middle Powers: Australia and Canada in a Changing World Order*. Vancouver: University of British Columbia Press.

Department of Foreign Affairs and International Trade (DFAIT). 2002. 'Canada's Point Man: Interview with Foreign Affairs Minister John Manley', *Canada World View*, Issue 14 (Winter). At: <www.dfait-maeci.gc.ca/canada-magazine/issue14/14t2-en.asp>. (28 Nov. 2008)

————. 2003a. *Performance Report for the Period Ending March 31, 2003*. At: <www.dfait-maeci.gc.ca/department/estimates/menu-en.asp>.

————. 2003b. 'Canada in Afghanistan: Building Bridges in Afghanistan', *Canada World View*, Issue 20 (Autumn). At: <www.dfait-maeci.gc.ca/Canada-magazine/issue20/01-title-en.asp>. (28 Nov. 2008)

————. 2006. *Stabilization and Reconstruction Task Force: Year in Review: Mobilizing Canada's Capacity for International Crisis Response*. Ottawa: DFAIT.

Dzedzic, Michael J., and Michel K. Seidl. 2005. *Provincial Reconstruction Teams and Military Relations with International and Nongovernmental Organizations in Afghanistan*, USIP Special Report 147, Sept.

Farhoumand-Sims, Chesmak. 2007. 'The Negative Face of the Militarization of Aid', *Human Security Bulletin* 5, 1 (Jan.–Feb.): 12–14.

Freeman, Alan. 2007. 'Does Harper Want Out of Africa?', *Globe and Mail*, 23 Nov., A16.

Grayson, Kyle. 2004. 'Branding "Transformation" in Canadian Foreign Policy: Human Security', *Canadian Foreign Policy* 11, 2 (Winter): 41–68.

Hammerstand, Anne. 2000. 'Whose Security? UNHCR, Refugee Protection and State Security after the Cold War', *Security Dialogue* 31, 4: 391–403.

Hynek, Nikola. 2007. 'Humanitarian Arms Control, Symbiotic Functionalism, and the Concept of Middlepowerhood', *Central European Journal of International and Security Studies* 1, 2: 132–55.

Lumsdain, David Halloran. 1993. *Moral Vision in International Politics: The Foreign Aid Regime 1945–1989*. Princeton, NJ: Princeton University Press.

Martin, Paul. 2005. 'Statement by the Rt. Hon. Paul Martin Prime Minister of Canada at the NATO Summit', 22 Feb. At: <www.nato.int/docu/speech/2005/s0502221.htm>. (28 Feb. 2008)

North–South Institute. 2007. *Fragile States or Failing Development? Canadian Development*

Report 2008. Ottawa: North–South Institute.

Nossal, Kim Richard. 1988. 'Mixed Motives Revisited: Canada's Interest in Development Assistance', *Canadian Journal of Political Science* 21, 1: 35–56.

Organization for Economic Co-operation and Development (OECD). 1997. *Conflict, Peace and Development Cooperation on theTthreshold of the 21st Century.* Paris: OECD. At: <www.oecd. org/dataoecd/57/55/33920283.htm>. (1 Nov. 2007)

———, Development Assistance Committee. 2001. *The DAC Guidelines Helping Prevent Violent Conflict.* Paris: OECD. At: <www.oecd.org/dataoecd/57/55/33920283.htm>. (5 Oct. 2007)

———. 2002. *Canada (2002), DAC Peer Review.* At: <www.oecd.org/document/61/0,2340,en_2 649_37413_2409533_1_1_1_37413,00.html>.

———, Development Assistance Committee. 2004. *The Security and Development Nexus: Challenges for Aid.* DCD/DAC(2004)9/REV2. Paris: OECD, Development Co-operation Directorate, Development Assistance Committee.

———. 2007. *Canada: Development Assistance Committee Peer Review.* Paris: OECD.

Pratt, Cranford. 1990. 'Middle Power Internationalism and Global Poverty', in Pratt, ed., *Middle Power Internationalism: The North–South Dimension.* Montreal and Kingston: McGill-Queen's University Press, 3–24.

———. 1994. 'Humane Internationalism and Canadian Development Assistance Policies', in Pratt, ed., *Canadian International Development Assistance Policies: An Appraisal.* Montreal and Kingston: McGill-Queen's University Press, 334–70.

———. 2001. 'Moral Vision and Foreign Policy: The Case of Canadian Development Assistance', in R. Irwin, ed., *Ethics and Security in Canadian Foreign Policy.* Vancouver: University of British Columbia Press, 59–76.

Suhrke, Astri. 1999. 'Human Security and the Interest of States', *Security Dialogue* 30, 3: 265–76.

Travers, James. 2006. 'In Full Retreat on Darfur', *Toronto Star*, 5 Nov., A1.

Treasury Board of Canada. 2007. At: <www.tbs-sct.gc.ca/rpp/0607/cida-acdi/cida-acdi03_>. (23 Nov. 2007)

United Nations Development Program (UNDP). 1994. *Human Development Report 1994: New Dimensions of Human Security.* New York: Oxford University Press.

———. 2006. *Human Development Report 2005: International Cooperation at the Crossroads: Aid, Trade and Security in an Unequal World.* New York: UNDP.

White House. 2002. 'Remarks by the President and Prime Minister Chrétien on U.S.–Canada Smart Borders', 9 Sept. At: <www.whitehouse.gov/news/releases/2002/09/print/20020909-4. html>. (26 Feb. 2008)

Winnipeg Free Press. 2007. 'Harper Announces $200 Million More for Afghan Aid', 26 Feb.

Additional Readings

Brysk, Alison. 2009. *Global Good Samaritans: Human Rights as Foreign Policy.* Oxford and New York: Oxford University Press.

Bzostek, Rachel. 2008. *Why Not Preempt? Security, Law, Norms and Anticipatory Military Activities.* Aldershot, UK: Ashgate.

Keenleyside, T.A. 1988. 'Development Assistance', in R.O. Matthews and C. Pratt, eds, *Human Rights in Canadian Foreign Policy.* Montreal and Kingston: McGill-Queen's University Press, 187–208.

Organization for Economic Co-operation and Development. 2007. *OECD DAC Handbook on Security System Reform: Supporting Security and Justice.* Paris: OECD. At: <www.oecd.org/ dataoecd/43/25/38406485.pdf>.

Penz, Peter. 2001. 'The Ethics of Development Assistance and Human Security: From Realism and Sovereigntism to Cosmopolitism', in R. Irwin, ed., *Ethics and Security in Canadian Foreign Policy.* Vancouver: University of British Columbia Press, 38–55.

Rutherford, Kenneth R., Stefan Brem, and Richard A. Matthew. 2003. *Reframing the Agenda. The Impact of NGO and Middle Power Cooperation in International Security Policy*. Westport, Conn., and London: Praeger.

Chapter 6

The Diplomacy of a Middle Power: Innovation and Its Limits

Jozef Bátora

Introduction

In recent decades, Canada has sought to maintain its middle-power aspirations through innovative diplomatic practices aimed at effective wielding of soft power. Conceptual issues and policy implications related to these foreign policy aspirations are dealt with in other parts of this volume. This chapter explores the somewhat more mundane aspects of Canada's middlepowerhood, namely the changing organizational and procedural foundations of Canadian diplomacy. I focus on two key elements in this respect—public diplomacy and reforms of the Canadian diplomatic apparatus supported by information technology. The former includes a focus on promoting Canada as an attractive country and co-operation with NGOs in foreign policy delivery, as well as new kinds of outreach activities where the Canadian public is being actively drawn into the foreign policy-making through consultation processes. The latter element includes innovative uses of information technology (IT) in support of diplomatic efforts, where the Canadian government has been in the vanguard among governments worldwide. Here, the focus is both on internal reforms at DFAIT and on broader use of the Internet in public consultations of foreign policy. Overall, Canada has pioneered a number of innovative diplomatic practices that have been instrumental in the occasional ability of this country to punch above its weight in foreign relations.

In the first section, the chapter discusses the institutional context of Canadian diplomacy with a focus on organizational characteristics of the Department of Foreign Affairs and International Trade (DFAIT) and traces the features that provide the organization with a comparatively high propensity to innovation. I then discuss DFAIT's activities in the field of public diplomacy and examples of innovative uses of IT in support of diplomatic operations. The third part provides a brief comparative perspective by looking at the dynamics of diplomatic innovations in Norway and the European Union (EU). The conclusion assesses the potential and limits of Canada's recent innovations in diplomatic practice.

The Institutional Context of Canadian Diplomacy[1]

For the greater part of its modern history, Canada had the status of a Dominion of the British Empire. It was formally granted independence by the Statute of Westminster passed by the British Parliament in 1931. Yet, the British Parliament retained the right to amend the Canadian Constitution until 1982, when the Constitution was repatriated from Britain and a new Constitution Act also was adopted. Despite this gradual emergence as an independent nation, Canada still formally remains a constitutional monarchy with the British monarch (today, Queen Elizabeth II) as its head of state. As a consequence of this complex history, the Canadian foreign ministry, as Burchill (1993: 59) proposed, has been 'less confident of itself than has likely been the case elsewhere, because it came into being and continues to operate in a constitutional lacuna'. Therefore, when Sir Wilfrid Laurier and his cabinet founded the Canadian foreign ministry on 1 June 1909, it was called the Department of External Affairs and not *foreign* affairs in order not to distort the principle of diplomatic unity within the British Empire (Eayrs, 1982: 96). Reflecting this situation, the purpose of establishing the department was, according to its first head, Sir Joseph Pope, merely to acquire 'a more systematic mode of dealing with what I may term, for want of a better phrase, the *external affairs* of the Dominion',[2] while the actual conduct of Canada's foreign affairs should remain in the hands of the British imperial administration.[3] From these humble beginnings developed what the former British ambassador, Sir William Hayter, referred to as 'one of the highest-powered foreign services in the modern world' (ibid., 97).

The aim here is not to provide a complete institutional history of the Department of Foreign Affairs and International Trade—such a comprehensive overview is available from DFAIT (2008) in connection with its 2009 centennial anniversary. The purpose, rather, is to review some of the key organizational characteristics of DFAIT that support its propensity towards innovative ways of conducting foreign affairs.

Organizational Structure

As in most other countries, the recent decades were characterized by increasing involvement of various parts of the Canadian government in the administration of foreign affairs.[4] This situation is reflected in numerous reorganizations that the federal foreign affairs administration has gone through in recent decades.

First steps towards the current organizational structure of DFAIT were taken in 1980, when, by a decision of Prime Minister Pierre Elliott Trudeau, the foreign service officers of the federal Department of Trade and Commerce and the federal Department of Employment and Immigration were merged with the Department of External Affairs.[5] The result of this consolidation was a 'new' Department of External Affairs established on 12 January 1982, which, according to the then Under-Secretary of State for External Affairs Gordon Osbaldeston, had 'a role in government which is essentially different from that of the old Department of External Affairs' (Nossal, 1993: 37). The difference was related mainly to the fact that the new department was to fulfill the function of trade promotion and also essentially become the main service provider to other governmental agencies active abroad. This brought about a new organizational culture, which, in simplified terms, was more business-like and less 'diplomatic'.[6] The department was then renamed 'External Affairs and International Trade' on 28 June 1989. The current name—'Department of Foreign Affairs and International Trade'—was introduced in 1995. In late 2003, by a decision of Prime Minister Paul Martin, DFAIT was formally split into two parts—Foreign Affairs Canada and International Trade Canada. This decision, which directly countered about two decades of sometimes challenging processes related to efforts of organizationally merging the two departments, had met with resistance within both parts of the organization. The departments continued to formally operate independent of one another for three years but remained located in the same building, and given the interconnectedness of the external agenda it eventually turned out that retaining a single amalgamated departmental structure is more effective.

At the time of writing, there were two ministers responsible for DFAIT: the Minister of Foreign Affairs and the Minister of International Trade. Through the two ministers the department reports to Parliament. In addition to the ministers, the DFAIT portfolio is also managed by Secretaries of State charged with geographical responsibilities. The development aid portfolio is managed by the Minister of International Cooperation responsible for the Canadian International Development Agency (CIDA), both placed outside the department in terms of political responsibility. Several organizations outside the department's portfolio have accountability relationships with one of the two ministers.

In 2008, the department operated through a network of 168 diplomatic missions in 109 countries (including embassies, high commissions, consulates, satellite offices, and nine missions to multilateral organizations), and was supported by 108 honorary consuls in 97 countries (accredited to 192 countries). In the departmental self-assessment published in 2002, the missions abroad were seen as providing the possibility of one-stop shopping for federal services and functions in other countries and thereby demonstrating the department's ability to manage issues horizontally and to co-ordinate a broad range of activities as indicated in the business lines (DFAIT, 2002–3: Section IV). In addition to the headquarters in Ottawa, the department was serving the citizens through 29 passport offices throughout the country and through a network of regional trade commissioners' offices. Overall, DFAIT employed about 9,700 staff members in 2008, of which about 20 per cent were rotational foreign service officers and about 50 per cent were locally engaged staff at missions abroad.

Organizational Culture

The organizational culture and working ethos of the departmental workforce have been characterized by informality and flexibility. Such attributes might be seen as being mostly the property of the trade officials, and the flexible business-like culture of the department certainly did owe a great deal to their presence within the organization. Yet, flexibility and teamwork also have characterized the foreign affairs officials since the early days of the department, albeit for different reasons than in the case of the trade officials. As Skilling (1945: 274) notes, referring to the Department of External Affairs in the 1940s:

> the work of the various divisions naturally overlapped considerably, and members of one division had frequently to be in contact with members of another, and with the Under-Secretary. In view of these facts and the smallness of the Department, the distribution of work was flexible and was not rigidly determined by the organization. ... The main burden of responsibility concentrated on the Under-Secretary himself, in informal consultation with several of the other top officials of the Department, without the need for a more formal committee on policy.

The fact that the departmental leadership encouraged such a culture of flexibility and consultation was crucial for further institutionalization of these features.[7] Maintenance of such an organizational culture also was enabled by the fact that 'the Department, questioning the worth of new management techniques and organization theory, tended to resist administrative innovation' (Eayrs, 1982: 98).[8] Somewhat paradoxically, this conservative approach to organizational change enabled the department to keep the culture of flexible mandates and consultation in times of a general rationalization and increased bureaucratization of Canadian governmental agencies. In general, the department had been relying on what Cooper (1999: 43) has termed *diplomatic improvisation*, 'geared to operational agility rather than to working within definitive guidelines [enabling the department] to deal flexibly with external situations'. As early as 1953, the economist B.S. Keirstead referred to these practices at the department as 'an exercise in pragmatic *ad hocery*' (Stairs, 2001: 17).

The consultative and flexible organizational culture that developed in early decades of the department's operation remains a strong characteristic feature of its workforce until today. This is reflected in the number of projects, special task forces, virtual teams, and task-related temporary divisions continuously formed and regrouped at the department and throughout the foreign service. These tendencies are strengthened by the pervasiveness of a client-oriented service ethos throughout the Canadian public administration in recent decades. Business-like methods inspired by the New Public Management are increasingly applied throughout the Canadian government, including DFAIT.

In 2006, in an internal review of the departmental mandate, the roles of DFAIT were identified as:

- an *interpreter* of international events and trends for the government and for Canadians, recognizing the growing importance of globalization on Canadian's life;
- an *articulator* of a distinctive Canadian foreign policy that expresses Canadians' view of the world in which they wish to live;
- an *integrator* of the government's international agenda and its representation abroad;
- an *advocate* of Canada's values and interests abroad;
- a *provider* of world-class consular and passport services to Canadians;
- a responsible *steward* of public funds charged with delivering common services abroad on behalf of all government departments (Blackwell, 2007: 49–50).[9]

Relations with the Domestic Environment

The domestic environment in which the department has been operating is characterized by a federal political structure, a bilingual society, and a lack of any clearly defined domestic support constituency for foreign affairs. The organizational changes the department has gone through since the 1980s have largely been attempts to respond to the challenges posed by the domestic environment. As Cooper (1999) suggests, the move towards adding trade officials who brought in managerial techniques and a business-like culture also could be read as an attempt by the department to gain legitimacy and support in the domestic business community and indeed throughout a society generally skeptical of empowering federal institutions. Similarly, ongoing attempts were made in recent decades to increase the percentage of francophone officials and to develop frameworks of co-operation with provincial governments (ibid.; Michaud, 2001).

A further challenge for the department is the system of foreign policy decision-making at the federal level, where the Prime Minister and the

Privy Council Office retain the lead in the overall political co-ordination of Canada's international policy. This creates a situation where the department continuously must jockey for its position as the co-ordinator of foreign affairs and tries to avoid being merely a service agency for the delivery of governmental policies abroad.[10] Furthermore, the growing internationalization of agenda administered by other governmental agencies has led to a situation where DFAIT also has had to fight to retain particular pieces of the international policy portfolio. As Copeland (2005) holds:

> Encroachment by other government departments into areas previously believed to be the exclusive preserve of the foreign ministry has been going on for years, but there has been no compensatory effort to insert the foreign ministry into domestic debates, to underline its relevance to the security and prosperity of Canadians; there has been no concentrated, sustained or strategic effort to develop a domestic constituency. The days of the foreign ministry cruising on its vestigial prestige and mystique, with its face to the world but its back to Ottawa, have long since passed.

To address this situation, comprehensive IT-supported efforts were initiated to engage the Canadian public in debates and national forums on foreign policy priorities and thereby to nurture some form of a broad-based political constituency in the domestic environment (see next section for more details). Moreover, since the early 1980s, the department has been encouraging its officers to take on secondments in other governmental departments so as to deepen their expertise in their respective fields of specialization; at the same time, experts from other governmental agencies would have been admitted on assignments within the department (Eayrs, 1982: 101; Balloch and Angell, 1992; Cooper, 1999, 2004). DFAIT's integration and co-operation with other governmental agencies have been facilitated by the fact that the department has been one of the pioneering agencies in the Canadian government in introducing IT in support of its organization and operations, not least as part of the Government On-Line Initiative. This was related to a more general pattern of innovation in foreign affairs administration in Canada focused on involvement of societal actors, which, as Cooper (2004: 253) suggests, could be a considered 'a model of how foreign policy should be restructured to facilitate competence and credibility and even how the "foreign" in international activity should be redefined'. A number of new practices emanated from these attempts at greater societal engagement.

New Practices for Wielding Soft Power: Public Diplomacy and Information Technology

The organizational structure and culture of the Canadian foreign affairs establishment and the societal context within which Canadian foreign policy has been conducted have fostered a number of innovative practices in the conduct of diplomacy. These have been providing the Canadian government with tools for an effective development and wielding of soft power. Canadian innovations have centred on two interwoven areas: public diplomacy, including involvement of societal actors in the formation and delivery of foreign policy; and advancements in uses of information technology in support of diplomatic operations. The rest of this section discusses these.

Canada's Public Diplomacy

The public diplomacy initiatives of the Canadian government have been developing in two dimensions. The first dimension involves efforts to foster involvement of Canadian societal actors in the formulation and conduct of foreign policy. The second dimension includes efforts to improve the image of Canada internationally, not least through involving societal actors.

Regarding the first dimension, this has taken on several forms. On the one hand, recent decades have seen a number of cases in which DFAIT and other government agencies have developed symbiotic relationships to promote particular policies. The best-known case of such co-operation is the so-called Ottawa Process, which led to the passing of the Convention to ban landmines in 1997. As this case is sufficiently covered in academic analyses (see, e.g., Cameron et al., 1998; Price, 1998; Thakur and Maley, 1999; Sending and Neumann, 2006; Hynek, 2008) and in other chapters of this volume, it will suffice to note here that through co-operation with the International Campaign to Ban Landmines, DFAIT was able to generate global awareness of the landmines issue on a level that would not have been possible through official governmental channels alone and/or if this had been seen as a governmental campaign aimed at raising public awareness of a particular agenda. In general, the shift from statecraft to 'society-craft' (Cooper, 2004: 40–4) has become a key element in the soft-power toolbox of the Canadian government in recent years.[11] Besides co-operation with issue-oriented policy advocacy NGO networks, this also includes development of relations with research think-tanks (Venugopal, 2001).

As the experience of the landmines campaign suggests, success in creating and managing successful symbiotic relationships between DFAIT and other governmental departments, on the one side, and societal actors involved in foreign policy, on the other, depends on shared values and priorities. In the 1990s, in the context of the information revolution and a repositioning of Canada in the aftermath of the Cold War, the role of 'Canadian values' has been increasingly stressed. As the 1995 *Canada in the World* report stated:

Canadians hold deeply that we must pursue our values internationally. They want to promote them for their own sake, but they also understand that our values and rights will not be safeguarded if they are not enshrined throughout the international environment. Canada is not an island: if the rights of people abroad are not protected, Canadians will ultimately feel the effects at home. They understand that our economic and security interests are served by the widest possible respect for the environment, human rights, participatory government, free markets and the rule of law. Where these are observed, there is a greater prospect of stability and prosperity—where they are not, of uncertainty and poverty. Their observance, therefore, is both an end in itself and a means to achieving other priority objectives. (DFAIT, 1995: ch. 5)

While the government sees values as central to Canadian foreign policy (see also Nossal, 1997), recent years have seen a weakening of the once fairly strong societal consensus in relation to what the Canadian values really are (IRG, 2005). In an attempt to contribute to the emergence of common value platforms with the societal actors, DFAIT has been involved in facilitating public dialogues on foreign policy. Building on a tradition launched in the 1970s by Pierre Trudeau, examples of such activities include the 1994 National Forum on Canada's International Relations and, most recently, the 2003 Dialogue on Foreign Policy.[12] In both cases, DFAIT and other federal agencies were involved in various forms of public debates on foreign policy priorities, including town hall meetings featuring the foreign minister, expert round tables, media debates, and web forums. The most recent strategic foreign policy documents, including *Canada in the World* and *Foreign Policy Dialogue: Report to Canadians*, were produced as a result of these public deliberations, and Canada has been leading the way internationally in 'responsive' foreign policy-making (Bátora, 2006a 2006b).

In relation to the second dimension of public diplomacy, the effort to improve the image of Canada abroad and thereby enhance its soft power has been a strategic priority for DFAIT. The challenge has been a stereotypical image of Canada as a country with a cold climate, rich in natural resources and wildlife, and short of the elements many Canadians would like others to associate their country with, such as multiculturalism, hi-tech industries, tolerance, and competitiveness (Potter, 2001). DFAIT has actively taken on the role as the lead co-ordinator of devising a strategy of external communication that would promote a more update vision of Canada. This was included in the activities related to the 'Canada–Cool–Connected' initiative launched in 2003, which involved identification of six characteristics of Canada— captivating, civil, competitive, creative, caring, and cosmopolitan. Each of the characteristics was then elaborated on with images and text modules distributed to Canadian missions abroad to bring about more consistency in the way Canada is presented around the world. A dedicated intra-net site has also been introduced in support of the activities, where governmental actors could access information and electronic image resources available for their respective promotional activities. This initiative met some severe challenges, though. A number of federal departments would not buy into the strategy as their promotion strategies often followed sector-specific priorities. The same applied to the provinces, where a number of them (most notably Quebec) chose to follow their own public diplomacy strategies. Finally, the overall mantra of this DFAIT public diplomacy initiative had to be adjusted in particular cultural contexts because in some countries the message would not be understood properly.[13] Most recently, the Inukshuk has been used as a symbol of Canada, not least in the campaign promoting the 2010 Olympic Winter Games in Vancouver. It has been associated with the role of the Inukshuk in aiding travellers in the wilderness of the Far North, which, as Keating points out in Chapter 1 of this volume, is meant to allude to the same role of Canada in guiding others through the uncertainties of the globalized world environment. In some sense, Axworthy (2003) makes the same point in envisioning the role for Canada as helping other nations to navigate the new global reality. This is in line with a notion associated with middlepowerhood, namely, the idea of Canada as a mentor state (see Fossum, 2006). Hence, while the doctrine of middlepowerhood may be in crisis in Canada today, uses of such imagery to refer to some of the essential role expectations pertaining to middle powers in descriptions of Canada's role indicate that the country continues to entertain aspirations as a middle power.

An important aspect in the processes of improving Canada's attractiveness abroad has been DFAIT's work in the domestic environment, in particular in relation to the public in the provinces. The program 'la diplomatie ouverte' (open diplomacy) managed by the Federal-Provincial Bureau at DFAIT in the early 2000s has been particularly focused on the youth in Quebec, where the goal has been to engage young Quebecers in debates of the international achievements of Canada and thereby raise their awareness and possibly their identification and sense of pride as Canadians. Indeed, as Nossal argues in Chapter 2 of this volume, the focus Axworthy had been placing on the promotion of Canada as a middle power was primarily aimed at a domestic audience. In this sense, the domestic outreach programs of DFAIT have also been playing an important role as nation-building mechanisms.

Information Technology in Support of Diplomatic Operations

The Canadian government and DFAIT in particular have been among the leaders in using advanced information technologies in support of diplomatic operations (Potter, 2002; Bátora, 2008). DFAIT was one of the first foreign ministries to establish a website (in July 1995), pioneered uses of virtual embassies and virtual teams, early on created on-line systems in support of trade promotion, and, not least, established a regular practice of web-based e-Discussions with the public focusing on topical issues on the foreign affairs agenda.

DFAIT's operations have been supported by state-of-the-art global electronic networks enabling classified and unclassified communication. By connecting to the system, Canadian diplomats have had access to a broad array of informational resources available to DFAIT, such as intra-net and databases dedicated to specific issues. Effective and entrepreneurial uses of information technology have also been supported by senior Canadian officials, including foreign ministers and their deputies, who have pioneered novel forms of IT-supported diplomatic work such as gathering policy information by accessing websites of terrorist organizations in a time when most foreign ministries in the Western world still did not have a website of their own (Smith, 1997; Smith and Sutherland, 2002). Obviously, in an information-intensive international environment, having an efficient IT infrastructure and being able to use it in non-orthodox ways provides a government with comparative advantages and an informational edge. As Cooper (1998) has demonstrated, this is essential for effective protection of soft-power resources, including credibility and favourable public perceptions abroad. It is also essential for effective conduct of humanitarian operations and generating public support for these operations at home and abroad (Smith, 1997; Smith and Sutherland, 2002).

The IT infrastructure of DFAIT enabled it to operate as a single global on-line organization. With the help of advanced software, such as the InfoBank system that was added throughout the organization in 2003 and 2004, different units can co-operate on tasks irrespective of geographic location and time zones. In some cases, this has led to a shift in the roles between headquarters in Ottawa and missions abroad. Here, the traditional division of labour in foreign ministry operations—where headquarters develops strategic policy guidelines and missions abroad implement them—was in some cases reversed. This concerned, for instance, the relations between the Japan Division in headquarters, with up to 15 employees, and the Canadian embassy in Tokyo, with 150 employees. Integration of electronic archives of embassies with divisions in the Ottawa headquarters also improves effectiveness by eliminating the waiting time due to time-zone differences, when officers on either side often would have had to wait for a whole working day to receive particular documents requested from their colleagues by e-mail. In this way, work on policy issues practically never stops and international developments can be followed up by virtual teams of officers in different geographic locations, often working away from office connected through mobile devices. Obviously, in the current information-intensive environment, such virtually integrated collaborative work of diplomatic officials is an essential precondition for any attempts of a country like Canada to wield effective influence.[14]

In addition to the high levels of interconnectedness within the Canadian foreign service, DFAIT has been innovative in using its website to reach out to the Canadian public. A flagship practice here is the so-called foreign policy e-Discussions. This involves a dedicated website on the main DFAIT site, where particular topics on the foreign affairs agenda are published with the aim of generating public interest and drawing the public into discussions. The website features topics such as 'Failed and Fragile States', 'Renewing Multilateral Institutions', and 'Showcasing Canadian Talent and Know-how Abroad', and includes topic-relevant resources from DFAIT, expert opinions and lectures in the form of videos or pod-casts, and a set of questions/issues raised for debate with the public. As I discussed in more detail elsewhere (Bátora, 2006b), the most innovative aspect of this exercise relates to DFAIT's work with the public inputs. Policy planning staff creates a synopsis of the public debate, including the most relevant points and suggestions. This is then circulated to the relevant policy-makers within the department, who can provide their opinions. Following up on such an internal review process, an official departmental response to a given discussion topic is drafted and posted on the website. Although the levels of public involvement in the e-Discussions have not been particularly high, the department has still seen the exercise as a useful tool for getting additional legitimacy for some of its policies and actions. For a middle power aspiring to play a role as a mentor state guiding others through the 'uncertain waters' of the current global environment, foreign policy-making needs to be based on higher degrees of legitimacy than has traditionally been the case (Fossum, 2006).

To set the Canadian developments into perspective, the next section takes a brief look at the diplomatic innovations of two international actors that may be used as comparative cases—Norway and the EU.

Diplomatic Innovation in Other Contexts: Norway and the EU

In a number of contributions to the international relations and political science literature, Norway and the EU have been used as comparative cases in relation to Canada. In the case of Norway, this is primarily in relation to the similarities in foreign policy agenda, priorities, and even conduct. Indeed, the landmark Ottawa Process was initiated at a meeting on the small island of Lysøen on the west coast of Norway and the meetings and negotiations prior to the final rounds in Ottawa were held in Oslo (Axworthy, 1998; Neumann, 2002). The EU has been compared to Canada in relation to its formation as a political entity comprised of individual political units (Fossum, 2004), as well as in relation to its external affairs priorities on human security and civilian power.

Norway

Like the Canadian government, the Norwegian government and, notably, its foreign ministry have had a long tradition of co-operation with the NGO sector in the delivery of its foreign policies. Some authors had even argued that this symbiosis represents 'a Norwegian model' of NGO-supported foreign policy conduct (Egeland, 1988; Tvedt, 1997; Bucher-Johannessen, 1999). In Neumann's (1999) somewhat critical assessment of this phenomenon, the Norwegian state maintains its power position in relation to the NGO sector though 'disaggregating' itself into the very processes of priority formation in the NGOs and, in some cases, there is hence a shift from NGO stimulation towards 'NGO simulation'. This has been facilitated by a broad consensus in the Norwegian society regarding basic values to be accentuated in foreign policy, such as promotion of peace, welfare state ideals, and environmental protection (Østerud, 1986; Dobinson and Dale, 2000). At the same time, though, the relations of the Norwegian foreign ministry with Norwegian society in general have been characterized as rather distant due to popular skepticism towards the perceived elitism of diplomats (Neumann, 1998).

In the development of public diplomacy, the Norwegian foreign ministry could rely on the high levels of societal consensus on core foreign policy values. This fact, in combination with the relatively distanced relations between the foreign ministry and the Norwegian public, has led to a somewhat paradoxical situation in which the foreign ministry does not seek much public consultation when developing its public diplomacy strategy. Instead, it hired the London-based Foreign Policy Centre to conduct a series of workshops in Norway and analyses outside Norway with the aim of identifying how Norway is viewed and how selected Norwegian societal actors would prefer to present their country abroad. The result of this exercise was a set of characteristics, including 'peace', 'equality', 'nature', and 'spirit of adventure', that were to become the guiding messages to be used by various actors in their presentation activities abroad (see Leonard and Small, 2003). Compared to the open and inclusive processes applied by DFAIT in the development of Canadian public diplomacy, the Norwegian foreign ministry has developed its public diplomacy strategy in a corporatist and centralized manner, but has managed to build it around value platforms that attract both the Norwegians at home and most public audiences abroad. As noted above, this may not be the case with the image and value platforms used for public diplomacy purposes by DFAIT (see Bátora, 2006a).

In terms of uses of information technology, the Norwegian foreign ministry has been among the laggards, introducing e-mail officially as late as 2000. While the situation has improved considerably in recent years, including the introduction of global virtual teams, the Norwegian foreign ministry has been a gradual and slow reformer. However, the organization used considerable resources for studying innovative practices and challenges associated with them in a number of other foreign ministries, including DFAIT. In this way, the Norwegian foreign ministry has been able to avoid some of the problems with information technology uses that fast reformers had to cope with in Canada and elsewhere (Bátora, 2008).

European Union

The EU has been compared to Canada in terms of it propensity towards acting like a civilian power and promoting human security. A number of EU member states are members of the so-called Human Security Network (Austria, Greece, Ireland, the Netherlands, and Slovenia) and the acting European Commissioner for External Relations, Benita Ferrero Waldner, was highly active in setting up the network in her previous role as Austrian foreign minister. A human security doctrine for the EU was elaborated by a high-level expert group and the suggestions were presented to the EU's High Representative for Common Foreign and Security Policy (CFSP), Javier Solana, in 2004 (Kaldor, 2004; Glasius and Kaldor, 2006). The human security doctrine also plays a key role in the 2003 European Security Strategy.

While this transformational foreign policy agenda is shared between the EU and Canada, a critical difference is that the EU also features a set of characteristics in its diplomatic apparatus that take it a step further in qualifying it as a transformational international actor. What is of interest here is the formation of what may be termed *EU-level foreign affairs administration* emerging in parallel to the continuously relevant and effective foreign affairs administrations of EU member states. This EU-level administration is based on a dual intergovernmental/supranational foundation of EU-level institutions involved in the conduct of the Union's external affairs: (a) the High Representative for CFSP, Solana, the Policy Unit supporting his work, the Political and Security Committee in the Council of the EU, and the EU Special Representatives in crisis regions; and (b) the external relations directorates general in the European Commission along with the External Service staffing the delegations in about 130 locations around the world. The putative European External Action Service and the planned post of the 'EU-foreign minister'[15] are expected to build institutional bridges across the organizational duality of the EU-level foreign affairs administration in its current form and further enhance its capabilities.

A central issue is what direction the development of the EU-level foreign affairs administration will take in its further development. In search of legitimacy as a member of the global diplomatic order, the EU-level foreign affairs administration may copy structures, practices, and routines established in the 'Westphalian' diplomatic order, which is maintained through peer pressure of foreign ministries that in their aggregate constitute the global organizational field of diplomacy. The processes through which, for instance, the EC external service has been increasingly seeking to gain recognition on par with state diplomatic services (Bruter, 1999; Dimier and McGeever, 2006) and to introduce diplomatic training with the aim of developing a 'standard culture of a diplomatic service' (Duke, 2002) would suggest that this is indeed the objective. Were that to continue and become the dominant pattern in the development of the EU-level foreign affairs administration, the EU would be on the way to becoming just another state actor and its diplomatic structures and practices would increasingly start to resemble those of federal states such as Canada featuring a federal diplomatic service and para-diplomatic structures and activities of provincial (member state) governments. A state-system-conformist development by the EU-level foreign affairs administration would hence bring Canada and the EU closer together in systemic terms in regard to the organization of their diplomatic apparatuses.

However, it is far from certain that such a development will become the dominant pattern in the development of the EU-level foreign affairs administration. Instead, we may continue seeing the burgeoning of structures and processes at the EU level, which will continue to function in a complementary fashion with the national foreign affairs administrations of member states and execute functions in niche areas pertaining to EU-level policies (see Hocking and Bátora, 2009). Thus, functions such as public diplomacy in the EU would continue to have a profoundly fragmented character, with much remaining on the level of member state governments and being complemented by EU activities focused on generating and maintaining attractiveness of the EU as a political project. Structures at the EU-level, however, might prompt the formation of similar regional structures elsewhere. This 'structural pull-factor' of the EU (Reiterer, 2006) would make the EU a system-transformative actor bringing about innovation and change not only *in* the global diplomatic order but *of* the global diplomatic order (Bátora, 2005). This potential, if realized, seems to be the principal difference between Canada, which remains a state and acts like one (and in innovative ways as a cosmopolitan vanguard), and the EU, which is a post-Westphalian entity learning to act like one.

Conclusion

The chapter focused on the organizational foundations of Canadian diplomacy and on its innovative potential in the context of foreign affairs establishments. The organizational features of DFAIT make it a foreign ministry prone to flexibility and open to learning new practices. At the same time, the highly complex co-ordination games that DFAIT has had to engage in for decades in relation to other governmental agencies and the governments of the provinces, notably Quebec, also provided the organization with experience in and readiness for highly complex domestic co-ordination of foreign policy, which most other foreign ministries are only just beginning to learn.

For effective conduct of middle-power foreign policy, the diplomatic apparatus needs to work with innovative diplomatic practices that the foreign affairs establishments of great powers do not need to follow and the foreign services of smaller countries are incapable of. The Canadian foreign affairs establishment has pioneered a number of such practices in the realm of public diplomacy and with respect to uses of IT in support of diplomatic operations. The central lesson that arises is the transformative potential of this set of practices in relation to diplomacy.

The transformative dynamics in DFAIT, however, is limited by the institutional context of interstate diplomacy featuring norms, rules, and routines embedded in the global organizational field of foreign ministries. Peer pressure mechanisms within the field foster isomorphic tendencies of adaptation, which make it difficult to maintain radically new practices. This relates, for instance, to standards of electronic information security, which DFAIT would be prepared to loosen as most of the classical middle-power agenda is semi-public in character anyway and involves multiple societal actors. Consequently, DFAIT would be best served by standards allowing for flexible electronic communication solutions that would enable efficiency gains from the IT investments. Yet, as previous research has shown, expectations of information protection by other foreign ministries create pressure on DFAIT, which does not allow for a too-abrupt departure from information security standards maintained within the organizational field (Bátora, 2008). The same applies to a number of other new practices in organizing diplomacy. One of the things DFAIT has had to do besides working out new practices has been to promote the usefulness and effectiveness of such new practices among partner governments. This is done, for instance, in delivering presentations at international conferences involving practitioners from other countries (see, e.g., Blackwell, 2007), receiving visits by foreign practitioners interested in learning about Canadian practices, and by sending DFAIT officials on multi-purpose promotion tours to foreign countries. An example of the latter was a visit by DFAIT staff involved in the organization of foreign policy e-Discussions in Afghanistan, the Middle East, and a number of European states in early 2006. The purpose was to gather video (and other) material for an upcoming e-Discussion on failed and fragile states, to inform staff at Canadian missions in the countries visited about e-Discussions, and also to introduce e-Discussions to foreign ministries of the visited countries and promote this innovative practice of public engagement. The latter point demonstrates the need to promote innovations in diplomatic practice and thereby create a more innovation-receptive environment within the organizational field constituted of foreign ministries.

A more general point that follows from this is that maintaining middle-powerhood involves legitimization not only of this identity in domestic political discourses and/or in relation to foreign public audiences, but also of organizational innovations in the conduct of diplomacy in relation to partner foreign ministries. Hence, a focus on organizational and administrative practices supporting the conduct of Canada's foreign policy should continue to provide us with insights about the changing nature of Canada's role in world politics.

Finally, as the cases of Norway and the EU show, the real test of Canada's innovative potential in the organization and conduct of its diplomacy is the issue of conformism with the standards of the global organizational field of diplomacy and/or the ability to break with it. As long as Canadian middle-power diplomacy works for the promotion of Canada as a state (whether as a cosmopolitan vanguard state or as a postmodern mentor state), its diplomatic innovations will not step out of the shadow of state sovereignty. The question is how to take such a step without a radical unsettling of the global diplomatic order. It is here that we might find the new vocation of middle-power diplomacy, which thereby would acquire an additional meaning as the diplomacy of a power that works in the middle between the state-system-conserving innovators of the world order such as Norway and state-system-transforming innovators of the world order such as the EU. Given its character as a contested state, Canada has the potential to play the role of such a systemic middle power.

Notes

I would like to thank the editors and the three anonymous referees for useful comments and suggestions on an earlier draft of this chapter.

1.   This part builds upon Bátora (2008: ch. 5).
2.   'Memorandum for Consideration of the Civil Service Commissioners, 25 May 1907', Civil Service Commission 1908: minutes of evidence, I, p. 48, *Sessional Papers of Canada*, 42, 15 (1907–8), quoted in Eayrs (1960: 15; italics in the original).
3.   This view derived not merely from Canadian hesitation or reluctance to undermine British supremacy, but reflected also an actual lack of personnel able to conduct foreign affairs. As Earl Grey, the British Governor General in Canada, complained in a letter to the Colonial Office in London in 1908: 'Bryce's [the then British ambassador to Washington who was also in charge of Canada's relations to the US] difficulties in conducting the negotiations [with the US government] have, I am sorry to say, been increased by the chaotic condition of the Administration here *qua* External Affairs. There is no Department, no official through whose hands all matters dealing with external affairs must go. Consequently there is no record, no continuity, no method, no consistency. . . . We have only three men in the [Canadian] Government Service, who have any knowledge of details connected with Canada's foreign relations. One drinks at times, the other has difficulty in expressing his thoughts, and conversation is as difficult as it is to extract an extra tight cork, and the third is the Under-Secretary of State, Pope—a really first class official' (Eayrs, 1960: 21).

4. As Under-Secretary of External Affairs, Allan Gotlieb argued in 1979: 'The fact that there is now a constellation of people and influences drawn from many parts of government, from the Prime Minister down, all having a legitimate stake in the planning, formulation and carrying out of foreign policy, means that External can seldom plan, formulate or carry out policy on its own. Practically everything it does is part of a collective endeavour' (Eayrs, 1982: 100).

5. To 750 External Affairs officials, 300 were added from the Department of Industry, Trade and Commerce, 250 from Employment and Immigration, and 150 from CIDA. Trudeau, in general, did not hide his view of the foreign service as an outmoded and largely obsolete organization, stating that: 'I believe it all goes back to the early days of the telegraph when you needed a dispatch to know what is happening in country A, whereas most of the time now you can read it in a good newspaper' (from a TV interview, quoted in Eayrs, 1982: 108).

6. As Eayrs (1982: 106) commented on the merger: 'If Big is Beautiful, External appears the winner, its influx from its rivals' ranks confirming its role as a department of supply and services abroad—perhaps at the expense of the traditional foreign office skills of intelligence analysis, policy formulation and the conduct of negotiation.'

7. As Eayrs (1982: 97) points out, O.D. Skelton, who was the Under-Secretary of State for External Affairs in the period 1925–41, 'imparted to [the department] through his character and his ways of looking at the world an ethos that outlasted him. . . . Skelton created contours that endured for decades.' Maintenance of the organizational culture that emerged under Skelton's leadership was helped by the fact the department was led in the years 1948–57 by Skelton's close apprentice, Lester B. Pearson. Hence, despite the post-World War II growth of the department in terms of the number of organizational units and employees, the organizational culture of internal informality that developed throughout the early decades remained a strong characteristic of the department.

8. In response to a 1963 report by a Royal Commission on Government Organization suggesting changes at the department inspired by the private sector, the departmental spokesman (backed by Pearson, who then was Prime Minister) quoted Viscount Falkland: 'When it is not necessary to change, it is necessary not to change' (Eayrs, 1982: 104).

9. In 2006, Adam Blackwell was Director General of the Strategy and Services Bureau at DFAIT.

10. DFAIT provides the infrastructure and other support for other governmental departments' activities abroad. See DFAIT (2002–3: Section III).

11. However, as the experience of the World Conference against Racism, Racial Discrimination, Xenophobia and Related Intolerance held in Durban, South Africa, in August and September 2001 had shown, involvement of societal actors can involve perils in the form of adoption of normative, emotive, and one-sided statements leading to and not fighting discrimination. This created a situation in which the Canadian Foreign Minister actually declined to participate in the event and denounced the statements of some of the participants after the conference. More generally, this experience raised a number of fundamental questions regarding assumptions about the efficiency, predictability, and reliability of state–society partnerships in the conduct of foreign policy (Cooper, 2004: 223–53).

12. For the political context of these processes in the 1990s, see Hynek, Chapter 4, this volume.

13. As the author's interviews with representatives of the Communications Bureau of DFAIT in 2003 indicated, this was a problem, for instance, in China, where the population would associate the word 'cool' with the meanings of cold or ice and not with the intended meanings of 'trendy' or 'modern'.

14. A challenge experienced by a number of officers I interviewed in 2003 and 2006 was the difficulty to separate between work life and private life due to the ease of carrying along hand-held electronic communications devices providing e-mail access, etc.

15. The official title proposed in the Lisbon Treaty is High Representative for the Union's Foreign Affairs and Security Policy.

References

Axworthy, L. 1998. 'A Ban for All Seasons: The Landmines Convention and Its Implications for Canadian Diplomacy', *International Journal* 53, 2: 189–203.

———. 2003. *Navigating the New World: Canada's Global Future.* New York: Knopf.

Balloch, H., and D. Angell. 1992. 'Foreign Policy Planning and Coordination in Canada: The Policy Planning Staff at External Affairs', *Canadian Public Administration* 35, 4: 449–63.

Bátora, J. 2005. 'Does the European Union Transform the Institution of Diplomacy?', *Journal of European Public Policy* 12, 1: 44–66.

———. 2006a. 'Public Diplomacy between Home and Abroad: Norway and Canada', *The Hague Journal of Diplomacy* 1, 1: 53–80.

———. 2006b. 'Emerging Tenets of Responsive Foreign Policymaking?', *International Journal* 61: 929–42.

———. 2008. *Foreign Ministries and the Information Revolution: Going Virtual?* Leiden and Boston: Martinus Nijhoff.

Blackwell, A. 2007. 'Result Based Diplomacy', in K. Rana and J. Kurbalija, eds, *Foreign Ministries: Managing Diplomatic Networks and Optimizing Value.* Geneva: Diplo Books, 45–52.

Bruter, M. 1999. 'Diplomacy without a State: The External Delegations of the European Commission', *Journal of European Public Policy* 6, 2: 183–205.

Bucher-Johannessen, B. 1999. 'Den norske modellen: Stat og samfunn hånd i hånd til fremme av Norge' [The Norwegian Model: State and Society Promoting Norway Hand in Hand], *Internasjonal Politikk* 57, 2: 199–220.

Burchill, R. 1993. 'Recent Structural Change in the Department', in Donald C. Story, ed., *The Canadian Foreign Service in Transition.* Toronto: Canadian Scholars' Press, 58–64.

Cameron, A., R. Lawson, and B. Tomlin, eds. 1998. *To Walk Without Fear: The Global Movement to Ban Landmines.* Toronto: Oxford University Press.

Cooper, A.F. 1998. *Snapshots of Cyberdiplomacy.* Leicester: DSP Paper.

———. 1999. 'Canada Trying to Get It Right: The Foreign Ministry and Organizational Change', in B. Hocking, ed., *Foreign Ministries: Change and Adaptation.* London: Macmillan Press, 42–51.

———. 2004. *Tests of Global Governance: Canadian Diplomacy and United Nations World Conferences.* New York: United Nations University Press.

Copeland, D. 2005. 'New Rabbits, Old Hats: International Policy and Canada's Foreign Service in an Era of Reduced Diplomatic Resources', manuscript, published in *International Journal* 60, 3: 743–64.

Department of Foreign Affairs and International Trade (DFAIT). 1995. *Canada in the World.* Ottawa: Government of Canada. At: <www.international.gc.ca/foreign_policy/cnd-world/chap5-en.asp>.

———. 2002–3. *Report on Plans and Priorities 2002–2003.* Ottawa: DFAIT. At: <www.dfait-maeci.gc.ca/department/rpp_2002_2003/section_04-en.asp>.

———. 2008. *'Punching above Our Weight': A History of the Department of Foreign Affairs and International Trade.* Ottawa: DFAIT. At: <www.international.gc.ca>.

Dimier, V., and M. McGeever. 2006. 'Diplomats without a Flag: The Institutionalization of the Delegations of the Commission in African, Caribbean and Pacific Countries', *Journal of Common Market Studies* 44, 3: 483–505.

Dobinson, K., and G. Dale. 2000. 'Den norske ryggsekk. En analyse av "norsk" fredsdiplomati' [The Norwegian Backpack. An Analysis of 'Norwegian' Peace-diplomacy], in G. Dale, ed., *Grenser for alt. Kritiske perspektiver på norsk utenrikspolitikk* [Borders of Everything. Critical Perspectives on Norwegian Foreign Policy]. Oslo: Spartacus, 45–69.

Duke, S. 2002. 'Preparing for European Diplomacy?', *Journal of Common Market Studies* 40, 5: 849–70.

Eayrs, J. 1960. 'The Origins of Canada's Department of External Affairs', in Hugh Keenleyside et al., eds, *The Growth of Canadian Policies in External Affairs.* Durham, NC: Duke University Press, 14–33.

————. 1982. 'Canada: The Department of External Affairs', in Zara Steiner, ed., *The Times Survey of Foreign Ministries of the World*. London: Times Books, 95–117.

Egeland, J. 1988. *Impotent Superpower—Potent Small State*. Oslo: Norwegian University Press.

Fossum, J.E. 2004. 'Why Compare Canada and the European Union—And How?', in P. Crowley, ed., *Crossing the Atlantic: Comparing the European Union and Canada*. London: Ashgate, 11–33.

————. 2006. 'Gidsland—Is There a Mentor State?', special issue of *International Journal*.

Glasius, M., and M. Kaldor. 2006. *A Human Security Doctrine for Europe: Project, Principles and Practicalities*. London: Routledge.

Hocking, B., and J. Bátora. 2009. 'Introduction', in 'Diplomacy and the EU', special issue of *The Hague Journal of Diplomacy* 4, 2: 113–20.

Hynek, N. 2008. 'Conditions of Emergence and Their Effects: Political Rationalities, Governmental Programs and Technologies of Power in the Landmine Case', *Journal of International Relations and Development* 11, 2: 93–120.

Innovative Research Group (IRG). 2005. *The Canadian Values Study*, Sept. Summary of findings at: <www.innovativeresearch.ca/Canadian%20Values%20Study_Factum%20290905.pdf>.

Kaldor, M. 2004. 'A Force for Intervention: A Human Security Doctrine for Europe, and Beyond', *International Herald Tribune*, 30 Sept.

Leonard, M., and A. Small. 2003. *Norwegian Public Diplomacy*. London: Foreign Policy Centre.

Michaud, N. 2001. 'Federalism and Foreign Policy: Comparative Answers to Globalisation', paper presented to the conference 'The Administration of Foreign Affairs: A Renewed Challenge?', Hull, Que., 1–3 Nov.

Neumann, I.B. 1998. 'Departemental identitet: Det norske utenriksdepartement' [Departmental Identity: The Norwegian Foreign Ministry], *Internasjonal Politikk* 56, 1: 75–103.

————. 1999. 'Norsk sørpolitikk: den disaggregerte stats diplomati' [Norwegian South Policy: Diplomacy of a Disaggregated State], *Internasjonal Politikk* 57, 2: 181–97.

————. 2002. 'Harnessing Social Power: State Diplomacy and the Land-Mines Issue', in Andrew F. Cooper, John English, and Ramesh Thakur, eds, *Enhancing Global Governance: Towards a New Diplomacy?* Tokyo: United Nations University Press, 106–32.

Nossal, K.R. 1993. 'Contending Explanations for the Amalgamation of External Affairs', in Donald C. Story, ed., *The Canadian Foreign Service in Transition*. Toronto: Canadian Scholars' Press, 37–58.

————. 1997. *The Politics of Canadian Foreign Policy*, 3rd edn. Scarborough, Ont.: Prentice-Hall.

Østerud, Ø. 1986. 'Nasjonalstaten Norge—en karakteriserende skisse' [The Nation State Norway—A Characterizing Sketch], in L. Alldén, N. Ramsøy, and M. Vaa, eds, *Det norske samfunn* [The Norwegian Society]. Oslo: Gyldendal Norsk Forlag, 14–35.

Potter, E.H. 2001. 'Information Technology and Canada's Public Diplomacy', paper presented to the conference 'The Administration of Foreign Affairs: A Renewed Challenge?', Hull, Que., 1–3 Nov.

————, ed.. 2002. *Cyberdiplomacy: Foreign Policy in the 21st Century*. Montreal and Kingston: McGill-Queen's University Press.

Price, R. 1998. 'Reversing the Gun Sights: Transnational Civil Society Targets Land Mines', *International Organization* 52, 3: 613–44.

Reiterer, M. 2006. 'Interregionalism as a New Diplomatic Tool: The EU and East Asia', *European Foreign Affairs Review* 11: 223–43.

Sending, O.J., and I.B. Neumann. 2006. 'Governance to governmentality', *International Studies Quarterly* 50, 3: 651–72.

Skilling, H.G. 1945. *Canadian Representation Abroad: From Agency to Embassy*. Toronto: Ryerson Press.

Smith, G.S. 1997. 'The Challenge of Virtual Diplomacy', paper presented to the Virtual Diplomacy Conference, Washington, DC, 1–2 Apr.

———— and A. Sutherland. 2002. 'The New Diplomacy: Real-Time Implications and Applications', in Potter (2002: 151–75).

Stairs, D. 2001. 'The Administrative Politics of Canadian Foreign Policy: Past Realities and Current Trends', paper presented to the conference 'The Administration of Foreign Affairs: A Renewed Challenge?', Hull, Que., 1–3 Nov.

Thakur, R., and W. Maley. 1999. 'The Ottawa Convention on Landmines: A Landmark Humanitarian Treaty in Arms Control?', *Global Governance* 5, 3: 273–302.

Tvedt, T. 1997. 'Norsk utenrikspolitikk og de frivillige organisasjonene' [Norwegian Foreign Policy and the Non-governmental Organizations], in T. Knutsen et al., eds, *Norges utenrikspolitikk* [Norway's Foreign Policy]. Oslo: Cappelen, 238–59.

Venugopal, R. 2001. 'Bridging the Gap between DFAIT and Civil Society: A Review of the CCFPD's Integration in the Foreign Policy Development Process', paper presented to the conference 'The Administration of Foreign Affairs: A Renewed Challenge', Hull, Que., 1–3 Nov.

Additional Readings

Bátora, J., and I.B. Neumann. 2002. 'Cautious Surfers: The Norwegian Ministry of Foreign Affairs Negotiates the Wave of the Information Age', *Diplomacy and Statecraft* 13, 3: 23–56.

Castells, M.. 1996. *The Information Age: Economy, Society and Culture*, Vol. 1: *The Rise of the Network Society*. Oxford: Blackwell.

Eldon, S. 1994. *From Quill Pen to Satellite: Foreign Ministries in the Information Age*. London: Royal Institute of International Affairs.

Fountain, J.E. 2001. *Building the Virtual State: Information Technology and Institutional Change*. Washington: Brookings Institution Press.

Frissen, P. 1997. 'The Virtual State: Postmodernisation, Informatisation and Public Administration', in B. Loader, ed., *The Governance of Cyberspace: Politics, Technology and Global Restructuring*. London: Routledge, 111–25.

Hay, J.B. 2000. *Practising Democratic Foreign Policy: DFAIT's Consultations with Canadians*. Ottawa: Canadian Centre for Foreign Policy Development.

Henry L. Stimson Center. 1998. *Equipped for the Future: Managing U.S. Foreign Affairs in the 21st Century* (Report). Washington, Oct.

Hocking, B. 1999. 'Foreign Ministries: Redefining the Gatekeeper Role', in Hocking, ed., *Foreign Ministries: Change and Adaptation*. London: Macmillan.

Kamarck, E.C., and J.S. Nye. 2002. *governance.com: Democracy in the Information Age*. Washington: Brookings Institution Press.

Melissen, J. 2005. *The New Public Diplomacy: Soft Power in International Relations*. London: Palgrave.

Orlikowski, W.J. 1992. 'The Duality of Technology: Rethinking the Concept of Technology in Organizations', *Organization Science* 3: 398–427.

Chapter 7

Canadian Middle-Power Identity, Environmental Biopolitics, and Human Insecurity

Andrew Baldwin and Simon Dalby

Policy versus Practice

December 2005 was a high point in Canadian environmental foreign policy. That month Canada was host to the 11th Conference of the Parties of the UN Framework Convention on Climate in Montreal (COP 11), which by many accounts was a major achievement in environmental multilateralism. Owing at least in part to the deft manoeuvring of Conference President Stéphane Dion, then Canada's Minister of the Environment, COP 11 moved international dialogue forward at a juncture when the future of the Kyoto Protocol seemed threatened by US obstinacy and its concomitant rejection of multilateralism. This was also the moment when Prime Minister Paul Martin took diplomatic licence by chastising the Bush administration's climate record and holding up Canada as a model of global environmental citizenship. This event exemplified Canada's Pearsonian tradition and middle-power status in the international order of things.

Yet it was saturated in paradox, a moment when Canada's virtuous international image stood in glaring contrast to the hard reality of its actual environmental record. Despite its ratification of the Kyoto Protocol in 2002, Canada's greenhouse gas emissions have risen faster than those of all other OECD countries with the possible exception of Spain. Investment in the Athabasca tar sands production is and continues to be fuelled by speculation over growing global demand for oil without even a hint of concern for its devastating environmental footprint. Canada continues to subsidize an outmoded forest sector, and water quality on First Nations reserves is chronically abysmal. Canadian mining companies have a dubious record overseas, while Canada's domestic mining record is equally questionable, not least when dealing with First Nations people on whose territories mining companies frequently operate. Even within the North American context, and despite Paul Martin's rhetoric, Canada has underperformed in both policy innovation and practical regulation in the area of environment (Vannijnatten, 2007). In comparison to European innovations on climate change in particular, Canada's performance has been embarrassingly tardy.

This chapter theorizes this contradiction not as an exception to Canada's image as a middle power, but as constitutive of it. Specifically, it complicates Canada's middle-power status by drawing attention to some of the contradictions that are foundational to Canada's political economy. Indeed, it is one thing to construct an image of Canadian foreign policy as progressive, virtuous, and intent on an internationalist world order based on peace, security, and environmental well-being. As many chapters in this book attest, such a framing has been a standard feature of Canada's foreign policy imaginary throughout much of the Cold War and into the present. But framing Canadian foreign policy through the middle-power idioms of good international citizenship are thrown into question when one considers the actual modes of economic life, resource production, and consumption that have been secured by the post-World War II Canadian state. That is, when one considers Canada's actual environmental record and reads this record against its middle-power image, a very different picture of Canadian foreign policy begins to emerge. Rather than a foreign policy committed to human security and well-being, one encounters instead a highly contradictory foreign policy that does not so easily square with its image and the relative innocence by which middlepowerhood is often construed. In the case of the asbestos trade, for instance, Canada maintains a foreign policy that seems to exacerbate environmental risk, and hence human *in*security, at the very moment Canadian foreign policy promises to do the opposite. Given the middle-power advocacy of human security through the 1990s and the first few years of the 2000s and Canada's role in formulating the doctrine of the 'responsibility to protect' (see UNDP, 1994; ICISS, 2001; Hampson et al., 2002), it is especially noteworthy that environmental security was frequently downplayed in the human security agenda. And insofar as Canada aspires to be an environmentally responsible citizen in today's globalized economy, Canada's steadfast reluctance to implement its Kyoto obligations seems wholly out of place.

In light of these contradictions, this chapter argues that any rethinking of Canada's status as a middle power ought to be done with an eye to Canada's political economies of resource extraction and consumption.

Indeed, assuming that environmental matters, specifically climate change, will continue to dominate international relations over the coming century alongside energy security, to rethink Canada's middle-power status must also factor in some of the very basic environmental contradictions that undergird Canadian political economy. The key point here is that in environmental matters, what Canada does at home is effectively international policy. Failure to abide by Kyoto is domestic activity with international effect—'pollution knows no borders', as environmentalists like to say. Likewise, the failure to take its rights and obligations to marginal First Nations peoples seriously, especially by favouring a political economy of extractive industries that perpetuates large-scale environmental disruptions, belies commitments to sustainability.

The chapter begins with a brief rendering of 'security' provided for in the writings of our main theoretical influence, Michel Foucault. Foucault may appear an unlikely figure to invoke in a volume about Canadian foreign policy and its supposed middle-power status. But his conceptualization of security prefigures and aligns very closely with the human security paradigm and the 'responsibility to protect', and thus provides a useful vocabulary for thinking about what is at stake in Canada's middle-power political imaginary, in particular the relationship between life and security. The chapter then considers three cases to highlight how the notion of human life is rendered insecure by specific actions taken by the Canadian state in relation to the environment. The chapter concludes with some ideas on how the rethinking of Canada's middle-power status would profit from a careful consideration of the contradictions embedded in Canada's political economy. In particular, this chapter questions which human lives are being secured by a foreign policy framed in terms of 'middlepowerhood'.

Biopolitics and Human Security

The discourse of human security that emerged in the mid-1990s marked a decisive shift in the way security would be defined as an element of foreign policy. No longer simply a discourse concerned with the state-led defence of national territory or interest, by adding to it the term 'human', security became linked to the encompassing notions of humanitarianism, human development, and universal well-being. This idea is consistent both with Foucault's notion of security, one of the main themes addressed in his 1977–8 Collège de France lectures recently published as *Security, Territory, Population*, and with his earlier theorizations on biopower and life (Foucault, 2007).

Perhaps the most useful of Foucault's elucidations on life and biopower can be found in his 1975–6 lectures, *Society Must Be Defended* (2003). Here, Foucault makes a broad distinction between sovereign power and biopower.

The former, claims Foucault, is most often framed as the power to take life and let live. That is, sovereign political authorities are invested with the right to kill. According to Foucault, what this means, in turn, is that the life and survival of a sovereign's subjects are a function of the sovereign's decision *not* to kill. The latter is a form of sovereign right that came into being in the eighteenth and nineteenth centuries. For Foucault (2003: 241), this emergent biopower embodied 'the right *to make live* and to let die'.

This emergent biopower is a state power that seeks to secure life in the polity by enabling *specific* kinds of political life to flourish. That is, rather than a sovereign right to kill or not kill, biopower names a new political right by which the state actively intervenes in the conduct of individual members of a polity such that people are made to live. But so, too, as a facet of this right, people are left to die, hence the abandonment of those lives framed as either outside the polity or as internal others.[1] In Canada, the treatment of First Nations peoples at various moments in the late nineteenth and early twentieth centuries provides a good example of state biopower. In late nineteenth-century British Columbia, for instance, First Nations peoples were simply forced to survive on dwindling areas of land as their traditional territories were subsumed under the expanding apparatus of British colonial law (Harris, 2002). The biopolitical state was, in this case, primarily concerned with making its citizenry live (by enabling colonialism), while simultaneously leaving to die all those who fell outside its purview.

Thus, even though biopower and sovereign power are counterposed in Foucault, they are never far removed, and it is here that we can begin to see their relevance for understanding the notion of human security and the international security principle set forth in the 'responsibility to protect'. As a discourse, human security stands in opposition to those state practices that deny citizens political life, practices, for instance, that limit individual rights, repress political dissent, and reward corruption. Indeed, and according to this framing of human security, it is precisely within these corrupt spaces that the causes of human *in*security are said to reside. Hence, human security discourse, and its explicit articulation in the 'responsibility to protect', implicitly obliges states to provide the essentials appropriate to liberal democratic governance. Human security discourses ushered in a concern for life at the level of the population by ensuring that people live healthy, productive lives, unencumbered by things like poverty, fear, and environmental despoliation. Indeed, the logic here suggests that conditions of insecurity take root in spaces where the lived experiences of people are left unattended and where people, reduced to 'bare life',[2] are simply left to fend for themselves. Human security, by contrast, seeks to forestall such conditions by directly intervening in bare life by enabling those reduced to such a condition to gain control in the deliberate unfolding of their lives.

Alongside Foucault's characterization of biopower as a concern for life, two additional sets of discourses are important to consider—environment and security. First, if biopower registers a concern for life, then it also registers a concern for the conditions that give life, including the effects of the so-called 'environment' on populations and bodies. In this sense, biopower frames a concern for *securing* specific conditions for life at the level of the population and the individual. This linkage is found not only in Foucault's essays and lectures of the 1970s, but much more recently in discussions of security and life related to the War on Terror and to the technological innovations for monitoring populations and modes of life, as well as to the commodification of risk in the insurance industry (Dillon, 2008).

We use Michel Foucault's notion of biopower to frame our analysis of human security discourse and its disjunctive relation to the rhetoric of Canadian environmental citizenship. We argue, then, that human security is an excellent example of biopower insofar as it promises to enhance, maintain, provide for, facilitate, and, above all, guarantee human life. It is a technique of security that is fundamentally about 'making people live' as opposed to one that simply seeks to secure them from foreign intrusion.

Neo-Liberal Environments

Human security seeks to cultivate neo-liberal subjects capable of governing themselves in accordance with the values of self-preservation, ethical awareness, and rational planning. It seeks to improve upon 'bare life' through a policy of 'making live' consistent with market capitalism. This corollary has been much less obvious until a recent cohort of graduate students turned its attention to the analysis of human security: human security requires a certain form of human to function—the neo-liberal, consuming human; other modes of life and death are simply excluded from its calculus and frequently from the rationales for government or international 'intervention' (Bell, 2007; Ozguc, 2007; Wilson, 2008). Economic neo-liberalism provides an important *dispositif* of human security insofar as it seeks to emancipate people from their poverty through the promise of market access and self-sufficiency realized through the commodification of their labour. Accordingly, the world would be made much more secure, if only the impoverished would simply embrace neo-liberalism, realize their common humanity through market-based consumption, and embrace the social contract guaranteed by the liberal state.

In the Canadian context, matters of urban consumption, far from the rural peripheries where resource extraction occurs, are frequently about privatized consumption where individual purchases, consumer waste recycling, and 'lifestyle' mark a mode of citizenship that substantially ignores its dependence on the infrastructure of suburban sprawl, car culture, and the lengthy commodity chains that supply consumer goods, 'green' and otherwise. That said, in the case of 'conflict diamonds' in particular, Canadian foreign policy has used arguments of good corporate practice as part of a discourse of Canadian virtue in contrast to the violent political economies of resource extraction of blood diamonds, especially in Africa (Le Billon, 2007). What this amounts to is that the environmental dimensions of Canadian human security policy are fraught with numerous contradictions, many of which allow image-making and foreign policy rhetoric to proceed divorced from the ecological consequences of both production and consumption. In short, this contradiction enables a policy that seeks to deliver human security in terms that frequently preclude *environmental* security.

The modes of life being secured, then, are those produced in the market economy. The ecological modernization of production, whereby toxic pollution is either avoided by technical innovation or removed by sophisticated engineering with a view to securing a 'clean' environment, is central to this environ-mentality (Christoff, 1996). But ecological modernization, especially its 'weak' variants,[3] has so far frequently failed to address the total throughput of materials and hence the ecological disruptions of the production and consumption systems as a totality. Capitalist economies rely on growth, and at least so far, despite high-profile Canadian participation in the Montreal Protocol deliberations in the 1980s, the Earth Summit in 1992, and right through to the Kyoto Protocol episode noted in the introduction to this chapter, the Canadian economy has produced petroleum, automobiles, and huge suburban houses, which use vast amounts of resources drawn from, among other places, Canada's boreal forest, with no apparent concern for the total ecological impact of this mode of life.

The Canadian economy perpetuates this mode of consumption because, in part, the notion of 'environment' enters into contemporary governmentality as either a technical matter of pollution control, or as a matter of resource management and related questions of parks, wilderness, and wildlife preservation. And important in this respect is the simple fact that 'environment' is here understood as *external* to humanity, something that frequently has practical effects should toxic substances be introduced into it in ways that come back to harm humans, or, if natural systems are disrupted, in ways that directly endanger health, the economy, or aesthetic dimensions of lifestyle. Ironically, contemporary biopolitics is frequently not about the biosphere. Modernity is premised on the separation of humanity from nature, which is to say we are modern precisely because our technologies and our practices of division have rendered nature external, something in need of protection, and something from which humanity, in turn, frequently needs protection (Walker, 2006).

Or at least when environment *is* connected to foreign policy and the practices of making 'foreign' or outside the purview of national life, threats are understood as externally sourced, having nothing to do with domestic matters and everything to do with how far 'they' are from the ideals of modern governance. That Canadian resource policy implemented either domestically or elsewhere might endanger others is not usually considered a matter of either security or foreign policy, but the inconsistencies between here and there are now a matter of political critique, especially in matters of ethical investment, and this directly challenges the preferred national image of Canada as a benign global citizen. As we show below, this is especially so in the case of Canadian failures to seriously tackle climate change. Much of the discussion of environment still relies on vaguely understood notions of external dangers, not matters that urban citizens in Canada's metropoles and suburban residents in particular are responsible for.

Canada and Environmental (In)Security

Environmental discourse is now often framed as an extension of liberalism in which 'the environment' is regarded as a social problem best mitigated by a state-led ecological modernization policy that privileges individual choice. The application of market rationality to all aspects of personal life, the state, and civil society, and the privileging of this rationality above all other values, is central to contemporary neo-liberal governmentality. Moreover, neo-liberal governmentality maintains a rhetorical commitment to preserving the basic institutions of liberal democracy (freedom, rights, civil liberties), while simultaneously working to undermine their presence as principles that govern policy, law, and rule. Indeed, to say 'we are working to protect the environment or climate' (a principle that values life and the preservation of life as its modus operandi) and at the same time ensuring that whatever is done conforms to a market rationality, in this case premised on cheap fossil fuels, actually works counter to the promise, as is the case, for example, with tar sands investment. And such an approach precisely enacts this neo-liberal rationality.

Canada's environmental record follows this pattern closely, as the three case studies illustrate: Canada's ongoing, deeply fraught practice of exporting asbestos; tar sands production; and conflicts around Aboriginal life in the boreal forest in which the forestry industry facilitates a neo-liberal mode of economy while leaving local peoples to their own devices. This latter case also allows us to emphasize the contemporary continuity with the colonial past of Canadian resource appropriation and the marginalization of Aboriginal modes of life, left to die as their resource base is compromised and the formal legal rights encoded in various treaties are flagrantly ignored, a pattern that is key to the blind spots in much of the discussion of environmental security elsewhere as well (Dalby, 2002).

Asbestos

It is important to emphasize that in today's global economy Canada's resource extraction industries, which have been important domestically in the expansion of the Canadian economy in the first few years of the twenty-first century and the consequent rise in the Canadian dollar in this period, have also been actively involved in exploration and resource extraction around the world, notably in Latin America (Gordon and Webber, 2008). In many instances these activities have generated opposition by local populations whose livelihoods have been endangered by mines, with all their resultant environmental disruption. The domestic patterns of despoliation are mirrored abroad, which complicates the relation between soft power and political economic realities. So, too, does Canada's involvement in promoting exports of hazardous substances, especially asbestos, where Canadian economic activities and domestic political considerations seem to weigh more heavily than the health and safety of people living elsewhere (Ruff, 2008).

Canada has been a long-time producer and exporter of chrysotile asbestos, a known carcinogen banned for use and sale in just about all developed countries. Up until 2000 Canada was the world's leading exporter of asbestos. It now ranks as the world's fourth largest asbestos exporter behind Russia, Kazakhstan, and Brazil. In 2007, Canada exported over $77 million in asbestos to the developing world, a large portion of which goes to India, China, and Mexico. Asbestos is, thus, an important Canadian export, and makes a significant contribution to Canada's trade balance. Yet this is a distressing export sector, since asbestos is a banned substance for most uses in Canada. Its use is restricted because it poses considerable health risks, most notably lethal mesothelioma cancer, to those who come into contact with it. Buildings across the country, including the Parliament buildings, have been renovated to remove asbestos, but Canada continues to promote its export and use abroad. Thus, asbestos provides an ideal commodity with which to think about the Canadian environmental paradox, specifically the contradictions that come to view when biopolitics rubs up against Canadian foreign policy framed as human security.

Central to the asbestos trade is the question of life, specifically *whose life* is worth securing and whose is not. The export of asbestos and the domestic ban on its use in Canada exemplify Foucault's formulation of biopolitics as the dynamic of making live and letting die. On the one hand, the Canadian citizenry is extended the right to live through the ban on a carcinogenic substance. Here, the Canadian citizenry is in effect made to live; its overall population health is secured through the ban in the hope that such a ban will reduce the incidence of cancer in the Canadian population. Clearly, through the domestic ban, Canadian citizens' lives are deemed worthy of being secured. This, of course, stands in stark contrast to the continued export of asbestos to countries with no commensurate ban, a practice that implicitly frames the inhabitants of these countries as unworthy of the ban.

The counter-argument to this, of course, is that asbestos-importing countries have every right to ban the domestic use of asbestos, a right enshrined in international trade law. If they fail to exercise this right, so the argument continues, this is a matter (even a failure) of domestic policy-making rather than one of international concern. In this sense, Canada can gain authoritative distance from the importer by claiming that the health and well-being of the inhabitants of importing countries fall well outside Canada's authoritative purview. Yet, such a policy seems to contradict the principle of the 'responsibility to protect' operative in the human security narrative. Indeed, is not the continued export of asbestos, given the knowledge of its carcinogenic properties, a flagrant violation of the intent, if not letter, of the human security doctrine? Similarly, this policy also contradicts the intent behind the principle of prior informed consent,[4] which, of course, serves as the basis of the Rotterdam Convention, a legally binding international convention that regulates the trade of chemicals with known health risks that Canada has played an important role in formulating. Nothwithstanding this role, Canada has actively resisted placing asbestos on the list of substances regulated by the Convention.

Canada endorses the 'responsibility to protect' principles, at least in development and foreign policy, as a means of making live (i.e., helping people overcome poverty by giving them the tools for success, such as capital, market access, technology, and capacity-building). However, Canadian asbestos export policy contradicts human security thinking precisely because asbestos is a life-threatening substance. Asbestos exports, by extension, are better understood biopolitically as a policy of 'letting die' or, more specifically, of letting *other*, non-Canadian people die due to a neglect of safety standards. It would appear, then, that the federal government apparently thinks these others are less important than jobs and investments in Quebec's asbestos mines. In short, environmental security occupies, at best, a marginal position in Canadian security policy as least as far as asbestos and its hazards are concerned. Canada's failure to support international measures to limit the health dangers of asbestos suggests that a much narrower formulation of national interest is driving this agenda, and middle-power good citizenship is of less importance than export revenues.

Forests

The practice of making live and letting die as a condition of biopolitical rule is foundational to Canada's forest economy. This is perhaps best exemplified in the case of Grassy Narrows First Nation in northwestern Ontario. Since 2002, Grassy Narrows has actively opposed forestry practices on their traditional territories as carried out by two of the world's largest forest products firms, AbitibiBowater and Weyerhaeuser. Both AbitibiBowater and Weyerhaeuser hold provincial forestry concessions, which grant them legal right to harvest timber in predetermined areas of northern Ontario. Grassy Narrows First Nation has long maintained that these forestry concessions were granted by the provincial government without adequate consultation, a legal requirement set forth in Canadian jurisprudence. Grassy Narrows First Nations also maintains that the continued clear-cut harvesting of timber on their traditional territory violates their treaty rights, specifically the right to make a livelihood from the land, and results in widespread flooding and mercury contamination in Grassy Narrows' water supply. Grassy Narrows maintains that the failure to consult and the environmental despoliation on its traditional territory violate their human rights, and thus the First Nation seeks greater control over natural resources on its traditional territory as a preliminary step in overcoming chronic poverty.

In this example, the Aboriginal residents of Grassy Narrows are unprotected *by* the law, yet they remain fully subject *to* the law, or in the words of Giorgio Agamben (1998), they occupy a zone of indistinction. This requires some explanation. In Canada, natural resource management is a constitutionally defined provincial right, entitling provincial authorities to manage natural resources in accordance with provincial objectives. The Canadian federal government maintains limited authority over natural resource management in some areas of taxation and in its capacity to negotiate international law. Significantly, however, First Nations are constitutionally defined as the fiduciary responsibility of the federal government as set forth in the contentious Indian Act. Routinely, these two bodies of law—natural resource law and the Indian Act—come into direct conflict as provincial authorities exploit ambiguities in the legal framework governing natural resources and First Nations. That is, even though First Nations throughout Canada frequently inhabit areas of intensive natural resource extraction, provincial authorities routinely suspend the rights of First Nations on the grounds that these rights are matters of federal, not provincial, jurisdiction. Similarly, when First Nations demand greater political authority over natural resources, or claim that natural resource extraction infringes on their legal entitlements, the federal government is able to suspend these concerns on the grounds that natural resources are under provincial jurisdiction. Thus, while subject to the law, the rights of First Nations are never adequately protected by the law.

This describes very well the situation faced by Grassy Narrows. Forestry continues on its traditional territory under the terms of the licence agreements between the province of Ontario and both AbitibiBowater and Weyerhaeuser, while the federal government has refused to intervene in this matter as per its fiduciary responsibility to protect. Indeed, the people of Grassy Narrows, as with so many other First Nations across Canada, are simply left to fend for themselves in an ambiguous legal arrangement that fails to protect their interests while simultaneously rendering them fully subject to Canadian law. The legal ambiguities that surround First Nations in respect of forestry policy generate intense insecurity, and seem to violate the doctrine of human security as set forth in the international principle of the responsibility to protect. First Nations, in this sense, are simply 'left to die', while the privileged agents of the market economy, in this case two large multinationals, continue to do business[5] in the production and export of relatively unprocessed forest commodities and, at the same time, generate considerable tax revenues for the state. This situation calls into question Canada's status as one of the world's leading environmental citizens. Although some visionary thinkers foresee the Canadian forest economy transforming into a leader in the provision of environmental services and green energy production, for the time being much of Canada's boreal forest continues to be allocated for low-grade bulk commodity export, an economy that demands high annual harvest levels and throughput and that routinely suspends subaltern political demands. This is very far from the international ideals of sustainable forest use, and of little use as a climate change policy that takes forests as 'sinks' for atmospheric carbon seriously.

Tar Sands

Perhaps the most egregious example of the divergence of rhetoric and reality in Canadian environmental policy is found on the issue of climate change (see Simpson et al., 2007; Weaver, 2008). Canada appeared to have taken the international high road with its support and ratification of the Kyoto Protocol. Stéphane Dion played a key role in moving the international process ahead when he served as Canada's Minister of Environment. But even as this international commitment was being asserted as critical to any strategy to tackle climate change, no realistic policies designed to constrain the expansion of tar sands projects in northern Alberta were being seriously considered, much less implemented. The enormous disruptions of the environment caused by the vast tar sands developments were not clearly linked to the impossibility of meeting Kyoto commitments, and emissions are only one part of the larger disruption caused by the massive excavation and huge energy and water uses of the processes to turn bitumen into petroleum. Once again, the extractive economy remained relatively untouched despite all the green rhetoric (Marsden, 2007).

Discussions of carbon markets were all premised on market rationalities, which partly overlooked the consequences of rapidly rising petroleum prices. Stéphane Dion, having moved on from being Environment Minister to become leader of the Liberal Party, tried to make a green tax shift a central theme in the October 2008 federal election campaign, but this policy proposal was lambasted by the producers in the Alberta oil patch and rejected by voters at the polls. While carbon taxes might work to reduce gasoline consumption and even encourage consumers to better insulate houses or even purchase smaller ones that needed less heating and cooling, the policies for tar sands development and for the rest of the major industrial sectors that use energy in large quantities remained relatively undeveloped. Provinces did begin to establish carbon markets, and trading arrangements emerged in preliminary form, but in comparison to European efforts they were in their infancy as of 2008.

The sheer scale of the tar sands development and the billions of dollars involved suggested clearly that taxes on consumption were highly unlikely to work in any way to stop this project. In part, this is because of traditional Liberal Party reluctance to antagonize Alberta oil industry leaders and Alberta provincial politicians, not to mention the governing Conservatives' active courting of business as usual in the energy sector. More generally, however, by focusing on retail politics, with the presupposition that environmental crises were to be dealt with by consumer choice, the hard issues of retooling the energy economy and making more radical industrial changes were avoided. Without these changes the retail economy, even if it became rapidly more efficient in energy use, could not cause enough reductions in carbon emissions to make Canada even close to compliant with Kyoto requirements. The retail economy, after all, directly involves only a fraction of the total national economic activity.

The international dimensions of this issue also play an important role. When Stephen Harper took over as Prime Minister in 2006, and then was returned to power with a second minority government in the 2008 election, one of the primary themes in his rhetoric was that Canada was now an energy superpower. While the craven desire to be seen to be playing in the big leagues might be explained in part by the personal psychology of the Prime Minister, clearly the larger geopolitical repositioning of Canada as a reliable supplier of energy to the United States was designed to appeal to American political and commercial interests nervous about growing dependency on imported petroleum. Coupled with a flat denial by the Conservative government that climate change was an issue needing attention and the consequent refusal to take environmental matters seriously, this version of neo-liberalism suggested that Canadian prosperity, and Canada's place among the big states of the planet, was dependent on both international oil markets and the geopolitics of supply insecurity. Neo-liberalism met neo-conservatism in the Harper government's determination to link its policies to those of the Bush administration, as energy supplies and the willingness to commit Canada to using force in Afghanistan in the War on Terror aligned Canada closely with then current American priorities.

The domestic consequences of such strategies, including the relatively high Canadian dollar, had deleterious effects on industrial exports from eastern Canada, but these difficulties were somewhat reduced later in 2008 when the Canadian dollar fell against the American dollar in part as a result of rapid reductions of oil prices. These changes, however, were increasingly subsumed in the more general economic crisis of the period, a crisis that the newly re-elected Conservative government seemed unwilling to seriously tackle, not least because of its neo-liberal assumptions that markets were the appropriate venues for decisions to be made about both the security of Canadian citizens and about the future place of Canada in the larger world.

Contemporary Policies

Globally, the relative neglect of environmental themes may finally be beginning to change, not least because of the dawning realization, articulated most clearly in the high-profile British *Stern Review* of 2006, that climate change is a massive case of market failure (United Kingdom, 2006). Understanding that the likely costs of continuing on the present course in terms of numerous forms of human insecurity are much greater than the costs of now taking preventive measures shifts the economic calculus, and with it the modes of governmentality invoked to tackle climate change. In recent years in the Canadian context, this is marked by increasing discussions of carbon trading systems and by the failed effort on the part of Stéphane Dion to initiate a 'green shift' in tax policy to facilitate industrial innovation and less carbon-intensive consumption. But market mechanisms are really the only preferred solutions to numerous environmental difficulties; this is what is to be secured in Conservative, New Democrat, and Bloc Québécois proposals for carbon cap and trade systems as well as in Liberal and Green Party proposals for green shift tax systems. In the immediate aftermath of the 2008 American presidential election, the Conservative government announced its plans to engage the new administration in negotiations for a continent-wide regime of carbon cap and trade arrangements (CBC, 2008). The Canadian government also suggested that energy security was so important that such arrangements would not penalize the production from the tar sands (Austen, 2009).

Ironically, Canada's international role as a middle power and its reputation as an innovative global player came back to haunt the new Conservative government. This coalesced in the climate denial debate where partisan rejection of the Kyoto agreement by the Conservatives was linked to the correct argument that Canada had no hope of meeting its Kyoto commitments. But the middle-power dimensions of national ideology portraying Canada as a good global citizen ran counter to the Harper government's arguments, made in particular by their hapless first Environment Minister, Rona Ambrose, that Canada should not participate in an agreement whose conditions it hadn't a hope of meeting. Coupled with the additional argument that the Kyoto agreements might constrain the development of the tar sands, a cornerstone of Stephen Harper's articulation of Canada as an energy superpower and as a crucial ally of the Americans in any search for independence from Middle East oil, partisan opposition was galvanized on green themes. But this was also done in a way that used Canada's international reputation as the leverage to force the government to at least pay some attention to international opinion. Critics invoked Canada's key role as a middle power as a compelling argument against the Harper government's lack of environmental policies.

Noteworthy, too, in all the discussion of climate change and the policy consequences necessary to deal with recognizing the reality of environmental change was the reinvention of sovereignty discourse. This can be identified both in rhetorical assertions by the Prime Minister that Canada is now an energy superpower and, explicitly, in renewed claims of territorial sovereignty in the Far North related to the realization that the Northwest Passage is likely to become a navigable waterway in coming years as the Arctic sea ice recedes. Canadian nationalists were quick to promote the presence of Canada in the Arctic in terms of national security and access to petroleum resources under the seabed. One popular book caught the mood, neatly punning meteorology and warfare in a title simply called *Arctic Front* (Coates et al., 2008). Less remarked upon is the huge irony of making claims that a Canadian presence in the High Arctic is necessary to monitor the environmental damage done by shipping in the region, a claim that requires ignoring Canada's substantial contribution to the changes that will shortly open the passage in the first place.

While Canada has taken a lead in international discussions on human security and played a high-profile role in facilitating ratification of the Kyoto Accord, its environmental record is much less 'green' than this image suggests. For Canada, the policy of environmental security, understood in terms of sustaining environments at home and abroad, has been a very low priority. Domestic environmental matters have been incorporated into a neo-liberal framework whereby managerial initiatives have cleaned up and regulated only some aspects of environmental affairs and not tackled the basic political economies of either extraction or suburban mass consumption.

With the accession of the Conservative federal government to power in 2006, climate change was simply denied and the exploitation of the tar sands in Alberta and other fossil-fuel energy projects has moved ahead rapidly, aided in part by speculation on the Canadian dollar but clearly more substantively driven by foreign investment in the then lucrative resources sectors of the

Canadian economy. While this has generated a political backlash, these policies emphasize the continuing importance of the resource extraction sector in the Canadian economy and the ambiguities in its political economy, allowing progressive image-making to coincide with business-as-usual industrial production at the cost of policies that are genuinely green.

Policies to tackle the global difficulties of environmental and human insecurities will require a substantial shift in geopolitical imagination in Canadian policy-making circles. The recognition that globalization ties humanity together in increasingly interconnected and artificial ways, and that human insecurities are hence a matter of social institutions, was a key insight in the early discussions of human security; it is even more important now as the multiple dimensions of global environmental change become obvious. Humans around the globe are now ever more dependent on the infrastructures that make contemporary modes of life possible (Dalby, 2009). Ironically, the financial crisis of 2008–9 has reactivated discussions of infrastructure provision and industrial strategies to revive flagging economies in many places. Whether Canadians will be able to take advantage of this moment to shape industrial strategy to make things that people need, to ensure basic needs are met without further disrupting ecological systems, and to diversify local production systems remains to be seen. The collapse in petroleum prices in late 2008 both reduced investment in tar sands development and also reduced the economic incentives to develop technologies not reliant on petroleum.

If such policy initiatives are to be undertaken in the near future they will require thinking much more carefully about sustainable modes of living, and will also require a coming to terms with Canada's legacy of dirty resource extraction industries as the basis for its wealth. Simple reliance on 'the market' is obviously no longer adequate as an economic strategy; likewise with matters of environment. If ecology is to be taken seriously as a key part of discussions of security, then a focus on what is produced and how is simply unavoidable. Correcting Canadians' self-image as good global citizens and simultaneously confronting the consequences of present modes of resource extraction are two necessary steps to help construct policies that promote life in all its diversity. If, as Tom Keating notes in his contribution to this volume, Prime Minister Harper wishes Canada to lead by example in getting things done, then in environmental terms Canadian biopolitics needs urgent attention. Given the unavoidable necessity for international co-operation on environmental matters, numerous contemporary security problems, and global economic difficulties, multilateral diplomacy is clearly going to be much needed in coming decades. But without good domestic performance on environmental matters in particular, Canada's claims to be a good international citizen remain highly suspect, and its middle-power role may remain as hollow as some of its critics have long suggested it has always been.

Notes

1. This is not to argue that the power to kill as a feature of sovereign authority is eclipsed by biopower. This mode of sovereign power continues to coexist with biopower. Foucault's main insight here is that to analyze sovereign power as merely the right to kill is an anemic reading of state power.
2. The term 'bare life' comes from Giorgio Agamben (1998). Glossing Agamben, 'bare life' refers to a political subjectivity that stands *outside* the law, but remains subject *to* the law.
3. Strong and weak variations on the ecological modernization theme have been advanced by Desfor and Keil (2004). To simplify, weak ecological modernization refers to the use of market-based instruments to internalize environmental externalities. Strong ecological modernization places greater emphasis on state regulation in reorganizing production and consumption along ecological lines.
4. The principle of prior informed consent means that importers of substances regulated by the Rotterdam Convention are entitled to know the legislative status of these substances in the exporting country. The principle holds that importers are entitled to this information prior to import. The Convention is an international safeguard designed to protect importers from substances banned for use in exporting countries. In our opinion, Canada's continued export of asbestos and steadfast refusal to include asbestos among the substances regulated under the Rotterdam Convention violate this principle of international environmental law.
5. The privilege extends to bankruptcy protection: AbitibiBowater filed for bankruptcy protection in the US in mid-April 2009.

References

Agamben, Giorgio. 1998. *Homo Sacer: Sovereign and Bare Life*. Stanford, Calif.: Stanford University Press.

Austen, Ian. 2009. 'The Costly Compromises of Oil from Sand', *New York Times*, 6 Jan. At: <www.nytimes.com/2009/01/07/business/07oilsands.html?_r=1>.

Bell, Colleen. 2007. 'Liberating Security: Governing Canada in the Age of Terror', Ph.D. dissertation, York University.

Canadian Broadcasting Corporation (CBC). 2008. 'Canada to Push Climate Agreement with Obama Government', CBC News, 5 Nov. At: <www.cbc.ca/canada/story/2008/11/05/canada-us-environment.html?ref=rss>.

Christoff, Peter. 1996. 'Ecological Modernisation, Ecological Modernities', *Environmental Politics* 5: 476–500.

Coates, Ken S., P. Whitney Lackenbauer, William R. Morrison, and Greg Poelzer. 2008. *Arctic Front: Defending Canada in the Far North*. Toronto: Thomas Allen.

Dalby, Simon. 2002. *Environmental Security*. Minneapolis: University of Minnesota Press.

———. 2009. *Security and Environmental Change*. Cambridge: Polity.

Desfor, G., and R. Keil. 2004. *Nature and the City: Making Environmental Policy in Toronto and Los Angeles*. Tucson: University of Arizona Press.

Dillon, Michael. 2008. 'Underwriting Security', *Security Dialogue* 39, 2 and 3: 309–32.

Gordon, Todd, and Jeffery Webber. 2008. 'Imperialism and Resistance: Canadian Mining Companies in Latin America', *Third World Quarterly* 29, 1: 63–87.

Hampson, Fen Osler, with Jean Daudelin, John B. Hay, Holly Reid, and Todd Martin. 2002. *Madness in the Multitude: Human Security and World Disorder*. Toronto: Oxford University Press.

Foucault, Michel. 2003. *Society Must Be Defended*. New York: Picador.

———. 2007. *Security, Territory, Population*. London: Palgrave Macmillan.

Harris, Cole. 2002. *Making Native Space: Colonialism, Resistance and Reserves in British Columbia*. Vancouver: University of British Columbia Press.

International Commission on Intervention and State Sovereignty (ICISS). 2001. *The Responsibility to Protect: Report of the International Commission on Intervention and State Sovereignty*. Ottawa: International Development Research Centre.

Le Billon, Philippe. 2007. 'Fatal Transactions: Conflict Diamonds and the (Anti)Terrorist Consumer', in Derek Gregory and Allan Pred, eds, *Violent Geographies: Fear, Terror, and Political Violence*. New York: Routledge, 133–52.

Marsden, William. 2007. *Stupid to the Last Drop: How Alberta Is Bringing Environmental Armageddon to Canada (and Doesn't Seem to Care)*. Toronto: Knopf.

Ozguc, Umut. 2007. 'In the Name of Emancipation: Interrogating the Politics of Canada's Human Security Discourse', MA thesis, University of New South Wales.

Ruff, Kathleen. 2008. *Exporting Harm: How Canada Markets Asbestos to the Developing World*. Ottawa: Rideau Institute.

Simpson, Jeffrey, Mark Jaccard, and Nic Rivers. 2007. *Hot Air: Canada's Climate Change Challenge*. Toronto: McClelland & Stewart.

Stern, Nicholas. 2007. *The Economics of Climate Change*. Cambridge: Cambridge University Press.

United Nations Development Program (UNDP). *Human Development Report 1994*. New York: Oxford University Press.

Vannijnatten, Debora L. 2007. 'Canadian Environmental Policy in a North American Context: Manoeuvring Towards Mediocrity', in Jean Daudelin and Daniel Schwanen, eds, *Canada Among Nations 2007*. Montreal and Kingston: McGill-Queen's University Press, 286–308.

Walker, R.B.J. 2006. 'On the Protection of Nature and the Nature of Protection', in Jef Huysmans, Andrew Dobson, and Raia Prokhovnik, eds, *The Politics of Protection: Sites of Insecurity and Political Agency*. London: Routledge, 189–202.

Weaver, Andrew. 2008. *Keeping Our Cool: Canada in a Warming World*. Toronto: Penguin.

Wilson, Rhea. 2008. 'Securing the Human: A Critique of Human Security and *The Responsibility to Protect*', MA thesis, University of Victoria.

Additional Readings

Barnett, Jon. 2001. *The Meaning of Environmental Security: Ecological Politics and Policy in the New Security Era*. London: Zed Books.

Dillon, Michael. 2009. *Biopolitics of Security in the 21st Century: A Political Analytics of Finitude*. New York and London: Routledge.

——— and Julian Reid. 2009. *Liberal Way of War: Killing to Make Life Live*. New York and London: Routledge.

Kuehls, Thom. 1996. *Beyond Sovereign Territory: The Space of Ecopolitics*. Minneapolis: University of Minnesota Press.

Roberts, J. Timmons, and Bradley C. Parks. 2006. *A Climate of Injustice: Global Inequality, North–South Politics and Climate Change*. Cambridge, Mass.: MIT Press.

Stanford, Jim. 2008. 'Staples, Deindustrialization, and Foreign Investment: Canada's Economic Journey Back to the Future', *Studies in Political Economy* 82: 7–34.

Superpower, Middle Power, or Satellite? Canadian Energy and Environmental Policy

Gordon Laxer

Introduction

En route to his first G8 meeting as Prime Minister of Canada, Stephen Harper stopped in London to proclaim Canada an 'energy superpower'. British investors, Harper stated, 'have recognized the emergence of Canada's global energy powerhouse. Or as we put it, the emerging energy superpower our government intends to build.'

Stephen Harper's claim to Canada's superpower ambitions was a dramatic departure from the more modest, middle-power pretensions of all previous prime ministers since 1945. It was ironic that Stephen Harper chose the 2006 G8 meetings to assert Canada's energy superpowerdom. This was the first time such meetings were held in Russia. If there is an emerging energy superpower today, surely it is Russia (Goldman, 2008: 14), a Saudi Arabia with nukes. Russia produces almost 10 million barrels of oil a day, just under 12 per cent of the world's total (EIA, 2008d),[1] and exports 7 million barrels, second only to the Saudis. Russia's natural gas stature is even greater. With 22 per cent of world production (EIA, 2008c),[2] Russia is the world's greatest natural gas power. It provides Europeans with 34 per cent of their supplies (Cohen, 2007), opening them to Russian blackmail.

Canada's daily energy production is puny by comparison: 4 per cent of the world's oil and 6.3 per cent of its natural gas (EIA, 2008c).[3] If Russia produces three times as much oil and natural gas and transforms its energy into international political power, can Canada credibly proclaim itself an energy superpower? What of the future? Stephen Harper qualified his boast by emphasizing Canada's 'emergence' as a superpower that his government 'intends to build'. For a staunch neo-liberal who usually trumpets markets as superior to governments in determining a country's economic strengths, it was uncharacteristic language. But Stephen Harper is right that the odds of Canada becoming an energy superpower will more likely be decided by state policies. Which policies are likely to lead to which desirable outcomes? Should Canada aim to be an energy superpower? To accomplish what ends? Or should Canada set its sights on a different sort of leadership on energy and the environment?

Although Prime Minister Harper's rhetoric differs from that of previous governments, the intent here is not to suggest that his government has broken with earlier Liberal governments on energy and environmental policies. It hasn't. The course the Conservatives have pursued involves the same US-oriented, resource-exporting policies.

The World in the 2020s

In the next 20 years, every country will face a triple enviro-energy crisis that will force it to make a paradigm shift towards a new balance with the natural world, or else be stuck in a declining fossil-fuel belt, analogous to the industrial Rust Belt of the US Midwest. How countries deal with the triple crisis will influence their position in what I anticipate will be the altered international order of the 2020s. What is the 'triple crisis'? First, more frequent and severe oil-supply shocks will likely accompany the end of cheap oil ('peak oil' theory) (IEA, 2008: 37–8). Second, expensive and less available oil will profoundly impact both a country's energy security and class justice issues regarding which citizens will have access to diminished energy supplies. Third, how will countries begin to make the transition to a powered-down, post-carbon society, to forestall climate change disasters? These crises show the inseparability of energy and environmental issues.

Meeting the Triple Crisis

How will Canada meet the triple crisis? Will it continue massive hydrocarbon usage and exports or be a world leader in building a green energy future? The determining issues include how Canada will use, develop, and save its energy. Will Canadian policies primarily ensure domestic or American energy security? Is it better to produce a unit of fossil-fuel energy or save it? Which policies would best serve the environmental future of humanity and other life forms?

Canada's lack of policy on energy security needs to be addressed in a volume such as this one on foreign and security policy. Although it is currently a political non-issue given that the country is a net exporter of energy, Canada is very unlikely to achieve domestic energy security based on domestic resources because of: (1) trilateral issues within NAFTA (the proportionality clause), which hinder Canada from ensuring that all Canadians have access to adequate energy supplies; (2) regional imbalances (the West as a net energy exporter, and eastern Canada as a net importer); (3) inadequate national pipeline infrastructure; and (4) environmental and physical limits to developing the full potential of Alberta's tar sands. Thus, while Canada is theoretically one of the few privileged countries in the world that does not need a national energy security policy, it is actually in desperate need of one because of poor political decisions in the past, historical wranglings between provinces and the federal government over control of energy policy and supplies, and pervasive but wrongheaded assumptions that Canada has unlimited energy resources. Canadian policies on energy and the environment are a weak, inconsistent, and problematic patchwork. These issues have important foreign policy implications: when Canada is finally forced to address them, after its citizens experience energy shortages that raise fears about freezing in the dark, the country will have to change its orientation to the United States. Ironically, Canada will have to distance itself from the US by showing it the greatest form of flattery—copying the US in developing *national* 'energy independence' and 'energy security' strategies.

Looking at these issues from the perspective of Canada's place in the international hierarchy of power relations is only one prism through which to view them. It emphasizes a country's tactics and capacity to influence events at home and abroad. Those only partially influence a country's policy direction. In their own ways, Denmark, Sweden, Germany, and Cuba are international enviro-energy leaders. But their international positions differ, showing that the latter do not necessarily determine policy direction. This chapter emphasizes the latitude countries have to make policy choices, regardless of their international relational position.

How likely are Stephen Harper's superpower ambitions to be realized in the next two decades? There are three possible trajectories for Canada's international enviro-energy future: superpower, middle power, or satellite. All three are compatible with Canada's role as a middle power in most respects. Countries can have superpower or satellite features within an overall intermediate frame, and the most defensible definition of middle power, is a relational one (Chapnick, 1999).

I start by outlining features to expect if Canada is an enviro-energy satellite, superpower, or middle power, and examine where the evidence lies. Since Canada's international position is relational, I use a comparative approach.

Energy Superpower, Middle Power, or Satellite?

There are competing ideas about the consequences of countries having lots of oil, or lots of resources including oil. Optimistic perspectives such as the energy superpower idea have precedents in Canadian scholarship. Writing in 1975, when the Organization of Petroleum Exporting Countries (OPEC) first flexed its muscles, and the US exited from Vietnam, James Eayrs (1975: 22–4) contended that Canada had become a 'foremost power' because of the growing stature of 'oil-sufficient industrial countries', a global shift to the power of countries with bountiful resources, and a decline in US confidence. In 1983, David Dewitt and John Kirton coined 'principal power' to elevate Canada above middle powers, only partially linking Canada's enhanced position to its oil and other resources.

An international literature has since emerged around the pessimistic concepts of 'resource curse' and the 'curse of oil', which, among other things, claims that petro-states suffer lessened democracy and growth rates (Sachs and Warner, 1999; Ross, 2001). Earlier, Harold Innis developed the 'staples approach', which argued that a bounty of resources tended to lead to dependency, at least among 'new countries' or hinterlands like Canada. Development, according to Innis and his political economy followers, was largely determined externally by the pattern of demand and technology level in metropolitan (great power) countries, and by the hinterlands' God-given geographic and resource endowments. Metropolitan countries largely initiated hinterland booms and busts. A reinforcing 'staple trap' tended to develop, which inhibited Canada from more diversified development (Watkins, 1977). Which approaches better explain Canada's energy and environmental policies and prospects, the optimistic or the pessimistic ones?

Superpowers

Politicians have licence to exaggerate more than academics, who are usually constrained by norms of accuracy. What are superpowers? According to Lyman Miller (2005), superpowers influence events by projecting economic, military, political, and cultural power on a world scale. When applied to enviro-energy superpowers, it implies that a country must be a world leader in energy output and have substantial reserves. Energy superpowers must also demonstrate that they put their own energy interests above those of other countries. No country is fully immune from outside influences. A continuum runs from independence to dependence. Superpowers are high on the continuum's independence end.

Energy superpowers also use their energy strengths to influence world supplies, and affect regional or world energy prices. Politically, energy super-powers use, or have the ability and determination to use, their energy to influence other countries' behaviour. Energy superpowers also use their massive energy supplies to strengthen their military capacity, through measures like guaranteeing fuel for their own armed forces and using taxes and economic rents from energy resources to fund their military might.

The environment is becoming more important in determining countries' international power in hard and soft terms. Energy conservation reduces a country's greenhouse gas (GHG) emissions, while enhancing its energy security position. US President Jimmy Carter understood this. In his famous 1977 television address, he stated that 'Ours is the most wasteful nation on earth. We waste more energy than we import.' He warned that if the US carried on its wasteful ways, 'Supplies will be uncertain.' America would become 'vulnerable to supply interruptions . . . . We will live in fear of embargoes. . . . Our energy problems have the same cause as our environmental problems—wasteful use of resources. Conservation helps us solve both at once. . . . We simply must balance our demand for energy with our rapidly shrinking resources' (Carter, 1977). Prophetic words.

Energy superpowers can strengthen their soft-power positions greatly by promoting a compelling, universal vision for the world's energy and environmental future. Facing the triple crisis of peak oil, climate change, and energy security, a paradigm shift that treated a unit of fossil-fuel energy saved as superior to one produced and consumed would enhance an energy superpower's world influence. To help shape the future, a country that has started the transition to a low fossil-fuel society would greatly enhance its energy superpower ambitions.

Middle Powers

Middle powers are different. Their position can be likened to that of the gap in a watermill to make flour. Middle powers struggle to maintain the space between the two millstones, so neither crushes them. The upper stone is comprised of several superpowers and great powers, while the lower stone encompasses the many countries with little influence or sovereignty. Middle powers struggle against becoming 'a functional part of empire', as Robert Cox (2005: 672) describes Canada's current position. They also resist descent onto the lower stone of international irrelevance. Middle powers usually support multilateralism, and make alliances with other middle powers to give their voices some weight, where often only the powerful matter. For most middle powers, becoming the dominant power in their region is a well-tested way to gain international recognition. Geography militates against this option for Canada. It is hard to be a regional power with only the US and Russia as your main neighbours.

Writing about India's long quest to become a great power, Nayar and Paul (2002: 5) highlight the threat from the upper millstone: 'The aim of entering the major power system is not simply for reasons of status or prestige, but rather for reasons of national survival and welfare, for middle powers are constantly confronted with the prospect of domination by the major powers.' I concur with Robert Cox (2006: 672) that during the Cold War, Canada stressed support for the United Nations and multilateralism 'as a counterweight against absorption into empire' and that this is 'realpolitik for a middle power'. As Cox notes, 'Recognition of sovereignty within a community of nations is a shield against the dominance inherent in a one-on-one unequal relationship.'

An energy middle power has sufficient sovereignty to be able to take care of its own citizens' energy and environmental security, while avoiding simply being a gas tank for empire. Working multilaterally 'to affirm the principle of adherence to acceptable rules of conduct for all powers, great and small' (Cox, 1989: 834), energy middle powers in the global North would do things like be good citizens of the International Energy Agency (IEA), strongly support European efforts to get broader adherence to curbing greenhouse gases, transition towards becoming low fossil-fuel societies, and fulfill commitments to post-Kyoto international agreements on climate change.

Satellites

Energy satellites are easy to describe. They are jurisdictions that lack the agency or determination to control their own resources. The corporations or government of another country or countries have first call on its energy resources, while the satellites' citizens stand at the back of the line in accessing their own resources. In 1959, Hugh Aitken captured the 'staples approach' view of this role for Canada:

> Canada, from the beginning of its history, has been a vulnerable economy, exposed to pressures and stimuli from more advanced nations. . . . Canada has never been master of its own destiny; as a satellitic staple-producing economy, it reflected, and still reflects, in its rate of development the imperatives of more advanced areas. (Aitken, 1959: 3)

Formulating his conception in the language of progress, Aitken saw more 'advanced' countries controlling their own fate. Does Aitken's view still hold, or has Canada climbed to the middle of the energy pack or to superpowerdom?

Energy Superpowers? Russia, Saudi Arabia, and the United States

Which countries are energy superpowers? Russia certainly is. Good cases can be made for Saudi Arabia and, surprisingly, the United States. Vladimir Putin's Russia makes the best case. We already looked briefly at Russia's prodigious oil and gas output and its use as a political weapon. The 1991 disintegration of the Soviet Union seemed to end Russia's overall superpower status. Russia's economy fell apart through the 1990s, and in August 1998 Russia defaulted on its debt. Most banks closed their doors (Goldman, 2008: 14). Russia was a basket case until rising oil and natural gas prices after 2000 revived it.

Under Putin, Russia began a global trend to re-nationalizing the oil industry. Corporations that are fully or dominantly government-owned now control about 80 per cent of the world's oil reserves (West, 2007). Today's big, private oil transnationals—remnants of the famed 'Seven Sisters' of oil that long dominated the oil world—are puny by comparison. ExxonMobil, BP, Chevron, and Shell now hold just 3 per cent of the world's oil reserves, and produce about 10 per cent of its oil and gas (Hoyos, 2007).

States can use private, domestically owned corporations as national champions to project foreign policy. The US and Britain have long used their big oil and gas companies to do that, as David Painter shows (1986). But, government-owned companies can be even better foreign policy instruments, since they are under direct state control. By their nature, they adopt economic nationalist strategies and generally put the interests of their citizens, or those of elites close to government, above those of exporters and other countries. Through its re-nationalized oil and gas corporations, Russia is also spearheading an Asian-based movement towards long-term oil contracts. The latter are undermining the dominance of the Anglo-American led spot-markets, where oil has been global, liberalized, open, and fungible (Stroupe, 2006). Fungible commodities are those whose individual units are capable of mutual substitution or interchangeability. If long-term oil contracts prevail, as in the 1970s, oil boycotts directed at particular countries could become effective weapons again, because targeted states would have difficulty obtaining oil from alternate sources (ibid.).

Russia cut natural gas exports to Ukraine in 2006 and 2009 to project its power. In doing so, it inadvertently sideswiped Western Europe and caused shortages there because the main gas pipeline to Europe runs through Ukraine. Russia has also cut natural gas exports to neighbouring Belarus and Georgia. Gas consumers feel the pain of supply cut-offs much more quickly than oil consumers because, unlike oil, it is difficult to store large quantities in strategic reserves. Liquefied natural gas, LNG, is very expensive. Russia is attempting to set up an OPEC-style cartel, the 'Gas Exporting Countries Forum', among 14 natural-gas exporting countries, including Qatar and Iran. Russia, Qatar, and Iran control 56 per cent of the world's natural gas reserves (Vasilyeva, 2008; IEA, 2008: 42). At present, gas has mainly regional rather than global markets (Yedlin, 2008). But, the cartel could become important if LNG exports rise substantially. Although Russian revenues fell substantially in the economic crisis of 2008–9, Russia had used its 'cash blizzard' from petroleum exports to repay most of its foreign debts and massively raise military funding (Goldman, 2008: 207).

Is Saudi Arabia the second energy superpower? At 10.7 million barrels/day of oil[4] and 12.6 per cent of global oil output, Saudi Arabia is the world's foremost oil producer and exporter. Saudi Arabia also claims to have the world's greatest oil reserves, although there is good reason to be skeptical (EIA, 2008e).[5] Unlike Russia, Saudi Arabia is big only in oil. It ranks tenth in natural gas, sixty-seventh in coal, and twentieth in electricity. The Saudis are the fourth largest producer of all forms of energy (EIA, 2008e).

Saudi Arabia's oil prowess alone gives it energy superpower credibility. It has used its great capacity to act as the world's 'swing producer', raising output when world prices are too high and dropping output when prices fall too low. The major question over its energy superpower claims is how independent Saudi Arabia is from US power. True superpowers must not be dependencies. When Franklin Roosevelt met Ibn Saud in 1945, it is thought that they struck a deal that remains intact today (Strahan, 2007: 171).[6] The US would guarantee the security of Saudi Arabia and the house of Saud in return for assured US access to Saudi oil. The Saudi regime is weakly legitimated. Most Saudis adhere to the Wahhabist or unitarian form of Islam, which advocates a return to early Islamic practices and warns against moral decline. Its puritanical values are contradicted by the 'venal, bloated, and Western-leaning' royal family (ibid., 170). Violent attacks against the regime have been frequent, including several against Saudi oil facilities. It is widely thought that the regime would fall quickly without US backing. Thus, claims to Saudi energy superpowerdom stand on shaky grounds. The country does not project economic, military, political, and cultural power on a world scale, even in energy. Saudi Arabia is not really an energy superpower.

What about the United States, which is a net importer of more oil (12.4 million barrels/day) than the world's next three largest oil importers combined (Japan 5.1 million barrels; China 3.4 million barrels; Germany 2.5 million barrels) (EIA, 2006)? Does oil import dependence rule out US energy superpowerdom? Perhaps. But American oil dependence hides its still bountiful energy supplies. America is the world's greatest 'primary energy producer'[7] when all forms of energy are considered—oil, natural gas, coal, and most forms of energy to produce electricity. The US is second in natural gas and coal production, and first in electricity. US petroleum output is still impressive. At 8.3 million barrels/day, its output is third, not that far behind Saudi Arabia (10.7) and Russia (9.7). US output is twice that of fourth-place Iran (EIA, 2008g; EIA, 2006). Only its super wasteful appetite for oil makes the US seem like an energy also-ran. The US has 4.6 per cent of the world's people (US Census Bureau, 2008),[8] produces 10 per cent of the world's oil, and consumes 24 per cent of it (EIA, 2008b).[9] If it achieved Jimmy Carter's 1977 goal of living off its own energy carrying capacity, it could achieve the long-sought goal of energy independence. The average American would still have access to more than double the world's per capita level of oil use. US profligacy makes it energy-insecure and pushes it towards imperial adventures to find oil under someone else's sands. 'Slowly but surely,' argues Michael Klare (2004:

Table 8.1   Canada: Energy Superpower? Oil and Natural Gas Production and Projections by Country

Country	Oil 2006–7	Oil 2030	Natural Gas 2006	Natural Gas 2030
Russia	9.9 mb/day (11.9% of world total)	9.5 mb/day	22% of world total	17.9% of world total
Saudi Arabia	10.7 mb/day (12.6% of world total)	15.6 mb/day	2.5% of world total	2.6–2.8% of world total
US	8.3 mb/day (10% of world total)	7.1 mb/day	17.8% of world total	11.6% of world total
Canada	3.4 mb/day (4% of world total)	7.8 mb/day	6.3% of world total	3.7% of world total

Source: Calculated from IEA (2008: 267, 272, 287, 290).

7, 11), 'the US military is being converted into a global oil-protection service . . . . Dependence often requires us to grant all sorts of favors to the leaders of our major foreign suppliers, whether we like them or not.' The imperial route chooses dependency, whereas energy conservation chooses independence. Despite such vulnerability, when total US energy output is combined with its military and diplomatic dominance, a strong case can be made that the US, along with Russia, is one of the world's two energy superpowers.

How does Canada rank as a primary energy producer? Canada is seventh in the world in oil, third in natural gas, twelfth in coal, and sixth in electricity (EIA, 2008a). Overall, Canada is the world's fifth greatest producer of primary energy. Does this make Canada an energy superpower? Not on current output (see Table 8.1). How many energy superpowers can the world support?

However, Stephen Harper's claims were for the future. Will Canada become the energy superpower of his dreams? The International Energy Agency (IEA, 2008: 249, 262) projects that Canada will produce 7.8 million barrels of oil per day in 2030, 7.5 per cent of the world's projected total of 103.8 million barrels/day. If so, Canada would almost double its share from the current 4 per cent level and be catapulted from seventh to third place. Counterbalancing Canada's projected oil gains, however, are anticipated declines in natural gas production. IEA figures project Canada's share of global gas output to fall from 6.4 per cent to 3.7 per cent, and its world ranking to fall from third to fifth place (2008: 290).

How good are IEA projections? The IEA explains that they should not be taken as forecasts of what is likely to happen. Rather they are 'a baseline vision of how energy markets are likely to develop should government policy making develop no further' (ibid., 61). Thus, unforeseen physical, political, and economic turns are likely to intervene in ways not currently anticipated. The further out the projections, the shakier they get. I am very skeptical that Canada's oil output will reach anywhere near the 7.8 million barrels/day forecast for 2030. The IEA projects that three-quarters (5.9 million barrels/day) of Canada's 2030 total will come from the tar sands, while it foresees Canada's conventional output to fall by 10 per cent, to 1.9 million barrels/day (ibid., 267).

Limits to Increasing Tar Sands Output

I have not analyzed IEA forecasts for other countries, but watch the tar sands closely. The development of oil from this source is fraught with more difficulties than conventional oil. There is good reason to believe that physical and political obstacles will limit tar sands output by 2030 to no more than about 3 million barrels/day, about half the IEA's forecast, and perhaps to less than that. If so, in two decades, Canada would produce 5 million barrels/day at most, or less than 5 per cent of the global total. This level would likely move Canada up the global oil ranking only moderately, all other things being equal.

Current technologies use vast amounts of water and energy to separate oil from the tarry sands in both surface mining and deep extraction methods. Studies show that the Athabasca River basin, the world's third largest, cannot support a fivefold increase in tar sands output from the 2007 level of 1.2 million barrels/day (Griffiths, 2006; Schindler et al, 2007). Two to 4.5 barrels of water are used to make one barrel of tar sands oil. Unlike municipal water systems, only 10 per cent of the water used in the tar sands is returned, in this case to the Athabasca River. Six cubic metres of toxic tailings waste is created for every cubic metre of bitumen mined. A 2006 Pembina Institute study concluded that 'though technologies are being developed, none are expected to reduce the oil sands' thirst for water before 2030' (Griffiths, 2006). There is growing recognition of the dire consequences. Peter Lougheed, former Conservative Premier of Alberta, insists that the province must treat water rather than oil and gas as Alberta's most important resource. 'Oil is a depleting resource', he observes. 'You could even consider a world where technological developments reduce the need for oil. But I don't see anything that's going to change with respect to water' (Finlay, 2008; Kom, 2007).

Equally troubling for tar sands expansion plans is its poor energy return on investment. This return is calculated by dividing the amount of energy produced by the amount used. The tar sands energy return is 'probably far less than one unit of energy consumed for every 5 units of energy produced', according to Thomas Homer-Dixon (2007: 51, 93).[10] Vast amounts of natural gas are needed to produce bitumen and upgrade it to more valuable synthetic crude. Söderbergh et al. calculated that to make one barrel of deep extraction (in situ) oil, it takes 1,700 cubic feet of natural gas, an equivalent energy expenditure of 30 per cent (Söderbergh et al., 2007: 1938). With only eight years left of 'established reserves' of natural gas for Alberta (Alberta Energy, 2007),[11] it is very unlikely that by 2015 to 2020 the province could simultaneously (1) supply most of Canada's gas market, as at present, (2) export more than half its gas to the US, as is virtually mandated by the proportionality clause in the Canada–US Free Trade Agreement (FTA; see below), and (3) fuel a fivefold expansion of the tar sands. Without additional sources of natural gas, alternative fuels, or spectacular efficiency improvements, the tar sands will not produce 5.9 million barrels/day by 2030.

On and off for 35 years, proposals have been in the works to bring natural gas from the Northwest Territories by pipeline down the Mackenzie Valley. In the current proposal, the line would end at the tar sands, for use there. If it gets built, an uncertainty at the time of writing, the pipeline would never be able to fuel more than 40 per cent of the natural gas demands of the tar sands projects (Moorhouse, 2006: 13). Furthermore, shipments would last for only 9–20 years, depending on the volume supplied (Cizek, 2007). After reviewing the fuelling of the tar sands, Söderbergh and his colleagues (2007: 1937, 1941) concluded that 'the current dependence on natural gas is unsustainable for the expanding Canadian oil sands.' Nuclear energy is a possible substitute fuel, but this could not be in place for at least a decade, and, needless to say, carries other serious hazards. A technique involving gasifying bitumen bottoms, or asphaltenes, to produce hydrogen, steam, and power, avoids using natural gas. It is touted as a solution to the looming gas shortage. The major drawback is that it emits more CO_2 than using natural gas (Toman et al., 2008: 21–2).

If physical problems to rapid tar sands expansion loom large, political obstacles also are building. This is especially true in the United States, the only importer of sizable amounts of tar sands oil, where a growing movement is attempting to block 'dirty oil' imports. California Congressman Henry Waxman inserted Section 526 in the 2007 US Energy Independence and Security Act. It states that no federal agency shall use a synthetic fuel, produced from non-conventional petroleum sources, unless its life cycle of GHG emissions are equal to or less than that of conventional fuel.[12] The military and post office are the US government's biggest oil consumers. Their use of tar sands oil could be stopped. A Rand study reports that without carbon sequestration, tar sands oil emits 15–20 per cent more CO_2 than conventional oil (Toman et al., 2008: xvi).

While interpretation of Section 526 was mired in controversy, its importance lies in whether it is a harbinger of US policy under President Barack Obama on all tar sands oil imports, not just those for government use. At the time of writing, Obama's stance on importing tar sands oil was unclear. During the election campaign, Obama vowed to break America's addiction to 'dirty, dwindling, and dangerously expensive' oil (Alberts, 2008). His energy advisers support low-carbon fuel standards, and Henry Waxman was elected chairman of the powerful Congressional Committee on Energy and Commerce in December 2008. Stephen Harper's government is clearly fearful (Simpson, 2009). Ottawa and Alberta talk bravely about exporting to other countries if the US blocks tar sands imports. But they can't walk the talk. The option to export to third countries is severely limited now and in the near future by a lack of pipeline capacity to Canada's coasts for transhipment overseas by tanker. Asia is the main alternative market discussed. At the moment, it is mainly a hypothetical possibility. In 2007, Canada exported 26,800 barrels of conventional and tar sands oil to Asia, about 1 per cent of Canada's total gross oil exports (CAPP, 2008: 14).

On the east coast, Newfoundland and Labrador produces 12 per cent of Canadian oil and exports about half of it (Tobin, 2005; Canada–Newfoundland Board, 2008).[13] It does not need pipelines to get its oil to market. Since its oil is sweet light crude, it does not figure in the dirty oil debate. Alberta is the source of 68 per cent of Canada's total oil output (Tobin, 2005: Annex, slide 3) and all of its tar sands output. Most of Canada's current and planned oil pipelines are aimed from Alberta southeast towards Chicago and US Gulf coast refineries. Only two pipelines, now in development, could bring tar sands and conventional oil to Asian markets. The first is Enbridge's Northern Gateway pipeline, being built from Edmonton to the Pacific port of Kitimat, BC. To be completed by 2012 to 2014, it is designed to carry 400,000 barrels/day of crude for transhipment by tanker either to the US west coast or to Asia (Tobin, 2005: 25–6; CAPP, 2008: 25–6). The second, and only other, pipeline system that could take significant quantities of oil to oceanside is that south of the Great Lakes, which brings conventional and tar sands oil from western Canada through Wisconsin, Illinois, and Michigan for sale in those states. Much of what is transported through this line goes on to Sarnia, Ontario, for refining and for the petrochemicals industry in that city. Enbridge proposed to reverse its Trailbreaker line from Sarnia to Montreal, which used to send western Canadian oil to Montreal between 1976 and 1999, but has since brought imported oil into southern Ontario. If re-reversed, at a cost of about $350 million, the pipeline would take western Canadian oil to Montreal. However, the plan is to ship 60 per cent or more of it past Montreal to the existing line to Portland, Maine. Although some of western Canada's oil (conventional and tar sands oil) may stay in Montreal, 128,000 barrels/day could go to Maine, to be shipped by tanker. The plan to re-reverse the line has been shelved indefinitely due to the economic recession of 2008–9. The earliest expected completion date is 2012 (Canwest, 2008). By combining Enbridge's Northern Gateway and Trailbreaker pipelines, Canada could divert future oil exports to third countries by an additional half-million barrels/day by 2012 to

2014, if the US barred dirty Canadian oil imports. This amount pales, though, compared to tar sands output of 1.3 million barrels/day in 2007 and projected tar sands output of 2.2 to 2.5 million barrels/day by 2014. It takes at least four to five years to build a new pipeline (CAPP, 2008: ii; Tobin, 2005: ii), so there will not be new capacity to add to possible exports to Asia soon. Thus, Canada's and Alberta's threat to take their dirty oil elsewhere is hollow.

Canada could conceivably export its conventional oil—about 2.1 million barrels/day—to the US, and reserve tar sands oil for domestic use. This is not a politically palatable option. Already, there is opposition in Quebec to taking Alberta's tar sands oil (Francoeur, 2008: A5). Popular opinion would likely be strongly opposed straight across Canada, and could well overturn governments that chose to pursue such a policy. Under this option, Canada's GHG count would rise alarmingly on a per capita basis, because GHGs are attributed to the country using the energy. International opinion would likely label Canada an environmental rogue state. A polar opposite strategy would be to find a big new market in eastern Canada for conventional oil from the West; today, eastern Canada imports almost one million barrels/day, much of it from insecure OPEC suppliers. This Canada-first option is expanded on below.

Finlandization

So far we have looked only at whether Canadian oil output will likely reach 7.8 million barrels/day by 2030. But very high energy production is only one criterion in assessing whether a country is an energy superpower. A superpower must also avoid what was called 'Finlandization' during the Cold War, to denote a country that, though formally sovereign, failed to challenge a more powerful neighbour in foreign policy. In contrast, energy superpowers put their own energy interests first and wield their massive energy resources to gain international influence. Canada fails on both counts, and could be said to be a contemporary exemplar of Finlandization on energy policy.

The 'Finlandization' of Canada began with the proportionality clause of the FTA (Laxer and Dillon, 2008) in 1989, coincidentally just as the Soviet empire was collapsing. An obscure sounding clause, proportionality was first placed in the Canada–US Free Trade Agreement. It gives the US first access to the majority of Canada's oil and natural gas output. The clause was transferred to the North American Free Trade Agreement (NAFTA) in 1994, as Article 605, prohibiting Canada from lowering the share of its total export shipments in specific energy goods relative to its total supply in the most recent three-year period, even if Canadians experience shortages. Currently, Canada exports two-thirds of its oil and about 56 per cent of its natural gas to the US, shares the clause effectively locks into place. In practice, proportionality guarantees the US first call on the majority of Canada's oil and natural gas in perpetuity, or until NAFTA and the FTA are renegotiated or ended. Or until the resources run out.

Mexico, too, is a major oil exporting country and the third country in NAFTA. But Mexico resisted strong pressure from US negotiators to cave on proportionality by refusing loss of sovereignty over oil and gas (Salinas, 2002: 72). Mexico's refusal was also a boon to the US, freeing the Americans from an obligation to maintain the current proportion of natural gas exports to Mexico in the event that the US experiences domestic shortages.[14] The proportionality clause formally applies to the US in its trade with Canada, but the US is not a significant exporter of oil, accounting for only 2.2 per cent of Canadian oil imports. Since the US imports almost 60 per cent of the oil it uses, it is, in effect, re-exporting oil it imports (EIA, 2008i).[15] Proportionality is thus a de facto Canadian obligation.

The proportionality proviso in the FTA and NAFTA is 'unique in all of the world's treaties', writes Richard Heinberg (2008), a noted California author on energy issues. 'Canada has every reason to repudiate the proportionality clause,' Heinberg continues, 'and to do so unilaterally and immediately.' Mexico's refusal on proportionality shows it is not prepared to surrender the same degree of energy sovereignty as Canada. Yet, no one calls Mexico an energy superpower.

Since signing the FTA in 1988, Conservative governments have been committed to strengthening Canada's role as an exporter of raw energy resources to the United States. The Liberals won the 1993 federal election on a promise to renegotiate NAFTA and get the Mexican exemption on proportionality. But the Chrétien government quickly caved in, and the Liberal position has been essentially the same as the Conservatives ever since. In 2005, Paul Martin's Liberal government signed the 'Security and Prosperity Partnership' (SPP), which deepens Canada's role as a major protector of US energy security and neglects Canadian energy security. Harper's Conservatives are even more enthusiastic backers of the SPP. On energy, Canada does not even act like an independent country, let alone a superpower.

Energy Middle Power

If Stephen Harper's claim that Canada is an emerging energy superpower can be dismissed as political hyperbole, is Canada credibly an energy middle power? As the world's fifth largest producer of primary energy, Canada easily has the capacity to claim the title. But, as we saw, Canada's poor policy choices tend to trump its energy potential. To be an energy middle power, a country must exercise sufficient sovereignty to take care of its citizens' energy security and environmental well-being. It must also resist alienating control over domestic energy resources to a more powerful neighbour and actively support multilateral action to cut carbon emissions and tackle the challenge of peak oil.

How does Canada measure up to these criteria? Not well. Canada is recklessly unprepared for the next global oil supply crisis. Despite its abundance of oil, Canada is more vulnerable than any other IEA country to short-term shocks because it is the only country in the 28-member International Energy Agency without strategic petroleum reserves (SPRs).[16] (The US has the world's largest SPRs.) While exporting 65 per cent of its oil, Canada imports 49 per cent of the oil it uses in refineries. In 2007, 49.6 per cent of those imports came from OPEC countries (Statistics Canada, 2008b), compared to 44.4 per cent for the US (EIA, 2008h). American presidents talk loudly about reducing dependence on Middle Eastern oil and gaining 'energy independence'. Canadian prime ministers never talk about Canadians' growing vulnerability from OPEC imports. Nor have any uttered the words 'energy independence' since the end of the National Energy Program in the early 1980s.

The world is about to experience a series of international oil supply shocks over the next decade. When the first one strikes, countries lacking at least one of the following alternatives will experience the severest crisis: (1) long-term oil supply contracts; (2) the military might to requisition other countries' oil; (3) prioritization of their own citizens' needs above exports; or (4) strategic petroleum reserves. Despite its oil abundance, Canada is in the severe-crisis camp. It currently lacks all four options.

Canada has insufficient oil pipelines to supply the whole domestic market and no plans for what to do when the era of cheap oil ends. SPRs are ideal to mitigate against temporary supply cuts. The IEA requires all members to maintain an emergency oil reserve of 90 days and exempts only net oil exporters, on the sensible assumption that they meet domestic needs before shipping surpluses abroad. Canada was specifically exempted from establishing reserves, the National Energy Board (NEB, 2007) explains, 'on the grounds that Canada is a net exporting country whereas the other members are net importers'. The NEB neglects to mention Norway, also a net oil exporter, which the IEA does not require to have SPRs. Despite this, Norway acts prudently and requires oil companies to stock a set level of oil reserves for use during an emergency (Hubbard and Weiner, 1985: 528). It ensures that its own citizens are supplied before exporting excess amounts.[17] When asked whether Canada needs SPRs, Matt Simmons, chairman of the Houston-based Simmons and Company International, the world's largest energy investment bank, replies, 'Do you Canadians use oil? Of course you need SPRs. Governments often don't look after their own citizens well, but they are not going to look after citizens in another country.'[18] Simmons adds that if Canada does not secure oil supplies for its own citizens, no one else will.

The IEA exemption for Canada regarding SPRs is not warranted. Canada acts like an oil importing country, and NAFTA's energy 'proportionality clause' undercuts the logic behind the IEA exemption. Thus, unknown to most Canadians, they are uniquely open to international disruptions in oil supplies. The NEB (2007), whose mandate is to ensure the long-term security of supply for Canadians, writes that, 'Unfortunately, the NEB has not undertaken any studies on security of supply.' This is an astonishing admission for a body started in 1959 to do precisely that. Canada does not act prudently because, it appears, current federal leaders and top civil servants are too intent on ensuring American security of supply rather than Canadian, and because they hesitate to take any action that might run counter to the short-term interests of the producer provinces (especially Alberta), their political leaders, and the provincial and national cash registers. The lesson of the savaged National Energy Program of the early 1980s is not soon forgotten: Canada's federal system of government makes it extremely difficult, and politically risky, for federal leaders to craft policy for the longer term that might intrude on provincial jurisdiction.

By not having SPRs, Canada is not acting like a good IEA member, something one would expect of an energy middle power. Unlike all other IEA members, Canada would not have SPR oil to share with member countries if an international emergency occurs (IEA, 2008).[19]

Strategic petroleum reserves help short-term crunches only. Unlike most countries, Canada has the potential to secure fossil-fuel energy supplies for the medium term and become a leader in moving towards a low-carbon society, but only if it reverses policy direction. To ensure the long-term security of supply, Canada could revert to the Canada-first policies in place before the 1985 Western Accord and 1989 Free Trade Agreement. Those policies disallowed the export of natural gas unless there were 25 years of 'proven' supply for Canadians' use. Reversion to such a policy would also mean that when Canadians cut fossil-fuel usage, the surplus energy saved would not be exported to the US—under an even higher proportion with NAFTA. Canada could become a leader in cutting carbon emissions. This strategy is outlined below.

Canada: A Green Middle Power?

Canada is quickly running out of natural gas, and has only 9.3 years of proven supplies left (Hughes, 2008). Yet, Canada cannot stretch out dwindling stocks for Canadian needs by cutting exports because it has to make over half of its natural gas available to the US under NAFTA's proportionality clause. If Canada ended natural gas exports, it could extend proven supplies to about 20 years. Canada will not run out of natural gas in either 9 or 20 years, because each year additional gas sources are found. Once discovered, they become 'proven'.

But the trend is downward. Canadian natural gas output peaked in 2002, and despite more rigs, new finds are not replacing drawdowns in most years.[20] Canadians could soon be relying on liquefied natural gas from politically unreliable Russia or Algeria to heat their homes in winter.

As we have seen, the fall in Canada's natural gas supplies is also due to the use of natural gas in the rapid expansion of tar sands oil, most of which is earmarked for US markets. Alan Greenspan, then chairman of the Federal Reserve, recognized this in 2003 when he told a US Senate committee that Canada had little capacity to significantly expand its natural gas exports, in part because of the role that Canadian gas plays in supporting growing oil production from tar sands (www.baglino.com/writing/LNGmemotoPOTUS. pdf). A prudent policy for an energy middle power would see Canada protecting diminishing domestic supplies for use in Canada's severe winters and for higher-end applications in petrochemical, fertilizer, and plastics industries. The Canadian government is not moving in these directions.

On the environmental front, Canada is dragging its heels, too. Instead of being a middle power in the idealistic sense of leading a moral campaign to cut greenhouse gas emissions, in the image of a Lloyd Axworthy (see Nossal, Chapter 2, this volume) on the environment, Canada is one of the world's great environmental laggards. By signing the Kyoto Accord in 1997, Canada pledged to reduce GHG emissions to 6 per cent below its 1990 level by 2008–12. Contrary to this commitment, however, it has done nothing serious to make it happen. By 2004, Canada's emissions were 25 per cent above the 1990 level and 'the underlying trend is strongly upwards', according to the Pembina Institute (2008). Emissions from oil and gas production, transmission, and distribution account for 20 per cent of the total, while electricity generation accounts for 16 per cent. Only government regulations and programs can have major influences over such emissions. In contrast, with passenger cars (which includes trucks) and residences, where individual decisions make a big difference, the share of emissions is only 10 per cent and 6 per cent, respectively. With energy-related CO_2 accounting for 61 per cent of GHGs (IEA, 2008: 407), curbing energy use and boosting non-fossil energy sources are crucial.

While paying lip service to the Kyoto Accord, Stephen Harper's government set a new goal of a 20 per cent reduction of GHGs by 2020. This was from the 2006 base, not from Kyoto's 1990 base year. If this goal were met, Canada would still fall short of its 1997 Kyoto commitments—a decade after the deadline. Furthermore, Canadian policy relies on annual 'intensity' improvements, not actual GHG reductions (ibid., 425). As it stands, there is little chance this revised goal will be met because little enforcement is envisaged. Canada's framework delays application of its emissions reductions for the tar sands by a decade, to 2018. The Pembina Institute concludes that the compliance options are complex, and some 'represent uncertain amounts of emissions reductions occurring at an uncertain future date' (Bramley and Demerse, 2008: 3). The 2009 Climate Change Performance Index ranks Canada second last of 60 countries on CO_2 emissions. Only Saudi Arabia was worse (Germanwatch, 2009).[21]

We have reviewed Canada's oil and natural gas policies and to a lesser extent its environmental policies. It is clear that while Canada could be an energy middle power, it is not acting like one. But, in one way, Canada is doing so—in its level of GHGs released. With 0.5 per cent of the world's population, Canada emits about 2.7 per cent of the world's GHGs (IEA, 2008: 382).[22] Canada would have to reverse direction if it were to assume an idealistic role of middle-power leadership in tackling the world's triple enviro-energy crisis.

Energy Satellite

The middle-power concept was developed by John Holmes and others as an alternative to the thesis that Canada is a US satellite (Cox, 1989: 823). There is a plausible argument that Canada is still a middle power in many respects, although since the end of the Cold War, Canada has moved from having had a distinctive foreign policy emphasizing multilateralism and peacekeeping to much greater dependence on the US, and has acted as a military deputy sheriff. As we have seen, Canada is highly unlikely to become the energy superpower of Stephen Harper's dreams. Canada is also not acting like an energy middle power. That leaves one possibility—that Canada is the energy and resource satellite that the staples approach long diagnosed it to be.

NAFTA's proportionality clause is the most important factor in making Canada an energy satellite. A colony or satellite loses control of its resources to a foreign power. Canada is prohibited from using its oil to supply half its citizens during international shortages. No other developed country is forbidden from using domestic resources to provide for its own citizens. When you cannot safeguard your citizens against freezing in the dark, or control how much you export, or set the price at which citizens buy back their own energy from foreign transnational corporations, you are more of a satellite than a superpower.

Canada used to hold two balls in the air at once. The first ball held up Canadian energy needs from domestic resources supplied by domestically controlled corporations, and used Canadian-owned pipelines located on Canadian territory. The 1980 National Energy Policy (NEP) represented the pinnacle of the first ball. The second ball has been that of a northern, satellitic energy supplier to the US. Now only the satellite ball is in the air. Canada, though, has a new NEP—No Energy Policy. If Canadian energy policies are now geared towards enhancing US rather than Canadian energy security, is there an alternative course?

Conclusion: Security and Powerdown

All US presidents since Richard Nixon have promised Americans energy independence. Their main worry has been the vulnerability of oil imports. In contrast, Canadian prime ministers never talk about energy independence, and enthusiastically support Canada's role as an energy satellite, which undermines energy security for Canadians. In a country where winter is the dominant season, energy insecurity could have serious consequences. The irony is that while American presidents have pledged energy independence, the US has gotten steadily more dependent. In contrast, Canadian prime ministers never talk about energy independence but could easily achieve it. Canada exports more energy than it uses. Why would Canada want energy independence? To achieve security of supply and a low-fossil-fuel society. Let's examine the latter.

Besides undermining Canadian energy security, NAFTA's proportionality clause cuts the umbilical cord connecting energy use with energy output in Canada. Every unit of oil, natural gas, or electricity that Canadians conserve will likely be exported to the US, and Canada consequently would be locked into an even higher proportional export obligation. The ratchet goes only one way. Thus, a big drop in Canadian oil and gas use, while good in itself, would not lead to a commensurate fall in domestic energy output and GHG emissions. The fastest-growing source of Canada's GHG emissions is oil production, not consumption. Would Canadians agree to drive smart cars or switch to transit or bicycles if it simply meant that more Americans could drive SUVs and Hummers, while GHG emissions remained constant? The perversity of proportionality is that if the US cuts energy consumption, it boosts their energy independence, whereas if Canadians cut energy use, more will be exported to the US. Canadians will substantially cut fossil fuel use only if the government adopts a Canada-first energy policy, so that when Canadians seriously conserve, fossil-fuel output drops commensurately.

The main US choice is to go really green and substantially cut fossil-fuel use, or adopt aggressive tactics, including war, to get other people's oil. Going green opts for independence. Empire opts for coercion, war, and dependence. Canada's main choice, in contrast, is to gain energy sovereignty so it can go green or to emit lots of GHGs by guaranteeing high oil and gas exports to the US, at the same time supporting American adventures abroad for oil.

There is a widespread, naive trust that if we start running out of cheap oil, we will easily find or substitute other cheap forms. Technology to the rescue. Business as usual. We can live in suburbia, drive SUVs, fly airplanes, and easily switch to the same quantity and price of energy from wind, solar, hybrid, nuclear, or other forms. Such faith has no basis in reality. The main solution lies in a paradigm shift towards a conserver society, where social, political, and lifestyle changes will lead to energy security and a powered-down society (Heinberg, 2004). Canada could set the goals of achieving the British and French levels of fossil-fuel use. Both countries have twice Canada's population, yet use less oil than Canadians. A Canadian energy and environmental security strategy is possible (Laxer, 2007).

Canada produces 3.23 million barrels/day of oil and consumes 1.8 million barrels daily. Tar sands production is currently about 1.3 million barrels/day. Since conventional oil output is 2.1 million barrels/day, Canadians can live on conventional oil and phase out tar sands production altogether. Canadians could then cut oil use to British and French levels, and easily live on slowly falling conventional supplies. Canada could become a world leader in learning to live within its own carrying capacity. Forget energy superpower pipedreams, Canada should become a super conserver and an international environment protector.

Notes

Thanks to Tom Keating for a very helpful discussion. The views and weaknesses of this chapter are mine.

1. In 2007, Russia produced 9.88 million barrels of oil per day out of a world total of 84.4 million.
2. Russia produced 23.2 trillion cubic feet of natural gas in 2006, out of a total of 103.98 trillion cubic feet in the world.
3. Canadian oil production was 3.42 million barrels/day in 2007 out of a world total of 84.4 million barrels/day. Canada's natural gas production in 2006 was 6.55 trillion cubic feet out of a total of 103.98 trillion cubic feet in the world. Its natural gas production rose to 6.6 trillion cubic feet in 2007. World production levels were not available for 2007. Russian gas production fell slightly in 2007, to 23.1 trillion cubic feet.
4. This is Saudi Arabia's normal level of oil production, but as the world's 'swing' producer it sometimes cuts production considerably when the world's oil price falls, as it did in the autumn and winter of 2008–9.
5. The Saudis claim 262.3 billion barrels of proven reserves. This number is as reliable as the government that provided the information. Saudi Arabia raised its official reserves by 50 per cent in 1989 after several OPEC countries raised theirs. Curiously, the Kingdom's reserves have not fallen after an additional 20 years. Official reserves have stayed in the 260 to 266 billion barrel range between 1990 and 2007.
6. The meeting was unminuted, but it is widely understood that this was the arrangement, confirmed by over 60 years of quite consistent practice (Strahan, 2007: 171).
7. The EIA defines primary power as the production of petroleum (crude oil and natural gas plant liquids), dry natural gas, and coal, and net generation of hydroelectric, nuclear, and geothermal, solar, wind, and wood and waste electric power.
8. The US had 303.8 million people in a world population of close to 6.7 billion.
9. US oil production averaged 8.48 million barrels/day in 2007. Total world supply was 84.64 million barrels/day. US consumption averaged 20.7 million barrels/day in the third quarter of 2007, compared to 85.25 million barrels/day. Oil is defined by the EIA as crude oil (including lease condensate), natural gas plant liquids, and other liquids and refinery processing gains and losses.
10. Homer-Dixon (2007) points out that the calorific output of 30 cubic metres of natural

gas is about one-fifth that of a barrel of crude oil. A complete estimate of energy return on investment must include energy involved in mining, transporting, pumping water, and disposing of wastes.

11. Alberta's Energy Department pegged 'remaining established reserves' at 41 trillion cubic feet (tcf), and annual production at 5.081 tcf (Alberta, 2008). That means there are 8.07 years of established remaining reserves for Alberta. The department estimates a further 51 tcf are 'yet to be established'.

12. Waxman was then chairman of the Congressional Committee on Oversight of Government Reform.

13. In a personal communication, 17 Jan. 2008, Professor Wade Locke, an energy economist at Memorial University, wrote: 'I do not know if anyone tracks where the oil is sold. None of it is processed within Newfoundland, but beyond it can go anywhere in the world.'

14. Thanks to Larry Hughes for making this point. The US imported 8.32 million barrels/day of oil in 2005 and exported 1.05 million barrels/ day in 2004. The US produced 490.1 billion cubic feet of natural gas in 2005 and exported 19.8 billion cubic feet that year. Thanks to Ryan Katz-Rozene for this research.

15. The EIA calculates that the US exports about 1.4 million barrels of oil daily, not an insignificant amount. This is about 12 per cent of US imports. Since the oil industry considers North America to be a single market, a lot of product goes back and forth across the border.

16. The IEA states that its main objective has been to 'increase energy security'. Member countries agree to undertake joint measures to mitigate the impact of oil supply emergencies. Establishing strategic petroleum reserves is one of these mitigating measures (IEA, 2007: 15–16).

17. Norway imports a small amount of specialty-grade oil from Russia. Ole Gunnar Austvik, e-mail to author, 14 May 2007.

18. Matt Simmons, telephone conversation with author, 31 Jan. 2008.

19. The IEA would call on Canada to supply 'surge' oil production in a crisis, but Canada could add little because there is not much shut-in potential.

20. In 13 of the first 18 years under the FTA (1989–2006), drawdowns exceeded new finds (Statistics Canada, 2008a).

21. The index ranks countries on a combination of three criteria: emissions trend (50 per cent weighting); emissions level (30 per cent weighting); climate policy (20 per cent weighting).

22. The IEA (2008: 382) puts total world GHG emissions at 28 billion tonnes per year. Canada emitted 747 million tonnes in 2005 (Pembina Institute, 2008).

References

Aitken, Hugh G.J. 1959. 'The Changing Structure of the Canadian Economy with Particular Reference to the Influence of the United States', in Aitken et al., eds, *The American Economic Impact on Canada*. Durham, NC: Duke University Press.

Alberta Energy. 2007. Natural Gas Statistics 2007. At: <www.energy.gov.ab.ca/NaturalGas/727. asp>. (28 Mar. 2008)

Alberts, Sheldon. 2008. 'Obama's Fight against "Dirty Oil" Could Hurt Oil Sands', *National Post*, 24 June. At: <www.nationalpost.com/most_popular/story.html?id=610810>. (16 Feb. 2009)

Bramley, Matthew, and Clare Demerse. 2008. *Evaluation of the Government of Canada's Greenhouse Gas Reduction Policies*. Drayton Valley, Alta: Pembina Institute. At: <pubs.pembina.org/reports/questionaire-ccpi-2009-final.pdf>. (3 Jan. 2009)

Canada–Newfoundland and Labrador Offshore Petroleum Board. 2008. At: <www.cnlopb. nl.ca/>. (16 Feb. 2009)

Canwest News Service. 2008. 'Quebec Eco Group Targets Oilsands Pipeline Project', *Edmonton Journal*, 6 Nov, A5.

Canadian Association of Petroleum Producers (CAPP). 2008. 'Crude Oil Forecast, Markets and Pipeline Expansions', June. At: <www.capp.ca/default.asp?v_DOC_ID=7638PubID=138225>. (14 July 2008)

Carter, Jimmy. 1977. 'The President's Proposed Energy Policy', 18 Apr. At: <www.mnforsustain. org/energy_speech_president_carter.htm>.

Cizek, Petr. 'A Choice of Futures: Cumulative Impact Scenarios of the Mackenzie Gas Project', Canadian Arctic Resources Committee. At: <www.ngps.nt.ca/Upload/Interveners/ Canadian%20Arctic%20Resources%20Committee/carc%20cumulative%20effects%20 presentation%20to%20JRP%20part%201.pdf>. (22 Dec. 2008)

Chapnick, Adam. 1999. 'The Middle Power', *Canadian Foreign Policy* 7, 2 (Winter): 73–82.

Cohen, Michael D. 2007. 'Russia and the European Union: An Outlook for Collaboration and Competition in European Natural Gas Markets', *Demokratizatsiya* 15, 4: 379–89.

Cox, Robert. 1989. 'Middlepowermanship, Japan, and Future World Order', *International Journal* 44, 4: 823–62.

———. 2005. 'A Canadian Dilemma: The United States or the World', *International Journal* 60, 3: 667–84.

Dewitt, David, and John Kirton. 1983. *Canada as a Principal Power*. Toronto: John Wiley & Sons.

Eayrs, James. 1975. 'From Middle to Foremost Power: Defining a New Place for Canada in the Hierarchy of World Power', *International Perspective* (Mar.–Apr.): 15–24.

EIA (US Energy Information Administration). 2006. 'Top World Oil Net Importers'. At: <tonto. eia.doe.gov/country/index.cfm>. (15 Dec. 2008)

———. 2008a. 'Canada Energy Profile'. At: <tonto.eia.doe.gov/country/country_energy_data. cfm?fips=CA>. (15 Dec. 2008)

———. 2008b. 'International Petroleum'. At: <www.eia.doe.gov/emeu/ipsr/t21.xls>. (2 Apr. 2008)

———. 2008c. 'Recent Natural Gas Production'. At: <www.eia.doe.gov/emeu/international/ RecentNaturalGasProductionTCF.xls/>. (10 Nov. 2008)

———. 2008d. 'Recent Total Oil Supply Barrels per Day'. At: <www.eia.doe.gov/emeu/ international/RecentTotalOilSupplyBarrelsperDay.xls/>. (10 Nov. 2008)

———. 2008e. 'Saudi Arabia Energy Profile'. At: <tonto.eia.doe.gov/country/country_energy_ data.cfm?fips=SA>. (15 Dec. 2008)

———. 2008f. 'United States Energy Profile'. At: <tonto.eia.doe.gov/country/country_energy_ data.cfm?fips=US>. (15 Dec. 2008)

———. 2008g. 'Top World Oil Producers'. At: <tonto.eia.doe.gov/country/index.cfm>. (15 Dec. 2008)

———. 2008h. 'United States Imports by Country of Origin'. At: <tonto.eia.doe.gov/dnav/pet/ pet_move_impcus_a2_nus_ep00_im0_mbblpd_a.htm>. (31 Dec. 2008)

———. 2008i. 'Weekly Imports and Exports'. At: <tonto.eia.doe.gov/dnav/pet/pet_move_wkly_ dc_NUS-Z00_mbblpd_w.htm>. (21 July 2008)

Finlay, Patricia. 2008. 'Lougheed, Edgar Peter', *The Canadian Encyclopedia*. Historica Foundation. At: <www.thecanadianencyclopedia.com/index.cfm?PgNm=TCE&Params=A1SEC900987 >. (18 Dec. 2008)

Francoeur, Louis-Gilles. 2008. 'Vers l'autonomie pétrolière. Le Canada pourrait arriver à satisfaire ses besoins pétroliers avec son propre pétrole à faible teneur en carbone', *Le Devoir*, 4 Oct., A5.

Germanwatch. 2009. 'The Climate Change Performance Index: Results 2009'. At: <www. germanwatch.org>.

Goldman, Marshall I. 2008. *Petrostate: Putin, Power, and the New Russia*. Oxford: Oxford University Press.

Griffiths, Mary. 2006. *Troubled Waters, Troubling Trends: The Need to Reduce the Oil Industry's Use of Water in Alberta and How to Do It*. Drayton Valley, Alta: Pembina Institute. At: <pubs.

pembina.org/reports/TroubledW7_Summary.pdf>. (18 Dec. 2008)

Heinberg, Richard. 2004. *Powerdown: Options and Actions for a Post-Carbon World*. Gabriola Island, BC: New Society.

———. 2008. 'Proportionality', *Energy Bulletin*, weblog, 7 Feb. At: <www.energybulletin.net/ newswire.php?id=40035>.

Homer-Dixon, Thomas. 2007. *The Upside of Down: Catastrophe, Creativity and the Renewal of Civilization*. Toronto: Vintage Canada.

Hoyos, Carola. 2007. 'The New Seven Sisters: Oil and Gas Giants Dwarf Western Rivals', *Financial Times*, 12 Mar. At: <www.ft.com/cms/s/471ae1b8-d001-11db-94cb-000b5df10621,dwp_ uuid=0bda728c>. (16 May 2008)

Hubbard, Glenn R., and Robert J. Weiner. 1985. 'Managing the Strategic Petroleum Reserve: Energy Policy in a Market Setting', *Annual Energy Review* 10: 515–56.

Hughes, David. 2008. 'The Energy Sustainability Dilemma: Powering the Future in a Finite World', PowerPoint presentation to the Logan Club, Ottawa, 25 Jan.

International Energy Agency (IEA). 2007. *Oil Supply Security*.

———. 2008. *World Energy Outlook*. Paris. At: <www.worldenergyoutlook.org/docs/weo2008/ WEO2008_es_english.pdf>. (17 Dec. 2008)

Kom, Joel. 2007. 'The Oilsands' Insatiable Thirst', *Calgary Herald*, 2 Dec. At: <www.canada.com/ calgaryherald/features/water/story.html?id=05f90a2a-d6c0-44aa-948c-0ff0d02afd2e>. (18 Dec. 2008)

Laxer, Gordon. 2007. 'Climate Change and Energy Security for Canadians', in Cy Gonick, ed., *Climate Change and Energy Security*. Halifax: Fernwood, 89–96.

——— and John Dillon. 2008. *Over a Barrel: Exiting from NAFTA's Proportionality Clause*. Edmonton and Ottawa: Parkland Institute and CCPA.

Miller, Lyman. 2005. 'China an Emerging Superpower?', *Stanford Journal of International Relations* 6, 1. At: <www.stanford.edu/group/sjir/6.1.toc.html>. (19 Dec. 2007)

Moorhouse, Jeremy, Matthew McCullogh, Greg Powell, and Ellen Francis. 2006. *Mackenzie Gas Project Greenhouse Gas Analysis—An Update*. Drayton Valley, Alta: Pembina Institute. At: <www.ngps.nt.ca/Upload/Interveners/Ecology%20North/EcologyNorth_MGP_GHG_ Analysis_An_Update_r2.pdf>. (16 Feb. 2009)

National Energy Board Communications Team. 2007. E-mail to author, 12 Apr.

Nayar, Baldev Raj, and T.V. Paul. 2002. *India in the World Order: Searching for Major-Power Status*. Cambridge: Cambridge University Press.

Painter, David. 1986. *Oil and the American Century*. Baltimore: Johns Hopkins University Press.

Pembina Institute. 2008. 'Climate Change: Federal Action'. At: <climate.pembina.org/issues/ federal-action>. (3 Jan. 2009)

Ross, Michael L. 2001. 'Does Oil Hinder Democracy?', *World Politics* 53, 3: 325–61.

Sachs, Jeffrey D., and Andrew M. Warner. 1999. 'The Big Push: Natural Resource Booms and Growth', *Journal of Development Economics* 59, 1: 43–76.

Salinas, Carlos De Gortari. 2002. *México: The Policy and Politics of Modernization*. Barcelona: Plaza & Janes.

Schindler, David, William Donahue, and John P. Thompson. 2007. *Running Out of Steam? Oil Sands Development and Water Use in the Athabasca River-Watershed: Science and Market-based Solutions*. Toronto: Munk Centre and University of Alberta.

Simpson, Jeffrey. 2009. 'Now the Hard Part: Waiting for U.S. Hints', *Globe and Mail*, 21 Jan., A19.

Söderbergh, Bengt, Fredrik Robelius, and Kjell Aleklett. 2007. 'A Crash Programme Scenario for the Canadian Oil Sands Industry', *Energy Policy* 35, 3: 1931–7.

Statistics Canada. 2008a. Table 128-0004. Petroleum and marketable natural gas, remaining established reserves in Canada, annual (cubic metres). Using E-STAT (distributor). Updated 1 Nov. 2008. At: <cansim2.statcan.ca/cgi-win/CNSMCGI.PGM?&Lang=E&ArrayId=128-0004&Array_Pick=1&Detail=1&ResultTemplate=CII/CII_&RootDir=CII/>. (16 Feb. 2009)

———. 2008b. *The Supply and Disposition of Refined Petroleum Products in Canada April 2008*.

Cat. no. 45-004-X p. 22. At: <www.statcan.gc.ca/pub/45-004-x/45-004-x2008004-eng.pdf>. (16 Feb. 2009)

Strahan, David. 2007. *The Last Oil Shock*. London: John Murray.

Stroupe, Joseph W. 2006. 'The New World Oil Order, Part 1', *Asia Times*, 22 Nov. At: <www.atimes.com/atimes/central_asia/hk22ag01.html> (10 Jan. 2008).

Tobin, Annette. 2005. 'Global Outlook for Oil and Gas: Focus on Canada'. Oil Division, Natural Resources Canada. At: <www.cna.nl.ca/oilandgas/ForumPresentations/AT%20Pres%20Oct%2011.ppt#2>. (29 Dec. 2008)

Toman, Michael, et al. 2008. 'Unconventional Fossil-based Fuels: Economic and Environmental Trade-Offs'. Rand Corporation. At: <www.rand.org/pubs/technical_reports/2008/RAND_TR580.pdf>. (29 Dec. 2008)

US Census Bureau. 2008. 'U.S. and World Population Clocks', Population Division.

Vasilyeva, Nataliya. 2008. 'Putin Says Gas Prices To Rise as Forum Takes Shape', *Globe and Mail*, 24 Dec., B5.

Watkins, M.H. 1977. 'The Staple Theory Revisited', *Journal of Canadian Studies* 12, 5: 83–95.

West, Robin. 2007. 'Panacea or Pipe Dream? Energy Policy and the Search for Alternatives: Session I: A Foreign Policy Mandate: Thirty Years of Oil And Gas', [US] Council on Foreign Relations, Washington, DC. At: <www.cfr.org/publication/12845/panacea_or_pipe_dream_energy_policy_and_the_search_for_alternatives.html?breadcrumb=%2Fissue%2Fpublication_list%3Fid%3D426%26page%3D3>. (16 Feb. 2009)

Yedlin, Deborah. 2008. 'Natural Gas Cartel Would Fail in Bid for OPEC-like Impact', *Calgary Herald*, 22 Oct. At: <www.canada.com/calgaryherald/news/calgarybusiness/story.html?id=6540f74f-f64e-4965-b276-9afa7400403b>. (5 Dec. 2008)

Additional Readings

Clarke, Tony. 2008. *Tar Sands Showdown: Canada and the New Politics of Oil in an Age of Climate Change*. Toronto: Lorimer.

Gonick, Cy, ed. 2007. *Climate Change and Energy Security*. Halifax: Fernwood.

Homer-Dixon, Thomas, ed. 2009. *Carbon Shift: How the Twin Crises of Oil Depletion and Climate Change Will Define the Future*. Toronto: Random House of Canada.

Klare, Michael. 2004. *Blood and Oil: The Dangers and Consequences of America's Growing Dependency on Imported Petroleum*. New York: Henry Holt.

Laxer, James. 1983. *Oil and Gas: Ottawa, the Provinces and the Petroleum Industry*. Toronto: Lorimer.

Nikiforuk, Andrew. 2008. *Tar Sands: Dirty Oil and the Future of a Continent*. Vancouver: Greystone Books.

McDougall, John N. 1982. *Fuels and the National Policy*. Toronto: Butterworths.

Warnock, John. 2006. *Selling the Family Silver: Oil and Gas Royalties, Corporate Profits, and the Disregarded Public*. Edmonton: Parkland Institute and CCPA—Saskatchewan Office.

Part II: Questions for Critical Thought

Chapter 4

1. Outline the basic tenets of Nye's conceptualization of soft power and discuss its strengths and weaknesses with regard to Canada's human security/international development.
2. What have been the main supporting discourses for the production and reinforcement of the overall discourse on Canada's soft power?
3. Critically discuss the argument that the landmine case has represented the victory of global civil society.
4. What are the main arguments of the alternative explanation of the landmine case and how does it differ from the mainstream account?
5. What has been the relationship between the human security agenda and the landmine case? Include the post-1997 development of the relationship in your discussion.
6. Outline Canada's government-initiated transformations of the third sector and explain why they are so important in understanding the nature of the country's human security.
7. Explain the argument that Canada's human security can be understood as a simultaneous desecuritization and domestication-at-a-distance of the international development agenda.
8. What has been the difference between involvement/citizenship and the new contractualism and when did the shift take place?
9. Why has results-based management (RBM) been introduced as a part of Canada's human security agenda?
10. Analyze key features of Canada's human-security risk assessment and discuss the two usually overlooked issues associated with it.

Chapter 5

1. How have security and development been redefined in post-Cold War CanFSP?
2. What constitutes the 'moral dimension' of CanFSP?
3. What have been the main features of the militarization of development aid?
4. What does 'identity crisis' in CanFSP refer to? Use some examples.
5. Is human security as practised by Canada a feasible goal in the twenty-first century?
6. What have been the main security issues Canada has been concerned about?

7. How might CanFSP be reformed to better meet the challenges of transnational terrorism?
8. What are some institutional and organizational consequences of the security–development approach?
9. Does the concept of human security eliminate the tension between ethical and security concerns?
10. Discuss Canada's security–development approach with regard to the country's involvement in Afghanistan.
11. What kinds of ethics are appropriate for governing development assistance?
12. Do Canadians have obligations to protect 'those beyond their borders'? If so, in what ways?

Chapter 6

1. What is the role of public diplomacy in the foreign policy of middle powers?
2. Why does DFAIT have a business-like culture?
3. What working methods does the term 'diplomatic improvisation' refer to?
4. What roles has DFAIT identified for itself and how do these roles support middle-power diplomacy?
5. Which steps has DFAIT been taking to improve relations with the domestic environment since the 1980s?
6. What do we mean when we say that Norway's government had been conducting the foreign policy of a 'disaggregated' state?
7. What were the challenges related to the Canada–Cool–Connected initiative?
8. Could the program 'la diplomatie ouverte' be considered a nation-building initiative?
9. Why is it important to have an efficient IT infrastructure supporting diplomatic operations?
10. Explain the meaning of 'systemic middle power'.
11. What are the similarities and differences between Canada and the EU in terms of innovations in diplomatic practice?

Chapter 7

1. Is the exclusion of environmental considerations from human security an oversight or strategic necessity?

2. What are the key tenets of biopolitics and what is the link to human security?
3. Outline key characteristics of neo-liberal environments?
4. On what grounds might the tar sands development be stopped?
5. Did Canada's stance on the Kyoto Protocol matter in the international arena?
6. Discuss the mismatch between Canada's obsession with international image and its record on the issues of asbestos and forests.
7. How might ecology and security now be linked in Canadian foreign policy?
8. What recent changes have occurred in the Canadian domestic political debate on environmental policies?
9. Why has the *Stern Review* perspective on the costs of climate change failed to register with Canadian policy-makers?
10. If Canada is an energy superpower, why does it then claim to be a middle power? Are these identities compatible?

Chapter 8

1. Discuss reasons why Canada is the only country in the International Energy Agency without strategic petroleum reserves.
2. What are the advantages for a country having a national energy policy as opposed to not having such a policy? Use the United States and Canada as examples in your discussion.
3. Why do most advanced countries have *national* energy security plans, while Canada does not?
4. If oil crises more than double or triple the price of transportation in the next decade, what will this do to globalization, which is premised on the death of distance?
5. Would drastically higher transportation costs renationalize and re-localize economies?
6. What is the triple crisis and how will Canada meet it?
7. What have been the key features of the 'Finlandization' of Canada in the realm of energy security?
8. Compare Canada to the putative energy superpowers (Russia, Saudi Arabia, and the US). What are the similarities between the former and the latter?
9. In regard to energy security, can Canada be considered an energy superpower, a middle power, or a satellite?
10. What have been the limits to increasing tar sands output?

11. While the US focuses on its own energy independence, why does Canada focus on American energy security rather than its own?

12. Are international efforts to combat climate change disasters likely to lead to the development of alternative, non-fossil forms of energy that will simply replace fossil fuels, or will these efforts include substantial powerdown to much less energy-intensive societies? What will be the implications for international relations?

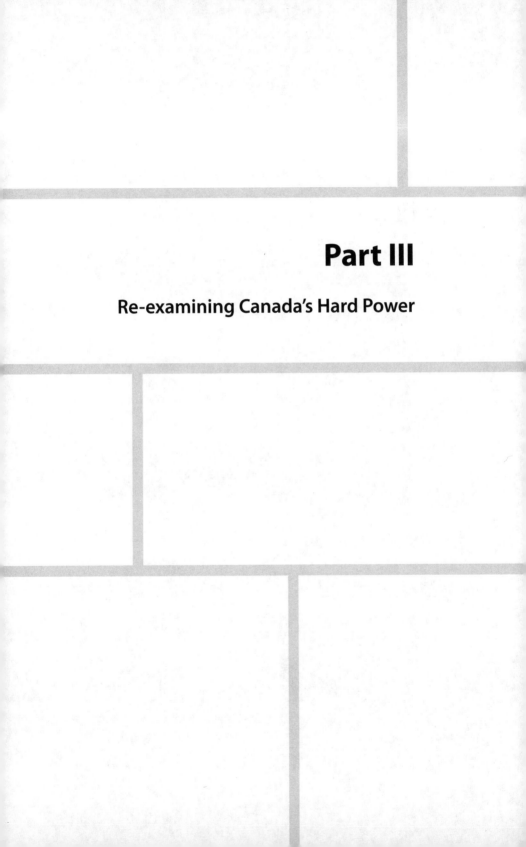

Part III

Re-examining Canada's Hard Power

Chapter 9

The Revolution in Military Affairs and the Dilemma of the Canadian Armed Forces

Wilfried von Bredow

Introduction

Canada is often seen from the outside as an ambitious middle power. As a member of the G8 and an assiduous actor in many international organizations, Canada seems to be rather successful in establishing itself in the upper ranks of this category with a special visibility in the UN system. Ranking is, however, difficult because no general consent exists on how to measure the 'political weight' of a country in the international system. Ingredients of hard power, such as a favourable geopolitical posture, a strong and stable economy, and efficient, well-trained, and well-equipped armed forces, may be substituted, up to a certain degree, by ingredients of soft power, such as a generally accepted domestic order with a high degree of legitimacy, an innovative educational system, and a comparatively good quality of life. Hard power and soft power, however, are not alternatives. A country with the ambition to contribute to the international order has to mix these ingredients in order to 'make a difference'.

Many Canadians perceive the international role of their country as that of a mediator, a peacekeeper, a driving force for the attempt to expand the realm of democracy and the rule of law, of individual rights and freedom, of peace, order, and good government, and also of sustainable economic well-being. The official and the public political discourses in Canada like to brand these as 'Canadian values' and to put them on the same level as the more material 'national Canadian interests', such as the development of the country's economy, political manoeuvrability, and long-term survival as a political entity.

Evidently, the armed forces play an important role in this self-perception of Canadians—as peacekeepers and armed protectors. This image, a part of which has always been a myth, was severely damaged by the Somalia affair in 1993. Soldiers of the Canadian Airborne Regiment participating in the humanitarian mission UNOSOM II tortured a Somali teenager to death and took photographs of the incident. When these photos became public Canadians were shocked, not only about the incident but also about the reaction of the military leadership. Eventually, the Airborne Regiment was disbanded. The *Report of the Somalia Commission of Inquiry* (1997) summarized the results of the 'Somalia debacle' by stating that a proud legacy was dishonoured. Only a year later, and although not directly attributable to any deficits in the Canadian peacekeeping culture, the political developments that led to the genocide in Rwanda in 1994 diminished even more the world's expectations in traditional peacekeeping as well as in the United Nations' mechanisms to cope with the kind of organized violence that had surged in Central Africa. In short, the international peacekeeping culture, which was not only but to a great extent developed by Canada, lacked the means to pre-empt the genocide. The deeply moving account of his abortive attempts to alert the 'international community' by Canadian General Roméo Dallaire (2003), who had been the helpless force commander of the United Nations Assistance Mission in Rwanda (UNAMIR) between October 1993 and August 1994, documents the pitfalls of so-called Chapter VI missions[1] in an environment of deeply rooted and easily mobilized 'inter-ethnic' fears and hatred.

These events were important in themselves. They also marked a deep structural change in military matters: the definition of the tasks of the armed forces, their organization, training, and equipment, and, last but not least, civil–military relations. These changes have mostly been initiated by the interplay of two developments, the emergence of a new international security landscape with new threats, risks, and dangers, and the remarkable dynamism of military technological innovations with a whole range of consequences for the armed forces. The term 'revolution in military affairs' (RMA) is often used to emphasize the dimensions of these consequences. Evidently, the international system is also changing considerably, which implies that the civil and military contributions of Western democracies to international peace and security are getting more important, both on the geopolitical (realist) level and on the level of values (idealist). These two levels do not converge, but they seem to gain mutual compatibility. They are getting more important, but they are also getting more difficult.

The following considerations start from a reflection on the 'revolution in military affairs'. What changes are perceived when this term is used and what socio-political changes may be overlooked when the focus is mainly on military affairs? The organizational development of Canada's armed forces and the professional development of Canada's soldiers have been considerably influenced by RMA, but also by constraints imposed on their performance in the partially new and non-traditional missions after the end of the Cold War. The literature on this subject mostly displays a certain melancholy, sometimes cool, sometimes more aggressive. Whether there was something like a 'post-Cold War military blues' (Cheeseman, 2001) in Canada or whether the Canadian military was really 'killed' (Granatstein, 2004) remains to be seen. But the transformation of Canada's armed forces was and continues to be a bit more of an ordeal than has been the case for the same processes in comparable countries. One could argue that one of the main reasons for this is the successful image of Canada's foreign and security policy during the East–West conflict of the Cold War era. In other words: the necessary changes here had to be more comprehensive than in countries such as the United States, France, or the United Kingdom.[2] Still, as we can assume that the Canadian military is pretty much alive, we have to look into the concepts and projects of the Canadian Forces to get a clearer picture of their new role in Canada's security policy.

The Revolution in Military Affairs

The term 'military revolution' has been used by historians to describe the emergence of large, centrally organized armies with sophisticated and expensive weapons in early modern Europe (Downing, 1992: 10). This development was instrumental for and accompanied by the rise of the modern state. As the title of Downing's book—*The Military Revolution and Political Change*—suggests, the revolution in military affairs was an element of a more comprehensive development that included change at various levels. If the concept of a revolution in military affairs is reduced to mainly illustrate changes in military technology and military operations, as important as these may ever be, certain historic eras gain the flavour of a permanent revolution. Some observers believe in a Napoleonic RMA and count up to four other significant military revolutions since (Cooper, 1997: 111). Undeniably, a lot has changed in the format of the armed forces and in the ways and means of warfare. But it does not appear to be really helpful to describe and analyze them by using the concept of revolution.

Today's concept of a 'revolution in military affairs' is based on the premise that information operations are becoming the most important element of modern warfare. The RMA literature has now been rather popular for nearly two decades, especially in the American and NATO security communities. Other terms that have previously been coined are 'information revolution' and 'military-technical revolution'. These terms have been regarded as too narrow insofar as they emphasize only the role of technology in the fundamental changes that have occurred and are occurring (Davis, 1997: 80).

As David Lonsdale (2007: 236) in his critical appraisal of the RMA concept writes, the increased application of information technology to the battle-space, the consequent digitization of forces, and the relationship between the increased availability of real-time information and precision-guided munitions form the core of the RMA belief that the nature of war is currently changing. It could be argued, however, that the revolutionary drive of this development is not so much generated by the technology but by dramatic doctrinal and organizational change, for technological innovations only open a window of opportunity. Whether and how the armed forces make use of this opportunity depends on many different factors: political determination by governments, military leadership skills, and money. The political determination of govern-ments to have the armed forces enter the path of RMA is again shaped by many different parameters. In NATO, the United States is the avant-garde in developing and introducing new technologies, which implies a reshaping of the armed forces' organization and training. Other NATO members lag behind. This divergence endangers the military interoperability in the alliance. If other NATO members do not want to lose the capacity to co-operate in the military theatre, they have no choice but to try to follow the American example. In terms of military security, Canada depends heavily on its southern neighbour. This generates a special incentive for the Canadian Forces to keep or regain military interoperability with the American military.

The process of adapting the military organization to the new technologies for military action is usually called *transformation*. Transformation is military change management without an end-state, a dynamic and quasi-permanent military reform. Transformation and RMA are conceptually similar and complement each other. For some observers they are even, as Sloan (2007: 3) remarks, interchangeable. Here again, a certain caveat seems necessary. Transformation should not be regarded as a mere technical and organizational change of the armed forces. The reorganization of the military apparatus, e.g., the intelligence bureaucracies, can certainly produce positive results. A broader notion of transformation is probably needed, for the process of transformation must also draw into the expected and unexpected political consequences of military behaviour in violent confrontations, conflict, and war.

New Missions of the Armed Forces

Under the umbrella of globalization, bad governance and escalating conflicts in remote parts of the world, from a Western perspective, may have a strong impact on one's own country. Western democracies have an interest in a functioning international order that embraces free trade, international co-operation, and human rights, probably in this order. Globalization augments the difficulties of many—if not most—states to effectively organize their societies, to remain the central institution of their citizens' loyalty, and to provide sufficient protection against risks and threats from beyond the borders. National economies are becoming more and more interdependent, which diminishes the ability of a state bureaucracy to plan and implement a national economic policy. Ecological problems can only be dealt with on a macro-regional or global scale— states as single actors are mostly incapable of ecological problem-solving. To resort to war as a traditional step in a mixed strategy to realize national interests has become either illegal or much too expensive.

This development comprises optimistic and pessimistic aspects. A bleak outlook into the future stresses the anarchical and disorderly features of the current international system, where violence remains the most important expression of power. On the other hand, optimists among political science experts point to the wave of democratization after the end of the East–West conflict. They claim that democratic societies would have serious problems in mobilizing their citizens for the purpose of waging war if the military enemy were also a democratic society. They conclude that the risk of war among authentic democracies is close to zero (Weart, 1998).

This is, however, only part of the overall assessment of future violence. In some regions, organized violence and war seem to be part of a political-military culture that is to a great extent immune to Western peace policies. Even in Europe, border conflicts and inter-ethnic wars continue to occur. On some continents, internal wars have become quite 'normal', as have military coups and periods of military dictatorships. The conflicts in question become militarized not because of the strength of a state but because of its instability and weakness. When a government and its agencies are unable to integrate the interests of different groups, when they lack the ability to contain internal tensions and to sustain law and order, the consequence may well be the outbreak of internal clashes and civil wars. Territorial control plays an important role in these wars, but mainly on the level of official war aims and the motivation to fight. The fighting itself can be transferred into other regions, e.g., into the urbanized parts of the world. International terrorism is a prominent and relatively cheap method to escalate local and regional conflicts.

These wars are certainly not a completely new phenomenon, and the literature on guerrilla warfare of the past few decades provides a vast array of empirical material to study their tactics and strategy. They combine primitive warfare and cruelty with high-tech sophistication and hyper-modern propaganda. Their intensity ranges from sporadic terrorism to secretly prepared genocide. It makes sense, however, to regard these violent conflicts as 'new wars', for they demand new modes of fighting and new ways of balancing ends and means.

When these conflicts spill over to Western countries, their governments have, as in the case of international terrorism, virtually no problems in legitimizing a military response, at least immediately after the violent inflictions on their societies. The case is more complicated when violent conflicts and violations of human rights in failed states seem to remain a local affair. In such cases, the Western response is contradictory. On the one hand, the human misery documented by television and other media arouses deep emotions that facilitate the call for 'humanitarian intervention'. On the other hand, governments are often rather cautious in deploying their troops in such trouble spots. The permanent difficulties of the United Nations to mobilize effective multinational crisis response missions or peace missions are notorious. The Western perception of what distinguishes these new wars from traditional ones and new missions from traditional war-fighting is still evolving. But general patterns can be identified: military missions have been widening and deepening at the same time, and they nearly always have been tightly interwoven with civil activities. Rupert Smith (2007: 271) identifies six major trends in contemporary war-fighting. The two most important of these trends are that there is no more a clearly defined battlefield, for the fighting takes place at any possible place among the people. Second, the new wars tend to be timeless, even unending—because the warring factions are intransigent in their demands and see no place for compromise in their zero-sum game, and because of the economic advantages that some warlords get out of the situation, which they therefore want to prolong as long as possible. The 'end' of such wars is not the victory of one side, but general exhaustion. The changes in the ways to wage war and the enlargement of the concept of security have led to new security strategies with a new canon of security threats and risks. The response to these new threats and risks is partly a military one, partly a civil one. To prevent and contain the horizontal escalation of conflicts and crises, the former Secretary-General of the United Nations, Boutros Boutros-Ghali, designed a complex *Agenda for Peace* (1992). Other important documents that have shaped the international debate on humanitarian interventions and peace missions are the *Report of the Panel on UN Peace Operations* (Brahimi Report) of August 2000 and the *Report of the International Commission on Intervention and State Sovereignty* of December 2001.

Humanitarian intervention by military means has had many different names in the past two decades. It is part of an international crisis management, which is mainly but not only organized in the framework of the United Nations. NATO now uses now the term 'crisis response operations' instead of the older term 'peace support operations'. Crisis response operations are of different types, ranging from support to civil organizations to combat missions. They are multinational, receive their legitimacy through the United Nations Security Council or another international organization, and include political, military, and civil actions with the goal to prevent the escalation of crises and to ensure crisis management in an effort to achieve peace and stability. Most often, these operations are 'military operations other than war'. In some cases they look like traditional warfare. But even when they include fighting, they are categorically different from traditional war operations. This is why these new missions demand a new profile and a renewed professional self-understanding on the part of the soldiers. They also demand a redefinition of civil–military relations (Hillier, 2008: 12).

The Evolution of Civil–Military Relations in Western Democracies

In most Western societies civil–military relations have developed over the last decades in a somewhat contradictory way. First, many changes of values and attitudes in civil society have also influenced the armed forces. Consider, for example, the role of women in the armed forces. Women first gained access to positions in civilian life that had been formally or informally reserved for men. There is a kind of reluctant parallelism between civil society and armed forces—an illustration of the contention that the gap between them cannot be too wide.

Second, this parallelism nonetheless seems to be interfered by another development that clearly is about to widen that gap. Interestingly, the most important impulse of this development stems not from the military, but from civil society:

- The abolition of universal conscription in many societies means that a traditional link between civilian society and the armed forces vanishes. A considerable number of young males previously had encountered military life. The armed forces were obliged to cope with new generations of youngsters. When this kind of mutual adaptation does not take place, it will be easier for all kinds of mutual prejudices and misperceptions to penetrate the minds of the people on both sides of the civil–military divide.
- Territorial defence is, so to speak, self-evident. It is also a common task of society and armed forces. The new missions of the armed forces, although regarded with cautious sympathy by society, are the job of specialists, often far away from home. Repression and humanitarian catastrophes demand intervention. But it is of secondary importance whether this intervention is in the hands of *our* soldiers or some other troops or perhaps even of some private security firms.
- Some military sociologists (Boëne, 2000) predict a return to radical professionalism, due mostly to the restoration of prestige, more frequent opportunities for military action, reduced military establishments, and a structural non-interest of the public in military matters. In terms of civil–military relations, the consequences will include—on the military

side—stronger professional identities, more forcefully expressed group interests, and less flexibility. This vision may stretch the argument a little too far. But the tendency exists.

If the distance between society and the armed forces is growing, it still remains a mostly friendly distance. Societies do not become pacifist. But they are only sporadically interested in the armed forces; with the exception of the United States, they do not want to spend too much money for their maintenance. The public will be proud of the armed forces when they intervene successfully and help to make peace. But public attention will turn away from their activities when problems occur and when there is no quick and visible success.

Canada: Continentalist Criticism

All of the above observations do not refer to a specific Western country. They need to be qualified according to the political and military cultures in every single country. The case of Canada is a very special case because of its military history in the first half of the twentieth century and because of its experiences with peacekeeping in multinational missions since the mid-1950s. The cosmopolitan peacekeeping tradition illustrates the internationalist and multilateral perspective of Canada's foreign policy. It was and continues to be rather popular among Canadians. This has been confirmed over the past decades in numerous public opinion surveys. A recent Angus Reid poll (June 2008) stated that Canadians are most proud of their flag (86 per cent), their armed forces (80 per cent), and, of course, hockey (71 per cent).[3] When asked whether the Canadian Forces should stick to a traditional peacekeeping role or should adopt a peacemaking role that might involve fighting, the answers are clearly in favour of the peacekeeping role, although a decided trend indicates greater acceptance of a more openly fighting role. In 2000, 65.8 per cent of those polled opted for peacekeeping, as opposed to 30.6 per cent who were amenable to peacemaking; in 2004, these percentages had shifted to 58.8 per cent (peacekeeping) versus 36.3 per cent (peacemaking), and by 2006, with greater Canadian activity and casualties in Afghanistan, which perhaps needed to be justified in the minds of many, the percentage for traditional peacekeeping had slipped to 51.4 while those aligning themselves with the more active peacemaking had climbed to 42.9 per cent.[4]

The end of the bipolar Cold War era initiated a deep change in the international system and the international security environment, a change further deepened by the ongoing process of globalization. Some of the threats of the bipolar world before 1990 faded away. This does not mean that the world today has become a safer place. But traditional military postures and strategies, according to many military analysts and those in uniform, had to be rearranged and transformed. Traditional peacekeeping and its military minimalism have lost some—though certainly not all—of their relevance as a method of freezing a violent conflict and hopefully restabilizing local order. In the peacekeeping literature, authors often distinguish between different generations of peacekeeping.[5] In the case of Canada, the 'proud tradition' (Dorn, 2005) was and still is mostly identified with the first generation of peacekeeping (Anker, 2005). The more dynamic and robust missions in the 1990s and the peacekeeping-turning-into-warfare mission in Afghanistan have, on the whole, not been really successful. This darkens the horizon of the transformation impetus. It was further darkened by the Liberal government's determination, since the mid-1990s, to cut public spending and to overcome the budget deficit that had become a trademark of the Mulroney era. Like most other Western countries, with one notable exception, Canada reduced the size of its armed forces and cut military expenditures. This was mostly well received by the Canadian public. At the same time, however, it generated some acidic criticisms from long-standing observers of the military, including the Council for Canadian Security in the 21st Century (2002), Scot Robertson (2002), Douglas Bland (2004), and J.L. Granatstein (2004). They criticized harshly the underfunding of the Canadian military:

In 2002, Canada spent the equivalent of $8.2 billion (US) on defence or about 1 per cent of its GDP, and given that the US effort is 3.5 per cent and Turkey's is 5 per cent, this relatively low figure for decades has ranked Canada ahead of only Luxembourg within NATO. (Holloway, 2006: 74)

The main difficulties of the transformation of the armed forces stem from a kind of negative synergy of four developments: (1) the fundamental change of the security landscape in the 1990s; (2) the necessity of radical organizational adaptations by the armed forces to the new security challenges; (3) a certain public reluctance to come to terms with the expanded canon of military missions; and (4) not least, severe financial restrictions. Most critical observers of the development of the Canadian Forces in the 1990s and beyond also emphasize the necessity for Canada to stay tuned or try to get tuned again with the military potential and perspectives of the United States. A typical example of this outlook is the last of five conclusions by Barry Cooper, Mercedes Stephenson, and Ray Szeto (2004: 30):

it seems clear that the implications of the RMA as well as the long-term interests of all Canadians in maintaining their liberty, their security, and their prosperity require that Canada defend itself by cooperating more closely with the United States and not by maintaining an exaggerated and narcissistic sense of its own distinctiveness.

The same perspective leads Joel Sokolsky (2004: 4), who maintains that 'Canada should occupy a unique place in the global calculus of US strategy.' And J.L. Granatstein argues that the recent developments of the armed forces in Canada are only the last stage of a long-term decay that started in the era of Lester Pearson and has continued without interruption to the present. According to his view, Pearson inadvertently 'killed' the Canadian military by introducing the concept of peacekeeping. Peacekeeping was a word that appeared sound and comparatively clean. Canadians fell in love with peacekeeping, which implied that they 'began to fall out of love with the true purpose of a military—to be ready to fight wars' (Granatstein, 2004: 15).

Peacekeepers versus Warriors: The Wrong Alternative

This juxtaposition, however, is not really correct. It currently underpins the self-perception of the top officers and political leaders of the Canadian military. The 'unexpected war' in Afghanistan, a war 'Canada slid in' (Stein and Lang, 2007: 289), has been used as an argument for the necessity to reshape the Canadian Forces more in terms of the warrior model. On the other hand, the lament of Walter Dorn (2006) that Canada has pulled out of peacekeeping in favour of offensive operations alongside with the United States is only partly justified, for traditional first-generation peacekeeping, like that in Cyprus or the Golan Heights, where Canadian soldiers have been serving for 32 years, is becoming outdated. Today and in the future, a more muscular form of peace mission is necessary, a mission that combines at least three different features.

First, peacekeeping will have to be combined with peacemaking and a well-planned participation in the reconstruction process. Peacekeeping is predominantly a task that comprises police and military aspects; it is best performed by a paramilitary police troop, a kind of *gendarmerie* like in France.

Second, peacemaking is a civil and a military business, which implies strong ties between the political and the military actors in the field. In cases of violence against the legitimate peace mission, the use of force is necessary. But it is always a precarious decision to resort to violence in the course of peacemaking because the adversary may fight without complying with traditional rules of engagement and international humanitarian law. As the West, and especially the 'coalition of the willing'[6] in Iraq, had to learn the hard way, the terms of the use of force have changed and these changes did not always confirm the optimism of the RMA literature or of democratic peace subscribers. And Western military peacemakers, facing new sorts of adversaries, can all too quickly find themselves rewriting and bending their own rules and those of the broad international community.

Third, reconstruction of basic infrastructure (schools, roads, wells, etc.) as part of the state-building and society-building process is predominantly a civil task, efficiently performed by state and non-state actors alike. In countries like Afghanistan, however, this task has to be protected by military force. Also, the equipment of the armed forces and the skills of some soldiers are sometimes very helpful in sustaining the reconstruction process. But this should be only at the margins of civil–military concepts of co-operation.

The contention here is that Western armed forces, presently and in the decades ahead, will have to be able to be both successful peacekeepers and efficient warriors. Western militaries have no choice between these two types of military activity, and it is short-sighted to emphasize only one of them and neglect the other. In other words, there is certainly more than one true mode of using the military. Public debates, but sometimes also debates among military experts, tend to simplify the complexities of political–military missions.

Out of Sync?

One of the problems Canada faces here are the discrepancies among political goals, the necessities to de-escalate the violence in local conflicts and asymmetric wars, and the military means needed to act successfully. The traditional Canadian emphasis on peacekeeping is still very much alive, but is has been severely tested during some of the missions since the end of the Cold War. Missions such as UNOSOM (Somalia) and UNPROFOR (the Balkans), and, more recently, ISAF (NATO's International Security Assistance Force in Afghanistan), are very different and have been staged in very different security environments. As Bouldin (2003: 270) writes, 'traditional war-fighting and peacekeeping missions and operations have been merging. Peacekeeping has become less peaceful, while wars are no longer simply wars between two military forces.'

The terrorist attacks on 11 September 2001 did not open a new chapter in the history of warfare, but they certainly changed Americans' perception of their country's security in a globalizing world. Whether Canadians like it or not, their security is tightly interwoven with the security of the US and, to a high degree, depends on American security decisions. From an American perspective, Canada has neglected its military for a long time because of the security umbrella afforded by the United States.

Even before 2001, Canada was out of synch in its global vision. Ottawa's peacekeeping orientation was no match for failed states and terrorism. While soft power may be an effective foreign policy approach in this millennium, it is largely ineffective without hard power to back it up. (Nunez, 2004: 89–90)

The geostrategic situation of Canada in North America is still the same. What did change is the new meaning of 'homeland security' for the United States since 9/11. This new meaning has had a considerable impact, also, on Canada's security policy (Lehmkuhl, 2007). In addition, the political-strategic priorities, the forms of organized violence, and consequently also the forms of military intervention in zones of instability have changed. The armed forces have to perform very different types of operations 'such as peace enforcement, delivery of humanitarian assistance, organizing elections, de-mining, rehabilitation of discharged soldiers, and economic and social development' (Wu, 2005: 25). All of these factors, plus a lot of military-technological innovations, necessitate a comprehensive reform or, to use the current buzzword, *transformation* of the armed forces.

Some Data on Transformation

In 2004, Canada's armed forces had about 62,000 active soldiers and an estimated 37,000 reservists, plus 9,000 paramilitary personnel. Defence spending came in at approximately 1 per cent of GDP, which situates Canada in the lower ranks of NATO members. The defence budget (actual expenditure) dropped from $12 billion in 1993–4 to $10.2 billion in 1998–9 and then climbed to $13.2 billion by 2003–4. The Department of National Defence labelled the 2005–6 budget the most significant investment in the military in the last 20 years and expressed some satisfaction with the commitment of an additional $3 billion over the next five years to support the expansion of the armed forces by 5,000 regular force and 3,000 reserve force personnel.[7] The budget for 2006–7 announced a further increase in defence funding of $1.1 billion over two years and a commitment of an additional $5.3 billion over the next five years. This increase will be spent for different purposes, the most salient of which is the acquisition of equipment to support a multi-role, combat-capable Canadian Forces.[8]

The *Canada First Defence Strategy* unveiled by Prime Minister Stephen Harper on 12 May 2008 defined three roles of Canada's military: to defend Canada, to defend North America, and to contribute to international peace and security. With these roles, the Canadian Forces are expected to deliver excellence at home, be a strong and reliable partner in the defence of North America, and project leadership abroad by contributing to international operations in support of Canadian interests and values. These are rather ambitious goals that still have to be made operational. This process, however, is not a kind of technical operation, but a political process with the participation of the public, the media, politicians, and military professionals. One of the driving motives for the transformation of the Canadian Forces is, of course, the experience with ISAF in Afghanistan. This experience underlines the necessity to prepare the forces for what some observers call Fourth Generation Warfare (4GW), where the boundaries between *civil* and *military* have imploded. The forces fight for the people among the people. Fighting among the people always implies the risk of fighting and killing the wrong people—civilians and other non-combatants who happen to be in the wrong place at the wrong time. The military must be aware of the counterproductive consequences of any so-called collateral damage. In such difficult situations the importance of special operations forces (SOF) is soaring. But not only SOFs are needed, as David Betz contends:

> You cannot fight 'wars amongst the people' without actually being amongst them, which means being able to maintain sustained contact with the local population to restore security and enable the re-emergence of civil life in areas disrupted by combat operations. And there's the crux: the West in general does not have enough of the right forces, especially infantry, for the task. (Betz, 2007: 221)

In the *Canada First Defence Strategy* the Canadian government promises the resources needed to expand the military to 70,000 regular force and 30,000 reserve force personnel. A 20-year plan starting in 2015 or later will replace 15 destroyers and frigates, 17 fixed-wing search-and-rescue aircraft, 65 fighter aircraft, and 10 to 12 maritime patrol aircraft. Land combat vehicles and systems will be purchased over the next years. The test for such long-term ambitious plans, which figure prominently in the political discourse, is their implementation. Visions and promises alone do not alter the conditions of Canada's armed forces when recession and turbulence on the international finance markets threaten government budgets.

The process of transformation of the Canadian Forces is foremost a process of modernization and adaptation to the new security challenges on the continent and in other parts of the world. One of the bigger challenges to all transformational dynamism is the rearrangement of the command structure. The three 'environments' (navy, army, air force) of the 1968 unified Canadian Forces are led by three commands under the umbrella of the Chief of the Defence Staff in the National Defence Headquarters. Under the same umbrella are also four operational commands: Canada Command, Canadian Expeditionary Force Command, Canadian Special Operations Forces Command, and Canadian Operational Support Command. The linkages within this structure are important and, as one can learn from many episodes in the past, difficult to implement.

The transformation literature (Rudner, 2002; Sloan, 2007) also emphasizes the need to rely more on unmanned aerial vehicles, i.e., drone aircraft, for intelligence, surveillance, and reconnaissance purposes. Canadian Forces will soon be able to make use of an earth-imaging satellite that will give them a ground moving target indicator capability. The government also has enhanced the airlift potential of Canadian Forces by purchasing and leasing medium- to heavy-lift helicopters for the troops in Afghanistan. Together with four C-17 strategic and 17 Hercules tactical transport aircraft, deployment of units to theatres in far places is going to be enhanced. This rough sketch demonstrates that a lot of changes in the Canadian Forces are underway. The current and projected increase in military expenditures and the introduction of new equipment seem to indicate a kind of normalization: Canada intends to reform its armed forces in order to keep up with other NATO members. This normalization, however, rests on fragile grounds. The outcome of the ISAF engagement in Afghanistan is more than doubtful. And the financial crisis plus economic recession could deeply disturb the normalization perspective.

Let us, for a moment, return to the Canadian public and their perception of the security policy of their country. How does the public view Canada's foreign policy and the role of the armed forces as a foreign policy instrument? A 2005 survey by the Innovative Research Group (IRG) emphasizes a relatively firm consensus on military issues. Two-thirds of Canadians agree (with 35 per cent strongly agreeing) that for Canada to play a significant role in international affairs, the country needs an effective military force and must also be willing to use the military when needed. One-half of Canadians (49 per cent) agree that Canada should increase aid to help in stabilization and recovery efforts in countries such as Haiti, Somalia, and Afghanistan. Almost as many Canadians (48 per cent) disagree with this position. These figures are not only relevant with respect to the armed forces. They also express a kind of identification with the middle-power status of Canada, which implies the ability and the determination to use military means. This identification weakens when the general acceptance is to be transferred into direct action. Here, the Canadian public is polarized.

In 2006, the IRG asked Canadians their opinion about terrorism and the war in Afghanistan. In this survey, 67 per cent of the sample agreed with the following statement: 'Canada should send troops to help when people in Asia and Africa are threatened by systematic human rights violations or countries collapse, even if no Canadian civilians are at risk and Canada has no direct interest at stake.' Fifty-nine per cent of the sample supported Canada sending troops to Afghanistan, with 23 per cent strongly agreeing with this action. About the same percentage—61 per cent—agreed that Canadian military involvement is providing critical assistance to local Afghans and is trying to create a peaceful and democratic society. Another survey in the same year, by Gregg, Kelly, Sullivan, and Woolstencroft, found only modest public support for the Canadian troops in Afghanistan. The inevitability of some casualties is accepted. There is, however, little knowledge about the mandate and the specific conditions of the mission. About 70 per cent of the sample believed that the main purpose of the Canadian troops in Afghanistan is more related to peacekeeping than to combat, and 47 per cent strongly opposed any combat role for Canadian troops. These findings come as somewhat of a surprise since the media coverage in Canada should have spread enough reliable information about the Afghanistan mission. In other words, the image of Canada as a peacekeeper is still strong enough among Canadians to trump empirical facts as presented in the media.

Wounded is the title of a September 2005 interim report by the Canadian Senate Committee on National Security and Defence. Two subtitles explain why this term is used: 'Canada's Military and the Legacy of Neglect' and 'Our Disappearing Options for Defending the Nation Abroad and at Home'. Is this a clear and correct diagnosis? Some observers of Canada's armed forces and Canadian military strategy argue that the defence policy statements of 2004 (*Securing an Open Society: Canada's National Security Policy*) and 2005 (*International Policy Statement: A Role of Pride and Influence in the World*) 'mark an important step forward in the articulation of both a national strategy and a national security strategy' (Richter, 2006: 31). Richter contends that the Liberal government, after years of abstinence, started again to think in strategic terms. He points, however, to what he sees as typical Canadian inconsistencies. For him, the tortuous debate of 2003–5 on missile defence in Canada must be seen as a reflection of 'Ottawa's reluctance to agree to any proposal that calls for closer defence ties' (Richter 2006, 38) between Canada and the US. This seems to be a correct interpretation. One should not forget, however, that American governments, especially the George W. Bush administration, sometimes did their best to frustrate their northern neighbour. Prime Minister Martin's decision in February 2005 against Canadian involvement in the American anti-missile plans of the National Missile Defense was certainly also motivated by domestic policy considerations. Another gap between strategic theory, policy decisions, and military capabilities seems to have opened in Afghanistan. The 'early' years of the Afghan mission (2003–4) were comparatively easy; but this changed in 2006 and has continued to change since. The last months of Paul Martin's Liberal minority government were marked by 'a new toughness in Canadian defence policy' (*The Economist*, 20 Aug. 2005) and by serious attempts to have the armed forces operate in new ways. When the Conservatives took over in 2006, Prime Minister Stephen Harper demonstrated an unprecedented enthusiasm for the Canadian involvement in ISAF. On 31 July 2006, ISAF assumed command of the southern region of Afghanistan from the US-led Operation Enduring Freedom. Approximately 2,500 Canadian soldiers were deployed in and around Kandahar (Operation Athena). Unfortunately, the resurge of the Taliban in the southern provinces of Afghanistan make successful operations much more difficult, and the number of Canadian soldiers who have lost their lives in Afghanistan has steadily climbed, to 127 by early August 2009. It has become evident that the involvement in Afghanistan will have to be much longer than originally thought of (Smith, 2007). Exit options are expensive in terms of NATO coherence, but are demanded with mounting pressure whenever there is an election in sight.

Conclusion: Double Dilemma

The government, its security policy, and the armed forces seem to be caught in a double dilemma. The first is the contradiction between the prevailing public self-perception of Canada as being the most arduous supporter of traditional peacekeeping, on the one hand, and the conditions and implications of the new missions for the armed forces, on the other. The long-developed and politically nurtured image of Canada as a 'soft' peacekeeper is, of course, to a certain extent nothing but a cliché. It gave Canada, however, the opportunity to shape its defence policy in a way that was compatible with the country's ambition to become a kind of global beacon of soft and multilateral security concepts without allocating too much funding to the defence budget. Today, the armed forces are inevitably drawn into the process of transformation. This process is designed to overcome certain disadvantages of equipment (due to the financial constraints on the military over recent decades), to allow for better interoperability with US and NATO forces, and to introduce new capabilities for responding to the challenges of asymmetric warfare. Such transformation is accompanied by a military-strategic debate divided between adherents of traditional peacekeeping capabilities (a minority in the military community but prominent in the general public) and adherents of robust warfare capabilities. This is, however, a wrong alternative, for the armed forces have to combine the skills of professional warriors and of civil-oriented constables and social workers with high intercultural competencies.

The second dilemma is made visible by the Canadian involvement in Afghanistan. The official defence strategy papers of the various governments have always emphasized the compatibility of territorial defence in North America and peace and stability missions abroad. The motives for such missions have always been a mixture of complex realist and value-oriented security interests. In the case of Afghanistan, the Canadian public not only remains unconvinced about the goals of that multilateral mission; a majority of Canadians also believe that the main purpose of Canadian Forces there is peacekeeping. Meanwhile, the government and the Canadian Forces have no choice but to take the war in Afghanistan as an example of the new security challenges that can only be met by a military establishment that has undergone transformation. This implies that the government and the military cannot accept a failure of the Afghanistan mission. If the progress in state-building and society-building, not to speak of nation-building, in Afghanistan is slowing down or even reversed, if the death toll of Canadian Forces continues to rise, it may well be that much of what public support exists will fade away. It is difficult to predict when the breaking point will be reached.

This double dilemma is further aggravated by the comparatively bleak economic perspectives at present. In the worst case, the revolution in military affairs and military transformation do not attain the projected goals and will be connected, in the public perception, with a failure in Afghanistan. In the best case, the flexibility and capability of the Canadian Forces are clearly enhanced and they can prove that they can participate successfully and honourably in difficult robust missions like Afghanistan. Neither of these cases is likely in its entirety. But it is practically impossible to predict whether, in the next decade, the political–military development will be nearer to the one or the other.

Notes

1. Chapter VI of the Charter of the United Nations enumerates various pacific means of settling disputes.
2. Other countries within NATO that have to overcome considerable (though different) difficulties in adapting to the new challenges for their armed forces are Germany and the new NATO members that until 1990 were Communist countries under Soviet authority.
3. <www.citynews.ca/news/news_24340.aspx>.
4. <www.queensu.ca/cora/_trends/armed_forces.htm>.
5. The first generation of peacekeeping is characterized by missions to impede an outbreak of violence between conflicting parties. Such missions are based on the consent of the conflicting parties. The second generation developed at the end of the Cold War and integrated measures to solve the conflict in question. The third generation is often called robust peacekeeping and involves the use of force to establish the conditions for a reconstruction of stability and order. The fourth generation of peacekeeping is the label for comprehensive actions with an executive mandate in fragile or failed states.
6. The 'coalition of the willing' in Iraq was literally a coalition without enough intelligence.
7. <www.forces.gc.ca/site/Reports/budget05/summ05_e.asp>.
8. <www.forces.gc.ca/site/Reports/budget06/summ06_e.asp>.

References

Anker, Lane. 2005. 'Peacekeeping and Public Opinion', *Canadian Military Journal* (Summer): 23–32.

Atkinson, Peter J. 2004. *Canadian Army Transformation: Where It Needs to Go*. Carlisle Barracks, Penn.: US Army War College.

Betz, David. 2007. 'Redesigning Land Forces for War amongst the People', *Contemporary Security Policy* 28, 2: 221–43.

Bland, Douglas L., ed. 2004. *Canada without Armed Forces?* Montreal and Kingston: McGill-Queen's University Press.

——— and Sean M. Maloney. 2004. *Campaigns for International Security: Canada's Defence Policy at the Turn of the Century*. Montreal and Kingston: McGill-Queen's University Press.

Boëne, Bernard. 2000. 'Post-Cold War Trends in the Civil Control of Armed Forces in the

West', in Gerhard Kümmel and Wilfried von Bredow, eds, *Civil–Military Relations in an Age of Turbulence: Armed Forces and the Problem of Democratic Control*. Strausberg: SOWI, 11–31.

Bouldin, Matthew. 2003. 'Keeper of the Peace: Canada and Security Transition Operations', *Defense and Security Analysis* 19, 3: 265–76.

Canada First. 2008. Defence Strategy. At: <www.mdn.ca/site/focus/first/defstra_e.asp>. (9 Nov. 2008)

Cheeseman, Graeme. 2001. 'Canada's Post-Cold War Blues and the Lessons for Australia', *Pacifica Review* 13, 2: 171–92.

Cooper, Barry, Mercedes Stephenson, and Ray Szeto. 2004. *Canada's Military Posture: An Analysis of Recent Civilian Reports*. Vancouver: Fraser Institute.

Cooper, Jeffrey R. 1997. 'Another View of the Revolution in Military Affairs', in John Arquilla and David Ronfeldt, eds, *In Athena's Camp: Preparing for Conflict in the Information Age*. Washington: Rand Corporation, 99–140.

Council for Canadian Security in the 21st Century, ed. 2002. *The People's Defence Review*. Calgary.

Dallaire, Roméo. 2003. *Shake Hands with the Devil: The Failure of Humanity in Rwanda*. Toronto: Random House Canada.

Davis, Norman. 1997. 'An Information-Based Revolution in Military Affairs', in John Arquilla and David Ronfeldt, eds, *In Athena's Camp: Preparing for Conflict in the Information Age*. Washington: Rand Corporation, 79–98.

Department of National Defence. 1999. *Shaping the Future of the Canadian Forces: A Strategy for 2020*. At: <www.forces.gc.ca/site/Reports/index_e.asp>.

———. 2005. *Canada's International Policy Statement: A Role of Pride and Influence in the World*. Ottawa.

Detomasi, David. 2002. 'The New Public Management and Defense Departments: The Case of Canada', *Defense and Security Analysis* 18, 1: 51–73.

Dorn, Walter. 2005. 'Canadian Peacekeeping: Proud Tradition, Strong Future?', *Canadian Foreign Policy* 12, 2: 7–32.

———. 2006. 'Canada Pulls Out of Peacekeeping', *Globe and Mail*, 26 Mar.

Downing, Brian M. 1992. *The Military Revolution and Political Change: Origins of Democracy and Autocracy in Early Modern Europe*. Princeton, NJ: Princeton University Press.

English, Allan D. 2004. *Understanding Military Culture: A Canadian Perspective*. Montreal and Kingston: McGill-Queen's University Press.

Granatstein, J.L. 2004. *Who Killed the Canadian Military?* Toronto: Harper Flamingo Canada.

Harrison, Deborah, and Lucie Laliberté. 2008. 'The Competing Claims of Operational Effectiveness and Human Rights in the Canadian Context', *Armed Forces and Society* 34, 2: 208–29.

Hillier, Richard J. 2008. 'Kanadas Streitkräfte und die öffentliche Unterstützung', *Europäische Sicherheit* 57, 5: 12–16.

Holloway, Steven Kendal. 2006. *Canadian Foreign Policy: Defining the National Interest*. Peterborough, Ont.: Broadview Press.

Horn, Bernd. 2006. 'Outside the Wire—Some Leadership Challenges in Afghanistan', *Canadian Military Journal* (Autumn): 6–14.

Innovative Research Group (IRG). 2005. *The World in Canada: Demographics and Diversity in Canadian Foreign Policy*, mimeo.

———. 2006. CDFAI Media Poll (for *Ottawa Citizen*), mimeo.

Jockel, Joe, and Joel Sokolsky. 2000–1. 'Lloyd Axworthy's Legacy: Human Security and the Rescue of Canadian Defence Policy', *International Journal* 56, 1: 1–12.

Leslie, Andrew. 2005. 'The 2004 Haycock Lecture. Boots on the Ground: Thoughts on the Future of the Canadian Forces', *Canadian Military Journal* (Spring): 17–24.

Lonsdale, David. 2007. 'Clausewitz and Information Warfare', in Hew Strachan and Andreas Herberg-Rothe, eds, *Clausewitz in the Twenty-First Century*. Oxford: Oxford University Press, 231–50.

Macnamara, W.D., and Ann Fitz-Gerald. 2002. 'A National Security Framework for Canada', *Policy Matters/Enjeux publics* 3, 10: 1–52.

Maloney, Sean M. 2007. 'Blood on the Ground: Canada and the Southern Campaign in Afghanistan', *Defence and Security Analysis* 23, 4: 405–17.

Nunez, Joseph R, 2004. 'Canada's Global Role: A Strategic Assessment of Its Military Power', *Parameters* 34, 3: 75–91.

O'Hanlon, Michael, and P.W. Singer. 2004. 'The Humanitarian Transformation: Expanding Global Intervention Capacity', *Survival* 46, 1: 77–100.

Privy Council Office. 2004. *Securing an Open Society: Canada's National Security Policy*. Ottawa.

Report of the Somalia Commission of Inquiry. 1997. At: <www.dnd.ca/somalia/somaliae.htm>.

Richter, Andrew. 2006. 'Towards a More Strategic Future? An Examination of the Canadian Government's Recent Defence Policy Statements', *Canadian Military Journal* (Spring): 31–40.

Robertson, Scot. 2002. 'The Defence Review: Attacking the Strategy-Resources Mismatch', *Canadian Military Journal* (Autumn): 21–8.

Rudd, David, and David S. McDonough, eds. 2004. *The 'New Security Environment': Is the Canadian Military Up To the Challenge?* Toronto: Canadian Institute of Strategic Studies.

Rudner, Martin. 2002. 'The Future of Canada's Defence Intelligence', *International Journal of Intelligence and CounterIntelligence* 15, 4: 540–64.

Senate Committee on National Security and Defence. 2005. *Wounded: Canada's Military and the Legacy of Neglect. Our Disappointing Options for Defending the Nation Abroad and at Home—An Interim Report*. Ottawa.

Sloan, Elinor. 2000. 'Canada and the Revolution in Military Affairs: Current Response and Future Opportunities', *Canadian Military Journal* (Autumn): 7–14.

———. 2006a. 'Canada's International Security Policy under a Conservative Government', in Andrew F. Cooper and Dane Rowlands, eds, *Canada Among Nations 2006: Minorities and Priorities*. Montreal and Kingston: McGill-Queen's University Press, 145–63.

———. 2006b. *The Strategic Capability Investment Plan: Origins, Evolution and Future Prospects*. Calgary: Canadian Defence and Foreign Affairs Institute.

———. 2007. *Military Transformation: Key Aspects and Canadian Approaches*. Calgary: Canadian Defence and Foreign Affairs Institute.

Smith, Gordon. 2007. *Canada in Afghanistan: Is It Working?* Calgary: Canadian Defence and Foreign Affairs Institute.

Smith, Rupert. 2007. *The Utility of Force: The Art of War in the Modern World*. New York: Knopf.

Sokolsky, Joel J. 2004. 'Realism Canadian Style: National Security Policy and the Chrétien Legacy', *Policy Matters/Enjeux publics* 5, 2: 1–43.

Stein, Janice Gross, and Eugene Lang. 2007. *The Unexpected War: Canada in Kandahar*. Toronto: Viking Canada.

Weart, Spencer R. 1998. *Never at War: Why Democracies Will Not Fight One Another*. New Haven: Yale University Press.

Wu, David A. 2005. 'Canada's Past, Present and Potential Future Contributions to a United Nations High-Readiness, Rapid Reaction Military Capability', *Canadian Military Journal* (Autumn): 25–32.

Additional Readings

Biddle, Stephen. 2004. *Afghanistan and the Future of Warfare: Implications for Army and Defense Policy*. Honolulu: University Press of the Pacific.

Boot, Max. 2006. *War Made New: Technology, Warfare and the Course of History 1500 to Today*. New York: Gotham Books.

Clausewitz, Carl von. 1989 [1833]. *On War*, ed. and trans. Michael Howard and Peter Paret. Princeton, NJ: Princeton University Press.

Dashwood, Hevina S. 2000. 'Canada's Participation in the NATO-led Intervention in Kosovo', in Maureen Appel Molot and Fen Osler Hampson, eds, *Canada Among Nations 2000: Vanishing Borders*. Toronto: Oxford University Press, 275–302.

Horn, Bernd, ed. 2006. *The Canadian Way of War: Serving the National Interest*. Toronto: Dundurn Press.

Mason, Dwight N. 2003. 'Canada and the Future of Continental Defense: A View from Washington', *Policy Papers on the Americas* 14, Study 10.

Pigott, Peter. 2007. *Canada in Afghanistan: The War So Far*. Toronto: Dundurn Press.

Segal, Hugh, ed. 2005. *Geopolitical Integrity*. Montreal: Institute for Research on Public Policy.

Tucker, David. 2007. *Confronting the Unconventional: Innovation and Transformation in Military Affairs*. At: <www.strategicstudiesinstitute.army.mil/pubs/display.cfm?pubID=729>.

Van Creveld, Martin. 2008. *The Culture of War*. New York: Presidio Press.

Wirick, Gregory, and Robert Miller, eds. 1998. *Canada and Missions for Peace: Lessons from Nicaragua, Cambodia, and Somalia*. Ottawa: International Development Research Centre.

Chapter 10

A Security Community—'If You Can Keep It': Societal Security, Demography, and the North American Zone of Peace

David G. Haglund

Introduction

The story has it that as he was leaving the federal constitutional convention that had gathered in Philadelphia midway through 1787 to design a new political framework for the fledgling American republic, Benjamin Franklin was asked what he and the other delegates had brought into existence through their heated deliberations. Franklin's cautionary response was, 'a republic—if you can keep it.' So, too, might we conceptualize a challenge facing the three North American countries in the twenty-first century: namely, the preservation of what, in historical terms, is a fairly new (i.e., twentieth-century) dispensation—their security community, or 'zone of peace'.

A few years ago, a report of a high-level task force commissioned to study the community-building prospects of Canada, the United States, and Mexico contained among its series of recommendations one major proposal: that the three countries establish, by 2010, a 'North American economic and security community' (Haass, 2005: xvii). The chairs of this 31-member task force were John Manley, William Weld, and Pedro Aspe, respectively from Canada, the US, and Mexico. Their work was sponsored by the New York-based Council on Foreign Relations, in conjunction with the Canadian Council of Chief Executives and the Consejo Mexicano de Asuntos Internacionales. Not surprisingly, given the ambitious nature of many of the report's recommendations, some task force members were moved to append dissenting, or otherwise modifying, views to the set of proposals (Council on Foreign Relations, 2005: 33–9). What is surprising, however, is that none challenged the contention that the three countries should be working towards the construction of a *security community*.

Why this is surprising is that it really does misstate the problem, at least in the realm of security, for it is generally conceded (though there are some skeptics, as will be discussed below) that for nearly three-quarters of a century, Canada, the US, and Mexico *have* constituted a security community. The real challenge is whether, given the variety of threats they face in this new century, they can preserve what is already built. By 'security community' is meant an order in which the use of force as a means of conflict resolution between members of the group has simply become inconceivable; i.e., they neither go to war against one another nor even consider doing so. Instead, whatever problems that inevitably arise between them, they undertake to resolve peacefully. With neither organized armed conflict nor the *threat* of such conflict playing a part in the resolution of intra-group problems, policy-makers and other policy elites are able to entertain 'dependable expectations' that peaceful change will be the only kind of change that occurs (Adler and Barnett, 1996: 73).

In this chapter, I examine two possible sources of upset to the North American security community. One of these concerns the prospect of massive migratory flows from one member of the community to another, bringing with them peril for the very 'identity' of the receiving country; in this regard, the challenge is sometimes conceived as a threat to 'societal security'. Indeed, this is seen in the fact that Mexican immigration to the United States recently has seized the imagination of more than a few writers who, in contemplating its meaning to American security, have conjured up a vision of a 'reconquest'— spiritual and possibly (who can say?) physical—of parts of the southwestern United States that once belonged to Mexico (Huntington, 2004).

The other source of upset is even more direct and long-standing: it inheres in the prospect of an attack on the territory and people of one member that has as its launching pad the territory of another member. This kind of apprehended threat coming from a neighbouring land is as old as international politics itself because, until fairly recently, neighbours have typically been anything but 'good' to each other and instead have usually ranked high on each others' lists of suspected enemies. In either case of upset, the argument goes, the response of the country feeling imperilled might be so vigorous as even to include the threat (veiled or otherwise) to employ *forceful* means of redress against the 'threatening' community member. If this occurred, it must logically put 'paid' to the security community itself, given what is said above about such a community being defined by the absence of such threats (as well, to be sure, by the absence of the actual *employment* of force in the resolution of intra-community disputes).

Now, the North American security community is a precious thing in its own right, an entity whose very existence demonstrates, *ex hypothesi*, that its trio of members have managed to find a way to live at peace with each other. In international relations, this is no trifling accomplishment. But the existence of a security community, though it is usually not commented upon, also affects in a significant way the 'power' standing of states, and while the analysis in this chapter locates the United States, not Canada, within the category of 'middle' power—certainly in the geographical though not in the normative sense, or in the context of relative capability—what I have to say in these pages does have much bearing on *Canada's* relative capability, not excluding the so-called 'hard-power' components thereof.

Perhaps an analogy with Germany can help make this point. Although the Federal Republic of Germany has sometimes been compared to Canada as an enlightened exemplar of a certain kind of policy that, *inter alia*, features a preference for multilateralism and a desire to minimize if not obviate the role of military force in international affairs, the historical sense in which Germany has been regarded as a 'middle power' is usually thought to be radically different from the Canadian understanding of the concept, with good reason. In the German case, middle power used to convey nothing if not the insecurity and vulnerability that came from being a country in the centre (in its case, of a European continent that had historically been violence-prone), surrounded by states few of whom could be assumed—at least until fairly recently—to be well-disposed towards it. To Germany, for far too long, the middle was anything but an irenic geopolitical locale. And this *geographical* 'middle-power' situation doomed Germany to figure prominently in the tragic geopolitical balancing that ultimately resulted in its economic and physical devastation, as well as the effective elimination, for nearly half a century, of its political sovereignty. It is in this sense that John Mearsheimer (2001: 127) has regarded America's geographical setting—its having, to its north and south, weak neighbours and being further protected, to its east and west, by the 'stopping power of water'—as contributing directly to its economic, political, and military might. By the same token, Canada's geographical setting, so long as its neighbourhood remains a 'zone of peace', also contributes mightily to *its* overall capability, enabling it to attain levels of economic development that would be impossible to reach, were it obliged to (mis)allocate scarce resources to the goal of trying to protect itself from a powerful and menacing neighbour.

Two Franklins and a Franklyn

As mentioned earlier, some dissent to the contention that there already *does* exist a North American security community can be encountered, usually in the case of the US–Mexican dyad.[1] However, in respect of the Canada–US tandem, one also confronts occasional skepticism on the part of those who really do believe that organized armed force might be employed by one country against the other. For instance, one Kingston (Ontario) based peace activist (an American expatriate from Maine) managed to publish a book in the early 1990s—during the first Clinton administration—purporting that the choice of nearby Fort Drum in upstate New York as the base of the US Army's 10th Mountain Division bespoke aggressive designs on Canada (Rudmin, 1993)! Even prior to the Clinton administration there had been some in Canada who worried about an American invasion, perhaps motivated by a desire to snatch oil or some other precious commodity, and at least one Canadian novelist dined out fairly regularly on the thesis during the early 1970s (Rohmer, 1973, 1974).

During the administration of President George W. Bush there were again some voices heard in Canada about possible future conflict with the United States, whether over scarce resources (including water) or over territorial disputes in the Arctic. The arrival in power of Barack Obama, more popular these days among Canadians than any *Canadian* politician, including and especially their own Prime Minister, Stephen Harper, has resulted in a near-total subsidence of such alarmist talk, just as it has brought about a dramatic halting of what had recently looked to be a wave of 'anti-Americanism' breaking over Canada, nowhere more so than in Quebec (Haglund, 2008). Still, it was not that long ago that even prominent Conservatives such as Harper, when he was campaigning to become Prime Minister in late December 2005, could promise to employ military means, if necessary, to defend Canada's claim that the Northwest Passage is an internal Canadian waterway and not, as the US, the European Union (EU), and many other entities argue, an *international* strait.[2] And while the EU, for instance, has made clear its apprehensions about certain Canadian 'unilateral' assertions regarding the Arctic (Dolata-Kreutzkamp, 2008), the US Navy primarily comes to mind when one thinks about potential military consequences of contested sovereignty in the Far North. Such thoughts have a way of quickly turning sombre, which is why Franklyn Griffiths (2006) could adjudge the Harper campaign promise to smack of a psychological disorder of the highest magnitude—in the event, the 'insanity' of Canada's possibly having to launch depth charges from an icebreaker onto an *American* nuclear-powered submarine!

Needless to say, should what Griffiths brands as 'insanity' come to pass, then we can all dismiss the Canada–US security community as a relic of the past. But as I will argue below, Canada–US armed conflict in the Far North is not a very real prospect; if we *are* to see any significant weakening of the Canada–US security community, it will not be as a result of tensions in the Arctic, and Benjamin Franklin's implied question will not derive its contemporary security-community significance in the scenario sketched by Griffiths. So, with

Benjamin Franklin's query in mind, we might want to ask, bluntly, whether the North American zone of peace really is 'idiot proof', in the sense that nothing can be imagined that would return any of the three countries of North America to their prior condition of having been bad instead of good neighbours.

I use the phrase 'good neighbours' advisedly, for it speaks to the historical period during which the North American security community became established over a span of years covering the administration of Franklin D. Roosevelt. Though it is sometimes argued that the Canada–US portion of North America constituted the world's first security community, the reality may be otherwise, with two Scandinavian states, Sweden and Norway, disputing the honours (after their peaceful, though far from friction-free, breakup in 1905).[3] As for Canada and the US, to the extent that planning for military action against one's neighbour can be taken as evidence of the non-existence of a regional security community (conveying, however *sotto voce*, a credible threat to employ force in conflict resolution), then not until such time as the two abandoned this kind of activity can we say that they had established a security community. In the Canadian case, it was not until the early 1920s that plans for military operations against the US ceased to be developed; for the US it would take until 1937, when the war and navy departments discarded the obsolete 'RED' plans (red being the colour code for the British Commonwealth and Empire) in favour of the new 'RAINBOW' plans directed at Germany, Italy, or Japan, or all three together (Morton, 1960). By contrast, the Scandinavians kicked this unsettling habit a few years earlier, during the 1920s (Ericson, 2000).

Certainly in respect of the continent's southernmost dyad, the US and Mexico, there can be no question of their contending for the title of world's first security community—not with Mexican irregulars invading New Mexico, as did Pancho Villa in March 1916, or American regular forces counterattacking on Mexican soil, as did General John Pershing later in the same month (see Cline, 1963: 176–81; Meyer, 1990). Withal, the Mexican–American dyad was not far behind the other two, as their security community also took shape during the interwar period, when (1) the Mexican revolution had consolidated to such a degree that no further insurrectionary raids into American territory were easily conceivable, and (2) American foreign policy towards the country's Latin American neighbours finally became characterized by a commitment to refrain from the use of force against any of them. Both conditions were fulfilled during these years, the first being the consolidation of the revolution under the 'Northern Dynasty' of Alvaro Obregón during the 1920s, and the second, Washington's formal renunciation of a right to intervene militarily in Latin America, made at two Pan-American conferences in 1933 and 1936, at Montevideo and Buenos Aires, respectively (Gellman, 1979).

Recently, it has been asserted by some that the heavy militarization of the US–Mexican border constitutes prima facie proof that the security community has come to an end. Some even speak of border 'wars' raging (Payan, 2006). Those who make this argument confuse border violence (usually drug-related) with something else, namely a state's intention to do those things that would put an end to the security community, such as planning or instigating armed conflict against the other. Tightened borders might be regrettable, all things being equal, but they can no more be said to signal the demise of a security community between sovereign countries (what Karl Deutsch and his colleagues would term a 'pluralistic security community') than can the presence of an armed Ontario Provincial Police be said to vitiate a security community *within* a sovereign state, in this case Canada (what Deutsch et al., 1957, call an 'amalgamated security community').

Some even argue that the *failure* to militarize America's southwest border will jeopardize US national security, and by extension the security community, by allowing into the country vast hordes of Mexicans, many of them said to be bent upon the demographic *reconquista* of territories lost to Mexico more than a century and a half ago. Those who invoke this argument, such as Patrick Buchanan,[4] are making implicit reference to the concept of societal security—a concept that can be expected increasingly to figure in discussions about the future of the North American security community. And though it may be incorrect to dispute the existence, today, of a security community between the US and Mexico, it remains to be seen whether that community will emerge unscathed from the emotional debate attending illegal immigration into the US from its southern neighbour. In this respect, should the forebodings harboured in a recent report by the US Joint Forces Command—of Mexico's becoming a failed state, with all that this might imply for American security—become a reality, then it would not be difficult to conceive that, at the very least, American military planners would be paying heed to the possibility of using force in defence of American interests.[5] But we are not there, yet, and may never reach that stage.

Societal Security: 'Mexicanization' or 'Canadianization'?

One of the contemporary ironies of discussions about borders within North America has been the growing frequency with which one encounters references to the 'Mexicanization' of the Canada–US border (see Andreas, 2005). The following section addresses why America's northern border has emerged as an object of physical security concern to many in Washington. In this section, we start by noting the irony associated with the current US anxieties about societal security, for in some respects these anxieties echo concerns first raised in the late nineteenth century as a result of virtually unchecked immigration from Canada (and elsewhere) into the US. Thus, from the point of view of societal security, we might more accurately depict the current debate as representing the 'Canadianization' of America's southern border.

Certainly, there is nothing singularly North American about the concept of societal security; in fact, the concept has figured largely in the work of European scholars associated with the 'Copenhagen School' of international relations theory. Nor is there anything odd about Europe's being the source of so much scholarly thinking on the topic, as recent developments connected with the growing (and substantial) immigration flows to Western Europe from Islamic countries testify. After all, societal security is about 'identity', those values and practices held in common by a people who see themselves making up a distinct (even if not unique) society. The menace in this case, then, is said to be to the 'collective identity' of a people, a term borrowed by international relations scholars from sociology (see Eisenstadt and Giesen, 1995).

For theorists associated with the Copenhagen School, there are three principal threats to societal security: (1) migration in such volumes that a country's identity and values are held to be at risk of profound alteration (much of the current European angst today, especially in the Netherlands, would fall under this category); (2) 'horizontal competition', meaning the linguistic and cultural pull exerted by a powerful neighbour on one's own identity (as evidenced, for instance, in long-standing Canadian anxieties about American cultural weight); and (3) 'vertical competition', with the threat here coming from within a country, where one collective identity with a regional base sets itself apart from the dominant identity (again, a familiar story in Canada, given the never-ending discussion over Quebec's place in the federation).[6]

But if the concept may not be specific to North America, there can be no gainsaying that concerns for societal security have a lengthy pedigree on this continent, and not just in the US. However, since so much of the current debate about the North American security community is framed by a sense of societal insecurity in the US, we first must focus on this country. What strikes the analyst who follows the vocal discussion currently going on in the US over illegal (and even some legal) forms of immigration is how unoriginal many of the concerns are, save that the first time Americans debated whether their national identity was being eroded by demographic pressure, it was often to the north not the south that they turned their gaze.

Consider the following demographic trends of an era that displayed all the hallmarks of what would later be termed 'globalization': the last decades of the nineteenth century and the first decade of the twentieth century, a time that began, to some, to look like the 'Americanization' of the world (Stead, 1902). Although it might appear that the dominant fact of that era was the outward projection of American economic and military power, it was also a moment when the world—or at least what would later be termed the 'Western' world—was coming to America. One population of one Western country—Canada—was especially showing up in American cities and states, though, more accurately, it was an intermingling of peoples (see Hansen and Brebner, 1940; Bukowczyk et al., 2005). Notes one chronicler of the population flow across the Canada–US border during the second half of the nineteenth century:

> While the population of the Republic was little more than tripling in fifty years, and that of Canada was being multiplied by less than two and a half, the little Canada south of the boundary line saw the number of its inhabitants multiplied by eight. Of all the living persons of Canadian birth in 1900, more than one-fifth were settled in the United States. (Moffett, 1972 [1907]: 10)

Though the process being limned by the above author was said to be 'Americanization', the statistics he deployed testified to a 'Canadianization' redolent in more than one respect of contemporary US discussions of inflows from Mexico. First there was the sheer magnitude of the phenomenon. In addition to the native-born Canadians living in the US at the turn of the last century (some 1.2 million), another half-million were born in the US of two Canadian parents, as well as three-quarters of a million born of one Canadian and one American parent. Adding all these groups together, one finds that 'there were in all 2,480,613 persons in the United States of at least half Canadian blood, which is more than half the number of similar stock in Canada.' Indeed, of the top 10 provincial/state jurisdictions in North America measured in terms of their Canadian 'stock', *half* were located in the United States, and Massachusetts was outranked as a 'Canadian' subnational jurisdiction in 1900 only by Ontario and Quebec (ibid., 10–11).[7]

A second factor was the qualitative dimension, and while it may strike us as odd today, more than a few observers of immigration flows from Canada to the US a century ago worried about the prospect of American identity being changed, and for the worse. In ways that bear similarity to Samuel Huntington's contemporary suspicions regarding the assimilability of America's large and growing Hispanic (mainly Mexican) population (Huntington, 2004: ch. 9), so, too, was there anxiety in the US—especially in New England[8]—about the strain on America's 'creedal' identity emanating from culturally distinctive groups of immigrants hailing from Quebec. The quantity was ominous enough, according to nativists who thought like this: over the course of the century spanning 1840 and 1940, a total of 2.825 million Canadians would establish themselves in the US, some 30 per cent (825,000) of them coming from Quebec. Most of these latter settled in New England, and at the height of the nativist anxiety over the 'new' (i.e., non-Anglo-Saxon) immigration of the late nineteenth and early twentieth centuries (see Higham, 1971), French Canadians constituted, at 575,000, 10 per cent of the six-state region's total population.[9]

But the quality of these immigrants was positively frightening to nativists convinced that American societal security was at risk, and perhaps even its physical security. Initially, the Roman Catholic Church in Quebec looked dimly upon the migrants who dared to make their lives in Protestant New England, but after 1880 or so a new spirit began to manifest itself among some ecclesiastical leaders in the province, for whom the diaspora raised the prospect of at least a spiritual reconquest of the once-disputed territories,[10] with maybe even a political reconquest looming in the bargain! This last was the dream of militants such as Jules-Paul Tardivel, who wondered whether 'l'Amérique française' could be expanded to include at least the northeastern part of the US, while some Catholic extremists allowed their imaginations freer rein, and foresaw an America that would be majority French within a century (Weil, 1989: 30–4).

The dream of Catholic militants became the nightmare of some Brahmin intellectuals, who had been digesting ideas related to the theory of 'Anglo-Saxon' supremacy that was at its height of popularity at the turn of the last century—a theory holding, among other things, that all the worthwhile political values and institutions, including and especially those that gave substance to America's creedal identity, could be traced back to the 'Teutonic' forests of antiquity, in which were to be encountered the first stirrings of democracy (Vann, 1958; Horsman, 1981). Some worried that the Teutonic virtues carried in the genes of freedom-loving Yankees would not be able to withstand the onslaught from what was being styled, by some, the 'Chinese of the East'— teeming masses of French Canadians steeped in medieval religious mumbo-jumbo, speaking a different language, and willing to work at any wage, thereby throwing out of employment virtuous and proud Anglo labourers.

Things turned out well, in the end. America survived, Franco-Americans assimilated, and if New England's textile economy went into long and painful decline, that was hardly the fault of the Quebecers. Not only did the region reinvent itself, but it remained an intellectual centre of the country, its very 'hub' for many New Englanders as well as other Americans. To be sure, the regional, and even national, identity had to have been affected as a result of the demographic flows that washed over America at the height of the new immigration, but it would be hard for anyone to make the argument that the country that would subsequently rise to global dominance had been hurt by the process. It was, in fact, much easier to maintain the opposite.[11]

And thus we might consider the current debate about the meaning of Mexican immigration for American societal security by thinking of it as a new phase of an established pattern. Obviously, although the nativist fears were proved wrong a century ago, when the continental focus was more on America's northern than its southern border, this need not mean that the fears of today are invalid. Still, there may be merit in invoking the 'Canadianization' analogy when we contemplate a possible societal security challenge to the North American zone of peace. What is said by some to be at stake, after all, is a deterioration in the US–Mexico relationship of such an order of gravity as to call into question the irenic *acquis* of the past 70 years and to open once again the prospect of America's having to plan to use force against its southern neighbour.

How could such deterioration occur? The crux of the contemporary alarmism about societal security is found in the nightmare scenario of the nativists—to wit, of the United States becoming, in effect, the Disunited States, and doing so as a result of the replacement of a unifying assimilationist ethic by a divisive multiculturalist one. This vision has been adumbrated in fairly recent statements about the impact of ethnic politics upon America's future, including and especially by the historian Arthur Schlesinger Jr (1998). In this divisive perspective, shared by Samuel Huntington and Patrick Buchanan, among others, the Mexican diaspora proves particularly troublesome, bent as it presumably is on a *reconquista* of lost territory in the US Southwest, whose proportions could only have been the envy of the Tardivels of the nineteenth century.

But there is reason to doubt that this scenario represents much of a threat. First, it still needs to be shown why the America of a century ago, with fully a third of its population foreign-born, should have been so thoroughly capable of preserving—indeed strengthening—its national unity, while the America of today, with only a tenth of its population foreign-born, must succumb to the pressure of ethnic diasporas.[12] Second, it needs to be demonstrated why fellow North Americans, which is what the Mexicans are, should prove to be more incapable of assimilation in the twenty-first century than were immigrants from the other side of the Atlantic—or for that matter, of the St Lawrence!—a century and more ago. Indeed, some authors have argued not only that America's Latinos are at least as readily assimilable as most previous ethnic influxes, but that their growing presence in American society gives the US a set of cultural (including linguistic) assets that will redound to its advantage in the future struggle for international influence, as well as market share, not only in the western hemisphere but throughout a world in which Spanish is exceeded only in importance by English as a global tongue. For this reason one Brazilian academic writing in France could proclaim, a dozen or so years ago (and not to French delight), that 'the twenty-first century will be American' (Valladão, 1996).[13]

On balance, the societal security dilemma that currently may (or may not) be affecting the US is unlikely to do much to unseat the US–Mexican security community.[14] This is not to say that political developments in Mexico itself, in particular drug-related violence, may not have a negative effect on the country's relationship with the US, but that need not, and probably would not, put an end to the security community. Instead, on the question of societal security and the North American security community, there is at least as much of a basis for an optimistic reading as for a pessimistic one because of the continuing power of assimilative factors even in an America that is thought to be 'multicultural'.[15]

Canada–US Security Relations: A New Fenianism?

If it is ironic to discover that today's American societal-security concerns stimulated by Mexican immigrants bear some resemblance to earlier anxieties about Canadian immigration, it is no less ironic to discover that American policy elites in recent years have been regarding their northern border—the much-ballyhooed 'longest undefended border' in the world—with trepidation from the point of view of physical rather than societal security, i.e., the kind of security woes that once were thought to be exclusively related to the border with Mexico. This is why, as noted above, one hears more and more references to the 'Mexicanization' of the Canada–US border, as inaccurate as the imagery may be. If it is true that, from the standpoint of societal security, America's southern frontier clearly is at the crux of the matter, the same does not necessarily apply when we turn to a discussion of America's physical security. Indeed, almost eight years after 9/11, Americans in high places continue to disseminate the fiction that at least some of the hijackers used Canada as a portal for entry to the US, as Janet Napolitano, the US Secretary of Homeland Security, claimed in late April 2009, and then, days later, was supported in this fiction by Senator John McCain, the defeated Republican candidate in the 2008 US election.

American policy elites in recent years have regarded Canada with a much more jaundiced eye than heretofore, even if for the grand American public, unencumbered as it is by much knowledge of its northern neighbour, Canada has continued throughout the past decades to be held in lofty esteem. Nor is there anything new in an American public's continually fawning over a people and a country that does not always reciprocate the affection (Freeman, 2005). What Frank Underhill related nearly half a century ago remains generally true, though there are moments, such as the present, when Canadians get swept up in a popular affection for an American leader: 'Americans . . . are benevolently ignorant about Canada, whereas Canadians are malevolently informed about the United States' (Underhill, 1961: 256–7).

This is not to suggest that those Americans who actually know something about Canada, i.e., the policy elites, have harboured aggressive designs on a neighbour that grew increasingly annoying to some of them during much of the early George W. Bush years, a time when it was possible to catch scholarly glimpses of Canada as a 'security threat to the United States' (Sapolsky, 2005: 31). What analysts such as MIT's Harvey Sapolsky have meant when they describe Canada as a threat to American security is that, starting in the mid-1990s and continuing for a decade, Canadian Liberal governments in their view had sought to constrain American power and influence by leading campaigns such as those that resulted in the ban on anti-personnel landmines and the establishment of the International Criminal Court. Not only did this kind of critique understate if not ignore completely those many things Canada did during those same years to assist the US,[16] but it also misidentified the real challenge. To the small extent that the Canada–US security community might be put into jeopardy in coming years, it would have much less to do with any ongoing Canadian tendency to wish to pluck the eagle's tail feathers and much more to do with a phenomenon that bears an ironic resemblance to a security challenge that once dramatically did affect security relations between the two North American neighbours. Let us refer to this phenomenon as the 'New Fenianism'.

As noted earlier, the Canada–US security community is one of the world's oldest. Emblematic of this North American zone of peace has been and remains a reciprocal commitment made by the two states to regard each other's legitimate physical security interests as being virtually tantamount to their own. It is no exaggeration to state that this commitment underpins the entire apparatus of Canada–US security co-operation, and it is a commitment that Prime Minister Harper recently, and wisely, explicitly restated when he spoke with the American and Canadian press on the occasion of President Barack Obama's visit to Canada in February 2009. This understanding took shape at the same moment the security community was forming, during the crisis atmosphere of the late 1930s, when a war in Europe was looming and when it seemed that American security might be imperilled should Canadian involvement in the European war make untenable the Monroe Doctrine.

We can call this norm the 'Kingston dispensation', as it first was made explicit in an address delivered by Franklin D. Roosevelt at Queen's University, in Kingston, Ontario, during the August 1938 Sudetenland crisis. The President told his audience that America would 'not stand idly by' were the physical security of Canada threatened by a European adversary as a consequence of the country's participation in a European war. For his part, Prime Minister Mackenzie King, speaking a few days later (though not in Kingston), pledged that Canada would ensure that nothing it did would jeopardize the physical security of the United States. Taken together, the two leaders' remarks constitute the normative core of the Canada–US security relationship: each country understood that it had a 'neighbourly' obligation to the other to demonstrate nearly as much solicitude for the other's physical security needs as for its own (see Haglund, 2003).

The Kingston dispensation was not quite an alliance, but within two years a bilateral alliance had been forged in North America when, in August 1940, the two leaders signed the Ogdensburg Agreement at the New York State border town, which established a formal security pact, including the Permanent Joint Board of Defence. This alliance remains America's longest-running bilateral security pact. Is there any reason to believe that this normative core could be subjected to severe challenge—so severe, in fact, as to put in jeopardy the North American zone of peace? Yes, though the chances of such occurring are extremely slight. Perhaps the only conceivable challenge to the security community resides in what Canada's former Minister of Transport, Jean Lapierre, termed his 'worst nightmare', that of a devastating terrorist attack mounted against American soil from Canada (Allison, 2005: 717).

This 'nightmare' scenario falls under the rubric the 'New Fenianism'. To be sure, analogies can never be anything other than imperfect, and this one looks, at first blush, to be more imperfect than most. To Canadian readers with historical knowledge, after all, the New Fenianism conjures up an earlier threat to physical security that really was a Canadian nightmare—the prospect of the country being invaded by swarms of Irish nationalists based in the United States and possessed of an abiding grudge, not so much against Canada as against Canada's then colonial ruler, Great Britain (Bell, 1991; Neidhardt, 1975). For the Fenians of old, whose ranks in America had been filled by the massive migration triggered by the Great Starvation of 1847, the most tempting target in the campaign for Irish independence was Canada; their 'jihad' envisioned seizing Canada, and though this central pillar of their strategic campaign may have failed to secure Irish independence, it certainly played a considerable role in uniting the British North American colonies in the tense period following the American Civil War (Jenkins, 1969).

Conceptually, what Fenianism in the nineteenth century represented was a diaspora's bid to achieve world-order aims by attacking targets on North American soil. The Old Fenians cared about Canada, but chiefly as a means to get Britain out of Ireland. The 'New Fenians' also have world-order objectives, the servicing of which could involve strikes on North American soil as a means of forcing the pace of developments elsewhere. In the case of the New Fenians, the aim is to dislodge America not from North America (a patent impossibility), but rather from the greater Middle East.

But if the comparison might be an apt one in terms of objectives, does not the difference in scale—tens of thousands of Irish-American jihadists versus a necessarily unknown but definitely tiny number of contemporary Canada-based jihadists—render nugatory the analogy?[17] Ordinarily, one would hesitate simply because of these scale differences to suggest the analogy, except that in the case of modern terrorism, as the events of 11 September 2001 showed, it does not require vast numbers to make a major impact on international security. Given the legitimate worry about terrorists acquiring weapons of mass destruction, small numbers can more than equal, in death and destruction, what in an earlier era would have required veritable armies to accomplish. As Robert Cooper (2004: ix) notes, ideological groups can today make do with only a minuscule fraction of the warriors who used to be required: 'Henceforth, comparatively small groups will be able to do the sort of damage which before only state armies or major revolutionary movements could achieve. . . . A serious terrorist attack could be launched by perhaps sixty people . . . [less than] 0.000001 per cent of the population is enough.'

To date, most of the Canadian jihadists involved in combat against America (and, when you think about it, Canada as well, given the involvement of the Canadian Forces in operations against the Taliban in Afghanistan) have done so outside of North American territory; one recalls in this regard the astounding saga of the Khadr family, made even more astounding by an early intervention of a Canadian Prime Minister, Jean Chrétien, to get freed from custody in Pakistan the now-deceased patriarch of the family, Ahmed Said Khadr, the Al Qaeda operative who enrolled his four sons in the jihad that would eventually take his own life and severely mess up theirs. As Colin Freeze (2005: A10) has written apropos the Chrétien involvement in this case, '[t]he widespread chill and embarrassment caused by the prime minister's intervention for Mr. Khadr a decade earlier still ripples through the Canadian government and its counterterrorism cases today.'

But there is the even greater embarrassment of one prominent jihadist, Ahmed Ressam, who did attempt to strike an American target—the Los Angeles international airport—from a base in Canada. Although the so-called 'millennium bomber' failed in his plan, his arrest in December 1999 by US border authorities in Washington State occasioned a great deal of concern on the part of US security officials, and did so well before the heightened mood of anxiety resulting from the attacks of 9/11. Needless to say, Jean Lapierre's 'nightmare' remains one for the entire Canadian security apparatus, and should a devastating terrorist strike against the US ever materialize from Canadian soil, it would be difficult if not impossible to overstate the severity of its impact, not just on Canada–US relations, but also on the North American zone of peace.

At the source of American security concerns regarding the Canada–US border is the perspective that terrorists can easily slip into Canada, as did Ressam and who knows how many others, as a result of the country's immigration policies, especially as they pertain to the processing of refugee claims. According to statistics compiled by the United Nations High Commission for Refugees (and published in its *2003 Global Refugee Trends*), Canada had an acceptance rate for refugee claims of 49.1 per cent, which translated into Canada *alone* accepting fully one-fifth of all the asylum seekers in an 18-state group of OECD countries (some 17,682 out of a total intake for the group of 80,219). The country's intake was disproportionately high because its acceptance rate was so out of line with the Western acceptance average of 15.1 per cent—an average that itself was exceeded by only two other OECD states: the US, at 21.8 per cent, and Italy, at 16.3 per cent (Collacott, 2006: 87).

Obviously, the overwhelming majority of these refugees constitute no threat whatsoever to Canadian or American—or anyone else's—security. But it strains credulity, particularly in light of the empirical evidence in both Canada and the US, to imagine that no terrorists have slipped and might still be slipping through the net. After all, most of those who struck New York and Washington on 9/11 had been residing *legally* in the US, and even those terrorists whose visas had expired had initially possessed valid entry documentation. This leads to the not unnatural suspicion among American security officials about Canadian policy and administrative practices, the logic being that if the US, which being the target of the terrorists (and therefore taking security more seriously than most other states) could have been so abysmally ineffective at keeping out those who meant it harm, then how much less attentive to security must be Canadian authorities, given that in Canada there is less anxiety than in the US about being in the crosshairs of Islamic terrorism? In this regard, Ressam has been, in the German sense of the word, the *Gift* that has kept on giving, for the memory of the administrative blundering associated with Ressam did for some long time continue to poison Canada's image in American intelligence circles.

But it is not just the patently illegal aspects of the New Fenianism that remain a constant source of concern for security experts in the US, as well as in Canada. There is also a completely legal aspect of the phenomenon that itself carries with it possible implications for the quality of the Canada–US relationship. Again, the analogy is instructive, for while most of the Irish diaspora did not, in the end, take part in the jihad against Canadian targets, that large diaspora did contribute to keeping Anglo–American relations from developing into a strategic partnership earlier than might otherwise have been the case. The Irish Americans were hardly the only immigrant group in the US to delight in urging politicians to tweak the tail of the British lion and otherwise adopt policies intended to harm British interests—the even larger German-American community also encouraged the pastime (see *American Review of Reviews*, 1910; Niebuhr, 1916; Dobbert, 1967)—but the Irish presence, especially in major urban centres of the Northeast, was a constant reminder to political leaders of the *electoral* danger in working too closely with America's fellow democracy across the seas, Great Britain.

So it bears pondering how current immigration sources and patterns in Canada might have an effect on the evolution of Canadian–American relations, given that considerable numbers of new arrivals are hailing from parts of the world that have hardly been sympathetic to America or its purposes, in this new century, dubbed by some the 'anti-American century' (Sweig, 2006). To be sure, anti-Americanism in Canada hardly needs offshore diasporas to stoke it; an electoral campaign and a well-publicized trade wrangle seemed to be all that was required to turn Paul Martin into Hugo Chávez, with the former Prime Minister attempting, unsuccessfully, to secure re-election in early 2006 by running against George W. Bush. But there is a difference between the variety of anti-Americanism as it has been articulated in those parts of the world where America was being seen, until the arrival of Barack Obama in the White House, as an implacable cultural and political enemy and the anti-Americanism bubbling up in parts of the world where America is considered still to be an ally and a partner, albeit an occasional annoyance.

If Canada's traditional so-called anti-Americanism is of the 'lite' (Naím, 2003: 95–6) and opportunistic variety (call it 'Martinism' after its latest iteration in the above-mentioned federal election campaign), it remains to be seen what will be the longer-term impact of immigration flows betraying a rather less salubrious form of anti-Americanism. If the US experience during the first half of the twentieth century in developing a stable partnership with Britain is any indication, one might expect the imported anti-Americanism of new immigrants, should it continue to colour American views on relations with Canada, to render more challenging the fashioning of a mature and rational 'America policy' in Ottawa, all things being equal.

However, it is not likely that Canada, were it to become more anti-American as it becomes more 'globalized', must necessarily live at greater risk of seeing the North American zone of peace turn into a historical artifact. Canada's relationship with the US, politically if not economically, would likely worsen in the process, but countries can have fairly mediocre relations with each other and still constitute a security community. One thinks, in this respect, of US relations with France: hardly the West's consistently most vibrant strategic couple (notwithstanding occasional outbursts of mutual affection), but still far from being enemies, alarums to the contrary notwithstanding (e.g., Miller and Molesky, 2004).

The key to the preservation of the Canada–US security community will be in controlling the illegal—from the point of view of both national and international law—side of the New Fenianism and preventing jihadists from reaching targets in the United States, should that be their intent. Only this last prospect—a Canada-based strike with significant casualties—has the ability to alter fundamentally a security status quo that has been incredibly beneficial to Canadian, as indeed to American, interests.

Conclusions

Although some readers might judge what has been discussed here to verge on the lugubrious, if not ridiculous, from the perspective of the query contained in the title, my conclusions are nevertheless rather upbeat. If no one should deem the North American zone of peace truly to be idiot-proof (for there are things that could yet go terribly wrong), the security community on the continent does remain a fairly robust entity. And though at times community-building enthusiasts in North America might show glimpses of 'EU envy', they would do well to reflect upon the reasons why some (not all) aspects of integration seem to be more fully developed in Western Europe than in North America.

Simply put, the Europeans understood only too well, after the second global conflagration of the twentieth century, that they had best develop means of dealing with one another different from the oft-tried, and painful, methods associated with the European balance of power. So they aspired to create, through the process of economic and political integration, a zone of peace among themselves. And by and large, aided by some considerable injection of offshore resources and attention, to say nothing of a looming Soviet threat, they succeeded in erecting a regional security community, the preservation of which must always remain the uppermost concern of sentient policy-makers, for whom the risk entailed by a stalling or reversal of integration continues to be that of intra-European war.[18]

By contrast, major war in North America has been a much more distant phenomenon, and hence the felt need for community-building *à l'européenne* has not been as great. The Europeans erected their security community in the immediate aftermath of their last intra-European bloodletting, so for them it is never a distant memory that links integration and community-building with the preservation of peace. For the North Americans, on the other hand, the same easy linkage cannot be drawn between community-building and the avoidance of regional interstate war. They have, in so many ways, had a much luckier recent past than the Europeans.

Nor should anyone lament that good fortune. Still, from time to time, it is well to reflect upon the possibility that there need be nothing inevitable about the continuation of the North American zone of peace. This is why an element of prudence is always desirable, and when it comes to national security, the symbol of prudence must remain efficient borders. Occasionally one hears discussions of a 'security perimeter', either around the entire North American continent or just its northern half. Such discussions miss the basic point that it would be in no one's interest if, say, the physical security of the US were ultimately to depend on decisions taken (or not taken) in Ottawa. At the very least, this would place an incredible burden on Canada.

It may once have been the case, as one student of Canada–US security relations has claimed, that 'no fences make good neighbors' (Shore, 1998). But in the current era of threat, even if this has become a diminished level of threat from that at the start of this decade (see Mueller, 2008), it must remain the function of America's borders to serve as the final barrier against those who would attack targets on American soil. It is simply unrealistic, the Kingston dispensation notwithstanding, to expect Canadian authorities to be able to provide that kind of barrier, even though they might and obviously do wish to do so.

As for the issue of societal security, which is what is mainly (though not exclusively) at stake in the matter of America's southern border, here an efficient frontier has to begin with a serious discussion about the meaning of Mexican immigration to the US. Anyone who thinks that nirvana can only be attained once the last Mexican illegal (or even legal!) immigrant has returned home would be well advised to watch Sergio Arau's film, *Un día sin Mexicanos*, which details the disastrous impact on the California economy of the sudden disappearance of the state's 14 million Hispanics (Aznárez, 2004). Contained in this far-fetched scenario is the kernel of an undeniable reality: that immigration from Mexico to the US does bring with it benefits to the American economy and, one can argue, to American society.

As with all things, there is a downside, and in this case it is easy to establish that many criminals, including drug smugglers, have been operating along the US–Mexican border. But to date no one has documented any 'New Fenians' seeking to harm America from a Mexican base. There are reasons for this, perhaps the most obvious being that the societal context that in Canada, the US, and Western Europe can facilitate (willy-nilly) the growth of Islamist cells, namely the presence of sizable immigrant communities from Islamic countries, is absent from Mexico.

Notes

An earlier version of this chapter was published under the title, 'A Security Community—"If You Can Keep It": Demographic Change and the North American Zone of Peace', *Norteamérica* 2 (Jan.–June 2007): 77–100. It is presented here in much revised form.

1. See González and Haggard (1998: 295–332) for a dissenting view, namely that the US and Mexico are 'still a long way from a deep or tightly coupled Deutschian security community' (326).
2. Though there is not much foreign objection to Canada's claim to sovereignty over the islands of the Arctic Archipelago, things are different in regard to the waterways separating some of those islands, specifically the seven channels that link the Atlantic to the Pacific Ocean and that collectively bear the name 'Northwest Passage'. See Charron (2005). For a discussion of the legal issues involved in determining whether a body of water is an international strait, see Haglund (1989).
3. For the argument that the two security communities arose at more or less the same time in the early twentieth century, and eventually merged into one transatlantic security

community, see Lebow (1994: 271–2). On the events leading to the rupture of Norway's union with Sweden a century or so ago, see Stolleis (2005).

4. Patrick Buchanan's comments were made on the television show, *The McLaughlin Group*, a weekly policy discussion aired by the Public Broadcasting System and hosted by John McLaughlin, 31 Mar. 2006.

5. According to the Joint Forces Command, there are two plausible, albeit worst-case, scenarios requiring policy consideration, and both concern an important American partner turning into a 'failed' state. One is Pakistan, the other Mexico, and in respect of the latter, the study's authors foresee that '[a]ny descent . . . into chaos would demand an American response based on the serious implications for homeland security alone.' Quoted in Debusmann (2009: 2).

6. For a thoughtful analysis of societal security within a broader conceptual framework, see Buzan et al. (1998: 119–40).

7. The top 10 'Canadian' jurisdictions were Ontario (with 1,858,787), Quebec (1,560,190), Massachusetts (516,379), Nova Scotia (435,172), Michigan (407,999), New Brunswick (313,178), New York (226,506), Manitoba (180,859), Maine (133,885), and Minnesota (114,547).

8. In 1894, members of Boston's Brahmin elite formed the Immigration Restriction League; see Anderson, (1981: 56).

9. This was when Quebec's own French-speaking population stood at less than 1.2 million, meaning that some 30 per cent of French Canadians were at the time living in New England.

10. After all, Samuel de Champlain had explored the coast of New England 15 years before the landing of the Pilgrims at Plymouth, and for a brief time the region was known as New France. And for many decades, beginning with the War of the League of Augsburg in 1689 and ending when the Seven Years War did in 1763, France and England disputed portions of present-day New England, with a savagery that at times matched anything seen elsewhere in the world during the contemporary era of so-called 'ethnic cleansing'. For the French exploration of the New England coast, see Forbes and Cadman (1929, vol. 3: 1; for the intercolonial warfare, see Pellerin (2001) and Leckie (1999). The entire period is ably chronicled in Havard and Vidal (2003).

11. For a good survey of the impact of immigration on American society, see Dinnerstein and Reimers (1999).

12. On the earlier tensions posed to, and surmounted by, the US political order as a result of ethnic diasporas, see Gerson (1964).

13. Predictably, Valladão's *The Twenty-First Century Will Be American* (1996), originally published in Paris under the title *Le XXIe siècle sera américain*, would soon occasion a direct rebuttal, in Pierre Biarnès, *Le XXIe siècle ne sera pas américain* (1998).

14. One writer even argues that America's Mexican diaspora has the effect of making Mexico a 'better' neighbour than it otherwise would be. See Shain (1999: ch. 5). For a more guardedly optimistic view, see Trillo (2006).

15. For optimistic readings of America's ability to resolve whatever identity crisis the country may be said to face, see Lacorne (1997); De Conde (1992); Hall and Lindholm (1999). But for a different, more pessimistic view, cf. Rieff (2009).

16. For a useful corrective, see Sokolsky (2006).

17. Consider that, during the Civil War, about 140,000 Irish Americans fought for the Union and another 30,000 fought for the Confederacy. While most of them had no desire actually to wage holy war against the object of their loathing, Britain, many did join the ranks of the Fenian movement, whose so-called 'armies' could boast of a paper strength of more than 7,000 men (see Dolan, 2008: 98–101).

18. This is the thesis starkly presented in Delmas (1999), which despite its provocative title is an ardent plea for the continuation of European integration primarily via close co-operation between France and Germany.

References

Adler, Emanuel, and Michael N. Barnett. 1996. 'Governing Anarchy: A Research Agenda for the Study of Security Communities', *Ethics and International Affairs* 10: 63–98.

Allison, Graham. 2005. 'Is Nuclear Terrorism a Threat to Canada's National Security?', *International Journal* 60 (Summer): 713–22.

American Review of Reviews. 1910. 'Do the German-Americans Dictate Our Foreign Policy?', 41 (Mar.): 349–50.

Anderson, Stuart. 1981. *Race and Rapprochement: Anglo-Saxonism and Anglo-American Relations, 1895–1904.* Rutherford, NJ: Fairleigh Dickinson University Press.

Andreas, Peter. 2005. 'The Mexicanization of the US–Canada Border: Asymmetric Interdependence in a Changing Security Context', *International Journal* 60 (Spring): 449–62.

Aznárez, Juan Jesús. 2004. '"Un día sin Mexicanos" se estrena entre Tijuana y San Diego', *El País* (Madrid), 24 Sept., 32.

Bell, Bowyer J. 1991. 'The Transcendental Irish Republic: The Dream of Diaspora', in Yossi Shain, ed., *Governments-in-Exile in Contemporary World Politics.* New York: Routledge.

Biarnès, Pierre. 1998. *Le XXIe siècle ne sera pas américain.* Paris: Éditions du Rocher.

Bukowczyk, John J., et al. 2005. *Permeable Border: The Great Lakes Basin as a Transnational Region, 1650–1990.* Pittsburgh: University of Pittsburgh Press, and Calgary: University of Calgary Press.

Buzan, Barry, Ole Wæver, and Jaap de Wilde. 1998. *Security: A New Framework for Analysis.* Boulder, Colo.: Lynne Rienner.

Charron, Andrea. 2005. 'The Northwest Passage: Is Canada's Sovereignty Floating Away?', *International Journal* 60 (Summer): 831–48.

Cline, Howard F. 1963. *The United States and Mexico*, rev. edn. New York: Atheneum.

Collacott, Martin. 2006. 'Canada's Inadequate Response to Terrorism: The Need for Policy Reform', *Fraser Institute Digital Publication*, Feb.

Cooper, Robert. 2004. *The Breaking of Nations: Order and Chaos in the Twenty-First Century.* Toronto: McClelland & Stewart.

Council on Foreign Relations. 2005. *Building a North American Community*, Independent Task Force Report no. 53. New York: Council on Foreign Relations.

Debusmann, Bernd. 2009. 'Among Top U.S. Fears, a Failed Mexican State', *International Herald Tribune*, 10–11 Jan., 2.

De Conde, Alexander. 1992. *Ethnicity, Race, and American Foreign Policy: A History.* Boston: Northeastern University Press.

Delmas, Philippe. 1999. *De la prochaine guerre avec l'Allemagne.* Paris: Éd. Odile Jacob.

Deutsch, Karl, et al. 1957. *Political Community and the North Atlantic Area.* Princeton, NJ: Princeton University Press.

Dinnerstein, Leonard, and David M. Reimers. 1999. *Ethnic Americans: A History of Immigration*, 4th edn. New York: Columbia University Press.

Dobbert, Guido A. 1967. 'German-Americans between New and Old Fatherland, 1870–1914', *American Quarterly* 19 (Winter): 663–80.

Dolan, Jay P. 2008. *The Irish Americans: A History.* New York: Bloomsbury Press.

Dolata-Kreutzkamp, Petra. 2008. 'Canada–Germany–EU: Energy Security and Climate Change', *International Journal* 63 (Summer): 665–81.

Eisenstadt, Shmuel Noah, and Bernhard Giesen. 1995. 'The Construction of Collective Identity', *European Journal of Sociology* 36: 72–102.

Ericson, Magnus. 2000. 'A Realist Stable Peace: Power, Threat, and the Development of a Shared Norwegian–Swedish Democratic Security Identity 1905–1940', Ph.D. dissertation, Lund University.

Forbes, Allen, and Paul Cadman. 1929. *France and New England.* Boston: State Street Trust.

Freeman, Alan. 2005. 'Americans Irk Canadians: Study', *Globe and Mail*, 24 June, A18.

Freeze, Colin. 2005. 'The Khadr Effect', *Globe and Mail*, 3 Oct., A10.

Gellman, Irwin F. 1979. *Good Neighbor Diplomacy: United States Policies in Latin America, 1933–1945*. Baltimore: Johns Hopkins University Press.

Gerson, Louis L. 1964. *The Hyphenate in Recent American Politics and Diplomacy*. Lawrence: University of Kansas Press.

González, Guadalupe, and Stephan Haggard. 1998. 'The United States and Mexico: A Pluralistic Security Community?', in Emanuel Adler and Michael Barnett, eds, *Security Communities*. Cambridge: Cambridge University Press, 295–332.

Griffiths, Franklyn. 2006. 'Breaking the Ice on Canada–U.S. Arctic Cooperation', *Globe and Mail*, 22 Feb., A21.

Haass, Richard N. 2005. 'Foreword', in Council on Foreign Relations (2005).

Haglund, David G. 1989. 'Canada and the Law of the Sea', in Paul Painchaud, ed., *From Mackenzie King to Pierre Trudeau: Forty Years of Canadian Diplomacy*. Québec: Les Presses de l'Université Laval, 609–29.

———. 2003. 'North American Cooperation in an Era of Homeland Security', *Orbis* 47 (Autumn): 675–91.

———. 2008. 'French Connection? Québec and Anti-Americanism in the Transatlantic Community', *Journal of Transatlantic Studies* 6 (Apr.): 79–99.

Hall, John A., and Charles Lindholm. 1999. *Is America Breaking Apart?* Princeton, NJ: Princeton University Press.

Hansen, Marcus Lee, and John Bartlet Brebner. 1940. *The Mingling of the Canadian and American Peoples*. New Haven: Yale University Press.

Havard, Gilles, and Cécile Vidal. 2003. *Histoire de l'Amérique française*. Paris: Flammarion.

Higham, John. 1971. *Strangers in the Land: Patterns of American Nativism, 1860–1925*. New York: Atheneum.

Horsman, Reginald. 1981. *Race and Manifest Destiny: The Origins of American Racial Anglo-Saxonism*. Cambridge, Mass.: Harvard University Press.

Huntington, Samuel P. 2004. *Who Are We? The Challenges to America's National Identity*. New York: Simon & Schuster.

Jenkins, Brian. 1969. *Fenians and Anglo-American Relations during Reconstruction*. Ithaca, NY: Cornell University Press.

Lacorne, Denis. 1997. *La Crise de l'identité américaine: Du melting-pot au multiculturalisme*. Paris: Fayard.

Lebow, Richard Ned. 1994. 'The Long Peace, the End of the Cold War, and the Failure of Realism', *International Organization* 48 (Spring): 249–77.

Leckie, Robert. 1999. *'A Few Acres of Snow': The Saga of the French and Indian Wars*. New York: John Wiley & Sons.

Mearsheimer, John J. 2001. *The Tragedy of Great Power Politics*. New York: Norton.

Meyer, Lorenzo, ed. 1990. *México–Estados Unidos*. México, DF: Centro de Estudios Internacionales/Colegio de México.

Miller, John J., and Mark Molesky. 2004. *Our Oldest Enemy: A History of America's Disastrous Relationship with France*. New York: Doubleday.

Moffett, Samuel E. 1972. *The Americanization of Canada*. Toronto: University of Toronto Press. Originally a Ph.D. dissertation, Columbia University, 1907.

Morton, Louis. 1960. 'Germany First: The Basic Concept of Allied Strategy in World War II', in Kent Roberts Greenfield, ed., *Command Decisions*. Washington: Office of the Chief of Military History, Department of the Army, 12–22.

Mueller, John. 2008. 'Terrorphobia: Our False Sense of Insecurity', *American Interest* 3 (May–June): 6–13.

Naím, Moisés. 2003. 'The Perils of Lite Anti-Americanism', *Foreign Policy* no. 136 (May–June): 95–6.

Neidhardt, Wilfried. 1975. *Fenianism in North America*. University Park: Pennsylvania State University Press.

Niebuhr, Reinhold. 1916. 'The Failure of German-Americanism', *Atlantic Monthly* 118 (Jan.): 13–18.

Payan, Tony. 2006. *The Three U.S.–Mexico Border Wars: Drugs, Immigration, and Homeland Security*. Westport, Conn.: Praeger.

Pellerin, Jean. 2001. *La Nouvelle-France démaquillée*. Montréal: Éditions Varia.

Rieff, David. 2009. 'Is Mexico Disintegrating?', *Globe and Mail*, 27 Feb., A15.

Rohmer, Richard. 1973. *Ultimatum*. Toronto: Clark Irwin.

———. 1974. *Exxoneration*. Toronto: McClelland & Stewart.

Rudmin, Floyd W. 1993. *Bordering on Aggression: Evidence of US Military Preparations against Canada*. Hull, Que.: Voyageur.

Sapolsky, Harvey M. 2005. 'Canada: Crossing the Line', *Breakthroughs* 14 (Spring): 31–7.

Schlesinger, Arthur M., Jr. 1998. *The Disuniting of America: Reflections on a Multicultural Society*, new and rev. edn. New York: Norton.

Shain, Yossi. 1999. *Marketing the American Creed Abroad: Diasporas in the U.S. and Their Homelands*. Cambridge: Cambridge University Press.

Shore, Sean M. 1998. 'No Fences Make Good Neighbors: The Development of the Canadian–US Security Community, 1871–1940', in Emanuel Adler and Michael Barnett, eds, *Security Communities*. Cambridge: Cambridge University Press, 333–67.

Sokolsky, Joel J. 2006. 'Walking the Line: Canada–U.S. Security Relations and the Global War on Terrorism', *Breakthroughs* 15 (Spring): 29–43.

Stead, William Thomas. 1902. *The Americanization of the World, or the Trend of the Twentieth Century*. London: Review of Reviews.

Stolleis, Michael. 2005. 'The Dissolution of the Union between Norway and Sweden in 1905: A Century Later', in Ola Mestad and Dag Michalsen, eds, *Rett, nasjon, union—Den svensknorske unionens rettslige historie 1814–1905*. Oslo: Universitetsforlaget, 35–48.

Sweig, Julia E. 2006. *Friendly Fire: Losing Friends and Making Enemies in the Anti-American Century*. New York: Public Affairs.

Trillo, Mauricio Tenorio. 2006. 'On the Limits of Historical Imagination: North America as a Historical Essay', *International Journal* 61 (Summer): 567–87.

Underhill, Frank H. 1961. 'Canada and the North Atlantic Triangle,' in Underhill, comp., *In Search of Canadian Liberalism*. Toronto: Macmillan of Canada, 255–69.

Valladão, Alfredo G.A. 1996. *The Twenty-First Century Will Be American*, trans. John Howe. London: Verso.

Vann, Richard T. 1958. 'The Free Anglo-Saxons: A Historical Myth', *Journal of the History of Ideas* 19 (Apr.): 259–72.

Weil, François. 1989. *Les Franco-Américains, 1860–1980*. Paris: Belin.

Additional Readings

Abu-Laban, Yasmeen, et al. 2007. *Politics in North America: Redefining Continental Relations*. Toronto: Broadview Press.

Andreas, Peter, and Thomas Biersteker. 2003. *The Rebordering of North America: Integration and Exclusion in the New Security Context*. New York: Routledge.

Burney, Derek H., Fen Osler Hampson, Michael Hart, Bill Dymond, and Colin Robertson. 2008. *From Correct to Inspired Relations: A Blueprint for Productive Canada–US Engagement*. Ottawa: Carleton University Canada–US Project (Dec.). At: <www.ctpl.ca/conferences/Canada-US-Project-2008.htm>.

Clarkson, Stephen. 2008. *Does North America Exist? Governing the Continent after NAFTA and 9/11*. Toronto: University of Toronto Press.

Farnham, Barbara. 2003. 'The Theory of Democratic Peace and Threat Perception', *International Studies Quarterly* 47: 395–415.

Harvey, Frank P. 2007. 'The Homeland Security Dilemma: Imagination, Failure and the Escalating Costs of Perfecting Security', *Canadian Journal of Political Science* 40 (June): 283–316.

Jones, David T. 2004. 'When Security Trumps Economics—The New Template of Canada–US

Relations', *Policy Options* (June–July).

Kergin, Michael, and Birgit Matthiesen. 2008. 'A New Bridge for Old Allies', Canadian International Council *Report* (Nov.). At: <www.canadianinternationalcouncil.org>.

Kydd, Andrew. 1997. 'Sheep in Sheep's Clothing: Why Security Seekers Do Not Fight Each Other', *Security Studies* 7, 1, 114–55.

Müller, Harald. 2006. 'A Theory of Decay of Security Communities, with an Application to the Present State of the Atlantic Alliance', Institute of European Studies, University of California (Berkeley), Paper no. 060409.

Poitras, Guy. 2001. *Inventing North America: Canada, Mexico and the United States.* Boulder, Colo.: Lynne Rienner.

Sloan, Elinor. 2009. 'Continental and Homeland Security', *International Journal* 64 (Winter): 191–200.

Studer, Isabel, and Carol Wise, eds. 2008. *Requiem or Revival? The Promise of North American Integration.* Washington: Brookings Institution Press.

Chapter 11

Canada's Responses to Terrorism: Human Security at Home?

Kent Roach

Introduction

Although Canada often is portrayed as a peaceable country relatively unaffected by terrorism, this is not the case. Two kidnappings, one ending in murder, by separate cells of a terrorist group committed to the separation of Quebec from Canada led to the invocation of the War Measures Act in 1970. Terrorism took a more international and more deadly turn when Sikh-Canadian terrorists simultaneously planted bombs on two Air India flights leaving Canada in June 1985. Prior to 9/11, these bombings—Air India flight 182 exploded in mid-flight on 23 June off the coast of Ireland, killing 329; explosives hidden in luggage on Air India flight 301 went off at Tokyo's Narita airport at about the same time, killing two baggage handlers—had been the world's most deadly act of aviation terrorism. The Air India bombings resembled the 9/11 acts of terrorism in several ways. They were inspired by grievances a world away. They employed modern technology. They were orchestrated multiple terrorist attacks in a nihilistic, unrestrained attempt to inflict mass casualties. The Air India bombings are now being re-evaluated as 'Canada's 9/11' as more people come to recognize how foreign conflicts can have devastating domestic consequences and how multicultural Canada can be a site for bitter homeland conflicts.

The terrorist acts of 9/11 had a major impact on Canada. Canada quickly responded by sending forces to participate in the invasion of Afghanistan, by enacting a massive Anti-Terrorism Act (ATA), and by agreeing to a 'safe third country' agreement that would deflect many refugee claimants back to the United States. The ATA enacted in the wake of 9/11 was defended by the government as consistent with Canada's constitutional bill of rights, the Canadian Charter of Rights and Freedoms (the Charter), and as necessary to respond to UN Security Council Resolution 1373. It also was defended as legislation designed to protect the human security of Canadians. In this way, Canada presented its anti-terrorism efforts as benign acts of good international citizenship that were consistent with human rights and aimed at promoting human security.

The use of the human security concept to justify the strong measures of the ATA was not totally unprecedented: the human security concept had been invoked in 1999 to justify bombing in Kosovo. In both cases, the human security concept was used to justify the exercise of hard power and the government stressed humanitarian motivations for coercive actions. By 2004, 'human security' was used by the Canadian government in a different manner—to justify an all-risk approach to threats to national security that focused not simply on terrorism, but also on threats presented by natural and man-made disasters and the need for emergency preparedness. This new approach echoed back to the softer aspirations of the human security concept used in Canada's promotion of the Ottawa treaty on anti-personnel land mines as a means to prevent needless suffering by vulnerable civilians.[1]

Many of Canada's immediate post-9/11 policies were designed to respond to American anxieties that Canada was a security threat. These anxieties were manifested in false but not implausible American suspicions that the 9/11 plotters might have entered the United States through Canada and a whole section of the US Patriot Act that was bluntly labelled 'protecting the northern border'. The ATA, including provisions that limited rights traditionally enjoyed by suspects and witnesses, was designed in part to show Americans that Canada was prepared to be tough on terrorism. Other measures, such as an agreement that provided that Canada would not accept refugee applicants who had reached the safe third country of the United States and 'Smart Border' security agreements, were designed in part to respond to American fears about Canada's more liberal immigration policies. In the immediate aftermath of 9/11, the Canadian police handed full investigative files to their American counterparts. Canadian spies facilitated the transfer of Canadian citizens to American authorities and conducted interrogations of a Canadian citizen held at Guantanamo. All of these events would generate subsequent controversy because of their impact on human rights and Canada's multicultural population. Although Canadian co-operation in American anti-terrorism efforts continues, the discovery of Canadian participation in some American abuses and Canada's decision not to participate in the invasion of Iraq constitute turning points in Canada's initial willingness to follow the American lead in the wake of the horrors of 9/11.

With almost 20 per cent of Canada's citizens having been born outside her borders, the national policy of multiculturalism has played a critical role in the development of recent security policy. Some attempts, not entirely successful, were made during the robust debate around the enactment of the ATA to respond to concerns raised by multicultural communities in Canada, most notably its rapidly growing and diverse Muslim population. At times, Canada has mirrored some American perceptions by acting as if its multicultural nature were a security threat. Canada has relied on immigration law as anti-terrorism law, even though such an approach is both under-inclusive and over-inclusive in identifying potential terrorists and departs from traditional due process standards in the criminal law. At other times, Canada's acceptance of multiculturalism has emerged as an important restraint and an asset in Canadian security policy. This is manifest not only in symbolic gestures such as the creation of a Cross-Cultural Roundtable on National Security, but by a more tangible commitment to review the national security activities of Canadian officials. Canada's commitment to multiculturalism has also produced a more liberal approach to defining terrorism and to prohibiting speech associated with terrorism than the position taken in Europe and Australia.

Canadian counter-terrorism policy bears the marks of Canada's concerns about human security, human rights, multiculturalism, and international good citizenship, as well as its need to live with its American neighbour. On these grounds a case can be made that Canada has pursued domestic security policies that are consistent with the aspirations of its foreign policy. That said, the devil is in the details of actual implementation. Even in the realm of aspirations, the ideas of human security, human rights, multiculturalism, and international good citizenship are ambiguous enough to justify a wide range of anti-terrorism policies.

Being a Good International Citizen

Canada has traditionally prided itself on being a good international citizen, which in the wake of 9/11, however, did not mean peacekeeping. Canada was one of the first countries to join American and other NATO forces in the invasion of Afghanistan. This followed trends started earlier in the 1990s of relying on NATO-sponsored military force more than UN-sponsored peacekeeping (see Keating, Chapter 1, this volume). Not much apparent deliberation or strategy lay behind Canada's decision to participate in the invasion of Afghanistan, a decision made less than a month after 9/11. Canada responded to the need to assure the United States that it was prepared to get tough on terrorists and to a notion of 'middlepowerhood' that Canada was neither big enough nor small enough to avoid participating in the invasion.[2] Canada's subsequent decision not to participate in the invasion of Iraq can be portrayed as an exercise of 'middlepowermanship' (see Nossal, Chapter 2, this volume) that distinguishes Canada as smarter if not more moral than other countries that acted on politicized and false intelligence. Nevertheless, the decision to stay out of Iraq also reflected the more mundane reality that Canada's very limited military resources were already stretched in Afghanistan.

In the wake of 9/11, Canada quickly enacted the ATA to comply with Security Council Resolution 1373 that required all nations to ensure that they had tough anti-terrorism laws, including laws targeting the financing of terrorism. The UN focused on terrorism financing because its most recent anti-terrorism convention related to that complex subject and it had already targeted the finances of Osama bin Laden, Al Qaeda, and the Taliban. Along with much of the rest of the world, Canada quickly enacted a terrorism financing regime despite evidence that deadly terrorism can be low-cost and in advance of investigations that revealed even robust financing measures would not have prevented 9/11 (Roach, 2007). Here, as in regard to Afghanistan, Canada followed the pack.

Canada's ATA criminalized a broad array of financial and other forms of support and facilitation of terrorism. It applied to a broad range of acts committed inside or outside of Canada in order to make clear that Canada was implementing various international conventions concerning specific forms of terrorism. People can be prosecuted in Canada for sending financial and other support to struggles fought in foreign lands even though the Canadian record of enforcement with respect to funds sent from Canada to groups such as the Tamil Tigers has been quite spotty. Nevertheless, on paper and in its periodic reports to the Security Council's Counter-Terrorism Committee, Canada is fully compliant with international anti-terrorism requirements.

Another central feature of the ATA was the ability of the cabinet to designate groups and even persons as terrorists. Forty-two groups have been listed in this fashion, including the Tamil Tigers and a domestic Tamil group. Although listing can be subject to judicial review after the fact, this has not happened in part because of laws that prohibit supporting terrorist groups. In addition, more than 450 groups and individuals have been listed as terrorists under regulations enacted under Canada's United Nations Act (RSC 1985 c. U-2). These lists are distributed to financial institutions and within government. Executive designation of terrorist groups and individuals is a common but problematic feature because it makes a person a terrorist outlaw without a trial or any discernible due process. At least one Canadian, Liban Hussein, was wrongfully listed as a terrorist under both UN and Canadian lists, an error that was corrected by the Canadian government after more than six months and considerable harm to Mr Hussein (Dosman, 2004: 15). Currently, controversy centres on Abousfian Abdelrazik, a Canadian citizen suspected of involvement with terrorism. He was unable to leave Sudan to return to Canada because he had been included, at American request, on UN and American lists. Documents revealed in July 2008 suggest that some Canadian officials feared American reactions if he were to be returned to Canada

(*Globe and Mail*, 2008a). Later, in June 2009, a decision by the Federal Court found that the Canadian Security Intelligence Service had been complicit in Abedlrazik's detention in Sudan and that the Canadian government had violated his Charter right to return to Canada by wrongly interpreting his listing by the UN as preventing his return and by refusing to issue him an emergency passport. This decision also criticizes the UN for the lack of due process in the listing process. Mr Abdelrazik has now returned to Canada pursuant to the Federal Court order.[3]

Although Canada has followed the international lead in enacting anti-terrorism measures, it has not always respected international human rights standards. In a 2002 decision,[4] the Supreme Court of Canada recognized that while international law would absolutely prohibit deportation of a non-citizen to a substantial risk of torture, there might be undefined 'exceptional circumstances' where such an act would not violate the Canadian Charter of Rights and Freedoms. The idea that Canada might possibly deport even a terrorist to torture has become a minor international embarrassment. The UN Human Rights Committee and its Committee against Torture have both pointedly reminded Canada of its absolute obligation not to participate in torture. The Canadian government has invoked the exception to torture in a number of cases involving security certificate detainees, but so far no judge has approved deportation to a substantial risk of torture in countries such as Egypt and Syria. In the immediate aftermath of 9/11, Canada was eager to invoke international obligations as a justification for anti-terrorism measures, but less eager to recognize international human rights law as a restraint.

Trying to Keep the Americans Happy

Canada was immediately affected by 9/11 as it accepted over 200 planes destined for the United States after the United States closed its airspace. False rumours were widespread that some of the 9/11 plotters had entered the United States through Canada. These rumours echoed the 1999 apprehension of Ahmed Ressam, who attempted to enter the United States from Canada to bomb the Los Angeles airport. Ressam had been denied refugee status in Canada but was at large. And as was mentioned, the Patriot Act reflected American concerns about security threats from Canada: part of it was labelled 'defending the Northern Border'.

In the immediate aftermath of 9/11, Canadian officials co-operated with American security officials in secret and problematic ways. As a result of a two-year, multi-million dollar public inquiry, we now know that that the Royal Canadian Mounted Police (RCMP) disclosed complete terrorism investigative files to their American counterparts in 2002 without vetting the information for its relevance, accuracy, and reliability or attaching the usual restrictions or caveats on the subsequent use of the Canadian information. Included in these files was inaccurate information that labelled Canadian citizens Maher Arar and his wife to be Islamic extremists linked to Al Qaeda. This information likely played a role in the decision to detain Arar when he was transiting the United States and then to render him to Syria where he was tortured (Commission of Inquiry, 2006). The Canadian government subsequently apologized to Mr Arar and paid him $10.5 million in compensation. The Bush government made no apologies and Arar remained on American watch lists. Arar's lawsuit against American authorities was shut down on grounds of state secrecy. Arar became something of a hero and his experience was a cautionary tale for Canada, but the American government apparently still considers him a security threat. A subsequent internal inquiry found that Canada's sharing of information and sending of questions to Syrian authorities played a role in the detention and mistreatment of a further three Canadian citizens who were held and tortured in Syria on suspicion of involvement with terrorism (*Internal Inquiry*, 2008; Pither, 2008).

Other problematic forms of co-operation were the actions of the Canadian Security Intelligence Service (CSIS) in facilitating the transfer of a Canadian citizen, Mohamed Jabarah, suspected of involvement in a terrorist plot in Singapore, into American custody in 2002. Although CSIS was created as a civilian security intelligence agency with no law enforcement powers in the wake of illegal activities targeting separatists in Quebec after the October Crisis of 1970, they detained Jabarah, denied him access to counsel, and transferred him to American custody where he subsequently pleaded guilty to terrorism charges (Security Intelligence Review Committee, 2008: 12ff.). On 12 September 2001 a refugee applicant suspected of involvement with terrorism also was summarily transferred to America authorities. After five years' detention in the United States, the man, Benamar Benatta, has been released from American custody and is claiming refugee status in Canada.

Canada acquiesced to the continued detention of a Canadian citizen, Omar Khadr, at Guantanamo Bay. Khadr is suspected of killing an American soldier in Afghanistan when he was 15 years old. Although Canada made some secret attempts to persuade the Americans that it was not appropriate to detain the severely wounded teenager in Cuba, it has refused publicly to criticize the American actions. In 2005, however, a Canadian court enjoined CSIS officials to cease interrogating Khadr at Guantanamo. In 2008, the Supreme Court of Canada held that the results of the interrogations and information that Canada supplied the Americans should be disclosed to Khadr because Canadian officials had breached the Charter by participating in violations of international human rights committed against Khadr at Guantanamo.[5] Khadr remains detained at Guantanamo despite the Obama administration's decision to attempt to close the military base. This situation raises the possibility that keeping the Americans happy in the future may require Canada to provide for Khadr's repatriation to Canada.[6]

In December 2002, Canada and the United States agreed to a 'safe third country agreement' as part of a 'Smart Borders' agreement to increase security and ease the flow of goods and people at the border. The agreement precludes most refugees who reach the United States from making a refugee application to Canada. The agreement responds to American perceptions that Canada's refugee policy is too liberal and generous. A report by the research division of the Library of Congress, for example, asserted that 'Canada's immigration laws are arguably the foremost factor in making Canada hospitable to terrorists.' The report also criticized 'the prevailing concern for or priority placed upon civil liberties in Canada' (Library of Congress Research Division, 2003: 152–3, 147).

The safe third country agreement was subsequently challenged by advocacy groups on the basis that Canadian actions in deflecting refugee applicants to the United States violated the Charter. A trial judge decided that the agreement violated both the Charter and Canada's international obligations towards refugees because of the more restrictive standards and greater use of incarceration in the American immigration system. Like the Arar affair, this decision had the potential to become a significant irritant in Canadian–American relations. It has recently been overturned by an appellate court,[7] and the Supreme Court has refused to hear a further appeal so that the safe third country remains in effect today.

All of the above forms of Canadian co-operation with the American War on Terror subsequently were subject to challenge and review in Canada. The Arar commission was headed by a respected judge appointed by the Martin government, but subsequently battled the Martin and the Harper governments over the release of secret information. CSIS actions with respect to rendering Jabarah into American custody were critically reviewed by the intelligence agency's review body, assisted by a retired Supreme Court judge. Canadian actions with respect to Omar Khadr and the safe third country were challenged in the courts under the Charter. Canada's commitments to human rights and multiculturalism have acted as an important restraint, albeit *ex post facto*, on Canadian efforts in the wake of 9/11 to co-operate with American anti-terrorism efforts.

Respecting Human Rights

As discussed above, Canadian concerns about protecting human rights, traditionally defined as the rights of individuals to be protected from state power, have restrained some Canadian security policies. The focus of these restraints has been the Charter, enacted in 1982 as a constitutional bill of rights in no small part as a reaction to concerns that Canada had overreacted to terrorism during the October Crisis. The police and the military during that crisis were given very wide powers to detain and search without judicial warrant. It was made an offence subject to five years' imprisonment to be a member of the terrorist Front de Libération du Québec or other organizations that advocated the use of force or the commission of a crime as a means of accomplishing government change. Almost 500 people were subject to arrest and temporary detention during the October Crisis. The vast majority never were charged with an offence.

Although the 2001 ATA was designed to ensure the US and the UN that Canada would have the necessary tools to prevent and punish terrorism, it was defended by the government as consistent with the Charter. A decision was made not to make membership per se in a terrorist group a crime. The police were given new powers within the law to make preventive arrests and to require a person with information about terrorism to tell a judge about the information, but these new powers were designed to comply with the Charter by giving targets a right to counsel and a right not to have compelled evidence used against them. In 2004, the Supreme Court held that the new powers of investigative hearings were consistent with the Charter when an attempt was made to compel a reluctant witness to talk about the 1985 Air India bombings. However, the Court stressed that because the hearings were conducted before a judge there was a presumption that they would be held in open court, and that any compelled evidence could not be used in any proceedings including immigration proceedings.[8] An investigative hearing was not used against the reluctant witness and in 2005, two accused were acquitted of the Air India bombing because of the trial judge's doubts about the credibility of all of the Crown's major witnesses, some of whom had to be placed in witness protection because of intimidation that included the murder of another potential witness. Investigative hearings may be a coercive and band-aid solution to larger and more difficult problems of protecting witnesses from intimidation.

As a concession to critics, the new powers of investigative hearings and preventive arrests were subject to a renewable sunset after five years. At the end of February 2007, Canada's minority Conservative government lost a resolution to extend investigative hearings and preventive arrests for a three-year period. The refusal of the opposition to support the minority Harper government was related less to principle than to the fact that Harper had made a reference to newspaper accounts of a relative of a Sikh Liberal member of the House of Commons possibly becoming subject to an investigative hearing in the continuing Air India investigation (Roach, 2008a: 5). The Harper government subsequently introduced new legislation to restore investigative hearings and preventive arrests; the legislation likely will be enacted in a new Parliament despite the government's continued minority status after the 2008 election.

Canada's commitment to human rights is closely related to its embrace of multiculturalism. The ATA was subject to a vigorous debate in Parliament and civil society in October and November 2001. Groups representing Canada's growing and diverse Muslim population raised concerns about the fact that terrorism, following recent British legislation, was defined as actions committed for a political or religious objective. In Canada, concerns about profiling or stigmatizing minorities on the basis of their political and religious beliefs were taken seriously. The government amended the bill to provide that the expression of political or religious thought or opinion would not in itself constitute terrorism. The first person charged under the ATA was able to have the political and religious motive clause struck down as infringing fundamental freedoms under the Charter. Canada's approach to the religious and political motive requirement is unique and demonstrates its concerns about human rights and multiculturalism. It stresses the unacceptable violence in terrorism as separate from its relationship with religious or political aims that might be shared by many non-violent people (ibid.). It has not been taken up, however, by other countries—contrary to the idea that multicultural Canada always leads the way as an influential moral middle power.

Human Security at Home: A Justification for Limiting Rights and/or a Sensible Security Policy?

The first use of the human security concept in counter-terrorism policy came when the Liberal government—in particular, noted human rights lawyer Irwin Cotler—defended the ATA as legislation designed to respect the rights of Canadians to human security (Cotler, 2001).[9] His use of 'human security' was to stave off civil libertarian criticisms of the Act and to argue that the security of innocent civilians from lethal acts of terrorism should be seen as a human right. The deployment of the human security concept to legitimate the ATA was only partially successful. A broad coalition of civil society groups continued to oppose the ATA on the basis that it gave the state excessive power (see Roach, 2003: ch. 3).

Human security is a sweeping and an elastic concept (Paris, 2001: 87); and it was subsequently used by the Martin government in 2004 to justify a subtle shift in direction in its domestic security policy from the 'hard power' of the criminal law reforms of the ATA, with its focus on punishing terrorists and their supporters, to a softer and broader all-risk approach that sought to limit harms to all Canadians from floods and pandemics as well as terrorism. This new approach to human security harked back to Canada's attempts to lead the way in protecting civilians from lethal landmines more than to its display of limited hard power in the bombing of Kosovo.[10]

In 2004, the Martin government enacted the Public Safety Act (SC 2004, c. 15), which provided a legislative framework for stepped-up aviation security efforts, more information-sharing within government, and greater ability of the executive to respond to emergencies. The Act also contemplated increased protection and surveillance of critical infrastructure such as pipelines, electricity lines, and airports, and increased control over dangerous materials such as explosives and toxins. This new 'public safety' phase in Canadian security policy was facilitated by the creation of a Department of Public Safety and Emergency Preparedness with responsibilities for border security, critical infrastructure protection, and emergency preparedness.

The Martin government also released the *Securing an Open Society* national security policy document in 2004. The policy was based on an 'all-risk' approach concerned with emergency preparedness for natural disasters and pandemics as well as with the dangers of terrorism.[11] In 2003, Canadians had been reminded that terrorism is not the only threat to public safety when more than 50 people died in Toronto as a result of a SARS outbreak. The Canadian policy can be contrasted with American policies that focused on the pre-emptive use of military force and homeland security measures aimed at terrorism but that were unable to respond to the devastation caused by Hurricane Katrina. Canada's use of the human security concept to justify an all-risk security policy and better emergency preparedness seems rather benign and sensible compared to its use with respect to the 2001 ATA to attempt to justify limits on the rights of terrorist suspects. The Harper government announced in November 2008 that it will produce a new national security statement. It remains to be seen whether this new policy will reject the all-risk approach and follow the American lead in placing the primary emphasis on terrorism.

Canada has used human security as an animating theme for its domestic security policy at a time where some have observed its declining influence in Canadian foreign policy (see Hataley and Nossal, 2004: 7). The Canadian government's use of the term 'human security' domestically has demonstrated its ambiguity. It was used immediately after 9/11 to help justify the hard power of expanding the criminal law and police powers in an attempt to apprehend and punish terrorists. The government sought to rebut civil libertarian critics by stressing its humanitarian goals. From 2004 on, however, the government used 'human security' to justify a very different all-risk security policy that relied on softer forms of administrative regulation and emergency planning. Critics will argue, however, that targeting all risks can mean that no particular risks or priorities actually are addressed. Moreover, there is a danger that the laudatory goals of human security may obscure a lack of capacity and co-ordination in government to actually achieve the sound goals of emergency preparedness (see Senate Standing Committee, 2008).

From Domestic to International Terrorism

Terrorism in Canada was transformed from domestic to international with the 1985 Air India bombings. These bombings by Sikh Canadian terrorists in the pursuit of Sikh independence killed 331 people, most of whom were Canadian citizens, many of them children. At the time, Canadians did not fully appreciate how global grievances and terrorism could affect their lives. Prime Minister Brian Mulroney alienated the Indo-Canadian community by offering condolences to the government of India even when the majority of those killed were Canadian citizens. In 1986, the government of India conducted a public inquiry into the bombings, but a similar full inquiry in Canada was not started until 2006. Only one person, a Canadian Sikh, has been convicted of manslaughter in relation to the bombing and two others were acquitted in 2005 after one of the longest trials in Canadian history. The alleged mastermind of the plot, Talwinder Singh Parmar, a Canadian citizen, eventually was killed in India. One terrorism prosecution against him in Canada collapsed when the state refused to disclose the identity of a key informant and Canada refused to extradite him to India because of concerns that he would be tortured.

If Canada had taken the Air India bombing more seriously it might have been more prepared for 9/11. The failure to prevent the Air India terrorist attack raised similar issues regarding the lack of co-ordination between intelligence and law enforcement and inadequate aviation security measures that played a role in 9/11. The Air India tragedy also demonstrated well before 9/11 how grievances a world away could cause lethal damage in privileged North America and how the technology of the West could be turned against it by terrorists. The current public inquiry into the bombing has a wide mandate that demonstrates the continued relevance of the Air India incident in the post-9/11 environment. The inquiry has been asked to examine the adequacy of intelligence and threat assessment, witness protection, terrorism financing law, aviation security, and criminal prosecutions in responding to the threat of terrorism. Finally, the Air India bombings underlined the fact that Canada's increasingly multicultural population had the potential to bring international terrorism to Canada.

Multiculturalism as a Security Threat: Reliance on Immigration Law as Anti-Terrorism Law

In many respects, Canada has treated its multicultural population as a security threat for its potential to bring offshore grievances to Canada; falling back on immigration law in the absence of anti-terrorism law. Canada's approach thus mirrors American concerns about Canada's immigration policies, including our rapidly growing Muslim populations, and the fear that multicultural policies designed to preserve homeland cultures have not produced sufficient integration or attachment to Canada. At the same time, multiculturalism, especially when combined with respect for human rights, has emerged as a restraint on Canadian anti-terrorism policy and an asset in Canada's fight against global terrorism.

Canada's reliance on immigration law targeted non-citizens in the immediate aftermath of 9/11. Immigration law provided broader liability rules and procedural shortcuts—including the use of secret evidence—than would be tolerated under the criminal law. Under Canadian immigration law, 'engaging in terrorism' or 'being a member of an organization that there are reasonable grounds to believe engages, has engaged or will engage' in acts of terrorism are grounds to make non-citizens inadmissible to Canada on security grounds.[12] Such persons can be detained pending review and can be deported under a complex administrative procedure known as security certificates. Six security certificates have been issued against men suspected of terrorism. In these cases, the persons have been detained, even though it is doubtful that they could be deported to their countries of citizenship—Algeria, Egypt (2), Morocco, Sri Lanka, Syria—without a substantial risk of torture.

The procedure for reviewing security certificates was extraordinary because it allowed a judge to uphold a certificate on the basis of intelligence never disclosed to the detainee or subject to any adversarial challenge. In a 2007 case, however, the Supreme Court held that the complete absence of adversarial challenge violated the Charter. Parliament responded with legislation that followed the British example of allowing security-cleared special advocates to see and to challenge the secret evidence (see Roach, 2008b: 282).[13] Despite this reform, the security certificate process remains subject to vigorous civil society criticism. Moreover, the future of security certificates remains in doubt given that neither indeterminate detention nor deportation to torture is a supportable alternative.

Immigration law applied as anti-terrorism law is both over-inclusive and under-inclusive. Policies such as the safe third country agreement will turn away many more legitimate refugees than terrorists. Security certificates can be used only against non-citizens suspected of terrorism. Indeed, there is a danger that Canada's reliance on security certificates has prevented it from developing expertise with criminal terrorism prosecutions that will have to be used with respect to Canadian citizens. The Air India bombings demonstrate that long before 9/11, Canadian citizens could be involved in international terrorism. In June 2006, 18 people, all of them Canadian citizens, were arrested in Toronto on suspicion of homegrown, Al Qaeda-inspired terrorism. One young person was convicted in October 2008 of participating in a terrorist group, largely on the basis of the testimony of Mubin Shakikh, an informer who had previously campaigned for allowing *shariah* law to be used to resolve family law matters. The young person was found guilty even though he did not know the specifics of a terrorist plot, which was alleged to involve plans to use truck bombs in Toronto and to storm Parliament in Ottawa (Roach, 2008c: 157).[14] In the same month, Canadian citizen Momin Khawaja was convicted of various terrorism offences in relation to his provision of funds, housing, and equipment in Canada, England, and Pakistan for a British-based plot, even though the judge gave him the benefit of the reasonable doubt about whether he knew about the fertilizer bomb plot in England (Roach, 2009: 279). In a globalized world, international terrorism can be committed by Canadian citizens acting at home or abroad and immigration law alone will be an inadequate response to such terrorism.

Multiculturalism as a Security Asset: Towards a Sophisticated and Sustainable Security Policy

Although multiculturalism can result in some security threats, it also provides a potential asset in combatting international terrorism. Multicultural sensitivities in Canada have been offended by the inclusion of a religious or political motive as a requirement in the definition of terrorist activities in the 2001 ATA, even though such a clause was taken from British legislation where it has not been seriously opposed. A court in Canada in 2006 struck down the requirement that terrorist activities be committed for a political and religious motive as an unjustified violation of freedom of expression, association, and religion.[15] This decision was based on the traditional principle that no motive justifies violence and had the effect of making it easier to prosecute terrorism cases. It may be more effective to stigmatize terrorism as murder than to conceive of it as a grander political or religious challenge to the state.

The 2006 report of the Commission of Inquiry into the Activities of Canadian Officials in Relation to Maher Arar underlined the risk that the innocent may be harmed by excesses and inaccuracies in anti-terrorism investigations, but it also made proposals for review that could improve national security activities in the future. For many Canadian Muslims, the Maher Arar case stands as an example of the vulnerable position they find themselves in. The targeting of the wrong people not only threatens civil liberties, but wastes limited resources. The alienation of Muslim communities by insensitive or heavy-handed tactics that inspire fear and distrust may dry up essential sources of information and co-operation with the state within those communities. The key informer in the Toronto terrorism prosecutions was a Muslim who had campaigned to allow the use of *shariah* law in divorce arbitrations before he penetrated the group at the request of Canadian security intelligence and policing agencies. Tactics such as racial and religious profiling offend equality values, but they may also be counterproductive to the task of developing sources that could help to identify potential terrorist plots. As part of its 2004 national security policy, Canada created a Cross Cultural Roundtable on Security Issues. Unfortunately, the Roundtable has not yet emerged as an active presence (Roach, 2006: 405).[16] However, it indicates a constructive desire to engage in cross-cultural dialogue on security issues.

The Harper government in 2006 appointed a public inquiry to examine the failure to prevent the Air India bombings, in part because of an election promise designed to court Indo-Canadian votes. A preliminary study 'found no evidence of racism on the part of anyone in a position of authority' (Rae, 2005: 4), but this finding does not bind the present inquiry, which has a wide mandate to examine not only the mistakes of the past but whether they could be avoided today. Increased independent review of the state's national security activities can respond to both excesses and deficiencies in Canada's anti-terrorism efforts.

United Nations Security Council Resolution 1624 of 2005 calls on all states to take steps to prevent incitement to commit terrorist acts. The resolution declares that states have 'obligations under international law to counter incitement of terrorist acts motivated by extremism and intolerance and to prevent the subversion of educational, cultural and religious institutions by terrorists and their supporters'. Resolution 1624 also calls on states 'to continue dialogue and broaden understanding among civilizations, in an effort to prevent the indiscriminate targeting of different religions and cultures'. Unfortunately, the targeting of what is considered by state officials to be 'extremist' speech that incites terrorism could inhibit intercultural dialogue, particularly if groups believe that some in their community have been unfairly stigmatized as supporting terrorism or fear that this may occur. The criminalization of speech is a problematic anti-terrorism strategy both because it burdens freedom of expression and because criminal prosecutions of such speech may be counterproductive.

Canada has so far resisted demands for new offences targeting speech associated with terrorism. To date, Canada's approach to terrorism speech has been more consistent with the more libertarian American approach than with the enactment of 'glorification of terrorism offences' legislation as in England and Australia. The enactment of such offences into law would raise concerns about both compliance with human rights and the effect on multicultural communities. Speech prosecutions will be a divisive strategy that could fuel fears that anti-terrorism efforts are based on hostility to Islam per se, rather than on a condemnation of violence. They may also distract police and prosecutors from more immediate threats. Canada's reluctance to enact new legislation against the glorification of terrorism, its rejection of the political and religious motive requirement for terrorism, and its emerging commitment to more effective review of national security activities demonstrate how multicultural sensitivities have affected Canadian security policies. Canadian security policy is better for these restraints.

Conclusion

Canadian security policy has been influenced by many of the themes that animate its foreign policies. The concept of human security was used in the immediate aftermath of 9/11 as a justification for the enactment of a new Anti-Terrorism Act that created new terrorism offences and gave the police increased powers in terrorism investigations. This use of the human security concept can be questioned both because it assumed that criminal law reforms would be effective in preventing terrorism and because it finessed the adverse effects of increased state powers on individual rights. Nevertheless, there were some precedents, including the use of hard military powers in the Balkans, for justifying the use of coercive state power in the name of human security. The subsequent use of the human security concept has been less coercive in inspiring an all-risk national security policy that places a premium on emergency preparedness and administrative regulation of sites and substances that can be used for terrorism. This use of the human security concept was more consistent with Canada's leadership in producing the landmines treaty. Canada's national security policy is balanced by focusing not only on the harms of terrorism, but also on the harms that can be caused by disasters and epidemics.

Canada's decision to participate in the NATO-led invasion of Afghanistan shortly after 9/11 demonstrated its status as a relatively weak middle power that could not afford to be seen as not supporting the American-led invasion. There seems to have been little strategy behind this quick decision and Canada is now committed to an exit from Afghanistan despite the resurgence of the Taliban and the Obama administration's decision to focus on Afghanistan rather than on Iraq. Although the invasion disrupted Al Qaeda, the long-term success of the invasion remains very much in doubt. Canada's subsequent decision not to participate in the 2003 invasion of Iraq can be seen as evidence that Canada still can claim to be a smarter and more moral middle power, but it also reflects the reality that Canada, as a weak middle power, had already committed its limited hard power to Afghanistan. Canada's performance on these issues will not resolve the long debate about whether it remains a middle power or the significance of such an ambiguous status.

Canada's post-9/11 security policy has been prepared for multiple audiences, including the United States with its concerns that Canada's multicultural population could pose a security threat, the United Nations with its desire to promote international co-operation in counter-terrorism, as well as Canada's own domestic communities. Initial attempts to co-operate with the Americans have had some unfortunate effects, most notably in the Maher Arar and Omar Khadr cases. In both cases, Canadian officials provided secret and questionable assistance to American anti-terrorism efforts that have subsequently been found by Canadian public inquiries and courts to violate human rights. Both the Charter and multiculturalism have restrained Canadian co-operation with the American War on Terror.

Canada's reliance on immigration law in the form of security certificates and the safe third country agreement as anti-terrorism law falls into a pattern that sees Canada's multicultural population as a potential security threat. The success of such strategies is very much in doubt. Indeterminate detention of suspected terrorists under immigration law is not sustainable and Canada will face huge international criticism if it deports suspected terrorists back to countries like Syria and Egypt where they will be tortured. The use of immigration law as anti-terrorism law responds to some American concerns that Canada's immigration policies are a security threat, but its over-inclusiveness in imposing harms on non-citizens who are not terrorists and under-inclusiveness in ignoring terrorist threats from Canadian citizens are problematic. The line between citizens and non-citizens is neither a firm nor reliable one for determining terrorism. All of the major suspects in the Air India bombings were Canadian citizens by 1985. The recent terrorism convictions in October 2008 affirm that Canadian citizens, including those born and raised in Canada, continue to be involved in international terrorism. Only the criminal law can be used to punish and incapacitate such persons.

There are some signs that Canada has been able to use its commitment to multiculturalism as an asset in developing a sophisticated and sustainable security policy. Canada's willingness to review critically its national security activities both in relation to the Maher Arar case and with respect to the Air India bombings suggests a willingness to learn from past mistakes that have harmed Canadians, whether they have been wrongly accused of or victimized by terrorism. Canada's caution about criminalizing extremist speech and interest in cross-cultural dialogue on security issues may have long-term dividends with respect to human rights and security. Members of multicultural communities should not be afraid to assist the state in its anti-terrorism efforts. Finally, Canada's sensible all-risk approach to national security has the potential to emphasize the interests shared by all Canadians in responding to a wide range of threats to human security.

Notes

1. For a discussion of the concept of human security as an animating theme of Canada's foreign policy in the 1990s, see Axworthy (2003: chs 7 and 8). See also Heinbecker (2000: 11).

2. Canadian Forces handed over some of their Afghan detainees to the Americans (Roach, 2003: 158–61) and subsequent attempts to challenge the treatment by Afghan authorities of those captured by the Canadians have been rejected on the basis that the Canadian Charter does not apply to the activities of Canadian armed forces outside Canada. *Amnesty International v. Canadian Forces* 2008 FCA 401, leave to appeal to the Supreme Court of Canada denied.

3. *Abdelrazik v. Canada* 2009 FC 580.

4. *Suresh v. Canada*, [2002] 1 SCR 3.

5. *Khadr v. Canada* 2005 FC 1076; Khadr v. Canada 2008 SCC 25.

6. In addition, a trial judge of the Federal Court has recently held that the Canadian government's failure to request the repatriation of Omar Khadr violated his Charter and international law rights as a youth accused of crime and declared that the Canadian government should request his repatriation from the Americans. *Khadr v. Canada* 2009 FC 405. The Harper government has refused to do so and is appealing this decision.

7. *Canada v. Canadian Council of Refugees* 2008 FCA 229.

8. *Re Section 83.28 of the Criminal Code* 2004 SCC 42; *Re Vancouver Sun*, 2004 SCC 43.

9. Professor Cotler, who subsequently became Minister of Justice, also made some more traditional civil libertarian criticisms, many of which were adopted subsequently.

10. But for arguments that even less controversial uses of the term are problematic instruments of 'advanced-liberal governmentality', see Hynek (2007: 132).

11. 'This system is capable of responding to both intentional and unintentional threats. It is as relevant in securing Canadians against the next SARS-like outbreak as it is in addressing the risk of a terrorist attack' Canada (2004: 10). For a defence of an all-risk national security policy, see Roach (2003: ch. 7).

12. *Immigration and Refugee Protection Act*, SC 2001, c. 27, s. 34.

13. *Charkaoui v. Canada*, [2007] 1 SCR 350 and *Act to Amend the Immigration and Refugee Procedure Act*, SC 2008 c. 3.

14. One adult, Saad Khalid, subsequently pled guilty (CBC, 2009).

15. *R. v. Khawaja* (2006) 214 CCC (3d) 399 (Ont. Sup. Ct.).

16. The Roundtable was reportedly briefed in March 2008 by government officials on a policy to move away from a policy of multiculturalism as 'celebrating differences' to one that is aimed at promoting 'Canadian identity' and a 'clash of cultures' (*Globe and Mail*, 2008b: A1). This briefing fits into the patterns of perceiving of multiculturalism as a potential security threat.

References

Axworthy, Lloyd. 2003. *Navigating a New World: Canada's Global Future*. Toronto: Knopf.

Canada. 2004. *Securing an Open Society: Canada's National Security Policy*. Ottawa, Apr.

CBC. 2009. 'Toronto-18 Member Pleads Guilty to Terrorism-related Charge', 5 May. At: <www.cbc.ca/canada/toronto/story/2009/05/05/toronto-bomb-plot005.html>.

Commission of Inquiry into the Actions of Canadian Officials in Relation to Maher Arar. 2006. *Report of the Events Relating to Maher Arar*. Ottawa.

Cotler, Irwin. 2001. 'Thinking Outside the Box', in Ronald Daniels et al., eds, *The Security of Freedom: Essays on Canada's Anti-Terrorism Bill*. Toronto: University of Toronto Press, 111–30.

Dosman, E. Alexandra. 2004. 'For the Record: Designating "Listed Entities" for the Purposes of Terrorist Financing Offences at Canadian Law', *University of Toronto Faculty Law Review* 62: 1–27.

Globe and Mail. 2008a. 'Canada Feared US Backlash over Man Trapped in Sudan', 24 July.

———. 2008b. 'Heritage Department Takes Aim at Religious Radicals', 1 Sept., A1.

Hataley, T.S., and Kim Nossal. 2004. 'The Limits of the Human Security Agenda', *Global Change, Peace and Security* 16: 5–9.

Heinbecker, Paul. 2000. 'Human Security: The Hard Edge', *Canadian Military Journal* (Spring): 11–15.

Hynek, Nikola. 2007. 'Humanitarian Arms Control, Symbiotic Functionalism and the Concept of Middlepowerhood', *Central European Journal of International and Security Studies* 1, 2: 132–55.

Internal Inquiry into the Actions of Canadian Officials in Relation to Abdullah Almalki, Ahmad El Maati and Muayyed Nureddin. 2008. Ottawa: Supply and Services.

Library of Congress Research Division. 2003. *Nations Hospitable to Organized Crime and Terrorism.* Washington, Oct.

Paris, Roland. 2001. 'Human Security: Paradigm Shift or Hot Air?', *International Security* 26: 87–95.

Pither, Kerry. 2008. *Dark Days: The Story of Four Canadians Tortured in the Name of Fighting Terror.* Toronto: Viking.

Rae, Bob. 2005. *Lessons to Be Learned.* Ottawa: Public Safety.

Roach, Kent. 2003. *September 11: Consequences for Canada.* Montreal and Kingston: McGill-Queen's University Press.

———. 2006. 'Multiculturalism, Muslim Minorities and Security Policy', *Singapore Journal of Legal Studies*: 405–38.

———. 2007. 'Sources and Trends in Post 9/11 Anti-Terrorism Laws', in Liora Lazarus and Benjamin Goold, eds, *Human Rights and Security.* Oxford: Hart, 227–56.

———. 2008a. 'The Role and Capacities of Courts and Legislatures in Reviewing Canada's Anti-Terrorism Law', *Windsor Review of Legal and Social Issues* 24: 5–56.

———. 2008b. '*Charkaoui* and Bill C-3: Some Implications for Anti-Terrorism Policy', *Supreme Court Law Review* 2nd series, 42: 281–354.

———. 2008c. 'The Toronto Terrorism Conviction', *Criminal Law Quarterly* 54: 157–60.

———. 2009. 'The Ottawa Terrorism Conviction', *Criminal Law Quarterly* 54: 1–4.

Security Intelligence Review Committee. 2008. *Annual Report 2006–2007.* Ottawa.

Senate Standing Committee on National Security and Defence. 2008. *Emergency Preparedness in Canada.* Ottawa.

Additional Readings

Bell, Stewart. 2007. *Cold Terror: How Canada Nurtures and Exports Terrorism around the World,* 2nd edn. Toronto: John Wiley.

Bolan, Kim. 2005. *Loss of Faith: How the Air-India Bombers Got Away with Murder.* Toronto: McClelland & Stewart.

Cohen, Stanley A. 2005. *Privacy, Crime and Terror: Legal Rights and Security in an Age of Terror.* Toronto: Lexis Nexis.

Commission of Inquiry into the Activities of Canadian Officials in Relation to Maher Arar. 2006. *Analysis and Recommendations.* Ottawa: Supply and Services.

———. 2006. *A New Review Mechanism for the RCMP's National Security Activities.*

Commission of Inquiry into the Investigation of the Bombing of Air India Flight 182. 2009. *Final Report and Research Studies,* 4 vols. Ottawa: Supply and Services.

Cotler, Irwin. 2002. 'Terrorism, Security and Rights: The Dilemmas of Democracies', *Journal of National Constitutional Law* 14: 13–69.

Daniels, Ronald, Patrick Macklem, and Kent Roach, eds. 2001. *The Security of Freedom: Essays on Canada's Anti-Terrorism Bill*. Toronto: University of Toronto Press.

Daubney, David, et al., eds. 2002. *Terrorism, Law and Democracy: How Is Canada Changing Following September 11?* Montreal: Les Editions Themis.

Diab, Robert. 2008. *Guantanamo North: Terrorism and the Administration of Justice in Canada*. Halifax: Fernwood.

Drache, Daniel. 2004. *Borders Matter: Homeland Security and the Search for North America*. Halifax: Fernwood.

Forcese, Craig. 2008. *National Security Law: Canadian Practice in International Perspective*. Toronto: Irwin Law. See also <www.nationalsecuritylaw.ca>.

———— and Nicole LaViolette, eds. 2008. *The Human Rights of Anti-Terrorism*. Toronto: Irwin Law.

Hamilton, Dwight, and Kostas Rimsa. 2007. *Terror Threat: International and Homegrown Terrorists and Their Threat to Canada*. Toronto: Dundurn.

Kymlicka, Will. 1998. *Finding Our Way: Rethinking Ethnocultural Relations in Canada*. Toronto: Oxford University Press.

McNaught, Kenneth. 1974. 'Canadian Political Trials', in M.L. Friedland, ed., *Courts and Trials*. Toronto: University of Toronto Press.

Mendes, Errol. 2002. 'Between Crime and War: Terrorism, Democracy and the Constitution', *National Journal of Constitutional Law* 14: 72–97.

Ramraj, Victor, Michael Hor, and Kent Roach, eds. 2005. *Global Anti-Terrorism Law and Policy*. Cambridge: Cambridge University Press.

Saywell, John. 1971. *Quebec 70: A Documentary Narrative*. Toronto: University of Toronto Press.

Wark, Wesley. 2006. *National Security and Human Rights Concerns in Canada: A Survey of Eight Critical Issues in the Post 9/11 Environment*. Ottawa: Privacy Commissioner.

Chapter 12

Canada and the Atlantic Alliance in the Post-Cold War Era: More NATO than NATO?

Benjamin Zyla and Joel J. Sokolsky

> *We often seek to define Canada's role in the world. Well, for whatever reason, we have one in Afghanistan.* (Manley, 2007: 12)

Introduction

In January 2008, an independent commission under the chairmanship of Canada's former Minister of Foreign Affairs, John Manley, published a report on Canada's future role in Afghanistan (Independent Panel, 2008). The minority Conservative government of Prime Minister Stephen Harper had established this panel to review, analyze, and advise the government on Canada's engagement in Afghanistan. The recommendations of the panel caused a storm of debate among Canada's NATO allies. The report threatened the North Atlantic Treaty Organization (NATO) by saying that if the alliance was unable to support Canadian operations in the southern province of Kandahar, Canada should terminate its military operations in support of NATO's International Security Assistance Force (ISAF). It was clear to the panel that the current ISAF mission shows significant deficiencies. First, there are insufficient numbers of military forces deployed against Taliban insurgents. The panel stated: '[A] successful counterinsurgency campaign in Afghanistan requires more ISAF forces. Despite recent indicators of imminent reinforcements, the entire ISAF mission is threatened by the current inadequacy of deployed military resources' (ibid., 35). The recommendation was to deploy 1,000 additional troops to Kandahar province to reinforce ISAF (ibid., 38). Second, the Manley report pointed to the lack of new equipment, such as medium-lift helicopters and high-performance unmanned aerial vehicles (drone aircraft) for the support and safety of Canadian soldiers. The conclusive recommendation of the panel was unequivocal: if those two main undertakings are not met in due time, 'the Government should give appropriate notice to the Afghan and allied governments of its intention to transfer responsibility for security in Afghanistan.' In short, the Canadian government then should leave its combat operations in Afghanistan.

Controversy over Canada's role in Afghanistan, long an issue in partisan politics in Ottawa, seemed to reach ahead following the release of the Manley report as the Harper government indicated that it would introduce a confidence motion in the House of Commons asking for support for continuing the current mission (including the combat role) until 2011. The Liberal Party, the largest opposition block, reached a compromise with the government, and on 13 March 2008 the House of Commons passed a motion that extended the mission, calling for increased emphasis on aid and training of the Afghan forces, but leaving to the commanders on the ground the determination of the extent of the combat role. However, all of this remained contingent upon receiving the requested support from allies (see ibid., n. 2).

Nonetheless, the fact that one of the smaller NATO countries like Canada could demand conditions on its future commitments in Afghanistan beyond 2009 is highly unusual. Such behaviour is generally associated with NATO's major powers, such as the United States, France, and Britain, not Canada. Nevertheless, Canadian contributions in Afghanistan since 2001 have brought Canada recognition among its allies. NATO's chief spokesman, James Appathurai, replied to the Manley report with appreciation of Canada's role:

> Canada has played, and continues to play a very, very important role in a strategically important part of Afghanistan, and we would like to see that role continued. And certainly NATO will, to the extent that we can, support any efforts to provide more . . . to garner more forces, including for the south. We have a long-standing request to nations to provide additional resources, and as Canada will lead this effort certainly NATO will be supportive where we can.

Appathurai also said: 'Let there be no ambiguity. Canada is playing a key role in this mission. We would like to see that role continue. We think Canada has accomplished a lot in Kandahar.'

This applause for Canada's role in and commitment to NATO has come a long way. In the 1990s, the accepted wisdom among Canadians and Canada's allies was that its military role within NATO had declined (Cellucci, 2005; Cohen, 2004). This analysis, however, appears to be inconsistent with Appathurai's blessing of Canada's current role in Afghanistan: assuming that the declinist school of Canadian foreign policy was correct that Canada indeed had declined in world politics in the 1990s, the logical conclusion could only be that Canada remained a laggard after 2001 when the alliance contributed to the so-called War on Terror.

However, by closely examining Canada's record of international engagements in the 1990s, it could be argued that Canada never was a laggard in NATO but a committed, dedicated, and capable ally that did not shy away from its international responsibilities. While this may seem surprising given the Canadian defence spending cuts in the 1990s and the withdrawal of forces from Germany in 1994, it should not be. In fact, during what senior military officers called the 'dark decade', partly because of low morale, Canada made major contributions to European security in the Balkans since it perceived threats to international peace and security overseas rather than at home. Canada made its forces available through UN missions and through NATO. Its forces were engaged continuously in multilateral peace support operations to secure and maintain international peace. These missions gained increasing support at home. While the Canadian Forces may not have been in great shape overall, they were nonetheless oriented towards deployments overseas, roughly similar in nature, although certainly not scale, to those of the US and quite unlike those of most other NATO allies, which were postured to defend their own European homelands. The Canadian bases in Germany were closed in 1994 and the Canadian government found itself with excess capability on its hands to deploy combat forces elsewhere in the world. Ottawa availed itself.

This threat perception also is the basis for allowing the government to uphold Canada's level of commitment after the terrorist attacks on 11 September 2001 and for emphasizing the importance of its expeditionary forces as the primary means to meet those threats abroad. Thus, for Canada, which is one of the few NATO allies that voluntarily deployed to the province of Kandahar, the Afghanistan operations have become the most salient dimension of its continued involvement in the Atlantic alliance. Indeed, Canada has demonstrated a dedication to the success of NATO that seems stronger than NATO's collective commitment to itself. Only this *fait accompli* could explain Canada's role in the alliance today.

Our aim in this chapter is to challenge the accepted wisdom in the literature on Canadian foreign policy, namely, that Canada had retreated from world politics in the post-Cold War era and, specifically, from NATO. We offer empirical evidence for the opposite view and argue that the notion of the 'decade of darkness' is a misrepresentation; Canada was a committed ally and, relative to its size, contributed more to NATO than some of its major NATO allies. We present a revisionist analysis of Canada's role in the post-Cold War era, first, by examining the argument of the declinist school in the Canadian foreign policy literature. Then we analyze Canadian burden-sharing in the early 1990s, making particular reference to Canada's contributions to the humanitarian crisis in the Balkans as well as to NATO's military and political responsibilities. Finally, we trace Canada's role in the Atlantic alliance from 9/11 to Afghanistan, finding that in this latter role Canada appears to be enacting NATO precepts in a manner more committed than other NATO allies.

Canada in the 1990s: The Declinist Argument

Distinguished historian Jack Granatstein (1998, 2004) and political scientist Andrew Cohen (2004) most eloquently represent the 'declinist' school in the literature on Canadian foreign policy. Indeed, their notion of an irrelevant Canada became a popular tool for explaining Canadian behaviour at home and abroad. Both analysts agree that Canada's relative standing in world politics diminished in the 1990s. However, they come to this conclusion from different angles: Cohen argues that domestic political conditions pushed Canada into an isolationist foreign policy in the post-Cold War era. Held responsible for this decline is the government's hesitation to fund key federal departments with international mandates, such as the Department of Foreign Affairs and International Trade (DFAIT) and the Department of National Defence (DND). The underlying reason for the fiscal cuts was Canada's budgetary crisis in the early 1990s that required fiscal restraint across the entire government. Particularly affected by these reductions were DFAIT and DND. The latter, for example, was forced to reduce its operating budget and to close its two bases in Germany.

Cohen suggests that Canada's irrelevancy in world affairs is a novelty for Canada. In the 1940s and 1950s, during the 'Golden Age' of Canadian foreign policy under the leadership of then Secretary of State Lester B. Pearson, Canada was a vital international actor making a difference in world politics (see Hillmer, 2008; Nossal, Chapter 2, this volume). Back then, Pearson, Hume Wrong, and Norman Robertson (the latter two career civil servants in the Department of External Affairs) worked hard to have Canada recognized internationally as a middle power at a time when the country had the reputation of being the 'helpful fixer' or 'honest broker'[1] in world politics. Since then, a debate has evolved in the literature about the explanatory value and veracity of the middle-power concept (see Nossal, Chapter 2, and Bosold, Chapter 3, this volume). However, according to the declinist school, this era ended with the post-Cold War era. In short, in the 1990s Canada is supposed to have vanished from world politics and has fallen behind on the list of the most influential countries in the world. Cohen (2004: 3) argues that:

> We did things abroad. We went to war, we kept the peace, and we died doing both. We fed, taught, and treated people in hard places, we brokered and proselytized in international councils. We bought goods from the corners of the earth and sold them there, too, and we became rich. We have a past. We come from somewhere.

Today, Canada is no longer 'as strong a soldier, as generous a donor, and as effective a diplomat, and it has diminished us as [a] people' (ibid., 2). Taken together, the fiscal cuts in the 1990s, according to the declinist school, resulted in a diminished international role for Canada. Particularly affected by the budget cuts was Canada's military, which had become 'undermanned, under funded, overextended, and ill-equipped' (ibid., 27).

Granatstein agrees with Cohen. However, he argues that Canadian politicians and the public at large 'killed' the Canadian military. In particular, the generation of Lester B. Pearson can be blamed for having started this decline:

> What no one remembers any longer is that, when Pearson cobbled the force together, few in Canada cheered . . . . But Canadians never really understood what their peacekeepers were doing, why they were good at their jobs, and why they were needed. And because they fell in love with peacekeeping, Canadians began to fall out of love with the true purpose of a military—to be ready to fight wars. (Granatstein, 2004: 13, 14–15)

Since the era of Pearson, Canadians have elected governments across party lines that continued the neglect of Canada's military and its foreign service. In the 1990s, Canadians starved the armed forces to the point where they had to 'do more with less': more operational deployments with less capabilities, equipment, and manpower.

Other analysts supported this view. *Canada Among Nations*, a well-acclaimed annual publication, argued in its 2002 edition that Canada was vanishing from world politics to the point where it became irrelevant (Hillmer and Molot, 2002). Others who have expressed similar views include Mel Hurtig (2003), Douglas Bland and Sean Maloney (2004), the Conference of Defence Associations (2002), a pro-defence lobby group in Ottawa, and the Conference Board of Canada (2000).

Indeed, the 1990s did not start well for Canadian foreign and defence policy.[2] The Mulroney government, while faced with a budgetary crisis at home, was forced to take actions to consolidate the federal budget. Even though all federal departments were ordered to save money, the Department of National Defence had high discretionary and capital spending, and became the primary target for reductions. DND was forced to tighten its belt and cut expenditures. It did so despite the fact that the same government had promised Canadians in 1984 that 'Canada will once again play its full part in the defence systems of NATO' (Canada, 1984: 7). Despite the government's review of Canada's foreign and defence policies (DND, 1987), when it promised to invest more than $183 billion over 15 years towards the modernization of Canadian armed forces in Germany, it was faced with reality at the end of the decade. A lack of funds and of public support as well as high inflation rates contributed to cutbacks at DFAIT and DND. With the end of the Cold War, Canadians questioned the rationale for large conventional militaries. A poll in 1995, for example, revealed that only 16 per cent of Canadians supported military investments, whereas redistributing Canada's wealth to the provinces was supported by 73 per cent, followed by youth employment measures (66 per cent), and health care (64 per cent) (Greenspon, 1998). The Mulroney government cut the military budget in two sets: first, the procurement programs for new nuclear submarines, battle tanks for the 4 Mechanized Brigade in Germany, new helicopters, a long-range patrol aircraft for the navy, and 1,200 additional troops for the brigade in Germany all were cancelled in 1989 (DND, 1992). According to some estimates, this saved the Canadian taxpayer more than $1.3 billion per year.[3] Canada also discontinued the Canadian Air–Sea Transportable Brigade Group (CAST) that was earmarked for the defence of Norway. Fifteen Canadian Forces bases in total across the country were closed as part of the fiscal consolidation process. The cuts took place at a time when Canada still had 6,600 troops forwardly deployed in Germany. The unilateral withdrawal of Canada from Germany cast doubts on Canada's commitments to the alliance. This fear was shared equally inside DND.

In 'Good Company' and Pulling Its Weight: Canada and NATO in the 1990s

These cuts were made, however, with regard to the fundamental consideration that Canada's national security policy was now being made in a new security environment. The fall of the Berlin Wall in 1989 transformed the international system and changed the way states interact. As a consequence of these systemic changes, the level of tensions among Cold War adversaries began to ease. This affected the conduct of foreign policy, and neither Canada nor NATO remained unchanged. If the Canadian defence effort exhibited elements of decline in the 1990s, it nevertheless was more than pulling its own weight when measured against what other NATO allies were doing. Canada did what mattered most to the alliance in the 1990s.

Notwithstanding the withdrawal of Canadian troops from Germany, Canada remained an active ally in the 'new' NATO. In fact, the decision to close two bases in Germany was consistent with NATO policies. Like Canada, other NATO countries cut the size of their troops. According to John Lis and Zachary Selden (2003) they did so quite drastically. For example, American troops sent to fight in Operation Desert Storm during the Gulf War in 1991 did not return to their bases in Europe and were redeployed back to the United States.[4] Generally speaking, the level of defence spending among NATO countries (measured against GDP) fell significantly; in the United States defence spending fell from 5.2 per cent on average for the years 1980–4 to 3.7 per cent for the 1990–5 period (see Table 12.1) (see Lis and Selden, 2003; NATO, 2003). France cut its

Table 12.1   Defence Expenditures as % of Gross Domestic Product (based on current prices)

Country	Average 1980–4	Average 1985–9	Average 1990–4	Average 1995–9
France	4.0	3.8	3.4	2.9
Germany	3.3	3.0	2.1	1.6
United Kingdom	5.2	4.5	3.7	2.7
NATO (Europe)	3.5	3.2	2.6	2.2
Canada	2.0	2.1	1.8	1.3
United States	5.6	6.0	4.7	3.3
North America	5.3	5.6	4.4	3.2
NATO Total	4.5	4.6	3.5	2.7

Source: NATO (2003).

level of defence spending from 4 per cent on average for 1980–5 to 3.4 per cent for 1990–5 (ibid.). The United Kingdom lowered its defence spending from 5.6 per cent on average for 1980–5 to 4.7 per cent for 1990–5.

While defence budgets shrank, NATO's military role became less important relative to its political functions, which have always been an integral part of the alliance but were less pronounced during the Cold War. During the Cold War, the numbers of troops and equipment, as well as levels of defence spending measured as a percentage of national GDP, were seen as an indicator of the extent of the member states' devotion to the alliance. However, the fall of the Berlin Wall in 1989 questioned these parameters of allied commitments.[5] In other words, while military capabilities at one time were a solid indicator of how much a NATO state shouldered allied burdens, the size and capabilities of the military do not necessarily translate into international influence in the post-Cold War era. The alliance has had less need for military commitments that were designed for the Cold War. Instead, flexible and highly mobile troops were needed to complete a range of tasks, including peace-building and reconstruction, as well as fighting in wars. NATO's London Summit in 1990, its first meeting after the fall of the Berlin Wall, provided guidance for NATO's new role by endorsing co-operation with NATO's former adversaries. There, NATO leaders officially determined an end to the division of Europe and offered countries from Central and Eastern Europe (CEE) a 'hand of friendship'. The Soviet Union had become a 'friend' of NATO.

NATO's new institutions, such as the North Atlantic Cooperation Council and the Partnership for Peace program, facilitated the outreach process and managed the evolving security vacuum in CEE. These institutions were based on three pillars: dialogue, co-operation, and collective defence.[6] Canada was responsive to this outreach process, and actively supported the Partnership for Peace program politically because it was in Canada's national interest to do so. It provided Canada with (1) transparency and a democratic control of the armed forces of CEE states; (2) a network of military and defence-related issues; (3) a co-operative relationship between CEE states and NATO; (4) confidence-building measures among new and old allies; and (5) it helped satisfy the United States for more Canadian globalism and solidified the Canada US relationship. Whether all of this made Canada the 'linchpin' in transatlantic affairs between Europe and North America is debatable. The idea of Canada's being a linchpin evolves out of the Canadian literature but is entirely absent from the US or European literature.

Militarily, NATO forces were ordered to become more flexible, more mobile, and more adaptable for the new security environment. Crisis management and multinational rapid reaction forces replaced large conventional force postures.

Canada quickly understood the new nature of NATO and put its armed forces under a transition process. Then Chief of the Defence Staff, General A.J.G.D. de Chastelain, noted that the ambition of the government and the Canadian Forces is to develop 'general-purpose combat capable armed forces, stationed in Canada for the most part, ready to deploy anywhere in the world in defence of Canada's interests' (quoted in Jockel and Sokolsky, 1993: 391).[7] Thus, it is not surprising that Canada was able to offer its services during an evolving crisis in the Balkans. It backed up its word with deeds and money when a major ethnic conflict unfolded in Southeast Europe that posed a significant threat: the crisis had the potential to seriously undermine European security (Mearsheimer, 1994–5). The transatlantic relationship also was strained (Vanhoonacker, 2001: 147–204). Canada's chief interest was to contain this conflict. While the United States demanded from its European allies more commitments for containing an ethno-nationalist conflict beyond their doorstep, it was apparent that Europe on its own was unable to stop it (see Cohen et al., 2003).

It started on 25 June 1991 with a referendum on Slovenian independence in which 88 per cent voted in favour. The leadership of the Yugoslav National Army (JNA) did not recognize this declaration of independence and used force to stop Slovenian secession (see Burg and Shoup, 1999). When the European Community failed to bring peace, the transatlantic alliance, represented chiefly by NATO, once again was called upon, this time, to help in a crisis-management operation. Canada was one of the first countries to answer the call, which marked the beginning of a deployment that lasted nearly a decade.

NATO's bold diplomatic and peacekeeping initiatives in Yugoslavia heralded a more interventionist doctrine of international affairs. It set a precedent in justifying on humanitarian grounds an intervention into the domestic affairs of a sovereign country. Canada was a strong supporter of a more active and interventionist NATO in former Yugoslavia, notwithstanding the fact that Canadian territory was not directly threatened by this crisis. However, Canada's interests were affected and it became one of the most outspoken advocates of a forceful intervention (Gammer, 2001: 80–5). What the government hoped for was a more forceful Chapter VII mission, which is a UN-mandated peace operation designed to ensure the peace by force if necessary. In that sense a peace-enforcement operation differs sharply from a peacekeeping mission.

Canadians first participated in the European Community Monitoring Mission (ECMM), and then in the United Nation's Protection Force (UNPROFOR) (see Maloney, 1997). UNPROFOR was a peacekeeping mission mandated to ensure the delivery of humanitarian aid, to establish so-called safe-zones, and to negotiate ceasefires (*United Nations Chronicle*, 1995). Canada's contingent— initially of 1,139 troops—(Operation Harmony) was tasked with monitoring UN Protected Areas (UNPAS) in Croatia (Bland and Maloney, 2004: 230). They were deployed to sector west, which, according to Carol Off, was one of the most dangerous sectors because it shared a hostile front line. Canada's contingent to UNPROFOR went through six rotations and was a significant contribution. Canada was the fifth largest country contributing to UNPROFOR (see Table 12.2). In total, Canada sent 2,091 soldiers, 45 police officers, and 15 observers (ibid.). Only France, Jordan, the United Kingdom, and Pakistan contributed more troops than Canada.

In view of Canada's fiscal situation, this commitment can be seen as a major contribution to upholding international peace and security in Southeast Europe. Furthermore, Canadian soldiers were better equipped, in relative terms, than some of its UNPROFOR allies. Canadians, for example, were the

Table 12.2   Allied Contributions to UNPROFOR

Country	Police	Troops	Observers	Total	%	Rank
France	41	4,493	11	4,545	11.5	1
Jordan	71	3,367	48	3,486	8.82	2
United Kingdom	0	3,405	19	3,424	8.66	3
Pakistan	19	3,017	34	3,070	7.76	4
Canada	45	2,091	15	2,151	5.45	5
Netherlands	10	1,803	48	1,861	4.71	6
United States	0	0	748	748	18.9	20

Source: Congressional Research Service (2003); UN (1996); personal interview with Lt. Col. Ross Fetterly, Government of Canada, Department of National Defence.

only ones having armoured personnel carriers, which made the Canadian contingent to UNPROFOR a fully mechanized brigade (Hewitt, 1998: 54). In 1993, Canadians encountered some of the worst fighting of the entire UNPROFOR operation when caught in the middle of the battle for the Medak Pocket (Off, 2004).

After the humanitarian situation had worsened and the Serbs disregarded NATO's list of compliances, the alliance answered with an air campaign (Operation Deliberate Force), which led to the Dayton peace agreement of 5 October 1995. In 1996 NATO's Implementation Force (IFOR) replaced an increasingly weakened and incapable UNPROFOR force. Canada sustained its Balkan commitments and dispatched 1,047 troops to IFOR (Bland and Maloney, 2004: 233).[8] The Canadian contingent consisted of a mechanized infantry company, an engineer squadron, and a national support and command element. Thus, Canadians helped to enforce the Dayton peace accord.

In December 1996, a Stabilization Force (SFOR) replaced IFOR and, again, Canada did not shirk its international responsibilities. It maintained its troops in the Balkans through Operation Palladium. This time, the government increased the number of troops to help stabilize the region. SFOR, like IFOR, operated under the authority of UN Security Council Resolution 1088. Canada sent 1,327 troops to SFOR. This commitment pushed the Canadian Forces to their limits: nearly all Canadian army units rotated through SFOR (ibid., 234).[9] Canada's relative standing in SFOR, again, was noteworthy. With its contribution, Canada ranked eighth of 18 countries in total (US Department of Defense, 2000: II–9).

In 1999, a second crisis shadowed the Balkans, this time in Kosovo. The conflict started in 1998 when ethnic Albanians began attacking the Serbian minority. The response of the Milosevic regime in Serbia was to violently repress the Albanian population, which created more than 400,000 refugees and caused 2,500 deaths (Congressional Research Service, 2001: 2).

As in Croatia and Bosnia, the Kosovo crisis posed a significant threat to the transatlantic alliance, in that NATO's most fundamental values were at stake. Again, Canada did not shy from shouldering some of that responsibility and was the seventh largest contributor (of 18 nations in total) to the 78-day Kosovo air campaign. Ottawa sent 18 CF-18 fighter jets and paid all of its own logistical costs. Although Canada provided only 2 per cent of the 912 jets, it flew 10 per cent of NATO's sorties (37,000 in total).[10] In addition, Canadian fighter jets, besides those of the US, were the only ones technologically capable of carrying precision-guided munitions. Thus, Canadian equipment provided NATO with a comparative advantage. Combining the contributions for the ground and air campaigns, Canada ranked third out of 13 countries in total. This was a disproportionate contribution to the NATO operation and one that Canada often does not get credit for.

In addition to its military commitments, Canada also was engaged diplomatically and financially in bringing stability and peace to the Balkan region. Relative to its size, Canada made a large contribution to the UN peace forces, which was used to pay for the common costs of the Bosnia and Herzegovina command. It gave $515,939 or 9.58 per cent of the total budget and was thus the third largest contributor (UN, 1996).

Moreover, as noted above, the new international security environment demanded that NATO's armed forces fulfill new roles and responsibilities. Large, conventional military force structures with highly inflexible, inefficient, and largely immobile troops had become outdated. Instead, capabilities for NATO's crisis management strategies established new demands in the post-Cold War environment. Thus, a state's contribution to NATO's rapid response forces can be seen as a benchmark of allied burden-sharing. During the 1990s, NATO's forces were sectioned into reaction forces[11]: rapidly deployable forces, main defence forces that are the 'classical territorial' defence forces, and augmentation forces earmarked for reinforcement functions. NATO's rapid response units are the forces that carry out NATO's new crisis management strategies. These units included multinational command structures and formations, such as the Allied Command Europe (ACE) Mobile Land Force, the ACE Rapid Reaction Corps for ground forces, and the Immediate and Rapid Reaction Forces (Air). The ACE force consisted of 5,000 troops and was supplied by 14 NATO states. Canada promised an infantry battalion group. In addition to the land forces, NATO also maintained standing naval units, for example, the Standing Naval Forces Atlantic (SNFL). This force consisted of six to 10 destroyers and frigates. Canada, Germany, the Netherlands, the United Kingdom, and the United States each sent one ship on a permanent basis. Canada's relative commitment to the NATO Reaction Force (NRF) ranked sixth among 16 allies (Congressional Budget Office, 2001).

After 9/11, there were further changes with the creation of the NATO Response Force (NFR) at the Prague Summit of 2002 and its subsequent activation at a full strength of 25,000 personnel in 2006. A fully joint and multinational force, the NRF is now a central crisis response mechanism where Canada plays a key role, especially in the maritime environment with its permanent contribution of a vessel to Standing NATO Maritime Group 1. SNMG1 drew public attention off the Horn of Africa in 2009, where it continues to conduct anti-piracy operations, with a Canadian frigate, HMCS *Winnipeg*, taking part.

In addition to more mobile and flexible forces, there was high demand for more UN peacekeeping forces in various global hot spots. Perhaps a more accurate indicator for measuring a country's relative commitment to these missions is the percentage of a country's total labour force made available to these peacekeeping operations. According to the numbers in 1999, Canada ranked sixth out of 26 countries that sent peace support personnel to UN peacekeeping operations (US Department of Defense, 1999: III–15). Canada, in fact, ranked higher than some of its major allies, such as the United States, the United Kingdom, and Germany, and Canada's 1999 contribution included a 15.8 per cent increase from 1998.

In addition to contributing to forces and operations, NATO also needs to sustain its common infrastructure, such as the headquarters building in Brussels, NATO's operational commands, and other costs. The salaries of NATO's international staff (NATO's civil servants), as well as of the support personnel, also need to be paid. The monies for this budget come from NATO member states. More specifically, NATO's budget is divided into three sub-budgets: the civil budget, the military budget, and the security and investment program. The level of contribution to the operating budget can be interpreted as an indication of the commitment states made to maintain NATO's operational effectiveness. In 1999, Canada contributed US $53.7 million (of US $1,114.8 million in total), or 4.8 per cent, to NATO's common budgets (Congressional Budget Office, 2001). This placed Canada sixth among 19 NATO allies in 1999.

Peace, security, and stability were clearly the priorities of NATO in the early 1990s. As part of NATO's 'hand of friendship', the alliance also donated aid to Central and Eastern Europe. Between 1991 and 1997, Canada gave US $251 million, or 5.94 per cent of its GDP, in support of nation-building projects in CEE (ibid.). This placed Canada fourth out of 17 nations in total. Only Germany, Denmark, and Norway offered more economic aid to CEE than Canada.[12]

In the post-Cold War era, Ottawa, largely with public support, had been dispatching forces overseas to participate in increasingly robust peacekeeping operations. Notwithstanding the fact that this meant the Canadian Forces engaged in some of their heaviest fighting since the Korean War, the peacekeeping myth did not go away (for a recent discussion, see Granatstein, 2007: ch. 2). Canadian peacekeeping was good politics for the government in Ottawa and kept the critics of Canada's armed forces at bay. Nevertheless, when it joined the US-led Operation Enduring Freedom in 2001–2 to topple the Taliban regime, Ottawa was operating in line with Canadian defence policy and the military experience of the 1990s. 'Here was still another multilateral "peace-enforcement" operation in a troublesome area of the world', which saw Canada deploying forces alongside traditional allies and friends in an operation that was fully sanctioned by both the UN and NATO (Jockel and Sokolsky, 2009: 329–30). Moreover, despite the cuts and budget reductions of the 1990s, Ottawa, as foreseen in the 1994 White Paper (DND, 1994), had the expeditionary forces to deploy. It sent six naval vessels, multiple aircraft, and 2,000 troops (see Standing Committee on Foreign Affairs and International Development, 2008; Lang and Stein, 2007).

The mission in Afghanistan was in Canada's national interest as that country was proven to have provided safe haven for international terrorists who continued to pose violent threats against Western cities and infrastructure, including those in Canada. Thus, the Canadian decision to deploy forces to Afghanistan in the fall of 2001 and early 2002 cannot be explained simply as an attempt to please Washington. All Canadian governments since 2001, as well as many Canadians, see the incidents of global terrorism that have arisen from radical Islam as a threat to Canada. The Martin government put it succinctly in the 2005 defence policy statement by saying that 'an increasingly interdependent world has tightened the links between international and domestic security, and developments abroad can affect the safety of Canadians in unprecedented ways. Today's front lines stretch from the streets of Kabul to the rail lines of Madrid to our own Canadian cities' (Canada, 2005: 5). One pro-defence pundit has said bluntly: 'We are at war. Ultimately the war against Islamist terrorism is our war' (Granatstein, 2007: 74).

Moreover, the decision to participate in the Afghanistan mission was in line with the approach to national security that had been championed by Lloyd Axworthy, Canada's Foreign Minister from 1996 to 2000. Garnering a large measure of popular support, and reflecting on the character of the UN and NATO operations of the 1990s, Axworthy had argued that the meaning of security had changed. It was no longer the security of states that was at risk, but that of the lives and rights of individuals, even from their own governments. Thus, Canada should be prepared to use its military to promote 'human security'. As Axworthy explained: 'When other means of addressing the threats have been exhausted, robust measures (including military action) may be needed to defend human security' (Axworthy, 1999). The atrocities committed by the Taliban and by the terrorists they harboured met the human security interventionist criteria.

In Washington and elsewhere, the regime of Saddam Hussein was viewed as another oppressive regime that mistreated its own population for its own benefit. Consequently, during the run-up to the American invasion of Iraq in 2003 and believing that Ottawa shared this view, the George W. Bush administration had put out its diplomatic feelers to elicit support from Canada. The Chrétien government dithered until the eve of war. As two analysts put it: 'To say the least, the Canadian government was hedging its bets and ducking the hard question until the very last minutes' (Brunnee and Di Giovanni, 2005: 378). It appeared in retrospect that Canada had worked with two strategies. Through diplomatic circles the US government was made to believe that Canada would support the mission in Iraq. The Canadian military, assuming the government would join Washington in an attack, co-ordinated with the US Central Command to send a Canadian battle group of 600–800 troops to Iraq. These steps were taken notwithstanding the fact that Canada's Minister of National Defence was publicly on record to committing 1,000 Canadian military personnel to the NATO-led ISAF mission. His commitment, in turn, meant that Canadian ground forces were not readily available to fight with the US in Iraq. Paul Cellucci, who then was the US ambassador to Canada, contends in his account of his efforts to secure Canadian participation that '[d]espite the obvious hesitations about the prospects of an invasion, we believed that Canada would be with us even without a second UN resolution on Iraq' (Cellucci, 2005: 135). At the same time, Canada's diplomats at the Canadian mission to the UN worked around the clock to solicit international support for a compromise resolution on Iraq. In retrospect, and in light of later revelations, it is evident that the United States was given no clear indication as to what the Canadian position was on the invasion of Iraq.

It was, therefore, still something of a surprise to Washington when, on 17 March 2003, the Prime Minister told a cheering House of Commons that Canada would not participate in the war. Coming after what seemed to be an inconsistent Canadian approach, the method by which the final decision was made illustrates a consistency in Canadian national security policy, namely, that decisions are made at the highest level, in either the Prime Minister's Office (PMO) or the Privy Council Office (PCO), and not in the Department of Foreign Affairs and International Trade. Indeed, during the 1990s DFAIT worked at arm's length from the PMO and PCO. The focus of the department had shifted to international trade issues, exploring ways of accessing new markets for Canadian businesses. NATO policy was of minor importance, if at all, to the department.

From the standpoint of the Bush administration the problem was not so much Ottawa's decision not to contribute forces but Prime Minister Chrétien's stated reasons for this decision. The Prime Minister openly rejected the US policy of regime change and associated Canada with the strong opposition coming from some other NATO allies, notably Germany and France. Moreover, Mexico and Chile, countries in a region of increasing interest to Canada, openly opposed the attack. Above all, Ottawa voiced its concern about what it saw as the unilateral nature of the invasion. In his remarks in the House of Commons, Chrétien criticized the United States for its lack of a clear UN mandate. What the Prime Minister did not mention was that a few years earlier, in 1999, the Canadian government had sent military forces to fight against Serbia, also without the explicit endorsement of the UN.

In addition, in spite of Chrétien's 'no', Canada indirectly supported the US by sending 31 exchange officers to serve with American and British ground forces in Iraq. Also, Canadian ships sailed to the Persian Gulf in support of enforcing UN sanctions against Iraq. Ironically, despite Ottawa's loud protestations that it was unwilling to join the 'coalition of the willing', Canada made a larger contribution than some who did join.

Still, Canada was acutely aware that steps were required to respond to Washington's irritation over how Ottawa had handled the Iraq issue. Not surprisingly, then, almost immediately after the 'no' to Iraq, the Chrétien government had moved quickly to say 'yes' to deploying the promised forces to the ongoing mission in Afghanistan. In a sense, the new deployment to Afghanistan had become Canada's substitute for participating in the Iraq war. Chrétien's successors, Paul Martin and Stephen Harper, continued to demonstrate to Washington, and to the American people and media, that, notwithstanding the recent disagreement over Iraq and despite unprecedented criticism of Canada in right-wing American media outlets, Canada has been a good ally. The embassy in Washington mounted a vigorous public relations campaign, which included placing posters in the Washington, DC, transit system assuring Americans that Canada took the War on Terror seriously and made a major contribution to the war in Afghanistan (Jockel and Sokolsky, 2008: 106). More concretely and importantly, both the Martin and Harper governments increased the level of defence spending and pledged to expand the Canadian military. They began to act on the military advice offered by the new and more forceful Chief of the Defence Staff, General Rick Hillier, who wanted to 'transform' the Canadian military by placing greater emphasis upon war-fighting and the need to provide the weapons to make this possible. The Martin government, acting on the recommendation of General Hillier, not only renewed the mandate in Afghanistan but also sent forces to the dangerous south. The Harper government, which came into office in 2006, fully endorsed that position and stayed the course.

Given the current number of American troops deployed and additional ones about to be dispatched to Afghanistan, the overall Canadian contribution of about 2,800 may not seem significant. Nonetheless, Canada's contributions to ISAF represent the fourth largest commitment of a NATO ally. Only the US, Britain, and Germany send more troops. Canada also is one of the few countries that engaged in combat. Thus, when measured qualitatively rather than quantitatively, Canada's ranking as an ally is high.

Canada was able to afford this commitment as its economy had recovered from the recession in the early 1990s. Since the end of the fighting in the Balkans, the Canadian Forces also had no other major military commitment overseas. Nonetheless, for a total force of 60,000 personnel, the Afghanistan commitment is a significant burden. DND's internal bureaucracy has pointed out that the Canadian Forces cannot undertake any other major military operation in the near future.

The Afghanistan operation also has been the first test of Canada's new military doctrine of a 'three-block war', in which the armed forces must be prepared to engage in the full spectrum of conflict, including peacekeeping, peacemaking, and assistance in humanitarian relief. The concept was first developed by General Charles Krulak of the US Marines. As noted, the Canadian version of the doctrine is rooted in the experience of Canadian service personnel in failed and failing states in the 1990s. During these conflicts, Canadian soldiers were called on by other allies, international organizations, and non-governmental organizations to perform a variety of tasks. Moreover, although the Canadian version of three-block war is based on human security, Canadian Axworthians were not eager, for their part, to recognize that human security dovetails very nicely with the arguments of the Bush administration and US neo-conservatives that terrorism can best be fought by encouraging democracy, development, and human rights in the Middle East's trouble spots.

Conclusion

Canada's contributions to the war in Afghanistan are just the latest demonstration, albeit the most dramatic and costly, of Canada's commitment to NATO since the inauguration of the alliance in 1949. Though criticized in some circles for being a laggard, especially after the Cold War, because of deep cuts in defence spending and force levels, Canada did maintain an expeditionary capability. Ottawa used its diminished forces to shoulder a significant portion of the burden through its peace-enforcement missions in the Balkans in the 1990s in support of European security and NATO when and where such support was most needed. When the post-Cold War decade ended, Canada had also gotten its fiscal house in order and enjoyed budgetary surpluses and a growing economy. Thus, despite the many problems that beset the Canadian Forces, Ottawa was strategically, politically, and materially predisposed and able to deploy military forces to Afghanistan again in 2001 when Canada was called upon by its allies to make a contribution in blood and treasure. This commitment spurred the Canadian government to markedly increase defence spending and to afford the forceful and outspoken Chief of the Defence Staff, General Rick Hillier, greater influence over the defence policy in general and the operations in Afghanistan in particular. The men and women of the Canadian Forces have risen to the challenge and the confidence placed in them, demonstrating a military prowess that has earned them the justifiable praise of allies and a new-found pride among the Canadian people.

During the Canadian federal election in the fall of 2008 Prime Minister Harper made a surprising public announcement that a re-elected Conservative government would withdraw Canadian troops from Afghanistan by 2011. The Conservatives won the election but with another minority government. In the Speech from the Throne of 20 November, which opened the new Parliament following the election, the Harper government stated that it would be 'transforming Canada's engagement in Afghanistan to focus on reconstruction and development, and to prepare for the end of the military mission there in 2011' (Canada, 2008). The following day, at a meeting in Canada of countries with troops in southern Afghanistan, the Minister of National Defence, Peter MacKay, was asked how Ottawa would respond to a request from US President-Elect Barack Obama for 'additonal help' in Afghanistan. MacKay responded that the US would have to look to other countries rather than those 'already carrying a disproportionate share of the load'. 'The reality is', he stressed, 'there are other NATO doors that president-elect Obama should be knocking on first' (CBC, 2008). Nevertheless, Ottawa has indicated that it will continue to contribute to the goal of promoting development, democracy, and stability in Afghanistan.

A consistently committed ally in war and peace, including during the 1990s, Canada is indeed now behaving in a manner more NATO than NATO when it comes to the alliance's stated objectives with regard to Afghanistan. The sacrifices, as well as the willingness of the government to expend political capital in the face of a still ambivalent public, have surely earned Ottawa the right to demand that there now be more NATO in Afghanistan.

Notes

The research for this paper has been supported by a grant of the Department of National Defence and its Special Projects Fund, the Social Sciences and Humanities Research Council of Canada (SSHRC), and a post-doctoral research fellowship from the Faculty of Social Sciences, Univerity of Ottawa. The authors also wish to thank Scot Davy for his assistance.

1. This notion became particularly popular after Canada helped to mediate international conflicts such as the Suez Crisis in 1956. See, e.g., Chapnick (2005).
2. To be fair to the declinist school, it should be acknowledged that their analysis extends beyond the Canada–NATO relationship. Yet, implicitly or explicitly, it still is a pivotal part of that analysis.
3. This sum excludes the money spent for training the forces in Germany. See, e.g., Rempel (1992: 232).
4. The literature on the Gulf War and the composition of Operation Desert Storm is vast. Collins (1991) provides a succinct overview. For US forces not returning to Germany but to the United States, see Campbell and Ward (2003). For a greater analysis of the transformation of post-1989 forces, see Moskos et al. (2000).
5. This change of the notion of security was affirmed by the then NATO Secretary-General, Javier Solana. See 'Press Point of Mr. Javier Solana, NATO Secretary General, and Minister Igor Rodionov, Russian Defence Minister', Meeting of the North Atlantic Council in Defence Ministers Session, NATO Headquarters, Brussels, 18 Dec. 1996.
6. As one aide to Secretary-General Manfred Woerner said, Woerner convinced NATO leaders that the window of opportunity to help shape the new democracies of CEE was very small. Interview with Jamie Shea, NATO Headquarters, 18 May 2007. For a detailed account of an evolving NATO in the 1990s, see, e.g., Kay (1998). Others accounts include Haglund (1996); Asmus (2002); Sloan (1989, 2002); Asmus et al. (1993).
7. Charles Moskos, while analyzing and comparing the transformation of Western armed forces, noted that Canada was one of the first countries that successfully transformed its armed forces to a post-modern military. See Moskos et al. (2000: 9).
8. Lenard Cohen counted a different number of Canadian troops and came to 1,035 in total (see Cohen, 2003: 127). The official DND number is 1,029, according to an interview with a DND official, June 2007.

9. The numbers provided by Bland and Maloney in *Campaigns for International Security*, it should be noted, are not identical with numbers available from other publications or official government documents. Cohen (2003: 127), for example, counted 1,800 troops as Canada's contribution to SFOR. DND lists 1,641 as the official number (interview with Senior Officer of DND, Finance Section, 2007).

10. Numbers have to be treated with caution. Daalder and O'Hanlon (2000: 4), for example, counted 'nearly 40,000' sorties.

11. All references to statistics and organization relate to the 1990s.

12. More specifically, the numbers for France between 1991 and 1997 are US $219 million (or 5.18 per cent), for the United Kingdom US $106.5 million (or 2.52 per cent), and for the United States US $244.6 million (or 5.79 per cent). Congressional Budget Office (2001).

References

Appathurai, James. 2008. 'Weekly Press Briefing', 30 Jan. At: <www.nato.int/docu/speech/2008/s080130b.html>.

Asmus, Ronald D. 2002. *Opening NATO's Door: How the Alliance Remade Itself for a New Era*. New York: Columbia University Press.

———, Richard Kugler, and Stephen F. Larrabee. 1993. 'Building a New NATO', *Foreign Affairs* 72, 4 (Sept.–Oct.): 28–40.

Axworthy, Lloyd. 1999. 'Message from the Honorable Lloyd Axworthy', Government of Canada, DFAIT, *Statements and Speeches* 99/35, 13 May.

Bland, Douglas L., and Sean M. Maloney. 2004. *Campaigns for International Security: Canada's Defence Policy at the Turn of the Century*. Montreal and Kingston: McGill-Queen's University Press.

Brunnee, Julia, and Adrian Di Giovanni. 2005. 'Iraq: A Fork in the Special Relationship?', *International Journal* (Spring): 60: 375–84.

Burg, Steven L., and Paul Shoup. 1999. *The War in Bosnia-Herzegovina: Ethnic Conflict and International Intervention*. Armonk, NY: M.E. Sharpe.

Campbell, Kurt M., and Celeste Johnson Ward. 2003. 'New Battle Stations?', *Foreign Affairs* 82, 4: 95–103.

Canada. 2005. *Canada's International Policy Statement: A Role of Pride and Influence in the World*. Ottawa: Government of Canada.

———. 2008. 'Speech from the Throne', 20 Nov. At: <www.sft.gc.ca/eng/media.asp?d=1364>.

———, Parliament. 1984. *House of Commons Debates*, 1st Session, 33rd Parliament, 5 Nov.

Canadian Broadcasting Corporation (CBC). 2008. 'Obama Must Knock on "Other Doors" for Afghanistan: MacKay', 21 Nov. At: <www.cbc.ca/world/story/2008/11/21/afghan-mackay.html?ref=rss>.

Cellucci, Paul. 2005. *Unquiet Diplomacy*. Toronto: Key Porter.

Chapnick, Adam. 2005. *The Middle Power Project: Canada and the Founding of the United Nations*. Vancouver: University of British Columbia Press.

Cohen, Andrew. 2004. *While Canada Slept: How We Lost Our Place in the World*. Toronto: McClelland & Stewart.

Cohen, Lenard J. 2003. 'Blue Helmets, Green Helmets, Red Tunics: Canada's Adaptation to the Security Crisis in Southeastern Europe', in Cohen et al. (2003: 125–34).

———, Alexander Moens, and Allen G. Sens. 2003. *NATO and European Security: Alliance Politics from the End of the Cold War to the Age of Terrorism*. Westport, Conn.: Praeger.

Collins, John M. 1991. *Desert Shield and Desert Storm: Implications for Future U.S. Requirements*, CRS Report for Congress. Washington: Congressional Research Service, 19 Apr.

Conference Board of Canada. 2000. *Performance and Potential 2002–03—Canada 2010: Challenges and Choices at Home and Abroad*. Ottawa: Conference Board of Canada.

Conference of Defence Associations Institute. 2002. *A Nation at Risk: The Decline of the Canadian*

Forces. Ottawa: Conference of Defence Associations Institute.

Congressional Budget Office. 2001. *NATO Burdensharing after Enlargement*. Washington, Aug.

Congressional Research Service. 2001. 'Kosovo and U.S. Policy', Report for Congress, RL31053. Washington, 4 Dec.

———. 2003. 'Bosnia: U.S. Military Operations', CRS Issue Brief for Congress, Order Code IB93056, updated 8 July.

Daalder, Ivo H., and Michael E. O'Hanlon. 2000. *Winning Ugly: NATO's War to Save Kosovo*. Washington: Brookings Institution Press.

Deblock, Christian, and Dorval Brunelle. 1997. 'De l'ale à la Zlea: Régionalisme et sécurité économiques dans les amériques', *Études internationales* 28, 2 (juin): 313–44.

Department of National Defence (DND). 1987. *Challenge and Commitment: A Defence Policy for Canada—A Synopsis of the Defence White Paper*. Ottawa: DND.

———. 1992. *Canadian Defence Policy*. Ottawa: DND.

———. 1994. *1994 Defence White Paper*. Ottawa: Minister of Supply and Services.

Gammer, Nicholas. 2001. *From Peacekeeping to Peacemaking: Canada's Response to the Yugoslav Crisis*. Montreal and Kingston: McGill-Queen's University Press.

Granatstein, J.L. 1998. *Who Killed Canadian History?* Toronto: HarperCollins.

———. 2004. *Who Killed the Canadian Military?* Toronto: HarperCollins.

———. 2007. *Whose War Is It? How Canada Can Survive in the Post 9/11 World*. Toronto: HarperCollins.

Greenspon, Edward. 1998. 'How We'd Spend Our Federal Surplus', *Globe and Mail*, 14 Feb.

Haglund, David G. 1996. *Will NATO Go East? The Debate over Enlarging the Atlantic Alliance*. Kingston, Ont.: Centre for International Relations, Queen's University.

Hewitt, Dawn M. 1998. *From Ottawa to Sarajevo: Canadian Peacekeepers in the Balkans*. Martello Papers 18. Kingston, Ont.: Centre for International Relations, Queen's University.

Hillmer, Norman. 2008. *Empire to Umpire: Canada and the World into the 21st Century*, 2nd edn. Toronto: Thomson Nelson.

——— and Maureen A. Molot, eds. 2002. *Canada Among Nations 2002: A Fading Power*. Toronto: Oxford University Press.

Hurtig, Mel. 2003. *The Vanishing Country: Is It Too Late to Save Canada?* Toronto: McClelland & Stewart.

Independent Panel on Canada's Future Role in Afghanistan. 2008. *Final Report*. Ottawa: Independent Panel on Canada's Future Role in Afghanistan.

Jockel, Joseph T., and Joel J. Sokolsky. 1993. 'Dandurand Revisited: Rethinking Canada's Defence Policy in an Unstable World', *International Journal* 48 (Spring): 380–401.

——— and ———. 2009. 'Canada and NATO: Keeping Ottawa In, Expenses Down, Criticism Out . . . And the Country Secure', *International Journal* 64 (Spring): 311–36.

Kay, Sean. 1998. *NATO and the Future of European Security*. Lanham, Md: Rowman & Littlefield.

Lang, Eugene, and Janice Stein. 2007. *The Unexpected War: Canada in Kandahar*. Toronto: Viking Canada.

Lis, John J., and Zachary A. Selden. 2003. *NATO Burdensharing after Enlargement*. New York: Novinka Books.

Maloney, Sean M. 1997. 'Operation Bolster: Canada and the European Community Monitor Mission in the Balkans, 1991–1994', in *The McNaughton Papers, no. 10*. Toronto: Canadian Institute of Strategic Studies.

Manley, John. 2007. 'Afghanistan: Meeting the Development Challenge', *Policy Options* 28 (Oct.): 6–12.

Mearsheimer, John. 1994–5. 'The False Promise of International Institutions', *International Security* 19, 3 (Winter): 5–49.

Moskos, Charles C., John Allen Williams, and David R. Segal. 2000. *The Postmodern Military: Armed Forces after the Cold War*. New York: Oxford University Press.

Nossal, Kim Richard. 1992. 'Succumbing to the Dumbbell: Canadian Perspectives on NATO in the 1990s', in Barbara McDougall, Kim Richard Nossal, Alex Morrison, and Joseph T. Jockel, *Canada and NATO: The Forgotten Ally?* Cambridge: Institute for Foreign Policy Analysis, 17–32.

North Atlantic Treaty Organization (NATO). 2003. Information on defence expenditures. Brussels.

Rempel, Roy. 1992. 'Canada's Troop Deployments in Germany: Twilight of a Forty-Year Presence?', in David G. Haglund and Olaf Mager, eds, *Homeward Bound? Allied Forces in the New Germany*. Boulder, Colo.: Westview Press, 213–47.

Sloan, Stanley R. 1989. *NATO in the 1990s*. Washington: Pergamon-Brassey's.

———. 2002. *NATO and Transatlantic Relations in the 21st Century: Crisis, Continuity or Change?* Headline Series, No. 324. New York: Foreign Policy Association.

Standing Committee on Foreign Affairs and International Development. 2008. *Canada's International Policy Put to the Test in Afghanistan: A Preliminary Report*. Ottawa: Standing Committee on Foreign Affairs and International Development, 2008.

United Nations (UN). 1996. *The Blue Helmets: A Review of United Nations Peace-Keeping*, 3rd edn. New York: UN Department of Public Information.

United Nations Chronicle. 1995. 'Fighting Escalates, UN Role in Question', 32, 3 (Sept.): 29–34.

United States Department of Defense. 2000. *Report on Allied Contributions to the Common Defense*. Washington: Department of Defense.

Vanhoonacker, Sophie. 2001. *The Bush Administration (1989–1993) and the Development of a European Security Identity*. Aldershot: Ashgate.

Additional Readings

Cellucci, Paul. 2005. 'The Relationship: A U.S. Perspective', *International Journal* 60: 509–15.

Dorn, Walter. 2005. 'Canadian Peacekeeping: Proud Tradition, Strong Future?', *Canadian Foreign Policy* 12 (Fall): 7–32.

Gotlieb, Allan. 2003. 'Foremost Partner: The Conduct of Canada–US Relations', in David Carment, Fen Osler Hampson, and Norman Hillmer, eds, *Canada Among Nations 2003: Coping with the American Colossus*. Toronto: Oxford University Press, 19–31.

———. 2006. *The Washington Diaries, 1981–1989*. Toronto: McClelland & Stewart.

Jockel, Joseph T., and Joel J. Sokolsky. 2008. 'Canada and the War in Afghanistan: NATO's Odd Man Out Steps Forward', *Journal for Transatlantic Studies* 6, 1: 100–15.

Maloney, Sean M. 2003. 'Are We Really Just Peacekeepers? Perception versus the Reality of Canadian Military Involvement in the Iraq War', *IRPP Working Paper Series*, No. 2003-02. Montreal: Institute for Research on Public Policy.

Middlemiss, Danford, and Joel J. Sokolsky. 1989. *Canadian Defence: Decisions and Determinants*. Toronto: Harcourt Brace Jovanovich Canada.

Morton, Desmond. 2003. *Understanding Canadian Defence*. Toronto: Penguin.

Nossal, Kim Richard. 1998–9. 'Pinchpenny Diplomacy: The Decline of "Good International Citizenship" in Canadian Foreign Policy', *International Journal* 54 (Winter): 88–105.

Polaris Institute. 2005. *It's Never Enough: Canada's Alarming Rise in Military Spending*. Ottawa, Oct.

Sokolsky, Joel. 2004. 'Realism Canadian Style: National Security Policy and the Chrétien Legacy', *Policy Matters* 5 (June): 1–43.

Stairs, Denis. 2003. 'Myths, Morals, and Reality in Canadian Foreign Policy', *International Journal* 58 (Spring): 239–56.

———. 2001. 'Canada in the 1990s: Speak Loudly and Carry a Bent Twig', *Policy Options* 22, 1: 43–9.

Tomlin, Brian, Norman Hillmer, and Fen Osler Hampson, eds. 2008. *Canada's International Policies: Agendas, Alternatives, and Politics*. Toronto: Oxford University Press.

Zyla, Benjamin. 2009. 'NATO and Post-Cold War Burden-sharing: Canada "the Laggard"?', *International Journal* 64 (Spring): 337–59.

Chapter 13

Canada's Arctic Policy: Transcending the Middle-Power Model?

Petra Dolata-Kreutzkamp

Introduction

Canada's middle-power model has been criticized for losing its validity in a changing world after the end of the Cold War (Welsh, 2004). This criticism is based on the assumption that Canada's position in the international system ('middlepowerhood') is contested by other emerging powers such as India, Brazil, and China and by the supposition that the disappearance of a stable bipolar system made the pursuit of an active multilateralist and internationalist policy ('middlepowermanship') more difficult for Canada (see Nossal, Chapter 2, this volume). Even if one stresses the importance of an identity-based middle-power model that focuses on identity politics and analyzes the popular constructions of the role Canada 'should' play in the world—'middle power is what Canada makes of it'[1]—the question remains how useful the middle-power category is for understanding Canada's current foreign policy.

To answer this, it may be helpful to employ a case study that highlights how assumptions about Canada's middlepowerhood and middlepowermanship frame both expectations (what Canada should do) and foreign policy behaviour (what Canada is doing). Canada's Arctic foreign policy is an interesting example for a number of reasons. First, one could argue that this is a fairly new foreign policy area, especially in the minds of the Canadian public, who hold no preconceived notions as to what the specific Canadian middle-power role should look like in this area. Second, only recently has the Arctic emerged as an international political space for global politics and global challenges. With the exception of maritime (UNCLOS) and environmental (Arctic Council) management institutions there are few global regimes and internationally accepted rules and norms in place that Canada—as a good international citizen—could support. Third, Canada's role in the Arctic cannot simply be explained by changes in the international system. The linkage of domestic and global levels of analysis, which found its analytical home in the concept of 'intermestic politics' (Manning, 1977), points to the importance of both national and international factors in understanding Canada's specific foreign policy behaviour. Fourth, any analysis of Canada's Arctic policy will expose the tension between the ideational and behavioural dimensions of the middle-power model. If the middle-power concept equates Canada's national interest with internationalism and multilateralism we are immediately confronted with an empirical puzzle in the Arctic, where we find a competing, alternative reading of Canada's national interest defined by Canadian sovereignty. Moreover, like the middle-power model, the concept of Arctic sovereignty can be seen as yet another expression of identity politics. If that is the case, the question becomes how far the two are compatible and, more importantly, whether the middle-power image inhibits our understanding of Arctic policy, which may be a contestation of that very image. Thus, Canada's Arctic policy may prove to be an important test case for the validity, relevance, and analytical usefulness of the middle-power model in the twenty-first century.

In analyzing Canada's Arctic foreign policy the middle-power model will be used in different ways. The historical development of foreign policy behaviour in Arctic affairs will be addressed in order to establish whether it was characterized by middlepowermanship. Did it involve an active internationalist and multilateral agenda? Did it include norm entrepreneurship[2] and the search for diplomatic niches (Cooper, 1993)? How can we best describe foreign policy behaviour in this area? Does it reflect popular ideas about taking on the role of a middle power? The middle-power model will also be held responsible for framing political analysis of Canadian foreign policy behaviour. It might be argued that the focus on Canada's role as a middle power limits the interpretation of Canada's foreign policy behaviour in the Arctic to dealing with questions pertaining to the international maritime legal regime (UNCLOS). This neglects the formative influence of bilateral relations with the United States, as well as domestic developments. The related question is how to best understand—as opposed to explain—Canadian foreign policy in the Arctic. The middle-power model may not be the best analytical tool to achieve such an understanding. Moreover, the middle-power image introduces a normative dimension to the crucial question whether the future political scenario in the Arctic will be characterized by a zero-sum race or by win-win co-operation.[3] Thus, a thorough understanding of where Canada stands on this issue is needed before Canada's middlepowermanship in the Arctic can be addressed.

In the twenty-first century the High Arctic has emerged as an important aspect of Canada's foreign policy agenda. While the world may not yet have entered 'the age of the Arctic' (Young, 1985–6; Osherenko and Young, 1989; Huebert, 2008), the region has increasingly attracted global attention because of its resource potential and its role as the 'canary in the coal mine' for climate change. Canadian interest in the region is not new; Ottawa has always pursued some form of Arctic policy. However, scholars agree that this was seldom more than 'reactive, piecemeal and ad hoc' (Huebert, 2006). Recently, calls for a coherent and comprehensive policy for Canada's North have resurfaced, and this time it appears that the Canadian government is determined to act. International developments, such as the depletion of fossil fuels, disagreement over the legal status of the Northwest Passage, and the intention, shared by all Arctic states, to extend the continental shelf to the North Pole, joined with domestic factors to make the Arctic a policy matter in its own right as well as an issue that will remain prominent in the twenty-first century.

In attempting to formulate and implement an Arctic policy, any government faces several structural difficulties. Like other regional issue areas in foreign policy (e.g., European policy), Arctic policy is defined through its spatiality and not by specific functional aspects such as defence or trade. It is characterized by the combination of a multitude of issues, which are not always compatible in their specific goals and policy instruments. They are part of both domestic northern and international circumpolar agendas, and include such diverse aspects as defence, economic development, indigenous governance, and human security, as well as energy and environmental security. In addition, as is the case with many other foreign policy areas, the dichotomy of domestic versus international settings is transcended because both levels—northern and circumpolar—are interlinked. Policies are characterized by interdependencies and by the intricate two-directional relationship between international and national factors (Putnam, 1988). Together they create an urgency for, and the framework of, any Canadian Arctic policy.

Canada's approach to foreign and security policies in this region is further characterized by its bilateral relationship with the United States as well as by its past policies, which were indicative of middlepowermanship. The active search for multilateral solutions and the attempt to introduce norms and rules constituted one facet of Canada's historical position in the Arctic. US–Canadian bilateral conflict over questions of sovereignty constituted another facet.

Undoubtedly, Canada's Arctic foreign policy has undergone a fundamental shift over the last decades. Not only has it become more important in the overall foreign policy agenda, but the very nature of that policy also appears to have changed. While international co-operation is still a proposed strategy, Arctic policy has become more proactive and assertive. This is due to changing domestic and international political environments, as well as to the emergence of new thinking about the Arctic and more generally about concepts of security in a post-Cold War world. Since these developments are closely interlinked they should be conceptualized as creating a multi-level and multivariate framework, in which the numerous aspects influence each other to create a specific situation. This, in turn, produces the shift in Canada's Arctic foreign policy. It also explains that while some of these developments can be seen as causal factors they are also constructed to some extent as justifications of specific policy decisions. Furthermore, to understand current policies, attention should be directed not only towards change. Underlying continuities equally inform today's Arctic policy. This applies to some of the prevalent ideas and images about the Arctic, and to the international legal dimensions of Canada's Arctic policy. More specifically, however, continuity characterizes the bilateral Canada–US relationship. After this chapter analyzes the various factors feeding into Canada's specific policy response towards perceived political challenges in the Arctic, the particularities of that response will be outlined.

The Changing International Environment

Climate Change and Energy

Recent global developments have combined to pose challenges to Canada's political and strategic position in the Arctic, and at the same time appear to offer economic prospects. Climate change and the concomitant melting of the ice pack generally cause better accessibility to the Arctic and its riches, both in the water column (fish) and in the seabed (oil, gas). The melting ice specifically leads to improved navigability of the Northwest Passage, the use of which would shorten the shipping route between Europe and Asia through the Panama Canal by some 7,000 kilometres. With increased shipping come both opportunities and risks for Canada. On the one hand, ships might be expected to rely on a support infrastructure such as deep-water ports, which in turn could become the catalyst for economic development and job creation in the Far North. On the other hand, increased shipping traffic raises the potential likelihood of oil spills and other environmentally disastrous incidents in this delicate ecological system. As an Arctic littoral state, Canada has to deal with the long-term prospect of the Arctic Archipelago becoming a commercial region and the Northwest Passage a much-frequented sea lane.

Changing Geopolitics

The opening up of the Arctic—in the sense of its accessibility and its international visibility—also affects Canada's spatial positioning on the geopolitical map as it puts emphasis on the country's third coastline. Canada, whose motto is 'a mari usque ad mare' (from sea to sea) now extends from sea to sea *to sea*. Historically, Canada's international position oscillated between being a transatlantic power and a continental power, but a third dimension has now been added to its international role, that of being an Arctic state. This has been facilitated by United States complacency regarding the region. It is further supported by the region's resource potential. In an international system based on the availability of cheap and secure energy, Canada has attained a new position, which Prime Minister Stephen Harper in June 2007 called an 'emerging energy superpower' and 'a bastion of world energy security' (Canada, 2007a).

Will Canadian foreign policy reflect the spatial shift in perspective from across the Atlantic and from its southern neighbour to Canada's North? More importantly, if Canada has indeed become a 'principal power' (Huebert, 2008: 5) in the Arctic, what implications does this new role have for Canada's middlepowerhood? Does this new geopolitical reality vest Canada with the power to be able to punch above its weight (cf. Cohen, 2004), and is this the diplomatic niche in which Canada should exhibit norm entrepreneurship? According to a number of commentators, Canada has a moral responsibility to bring about rules-based co-operation in the region and to address future global challenges, including climate change (Byers, 2007; Griffiths, 2008; Pharand, 2007). One of the immediate geopolitical challenges will be to secure Canada's northern flank, which, because of melting ice, in the foreseeable future could allow for easier approaches to the mainland from the Arctic by smugglers, illegal immigrants, and terrorists, and facilitates 'foreign encroachments on Canada's natural resources' (National Defence Canada, 2008: 6). Since this involves the continental security perimeter, it will necessitate future security co-operation between Canada and the United States.

Competition in the Arctic

Climate change and energy scarcity have combined to initiate what some commentators likened to a 'race' to the North. Not only are Arctic neighbours—Denmark, Norway, Russia, the United States—engaging to different degrees, but Europe and Asia are also involved, where commercial interests press for icebreaker construction programs and politicians address issues of climate change and energy security in the High Arctic (Steinmeier and Miliband, 2008). Of immediate relevance for Canada are territorial claims by other Arctic states. The underwater planting of a Russian flag at the North Pole, Danish contestations in the Kennedy Channel, and US disregard of Canadian claims to the Northwest Passage are all interpreted as potentially posing threats to Canada's sovereignty. As a consequence, Canada's territorial jurisdiction is seen as at least partly contested in four areas: (1) Arctic islands, (2) Arctic waters, (3) maritime boundaries, and the (4) Northwest Passage.[4] Jurisdiction over islands is not really an issue today with the possible exception of Hans Island, which both Canada and Denmark claim as theirs. Boundary disputes may arise in the Western Arctic where Canada and the United States have still not agreed on territorial demarcations in the Beaufort Sea, one of the most resource-rich areas in the North American Arctic. Jurisdiction over

Arctic waters relates to the international space beyond the 200-mile exclusive economic zone (EEZ). This maritime region, which gives contiguous coastal states exclusive rights to the resources in that area, can be extended further if the continental shelf reaches beyond the 200-mile limit. Thus, in the Arctic it would be possible to stretch the EEZ to the North Pole if a country were able to prove that the Lomonosov Ridge is in fact an extension of its underwater shelf. This is the rationale behind Russia's planting of a flag in the Arctic in August 2007. It also drives scientific mapping endeavours in the region.

Others have criticized this popular reading of events in the Arctic and instead offer an interpretation stressing the orderly fashion and co-operative nature of the process (Riddell-Dixon, 2008; Koivurova, 2008). They refer to the existence of an international legal regime, under which Canada already has the right to extend its continental shelf. The 1982 United Nations Convention on the Law of the Sea (UNCLOS) stipulates the different degrees of state ownership to the sea and puts a process in place for extending EEZs. Under this regime Arctic states will have to submit their delineation of the outer limits of the continental shelf to an international commission. This commission then makes recommendations on the basis of the legal and scientific validity; it is up to the state to delimit the shelf on the basis of these recommendations. The necessary scientific data are often collected in a co-operative manner. However, the process is at the same time political. First, while UNCLOS may provide 'rules and procedures . . . guiding state behavior' (Riddell-Dixon, 2008: 343–4), one might argue that what has been perceived as the race to the North Pole has been facilitated by the changing legal regimes of international maritime spaces. Second, since the states ultimately delimit the continental shelf, competing claims may not necessarily be resolved in a co-operative fashion. It will be analytically paramount to differentiate between the orderly legal framework and the potentially conflict-ridden political process. This is not to say that technological and scientific co-operation does not exist among Arctic states, as well as interdepartmental co-operation in Canada. The more interesting observation, however, is that in the public and political discourse this co-operative moment has only recently been stressed.

For most Canadians, international competition in the Arctic consists mainly of sovereignty contestation and rivalry. This rivalry is best crystallized in the dispute with the United States over the status of the Northwest Passage, which 'conjures up images of Canada losing its national heritage in the North' and 'of the United States asserting rights over what is rightfully Canadian' (McRae, 2007: 1).

The Bilateral Dimension: US–Canada Relations

The United States has always figured prominently in Canadian Arctic policy, informing the Canadian Arctic sovereignty discourse. After Canada acquired the Arctic islands in 1880, the US government, and even more so American whale hunters, posed one of the most persistent threats to Canada's claim to the High Arctic in the late nineteenth and early twentieth centuries. Yet world events brought the two countries closer together and fostered close military co-operation in the region, first during World War II and then in the ensuing Cold War confrontation between the United States and the Soviet Union. Security considerations and strategic objectives reigned supreme in the Arctic, especially in the 1950s when the area was seen as a potential battleground and thoroughfare for any Soviet attack directed at the United States. Since the early 1940s a series of bilateral projects, chiefly under the direction of the US Army, including the construction of roads, pipelines, airstrips, weather stations, and, most importantly, radar warning lines and joint military exercises, paved the way for US military presence in the Canadian Arctic. This 'militarization of the North American Arctic' was further manifested through the 1957 NORAD agreement between Canada and the US (Lackenbauer and Farish, 2007; Elliot-Meisel, 1998).

For US policy-makers, interest in the Arctic was almost exclusively driven by continental security considerations. In Canada, continental security helped assuage concerns over US encroachment on Canada's effective control of the region. However, sovereignty never ceased to be an issue. US military presence in the Arctic was seen by some as an act of aggression. A number of Canadian officials even called for plans to 're-Canadianize the Arctic' (Grant, 1991). This sovereignty discourse fulfilled an important political function; it allowed Canada to construct its ally, the United States, as an adversary at a time when the overriding security threat of a Soviet strategic attack was felt by both countries, a threat that facilitated military co-operation on a truly integrated and continental level, and forbade any intra-alliance dissension. While it allowed Canadians to develop a national identity different from the United States, it also perpetuated the differentiation between security and sovereignty. This separation echoes the dichotomy of continental and transatlantic (NATO) versus national Canadian interests. It endures today and continues to inform most of the debate on Canada's Arctic policy while giving meaning to 'Arctic sovereignty' (see Huebert, 2005–6, 2006, 2008).

With the increasing range of ballistic missiles in the 1960s the importance of defending the Arctic approach through military instalments and surveillance diminished, as did Canadian apprehensions about US behaviour in the North. It re-emerged in 1969–70 and in 1985, when Canadians felt that the United States was blatantly disregarding Canada's claim to the Northwest Passage. In 1969, shortly after oil was found in Prudhoe Bay, Alaska, the US oil company Humble Oil sent the tanker SS *Manhattan* through the Northwest Passage to assess its viability as a commercial route. The Americans did not seek prior authorization from the Canadian government. This event caused a public uproar in Canada and in 1970 the Trudeau government passed the Arctic Waters Pollution Prevention Act (AWPPA), which prohibited the deposit of waste in Arctic waters from either ship or land source—environmental legislation that was later incorporated into the United Nations Convention on the Law of the Sea as the Arctic clause (Article 234). A second incident took place in the mid-1980s when the US icebreaker *Polar Sea* crossed the passage on its way from Greenland to Alaska. This time the Canadian authorities had been informed and the US, to appease Canadian sensitivity on the subject, affirmed that this would in no sense compromise Canada's legal position. Still, the public outcry in Canada was considerable. The government reacted very quickly and in 1986 announced straight baselines to enclose the Arctic Archipelago as internal, territorial Canadian waters (see *Northern Perspectives*, 1986). As before, the US did not accept the claim. Instead, in 1988, the two countries signed an Arctic Cooperation Agreement, which stipulated that US icebreakers had to notify Canadian authorities when travelling through the Northwest Passage. A closer look at the agreement reveals that the two countries essentially agreed to disagree, since the notification did not entail acceptance of Canada's legal claim. Equally important, it did not apply to any other type of ship—not commercial ships but also, and especially, not submarines, which, according to most military specialists, have been regularly traversing the passage. Here the Canadian government finds itself in a dilemma, because criticizing the US for submerged crossings of the passage would mean recognizing routine usage, which in fact could compromise Canada's position that the passage is not an international strait due to its exceptionally rare historical use.[5] At the same time, of course, the US military is not in the habit of making public the transit routes of its submarine fleet.

Path Dependencies

This overview of events in the twentieth century shows how specific historical experiences and decisions inform the current situation, but also limit the scope of solutions available today. First, Arctic sovereignty is not a new topic. It has resurfaced time and again since Canada acquired the Arctic islands from the UK in 1880. At the same time, Canada has been complacent about enforcing its territorial claims in the Far North. Accordingly, its Arctic policy has been reactive and seldom proactive. Only when it perceived its position in the North to be jeopardized did the government respond. Second, because the more recent contestations of sovereignty have been with regard to the Northwest Passage, this specific aspect of Arctic policy has occupied most public and media attention, and this issue has put the most pressure on policy-makers to propose solutions. Third, because of the events in the 1940s and 1950s—which were formative in the construction of a dichotomous security–sovereignty discourse and targeted the United States as the adversary in terms of sovereignty—today's threats to Canadian jurisdiction in the Arctic are seen as mainly emanating from its closest ally and neighbour to the south. This is aggravated by the fact that the two key conflicts in the Arctic involved the United States disregarding Canada's legal claims to the Northwest Passage. While the bilateral relationship between the two countries certainly frames Canada's Arctic policy, Canadian governments have tended to limit the issue to one of bilateral conflict. This perspective disregards the fact that other international actors, including the European Union, also fail to acknowledge Canada's claims to the Northwest Passage, and that in the early twentieth century Canadian jurisdiction over the islands and the waters was contested by other Arctic nations, namely Denmark, Norway, and Russia.

Maritime Power versus Coastal State

Canada–US relations in the Arctic and the issue of Arctic sovereignty are inextricably linked and are epitomized by the question of who owns the Northwest Passage and who can enforce regulatory regimes to protect the region. Canada's interests are also influenced by its status as a coastal state, which typically aspires to exert as much control as possible over its adjoining seas in order to be able to deal with questions of environmental, social, and maritime governance. The US position in the dispute is mainly informed by its maritime agenda. As an economic and maritime power Washington has historically been a propagator of the freedom of the seas. The US is determined to safeguard global maritime trade and to secure vital sea lines against disruption through acts of piracy or terrorism, through collisions, or through regional instability. Free passage through international straits is an important policy objective for Washington and thus any extensive jurisdictional claims by littoral states on the grounds of sovereignty or environmental aspects are (tantamount to being) unacceptable. Furthermore, the US defends navigational rights for international oil companies. While Washington may not have a great interest in the Northwest Passage as such, it fears that any concessions to the Canadians on this issue would compromise the US position on international straits elsewhere, especially concerning the Strait of Malacca (Nincic, 2002).

Security Co-operation in the Arctic

Washington's policy in the Arctic is not only determined by its international role as a maritime power, it is also characterized by its relative disinterest in the Arctic region. In general, the Arctic in recent years has not figured prominently in current US strategic thinking. However, this could change as there has been some renewed interest in the security dimension recently (White House, 2009). First, Washington has become increasingly apprehensive of Russia's intentions in the Arctic and towards the United States in general. Second, the Arctic has now entered the US energy security and thus national security discourse because of its potential oil and gas reserves.[6] Third, decision-makers fear that the increasing accessibility of the Arctic will make transit by hostile nations and non-state actors (e.g., terrorists) probable, and that climate change in the Arctic will adversely affect existing infrastructure as the thawing of permafrost damages pipelines and other vital energy and military installations. In combatting security threats in the North the US sees Canada as its partner, a view institutionally reinforced by existing integrated defence structures and future security co-operation under NAFTA.[7] Hence, Washington is hesitant to forcefully push its standpoint on the Northwest Passage and overtly challenge Canada's position. Rather, the US administration appears to be quite happy with a functionalist solution whereby Canada would be responsible for monitoring the passage—which, after all, constitutes a northern approach to the North American mainland—as well as for dealing with any potential threats to the North American security perimeter, such as smuggling, illegal immigration, and terrorism. Because this falls well short of officially accepting Canada's sovereignty claim, Ottawa is unlikely to agree to such a solution. The exercise of functional jurisdiction will not be enough to solve Canada–US differences in the Arctic if sovereignty remains so important for Canada. Both countries, it seems, prefer to continue to agree to disagree since there is no politically easy way out of this dilemma. In the meantime, the focus is directed towards legal solutions to the dispute.

The Domestic Setting: Changing Actors and Processes

Indigenous Agency

The domestic counterpart to Canada's Arctic foreign policy is regional northern policy. As Ottawa's policy towards indigenous communities in general became more important in the 1990s so did relations with the territories in the Canadian North. Land claims agreements and devolution negotiations have boosted indigenous political action. Inuit representatives have not only assumed domestic political importance but they also became transnational actors dealing with Arctic Aboriginal groups outside Canada as well as with other Arctic states. The Canadian government acknowledged this indigenous agency, and the linkages between domestic regional policy and circumpolar affairs, by creating the post of ambassador for circumpolar affairs in 1994. This position had been filled by Inuit representatives, who have been mainly responsible for fostering transnational, circumpolar co-operation and liaising with the Arctic Council.

Indigenous actors play another important foreign policy role: they underscore Canada's historic title as they have occupied both Arctic land and sea for centuries. More specifically, they have ensured military presence in the Arctic.

From the 1970s to the 1990s Arctic Rangers, who are part of the Canadian Forces reserves and primarily made up of Inuit volunteers, were the only military presence in the Arctic (Lackenbauer, 2005–6). Today, indigenous spokespersons, such as Nunavut Premier Paul Okalik, make use of the role Inuit play in the historic claim to sovereignty in order to gain federal support for a 'thriving Nunavut' (Okalik, 2008: 4; Simon, 2007). Because of the commercial prospects of the Arctic—both as a resource extractive and commercial space—Inuit spokespersons have already called for more far-reaching devolution agreements, which would allow them to receive the proceeds from resource activities, diversify their economy, and create jobs, as well as provide (vocational) training in the North (Okalik, 2008: 5). In particular, the questions of resource management and who owns the resources in the Arctic affect Canada's indigenous foreign policy agenda. The ongoing negotiation process could explain Ottawa's rejection of the 2007 UN Declaration on the Rights of Indigenous Peoples, which included a passage on indigenous resource rights. This complex interweaving of *foreign* and *domestic* policy dimensions has created the need for a comprehensive approach integrating issues of good governance (social programs and economic development), environmental stewardship, and national security and sovereignty. Such an approach would reflect the ideal of middlepowermanship (Griffiths, 2008).

Bringing the State Back In

Northerners assumed an important political role in the Arctic policy debate. This development has repercussions for the scope of the government's response to international challenges in the Arctic. One of the responses by the current Harper government has been to emphasize the federal government's decision-making and policy formulation authority. Thus, circumpolar affairs are carried out by state actors. Accordingly, in 2006 the Canadian government abolished the post of ambassador for circumpolar affairs. This move was all the more surprising since the International Polar Year was to commence in 2007. The approach of pushing back non-state and transnational actors is shared by other Arctic states as energy and security considerations have made Arctic policy a top priority. Such a trend is aptly illustrated by the meeting of the five states with legitimate claims to sovereignty in the High Arctic (Canada, the US, Russia, Norway, and Denmark) in Ilulissat, Greenland, in May 2008. The declaration from this meeting reaffirms nation-states as the most important and indeed the only legitimate actors with respect to maritime jurisdiction in the Arctic, and the existing legal frameworks as sufficient. Notably, participation in the meeting was limited to sovereign states and did not involve the somewhat larger Arctic Council (which has eight members, including Iceland, Sweden, and Finland, as well as a number of states and organizations with observer status), nor did it include transnational circumpolar organizations (e.g., the Saami Council and the

Inuit Circumpolar Council) or supranational actors (European Union). Clearly, non-state and transnational actors—and those states without a sectoral claim extending to the North Pole—have been relegated to playing a minor role in today's Arctic policy. This is not to say that questions of good governance are not a factor in Canada's policies towards the High Arctic; however, such concerns are secondary and are decoupled from what the government sees as its *foreign* policy agenda in the Arctic. This development also undermines middlepowermanship, because it fails to emphasize co-operation and compromise.

A Changing Bureaucracy

Within the national bureaucracy we find a multitude of actors involved in formulating and implementing Arctic policy, each of which has its own particular stake in the region.[8] As Arctic policy was mainly seen through the lens of military security during the Cold War, the Defence and External Affairs departments[9] were primarily responsible for Canada's international Arctic affairs. In addition, surveillance capacities in the Arctic rest with civilian organizations such as the Canadian Coast Guard and the Royal Canadian Mounted Police, and so their respective departmental umbrella organizations have also been involved. When NORDREG—a voluntary vessel traffic system— was introduced in 1977 Transport Canada was added as another bureaucratic actor (see Pharand, 2007: 48–51). As further policy dimensions have emerged, such as the environment, development, societal security, and energy, the respective departments have become more involved.

As a result of this fragmentation of departmental authorities, the Department of Indian Affairs and Northern Development (DIAND—now officially called Indian and Northern Affairs Canada, or INAC) was singled out as the responsible agency for designing an overall strategy. Yet several aspects, both historical and structural, have inhibited this department from reaching policy formulation pre-eminence. While it may be the obvious candidate for formulating any Arctic policy, the emergence of Arctic sovereignty as a national interest has often meant that prime ministers have given top priority to the issue and thus the Prime Minister's Office (PMO) and the Privy Council Office (PCO) have been prominent in formulating strategies for the North. In addition, because the department combines Indian Affairs and Northern Development it sometimes works against its own goals, especially when questions of environment and social cohesion collide with development proposals. Finally, the department seems to lack legitimacy in the sense that indigenous actors do not respect the department. The division of the foreign (Department of Foreign Affairs and International Trade, DFAIT) and domestic (DIAND) aspects of Arctic policy have meant that a comprehensive approach has been difficult to achieve. This has further facilitated the shift of policy-making authority to the PMO and PCO (Griffiths, 2008: 3).

While in specific functional areas interdepartmental relationships might be characterized by co-operation—e.g., among DFAIT, Natural Resources Canada, and the Department of Fisheries and Oceans in their combined effort to delineate the continental shelf (Riddell-Dixon, 2008: 346–7)—overall the fragmentation of authorities and responsibilities impedes the formulation of a comprehensive Arctic policy, thereby giving rise to calls for a new 'Department of Northern and Arctic Affairs' (Pharand, 2007: 52).

Changing Ideas and Perceptions

Changing Concepts of Security

Security and sovereignty have played central roles in formulating Canada's diplomatic standpoints on the Arctic. Any understanding of how they influence decision-making and the political process is complicated by the fact that the two concepts have evolved historically. While sovereignty has retained its meaning as the insurance of territorial integrity and jurisdiction in the Far North, the interpretation of security has undergone fundamental change. With the end of the Cold War and the emergence of critical security studies in the 1990s, the security concept has been broadened to include implicit threats to states as well as direct threats to individuals and communities (Krause, 1998). Concepts such as environmental, energy, and human security were added to traditional notions of national security. These new definitions did not supplant older concepts but supplemented them; they informed the Canadian foreign policy discourse in the 1990s and in the early years of the new millennium. This is not to deny that some of these new threats had gained prominence before the 1990s; however, they were not sufficiently conceptualized and theorized as national security challenges.

Environmental Security

Threats to the environment lay at the heart of Canada's legal response to US contestations of its sovereignty claim on the Northwest Passage in 1969–70. The journey of the SS *Manhattan* pointed towards future traffic of oil tankers in the Arctic. Several major oil spill incidents at the time had sensitized decision-makers to the potential environmental threats of such commercial transits. In addition, negotiations of the Convention on the Law of the Sea were in full swing. Canada's policy response to encroachments on sovereignty was the unilateral enactment of the AWPPA. The Canadian government based its decision on environmental arguments, reasoning that existing international regimes provided insufficient protection of the Arctic environment. Furthermore, it insisted that 'a danger to the environment of a state constitutes a threat to its security.'[10] Even today, aspects of environmental security play a crucial role in supporting Canada's claims for controlling and monitoring the Northwest Passage, as well as in justifying Canada's unilateral action in the region.

Since the passing of the AWPPA in 1970, 'environmental unilateralism' has become a controversial aspect of Canada's maritime and Arctic policies. During the so-called 'turbot war' between Canada and the EU in 1995, Canada's legal basis for action was conservation-related law, also unilaterally passed. While Europeans condemned the *style*—i.e., Canada's unilateralism—as immoral, Canada in turn insisted that the *objective* of such unilateral action was ethical since it aimed to protect the environment where multilateral institutions had failed to do so. In accordance with the latter view, some have argued that the 1970 legislation 'was particularly *avant-garde* in its custodianship concept' (Cooper, 1997; Hellmann and Herborth, 2008). What complicates this discussion is the fact that questions of environmental security intersect with those of territorial jurisdiction. Hence, the more fundamental question still relevant today is whether unilateral action can contribute to multilateral co-operation and regimes and whether Canada should follow such a foreign policy approach. A second question raised is whether this constitutes a new version of middlepowermanship, which is characterized by its norm-setting— at the expense of its multilateral approach. On the one hand, Canadian unilateralism has indeed moved the international jurisdiction of maritime pollution forward. After all, the 1982 UNCLOS incorporated the idea behind the AWPPA in its Arctic clause. On the other hand, Canada risks eventually losing its credentials as a champion of multilateralism and international law, especially if it exempts its unilaterally enacted regulations from the jurisdiction of the International Court of Justice.

Human Security

In addition to considerations of environmental threats, which predate the end of the Cold War, human security began to gain prominence in Canadian foreign policy in the 1990s. The concept emphasizes threats to individuals' and communities' security by acknowledging the existence of transnational threats and expressing concerns about human development. In the eyes of some, Canada assumed the role of a trailblazer with respect to human security in the Arctic when it took on a leadership role in establishing the Arctic Council, an intergovernmental institution that brings together Arctic states as well as non-state actors such as the various indigenous groups and organizations in the Arctic. The end of the Cold War, and the disappearance of conventional military threats in the Far North, had introduced a phase of increasing interdependence in the Arctic, with non-state actors assuming responsibilities for the region. Several transnational institutions were founded and indigenous representatives pushed for the demilitarization of the area. For them, US–Canada military co-operation and past activities in the Arctic had infringed on indigenous security by posing environmental risks and disrupting traditional lifestyles (Lackenbauer, 2005–6). Their demands were in part based on a similar proposal by former Soviet President Mikhail Gorbachev to found an Arctic 'zone of peace'. In addition, Arctic experts advised Ottawa to 'explore the possible role of the Conference on Security and Cooperation in Europe (CSCE) in regard to Arctic security' (Åtland, 2008; Fraser and Harker, 1994–5; Special Joint Committee, 1986: 127–35; Richstone, 1986).

While the Canadian government was hesitant to propagate a weapons-free Arctic, it did become a champion of multilateral co-operation (Lackenbauer, 2008). Indeed, Canada was instrumental in convincing the United States to join this circumpolar forum. Of course, it helped that in reviewing its Arctic policy in the immediate post-Cold War years, Washington had become more receptive to ideas of collaboration in environmental areas, one of the strongest mandates of the Arctic Council. Nevertheless, classic security assumptions persisted. As one of the founding members of the Arctic Council, Washington was successful in excluding any military security-related matters from the organization's mandate. Instead, the Council has concentrated on environmental and societal issues.

Changing Securitizations of the Arctic

As the above discussion of environmental and human security has shown, the immediate post-Cold War era and the concomitant changes in the international environment facilitated a broader understanding of security that led, in turn, to a comprehensive security approach combining policy fields previously unrelated to security or to one another. In addition, Arctic issues shifted into 'emergency mode and [out of] the normal bargaining process of the political sphere' (Buzan et al., 1998: 4). This kind of securitization differed from strategies current at the time, which stressed the possible loss of sovereignty in order to prioritize classic military responses to perceived threats to Canada's territorial and jurisdictional integrity. The latter catered to a 'military set-piece' (Lackenbauer, 2008) and formed the argumentative basis for a conventional military buildup. It also had a bureaucratic impact; the only truly interdepartmental structure with regard to Arctic affairs was set up as an integral part of a Canadian security agenda. The Arctic Security Working Group was founded in 1999 and its semi-annual meetings continue to bring together 15 federal departments, as well as academics and representatives from the territories, to discuss Arctic issues. It has grown so much in recent years that subcommittees have been created to address questions of Arctic security and sovereignty (Huebert, 2005–6: 22–3).

Because the Canadian government has defined challenges in the Arctic as a threat to sovereignty, it has not only assumed policy control but also created an expectation that these threats would be met by conventional security strategies. As a result, symbolic politics constitute an integral part of Ottawa's Arctic policy and announcements of military programs such as icebreaker construction projects and expanding the Arctic Rangers become important media events. Prime ministerial visits to the Arctic have become frequent and photo ops with Rangers and icebreakers a staple of the media coverage. Together with the aforementioned return of the nation-state as the only legitimate actor, the re-emergence of classic military security signifies a return to realist conceptions of the international system.

These differences are also reflected by the distinction between hard and soft power. As Joseph S. Nye has argued, there are different ways of achieving one's goals. Power can be exercised directly and indirectly. If exercised indirectly it means 'getting others to want what you want'. Because it is indirect or co-optive and relies on 'the attraction of one's ideas or on the ability to set the political agenda in a way that shapes the preferences that others express', and because influencing these preferences is 'associated with intangible power resources such as culture, ideology, and institutions', Nye calls this 'soft power' (Nye, 1990a: 181; 1990b: ch. 2; 2002–3: 552–5). Thus, where hard power is militaristic and coercive, soft power is diplomatic and persuasive. The latter describes what Canadians expect a middle power to do; thanks to the 'discursive continuity' (Hynek, 2007: 139) in Canadian politics, middlepowermanship has been constructed along the lines of soft power. However, at the moment there appears to be more emphasis on an assertive hard-power approach as conventional security and sovereignty challenges continue to drive Canada's Arctic policy, particularly in the wake of reconsiderations of security threats after 9/11. Admittedly, some of the Cold War security threats have endured; nuclear submarines, for example, are still operating in the Arctic without Canada knowing the specifics of these operations.

The Public Debate: From Decline to Grandeur

Another factor that has contributed to the current emphasis on a military posture in the Arctic is the 'declinist' debate, which originated in the late 1990s and early 2000s, when some authors criticized Canada for wanting to play a role in international affairs without providing sufficient funding for its military and diplomatic infrastructure and personnel. They argued that Canada was relying too much on its past reputation. This, in effect, started a public debate about the country's future international role (Cohen, 2004; Granatstein, 2004). One of the ways the incoming Conservative government distinguished itself from its predecessor and introduced change was to actively engage in this debate and announce increased defence spending. A similar response was also applied to the Arctic by focusing on Arctic sovereignty.

To understand why such an assertive Arctic sovereignty rhetoric resonates with the Canadian public, one needs to conceptualize Arctic policy as an active nation-building process. It creates cohesion and gives meaning to the otherwise amorphous concept of Canadian identity. After all, the notion that 'the Arctic is ours' is shared by almost all Canadians, whether anglophone or francophone, indigenous or new immigrant, liberal or conservative, westerner or easterner, young or old. The Arctic sovereignty discourse not only creates pan-Canadian cohesion, it also is supported by bipartisanship. The current Arctic sovereignty agenda emerged under the Liberal Chrétien and Martin governments, and in the 2008 federal election all party programs included a section on the Arctic, making it the one issue where parties disagreed least. Not surprisingly, then, most Canadians support a policy that aims to ensure the continuance of Canada's claim to the North. Besides geography, literary traditions, historical narratives, and cultural expressions have helped construct Canada as a northern nation, so the 'the true North, strong and free' will continue to play a formative role in any public discourse on Canada's identity and its future international role (Coates et al., 2008). The imagery is so strong that it even overrides the other powerful image of Canadian foreign policy, that of the middle power.

Arctic Policies

The Legal Response

Canada's foreign policy responses to challenges in the Arctic can be subdivided into legal, military, and diplomatic activities. The legal claim to the Arctic is the most prominent aspect of Canada's Arctic policy and is a constant in Canadian foreign policy. However, the specific substance of that claim has been rather inconsistent. In the early twentieth century it rested on a sectoral claim, whereby all the area between the country's eastern and westernmost longitudes up to the North Pole was claimed as Canadian. Yet, it was unclear whether this claim included both land and water. Since the late 1960s there have been several attempts at extending coastal areas to include internal waters. In 1986, in response to US encroachment on the Northwest Passage, the concept of straight baselines was espoused in order to enclose the waters of the Arctic Archipelago within Canadian territorial waters. At the same time, the sovereignty claim was framed as a historic title based on concepts of cession and occupation. This interpretation emphasizes the fact that the UK had officially ceded the territory to Canada and that it has since been occupied by the Canadian Inuit (see Pharand, 2007). Reactions have changed over time as new legal regimes emerged and as the challenges in the Arctic began to include environmental threats. The 1982 UNCLOS forms the international legal framework for much of Canada's activity in the area.

The Military Response

Another response format to challenges in the Arctic is military. One of the first reactions to encroachments in the High Arctic is to show presence—on land, on water, and in the air—to enforce sovereignty and exert control and authority. This differs from the military deterrence strategy used in a Cold War context, and includes civilian surveillance and law-enforcement institutions such as the Coast Guard and RCMP. Operationally, it translates into increased surveillance flights, military exercises, and proposals to construct icebreakers. This was the case in 1969–70, immediately after the *Polar Sea* crossing in 1985, and again in recent years. In 1970 and 1986, programs for the construction of polar icebreakers were announced, but both were shelved or failed to materialize. Arguably among the reasons for this failure were the enormous costs and the minor political role the Canadian navy and coast guard play, as well as the minimal electoral gain to be expected from such policies (Pullen, 1986). Yet, whenever sovereignty is imperilled these programs reappear, prompting commentators to warn of a remilitarization of the Arctic. Since 2002 military exercises in the Arctic have been revived and have been complemented by the promise to increase military capabilities in the North (Huebert, 2005–6: 25). The need for a renewed Arctic policy was outlined in the 2005 *International Policy Statement* and was accompanied by a general call for a military buildup in the North. Strengthening military and civilian law enforcement capabilities also characterized the Conservatives' 2005–6 election platform and subsequent initiatives of the Harper government, including the 2007 Northern Strategy and the 2008 *Canada First Defence Strategy*.

Strengthening Canada's sovereignty is one of the four pillars of Canada's Northern Strategy, as outlined in the October 2007 Speech from the Throne. It promised 'new Arctic patrol ships and expanded aerial surveillance' to guard the Arctic and the Northwest Passage, as well as expansion of the size and capabilities of the Arctic Rangers (Canada, 2007c). The 2008 budget substantiated a number of these promises. Among other things, it provided funding for a new polar-class icebreaker for the Canadian Coast Guard and Arctic seabed mapping. Only two months later, in May 2008, the Canadian government unveiled a military blueprint, the *Canada First Defence Strategy*. It spelled out six core missions, the first of which was to 'conduct daily domestic and continental operations, including in the Arctic' (National Defence Canada, 2008a: 3). Most importantly, it included plans to acquire 6–8 Arctic patrol ships as well as radars and satellite to improve surveillance capabilities in the Arctic. In its backgrounder, the Canadian Defence Department stressed the importance of the Canadian Forces with respect to Arctic sovereignty: 'The Canadian Forces have a significant role to play in asserting Arctic sovereignty and will be called upon to provide that all-important presence' (National Defence Canada, 2008b). Still, military experts warn that Canada may not be able to monitor the whole area, let alone enforce law. They agree that military and civilian capabilities to date have been insufficient to ensure a comprehensive control of the vast and often inaccessible region.

The Diplomatic Response

In contrast to the Cold War, when much of Canada's foreign policy in the Arctic was driven by military and strategic considerations, the 1990s were characterized by a multilateralist approach and a focus on circumpolar affairs. This middlepowermanship was reflected in the 'Northern Dimension' approach that espoused a comprehensive northern policy by integrating the various conventional and new challenges in the Arctic and by addressing both the national and international levels. This approach goes back to initiatives by the transnational indigenous Inuit Circumpolar Conference (today named the Inuit Circumpolar Council), which found attentive ears in the Special Joint Committee on Canada's International Relations when this committee studied Canada's role in the Arctic and its relations with the United States after the *Polar Sea* incident in the mid-1980s. The joint committee's final report, *Independence and Internationalism*, included a chapter on the 'northern dimension' of Canada's foreign policy. Against a hard-power approach of flexing military muscle, it called for good governance strategies, which would include devolution of political and economic power to the Inuit, something that occurred through the creation of the territory of Nunavut in 1999. Furthermore, this report proposed closer co-operation with Arctic neighbours and closer attention to environmental issues (Special Joint Committee, 1986: 127–35; Richstone, 1986).

Following the foreign policy dimension of these recommendations, Canada began to actively champion an intergovernmental circumpolar forum, and the Arctic Council was founded by the 1996 Ottawa Declaration. In 1997 the Standing Committee on Foreign Affairs and International Trade issued its report, *Canada and the Circumpolar World: Meeting the Challenges of Cooperation in to the Twenty-First Century*, DFAIT published *Towards a Northern Foreign Policy: A Consultation Paper* in September 1998, and in 2000 DFAIT produced *The Northern Dimension of Canada's Foreign Policy*. Its four main objectives were to provide security and prosperity in the North, to assert sovereignty, and to 'establish the Circumpolar region as a vibrant geopolitical entity integrated into a rules-based international system; and to promote the human security of northerners and the sustainable development of the Arctic' (DFAIT, 2000: 2). In these documents sovereignty and security were not only and directly linked to military capabilities. In addition, Arctic sovereignty was reinterpreted to include issues of good governance as an 'important value' (McRae, 2007: 3). This is the fundamental analytical difference between the *Northern Dimension* approach and the 2007 *Northern Strategy*. While the 2007 *Northern Strategy* sets out comparable objectives ('economic and social development, governance, environmental protection, and sovereignty'), subsequent announcements and budgetary decisions to support icebreaker construction programs and seabed mapping clearly point to the priority of sovereignty in Canada's current foreign policy for the Arctic. Furthermore, the 2000 and 2007 documents differ in the proposed means to achieve Arctic sovereignty. Where the *Northern Strategy* proposes an increase in military and civilian control capabilities, the *Northern Dimension* promulgated multilateral co-operation.

Arctic Foreign Policy under Harper

Current Arctic policy is characterized by an emphasis on sovereignty and reliance on classical military security. Hence, the Canadian government has insisted on highlighting the threats to the country's security and sovereignty by making their protection a top priority. This 'securitization' of challenges has pushed perceptions of economic opportunities to the background. The move is epitomized by the constant reference to 'Arctic sovereignty', which alludes to a possible loss of territorial jurisdiction if not territory and calls for a strong response with a military defence posture. This sovereignty discourse is accompanied by an assertiveness and determination not to yield an inch from current Canadian positions on the Arctic. In July 2007 Prime Minister Stephen Harper reaffirmed Canada's uncompromising stance when he introduced the 'use it or lose it' dictum: 'Canada has a choice when it comes to defending our sovereignty over the Arctic. We either use it or lose it. And make no mistake, this Government intends to use it' (Canada, 2007b).

The current prominence of the Arctic sovereignty discourse in Canada's policy agenda indicates that the circumpolar, multilateralist outlook has been replaced by one that emphasizes state actors, the assertion of sovereignty, and possible unilateralist action to safeguard national interests. This shift explains various calls from analysts and academics for a 'whole of government' and 3D (defence, diplomacy, and development) approach, which combines questions of sovereignty and security, good governance, and economic development. Others hope that Canada will once again become a champion of multilateralism and return to middlepowermanship. They fear that in the long run Canada's assertive and uncompromising position on the Northwest Passage could undermine its credibility as an environmental steward in the Arctic (Lackenbauer, 2008: 2, 4).

As the above discussion indicates, Canada's Arctic policy has changed because of shifting international and domestic environments. Furthermore, shifts in the perception of security, and ideas about the Arctic, have influenced policy decisions. At the same time, Arctic policy has also been informed by continuities such as the construction of Canada as a northern nation and the importance of Arctic sovereignty in identity politics. As the study of Canada–US relations illustrates, historical path dependencies also play a role in that they frame the sovereignty discourse to include the contestation of Canada's jurisdictional authority by the United States. In conclusion, there have been clear moves on the part of recent Canadian governments from a multilateral, circumpolar policy outlook to a unilateral Arctic sovereignty policy, from reactive to proactive, and from co-operative soft power to military hard power. At the same time, Canada's Arctic policy remains inconsistent and ambiguous as it tries to accommodate the different shifts in the international, national, and conceptual arenas.

Conclusion: Canada between Arctic Power and Middle Power

Does the current nature of Arctic policy mean that Canada has moved away from being a middle power? If middlepowermanship is characterized by multilateralism and active internationalism, this may well be the case. The relatively minor role that Canadian middlepowermanship plays at the moment is the more surprising considering that US complacency and relative disinterest in the region would allow Canada to pursue niche diplomacy and also push for a functionalist agenda. Thus, it could be through precisely its Arctic policy that Canada would be able to reclaim its internationally visible position as middle power. However, for this to work Canada would need to reconcile its middlepowerhood in the region with middlepowermanship. It should champion multilateralist solutions and actively engage in norm entrepreneurship in the circumpolar Arctic. As a middle power, Canada should welcome non-state actors back onto the scene and push for international regimes to meet the global challenges in the Arctic.

Such an interpretation, however, would depend on the analytical validity of the middle-power idea for Arctic policy. If the middle-power idea is in fact no objective analytical category but simply what Canada makes of it, one could argue that the 'discursive continuity' (Hynek, 2007: 139) of that concept lost its power once a new policy field, i.e., Arctic policy, entered the foreign policy discourse. Moreover, this new foreign policy discourse was driven by another discursive construction, that of Arctic sovereignty. Thus, it may be more helpful to interpret Arctic sovereignty and middle power as two separate ideas feeding into and defining what Canada sees as its national interest. This way we should not be surprised that Arctic policy does not easily fit into the analytical category of middle power. Furthermore, it would mean that the middle-power concept impedes our understanding of Arctic policy.

Ultimately, regardless of whether we see Arctic policy in terms of the middle-power concept or not, any analysis of Canada's foreign policy in the Arctic has to position itself in relation to that powerful idea.

Notes

1. Following Alexander Wendt's famous dictum that 'anarchy is what states make of it', the argument is that the middle-power image is not a static objective category or a set of foreign policy behaviours; instead, it affirms that what constitutes a middle power is historically contingent and it recognizes that national interests are constructed and follow a set of distinct ideas and values (Wendt, 1992). Nikola Hynek (2007: 139–40) has shown the political function of the continuous construction of that middle-power image.

2. Ann Florini (1996: 375) defines a norm entrepreneur as 'an individual or organization that sets out to change the behavior of others'.

3. Elizabeth Riddell-Dixon (2008: 343) has challenged the popular assumption that 'Arctic countries are engaged in a highly competitive scramble to stake claims.' A good example of such an alarmist interpretation is Borgerson (2008).

4. For the most recent and comprehensive discussion of the complex jurisdictional aspects, see Pharand (2007). Donat Pharand (1988; Pharand with Legault, 1984) and Donald McRae (2007: 4–6) have commented on the legal aspects of Canada's Arctic policy.

5. Pharand (2007: 37) argues that this is only a problem in those cases where Canada does not know of submarine crossings. If they took place under some continental defence arrangement these crossings would not qualify as transits by foreign ships.

6. For a good example of the official US perspective on the Arctic, see McMurray (2008). See also President Obama's 'New Energy for America' agenda, at: <www.whitehouse.gov/agenda/energy_and_environment/>.

7. The trilateral Security and Prosperity Partnership launched in 2005 is a good example.

8. Pharand (2007: 52) counts at least 15 departments and agencies 'that have some kind of jurisdiction or interest in northern and Arctic Affairs'.

9. In the 1990s the Western Europe desk within Foreign Affairs dealt with circumpolar matters as these were mainly relating to Greenland. Today this responsibility has been assumed by the Directorate of Aboriginal and Circumpolar Affairs.

10. 'Summary of Canadian Note of April 16 Tabled by the Secretary of State for External Affairs in the House April 17', 9 Int. Legal Materials 608 (1970), quoted in Henkin (1971: 133). On the AWPPA, see Pharand (1973).

References

Åtland, Kristian. 2008. 'Mikhail Gorbachev, the Murmansk Initiative, and the Desecuritization of Interstate Relations in the Arctic', *Cooperation and Conflict* 43, 3: 289–311.

Borgerson, Scott G. 2008. 'Arctic Meltdown: The Economic and Security Implications of Global Warming', *Foreign Affairs* 87, 2: 63–77.

Buzan, Barry, Ole Wæver, and Jaap de Wilde. 1998. *Security: A New Framework for Analysis*. Boulder, Colo.: Lynne Rienner.

Byers, Michael. 2007. *Intent for a Nation: What Is Canada For?* Vancouver: Douglas & McIntyre.

Canada. 2007a. 'Prime Minister Stephen Harper Calls for International Consensus on Climate Change', Berlin, 4 June. At: <www.pm.gc.ca>.

———. 2007b. 'Prime Minister Harper Announces New Arctic Offshore Patrol Ships', 9 July, At: <pm.gc.ca/eng/media.asp?category=2&id=1741>.

———. 2007c. 'Speech from the Throne: A Proud and Sovereign Canada', 16 Oct. At: <www.sft-ddt.gc.ca/eng/media.asp?id=1368>.

Coates, Ken, P., Whitney Lackenbauer, and Greg Poelzer. 2008. *Arctic Front: Defending Canada in the Far North*. Markham, Ont.: Thomas Allen.

Cohen, Andrew. 2004. *While Canada Slept: How We Lost Our Place in the World*. Toronto: McClelland & Stewart.

Cooper, Andrew F. 1993. 'Niche Diplomacy: A Conceptual Overview', in Cooper, ed., *Niche Diplomacy: Middle Powers after the Cold War*. Vancouver: University of British Columbia Press, 1–24.

———. 1997. 'The Politics of Environmental Security: The Case of the Canada–Spain "Fish War"', in Cooper, *Canadian Foreign Policy: Old Habits and New Directions*. Scarborough, Ont.: Prentice-Hall Allyn and Bacon Canada, 142–72.

Declaration of Ilulissat, 28 May 2008. At: <arctic-council.org/filearchive/Ilulissat-declaration. pdf>,

Department of Foreign Affairs and International Trade Canada (DFAIT). 2000. *The Northern Dimension of Canada's Foreign Policy*. Ottawa.

Elliot-Meisel, Elizabeth B. 1998. *Arctic Diplomacy: Canada and the United States in the Northwest Passage*. New York: Peter Lang.

Farish, Matthew, and P. Whitney Lackenbauer. 2007. 'The Cold War on Canadian Soil: Militarizing a Northern Environment', *Environmental History* 12, 4: 920–50.

Florini, Ann. 1996. 'The Evolution of International Norms', *International Studies Quarterly* 40, 3: 363–89.

Fraser, Whit, and John Harker. 1994–5. 'A Northern Foreign Policy for Canada', *Northern Perspectives* 22, 4. At: <www.carc.org/pubs/v22no4/policy.htm>.

Granatstein, Jack L. 2004. *Who Killed the Canadian Military?* Toronto: HarperCollins.

Grant, Shelagh D. 1991. 'A Case of Compounded Error: The Inuit Resettlement Project, 1953, and the Government Response, 1990', *Northern Perspectives* 19, 1. At: <www.carc.org/pubs/v19no1/2.htm>.

Griffiths, Franklyn. 2008. 'Towards a Canadian Arctic Strategy', Canadian International Council, Preliminary Paper, July 2008. At: <www.igloo.org/canadianinternational/research/franklyngr>.

Hellmann, Gunther, and Benjamin Herborth. 2008. 'Fishing in the Mild West: Democratic Peace and Militarised Interstate Disputes in the Transatlantic Community', *Review of International Studies* 34, 3: 481–506.

Henkin, Louis. 1971. 'Arctic Anti-Pollution: Does Canada Make—or Break—International Law?', *American Journal of International Law* 65, 1: 131–6.

Huebert, Rob. 2005–6. 'Renaissance in Canadian Arctic Security?', *Canadian Military Journal* 6, 4: 17–29.

———. 2006. 'Reenforcing Sovereignty, National Security and Circumpolar Cooperation', *Northern Perspectives* 30, 1: 7–10.

———. 2008. 'Canadian Arctic Security: Understanding and Responding to the Coming Storm,' Canadian International Council, Preliminary Paper, July 2008. At: <www.igloo.org/canadianinternational/research/robhuebert>.

Hynek, Nikola. 2007. 'Humanitarian Arms Control, Symbiotic Functionalism and the Concept of Middlepowerhood: Initial Remarks on Motivation, or Why Another Study on the Landmine Case', *Central European Journal of International and Security Studies* 1, 2: 132–55.

Koivurova, Timo. 2008. 'Alternatives for an Arctic Treaty: Evaluation and a New Proposal', *Review of European Community & International Environmental Law* 17, 1: 14–26.

Krause, Keith. 1998. 'Critical Theory and Security Studies', *Cooperation and Conflict* 33, 3: 298–333.

Lackenbauer, P. Whitney. 2005–6. 'The Canadian Rangers: A "Postmodern" Militia That Works', *Canadian Military Journal* 6, 4: 49–60.

———. 2008. 'Arctic Front, Arctic Homeland: Pre-Evaluating Canada's Past Record and Future Prospects in the Circumpolar North', Canadian International Council, Preliminary Paper, July 2008. At: <www.igloo.org/canadianinternational/research/whitneylac>.

Manning, Bayless. 1977. 'The Congress, The Executive, and Intermestic Affairs: Three Proposals', *Foreign Affairs* 55, 2: 306–24.

McMurray, Claudia A. 2008. 'Emerging from the Frost: The U.S. Perspective', in Kjetil Skogrand, ed., *Emerging from the Frost: Security in the 21st Century Arctic*. Oslo: Norwegian Institute for Defence Studies, 31–7.

McRae, Donald. 2007. 'Arctic Sovereignty? What Is at Stake?', *Behind the Headlines* 64, 1: 1–23.

Miliband , David, and Frank-Walter Steinmeier. 2008. 'Europe Has to Face Up to the Security Policy Impact of Climate Change', 13 Mar. At: <www.auswaertiges-amt.de/diplo/en/Infoservice/Presse/Interview/2008/080313-klimasicherheit.html>.

National Defence Canada. 2008a. *Canada First Defence Strategy*. Ottawa.

————. 2008b. 'Backgrounder: Canada First Defence Strategy—Canadian Forces' Contribution to Sovereignty and Security in the North', 12 May. At: <www.forces.gc.ca/site/Newsroom/view_news_e.asp?id=2645>.

Nincic, Donna J. 2002. 'Sea Lane Security and U.S. Maritime Trade: Chokepoints as Scarce Resources', in Sam J. Tangredi, ed., *Globalization and Maritime Power*. Washington: Institute for National Strategic Studies, National Defense University, 143–70.

Northern Perspectives. 1986. Special issue: 14, 4.

Nye, Joseph S., Jr. 1990. 'The Changing Nature of World Power', *Political Science Quarterly* 105, 2: 177–92.

————. 1990. *Bound to Lead: The Changing Nature of American Power*. New York: Basic Books.

————. 2002–3. 'Limits of American Power', *Political Science Quarterly* 117, 4: 545–59.

Okalik, Paul. 2008. 'Arctic Priorities: A Northern Perspective', *Behind the Headlines* 65, 4: 3–8.

Osherenko, Gail, and Oran R. Young. 1989. *The Age of the Arctic: Hot Conflicts and Cold Realities*. Cambridge: Cambridge University Press.

Pharand, Donat. 1973. *The Law of the Sea of the Arctic with Special Reference to Canada*. Ottawa: University of Ottawa Press.

————. 1988. *Canada's Arctic Waters in International Law*. Cambridge: Cambridge University Press.

————. 2007. 'The Arctic Waters and the Northwest Passage: A Final Revisit', *Ocean Development & International Law* 38, 3: 3–69.

———— with Leonard H. Legault. 1984. *Northwest Passage: Arctic Straits*. Dordrecht: Martinus Nijhoff.

Pullen, T.C. 1986. 'That Polar Ice-Breaker', *Northern Perspectives* 14, 4. At: <www.carc.org/pubs/v14no4/5.htm>.

Putnam, Robert D. 1988. 'Diplomacy and Domestic Politics: The Logic of Two-Level Games', *International Organization* 42, 3: 427–60.

Richstone, Jeff. 1986. 'Arctic Sovereignty: The Search for Substance', *Northern Perspectives* 14, 4. At: <www.carc.org/pubs/v14no4/2.htm>.

Riddell-Dixon, Elizabeth. 2008. 'Canada and Arctic Politics: The Continental Shelf Extension', *Ocean Development & International Law* 39, 4: 343–59.

Simon, Mary. 2007. 'Canada Needs More Than New Patrol Ships', *Nunatsiaq News*, 3 Aug.

Special Joint Committee on Canada's International Relations. 1986. *Independence and Internationalism: Report of the Special Joint Committee*. Ottawa: Queen's Printer for Canada.

Welsh, Jennifer. 2004. 'Canada in the 21st Century: Beyond Dominion and Middle Power', *Behind the Headlines* 61, 4: 1–15.

Wendt, Alexander. 1992. 'Anarchy Is What States Make of It: The Social Construction of Politics', *International Organization* 46, 2: 391–425.

White House. 2009. 'National Security Presidential Directive and Homeland Security Presidential Directive: Arctic Region Policy', 9 Jan. At: <georgewbush-whitehouse.archives.gov/news/releases/2009/01/20090112-3.html>.

Young, Oran R. 1985–6. 'The Age of the Arctic', *Foreign Policy* 61: 160–79.

Additional Readings

Cooper, Andrew F., and Whitney Lackenbauer. 2007. 'The Achilles Heel of Canadian Good International Citizenship: Indigenous Diplomacies and State Responses in the Twentieth

Century', *Canadian Foreign Policy* 13, 3: 99–119.

Dosman, E.J., ed. 1976. *The Arctic in Question.* Toronto: University of Toronto Press.

Elliot-Meisel, Elizabeth B. 1999. 'Still Unresolved after Fifty Years: The Northwest Passage in Canadian–American Relations, 1946–1998', *American Review of Canadian Studies* 39, 3: 407–30.

Grant, Shelagh D. 1988. *Sovereignty or Security? Government Policy in the Canadian North 1936– 1950.* Vancouver: University of British Columbia Press

Griffiths, Franklyn, ed. 1987. *Politics of the Northwest Passage.* Montreal and Kingston: McGill-Queen's University Press.

———. 1988. *The Arctic as an International Political Region.* Toronto: Science for Peace/Samuel Stevens.

———. 1996. *Strong and Free: Canada and the New Sovereignty.* Toronto: Stoddart.

———. 2004. 'Pathetic Fallacy: That Canada's Arctic Sovereignty Is on Thinning Ice', *Canadian Foreign Policy* 11, 3.

——— et al. 2008. 'Canada's Arctic Interests and Responsibilities', *Behind the Headlines* 65, 4.

Heininen, Lassi, and Heather N. Nicol. 2007. 'The Importance of Northern Dimension Foreign Policies in the Geopolitics of the Circumpolar North', *Geopolitics* 12: 133–65.

Fogelson, Nancy. 1992. *Arctic Exploration and International Relations 1900–1932: A Period of Expanding National Interests.* Anchorage: University of Alaska Press.

Lasserre, Frédéric. 2001. 'The North-West-Passage: A Future Maritime Route?', *Relations internationales et stratégiques* 42: 143–60.

Lindsey, George R. 1977. *Strategic Aspects of the Polar Regions.* Toronto: Canadian Institute of International Affairs.

Morrison, William R. 1987. 'Eagle Over the Arctic: Americans in the Canadian North, 1867– 1985', *Canadian Review of American Studies* 18, 1: 61–75.

Möttölä, Kari, ed. 1988. *The Arctic Challenge: Nordic and Canadian Approaches to Security and Cooperation in an Emerging International Region.* Boulder, Colo.: Westview Press.

Nord, Douglas C. 2006. 'Canada as a Northern Nation: Finding a Role for the Arctic Council', in Patrick James, Nelson Michaud, and Marc J. O'Reilly, eds, *Handbook of Canadian Foreign Policy.* Lanham, Md: Lexington, 289–316.

———. 2007. 'Looking for the North in North American Foreign Policies: Canada and the United States', *American Review of Canadian Studies* 37: 205–17.

Nuttal, Mark, and Kathrin Wessendorf, eds. 2006. 'Arctic Oil and Gas Development', *Indigenous Affairs* 2–3.

Øvrik, Nils, and Kirk R. Patterson. eds. 1976. *The North in Transition.* Kingston, Ont.: Centre for International Relations, Queen's University.

Seyersted, Per, ed. 1991. *The Arctic: Canada and the Nordic Countries.* Lund: Nordic Association of Canadian Studies.

Tynan, Thomas. 1979. 'Canadian–American Relations in the Arctic: The Effect of Environmental Influences upon Territorial Claims', *Review of Politics* 41, 3: 402–27.

Young, Oran R. 2009. 'Whither the Arctic? Conflict or Cooperation in the Circumpolar North', *Polar Record* 45, 232: 73–82.

Part III: Questions for Critical Thought

Chapter 9

1. What are the main features of the current concept of RMA?
2. What is the connection between the RMA and the process that drives the transformation of the armed forces in NATO and some other countries?
3. The armed forces of Western countries, including Canada, have to prepare themselves for new and non-traditional military missions. What are the salient features of these missions?
4. In the self-perception of the Canadian public, what 'Canadian values' should the government promote in its external relations, and to what extent do these values differ from 'ordinary' national interests?
5. Canada perceives itself as a 'proud peacekeeper'. What are the roots of this perception? Is it more of a political myth or has it reflected Canada's behaviour in international politics?
6. What are the differences between traditional peacekeeping during the Cold War and more robust forms of peacekeeping since the 1990s?
7. Explain the term 'Fourth Generation Warfare' and outline its main features.
8. Why is Canada's security policy so heavily dependent on the US?
9. What does military interoperability mean? Discuss its relevance for the Canada–US relationship.
10. Why did Canadian governments in the 1990s reduce the budget of the Canadian Forces?
11. What are the three roles of Canada's military according to the *Canada First Defence Strategy* of May 2008?
12. Do the processes of RMA and military transformation of the Canadian Forces and their mission in Afghanistan reinforce or dilute the perception and self-perception of Canada as a middle power?

Chapter 10

1. How does a 'security community' differ from other forms of institutionalized security co-operation, such as an 'alliance' or 'collective security'?
2. What is the difference between 'societal security' and more traditional concepts, such as 'physical security'?
3. How does the North American security community contribute to Canada's 'power' in the international system?

4. What is the crux of the dispute between Canada and several other political actors (including the US and the EU) regarding the status of the Northwest Passage?
5. Is the Canada–US security community the world's oldest such community?
6. What other pairing of neighbouring states can you think of as having a claim to the 'title' of being the first to have forged a regional 'zone of peace'?
7. Is there a security community between the US and Mexico? If so, when did it arise?
8. From the point of view of 'societal security', why is it more appropriate to speak of the 'Canadianization' of the US–Mexican border than of the 'Mexicanization' of the Canada–US border?
9. To what security issue does the expression the 'New Fenianism' refer?
10. Is the North American security community 'idiot proof'?

Chapter 11

1. What major acts of terrorism have affected Canada?
2. How has Canadian security policy adjusted to trends away from domestically inspired acts of terrorism to internationally inspired acts of terrorism?
3. Assess Canada's initial response to 9/11? Was it primarily driven by a desire to respond to American perceptions of its northern neighbour as a potential security threat?
4. Given subsequent experience, was Canada's initial reaction to 9/11 an overreaction, an underreaction, or an appropriate reaction? Has Canada paid too little, too much, or an appropriate amount of attention to human rights since 9/11?
5. Explain the different meanings of 'human security' and how it has affected Canadian national security? What are the similarities and differences between the use of the human security concept at home and in Canada foreign policy?
6. What was the significance of Canada's first official national security policy, *Securing an Open Society*, issued by the Martin government in 2004?
7. How is Canada's 'all-risk' national security policy different from American national security policies? Does it make sense for Canada to have a policy that addresses all risks, including natural or man-made disasters, or should Canadian policy be more focused on the risk of terrorism?

8. Has Canada done anything in terms of its security policy that would support claims that it is a leading middle power that can exercise global leadership?

9. Who is Maher Arar and why is he a significant person who still has an impact on Canadian attitudes towards anti-terrorism investigations and Canadian–American relations?

10. How has and how should Canada's multiculturalism influence its national security policy?

Chapter 12

1. What are the scope and extent of the 'Canada in decline' argument in Canadian national security policy? Why was the argument so palpable in Canada? Discuss.

2. What are the main criticisms of the 'declinist' argument and why? Discuss.

3. How does the declinist school argument relate to the three schools of Canadian foreign policy?

4. Explain the concept and scope of the so-called 'decade of darkness' in Canadian defence policy.

5. The Canadian government has been criticized for not being able to think 'strategically' about defence policy. Has this been the case in the post-Cold War era? If so, why?

6. In what ways did Canada remain an active member of NATO despite declining defence budgets at home?

7. Describe, contrast, and explain Canada's national interests in the 1990s vs those in the post-9/11 world?

8. What was the impact of UN and NATO peacekeeping operations on Canadian defence policy and how did Canada perform in those operations?

9. What, if any, were some of the domestic constraints on Canada's involvement in NATO in the 1990s?

10. Why does Ottawa always seem concerned about having 'influence' in the international arena? To what extent, if any, does Canada's role in NATO give Canada that influence?

11. What is the major external national security threat to Canada today? How is that threat different from threats during the Cold War and the immediate post-Cold War periods?

12. Has Canada abandoned its once well-respected role as a 'peacekeeper'? And if so, why?

Chapter 13

1. In what ways does Canada's Arctic policy reflect changes in the international system?
2. How useful is the middle-power model for studying Canada's Arctic policy?
3. Why has Arctic policy become an important aspect of Canada's foreign policy agenda?
4. What issues constitute Canada's Arctic policy?
5. Should we understand Arctic policy as foreign or domestic policy?
6. How important are history and geography in analyzing Arctic policy?
7. How 'new' is Arctic policy?
8. To what extent is the national bureaucracy responsible for providing competing Arctic strategies?
9. Which non-state actors have become active in the Arctic? What are their interests and what do they advocate?
10. In what sense is the Northwest Passage a bilateral foreign policy issue?
11. What do we mean by Canada's Arctic sovereignty and what role does Prime Minister Harper's dictum 'use it or lose it' play in it?
12. To what extent do international regimes and institutions such as UNCLOS and the Arctic Council influence Canada's Arctic policy?
13. What is the relationship between northern and Arctic policy?
14. What have been the key trends of Canada–US relations in the Arctic?
15. To what extent do security considerations drive Canada's Arctic policy and what have they been?

Conclusion

David Bosold and Nik Hynek

'The Arctic and the North are part of our national identity', Lawrence Cannon (2009) recently stated in a speech delivered in Whitehorse, Yukon. Canada's Foreign Minister went on to state that he was 'committed to ensuring that the international spotlight stays focused on the challenges and opportunities facing the Arctic'. Cynics may argue that this commitment may be rather short-lived, especially given the number of reshuffles in the ministerial portfolio over the last five years. More importantly, however, and bearing in mind the points raised in Chapter 13 by Petra Dolata-Kreutzkamp, one might also question Cannon's claim that the Arctic really forms part of Canada's collective identity. At any rate, his statement implicitly affirms one of the central arguments of this volume: that the way Canadian policy-makers have perceived their country's role in international affairs is highly contingent and that their perception has varied from issue to issue. Carving out niches, shifting the attention to other policy fields, and relabelling the country's (self-)image—be it middle power, model power or, nowadays, Arctic power—has been a consistent feature of CanFSP that is destined to stay with us for the years to come. As the preceding chapters make clear, a number of commonly held wisdoms of CanFSP have been myths rather than proven historical facts. Canada's supposedly benign involvement in global affairs, exemplified by metaphors such as the 'good international citizen', 'honest broker', and 'do-gooder', is less obvious if not outright contradictory if one shifts the attention from the mainstream readings of history to the concrete policies on the ground in the domain of environmental politics or to (at least some) security policies in Afghanistan.

The mythology, of course, is not a feature unique to Canadian foreign and security policy but is common to the policy of any country. A quite specific feature has thus been the *degree* to which myths, clichés, and stereotypes have penetrated and colonized the field of Canadian foreign and security policy *analysis*. Hence, instead of simply taking for granted myths such as Canada's role as the peacekeeper par excellence, one should embark upon their critical examination (see Thomsen and Hynek, 2006). This does not imply that only the readings and interpretations collected in this volume are 'correct' and 'true'. It does, however, highlight that critical takes on CanFSP, such as the ones presented here, vary from more traditional approaches in a number of ways and that there are good reasons for skepticism when confronted with seemingly objective historic accounts. In that sense, the chapters in this volume have sought to contextualize and reassess the key narratives of CanFSP in order to present a more encompassing picture of Canada's past and recent processes, results, and performances. A number of issues were tackled in that respect.

A Reassessment of Middle-Power Narratives

The first part of this volume (Chapters 1–3) offered an encompassing review of the concept of a middle power. Starting with a closer historical examination of middle power in terms of Canada's external behaviour since 1945, the argument was put forward that there is currently a growing discrepancy between Canada's ambitions and its record in what it actually delivers. According to Keating, putting more money where the mouth is will be central to remedying the growing disenchantment of Canada's current role in the world. This is even more pressing since the number of states willing and capable of exploiting functional niches traditionally reserved to middle powers has increased over the past few years, a phenomenon Parag Khanna (2009) has aptly characterized as the rise of the 'second world'. Yet, despite the geopolitical changes that have allowed for transcending the national security straitjacket of the Cold War era, the new latitude in Canadian foreign and security policy has so far not resulted in a quasi-reinvention of that policy, as Nossal reminds us. The resilience of middle power, understood as both middlepowerhood and middlepowermanship, he states, has illustrated less the continuous usefulness of the concept for academic research than the fact that the narratives about Canada's place in the world have changed little during the past few decades.

Changes in Labels and Practices

The value-added of the concept or image of middle power—the subject of the chapters in the second part of this book—does not lie in its quality for a rigorous scholarly analysis. Rather, it is a prism through which we can see how the idea has repeatedly been used by Canadian policy-makers to highlight the distinctiveness of the country, its citizens, and its position and role in global affairs. This domestic dimension of middle-power identity politics is also reflected in the repeated attempts to rejuvenate foreign policy by creating new and catchy labels such as the 'model power' or, as Bátora noted in Chapter 6, the 'Canada–Cool–Connected' slogan. It is in that respect that Bosold, in Chapter 3, sought to pinpoint the fallacies of rebranding the country's role in foreign and security policy and to show that real change requires more than a play of words. Semantic changes must reflect—and also lead to—changes in practices. While the proponents of the 'model-power' concept are undoubtedly right in arguing that the diplomatic toolbox of CanFSP has significantly changed over the last decade, this change does not mean that anything can be gained from a new semantic label. This is mainly due to the persistent popularity of the notion of middle power at home. Moreover, though, this is the case because charting a new path for CanFSP requires more than a governmental decision to use different role conceptions. Diplomatic success and military success ultimately both depend on the congruence of the domestic and the external perceptions of Canada's leverage and its legitimization.

That this leverage is perceived to be larger within Canada than outside the country is only one of the conclusions we can draw from one of the defining diplomatic events in recent Canadian history, the Ottawa Process to ban landmines. Nik Hynek, in Chapter 4, offered an alternative reading to the triumphalist, ethical, and often self-righteous perception of the ban on landmines (see also Latham, 2001). This alternative view suggests that the broader political-economic changes that have occurred within Canada since the 1960s, and especially after 1993, also need to be analyzed more closely. Hynek has challenged the prevalent accounts of this new era of humanitarianism by not placing the landmine ban within a somewhat awkward architecture of global governance but instead by shedding light on the domestic setting that has been regulating and defining the scope and nature of NGOs' involvement. The oft-cited myths that states have lost power at the expense of civil society actors—and that new roles for NGOs are the best illustration of the process of democratization of CanFSP—do not hold up to scrutiny of the actual record. Political practices allow for a divergent interpretation of the landmine ban in which Nye's definition of soft power (and, with it, the entire mainstream narrative on landmines built upon it) is found to be conceptually flawed and empirically absent.

New Modes of Foreign and Security Policy-Making

Contemporary changes in CanFSP are not exhausted by the process of government appearing to do less by outsourcing its previous tasks to NGOs that compete for governmental funding in their respective issue areas. Likewise, the degree of inter-ministerial co-ordination to allow for the efficient and effective administration of joint missions and programs has increased significantly over the last decade. During this process, the autonomy of line departments has been undermined and the ministerial rules of foreign and security policy-making have been changed. In addition, the security–development nexus has been one of the most recent forms of how traditional foreign, security, and development policy intersect. In spite of its introduction under Paul Martin's Liberal government, the so-called 3D approach is still informing the strategies of Canada's engagement in Afghanistan and has led to a redefinition of political purposes formerly associated with the delivery of foreign aid and peace-building activities. Besides the changes depicted in Chapters 4 and 5, Bátora in Chapter 6 illustrates that Canada's soft power also depends on innovations within DFAIT. Most notably, the potential of DFAIT to engage in a dialogue with peers by harnessing new information and communication technologies can be said to contribute procedurally to a reinvigoration of middle-power diplomacy. In addition, wielding soft power also depends, to an ever greater extent, on the possibilities to interact directly with citizens outside of Canada by means of public diplomacy. While Canada is undeniably leading in terms of its expertise in this field, it remains to be seen how other countries will position themselves vis-à-vis the ideas that have been promoted by DFAIT in recent years.

A Broadened and Deepened Security Paradigm

Besides changes in the foreign policy process, the broadened and deepened understanding of security (see Buzan, 1991; Krause and Williams, 1996) has left an imprint on CanFSP that goes beyond the issues associated with human security. Most importantly, it also includes energy security and environmental security. Both are illustrative of global and regional interdependencies, and diplomatic success in these issue areas ultimately depends on a viable combination of a domestic consensus and a suitable strategy for co-operation with other states. As the example of the tar sands shows, Canada is a country that could potentially be energy independent. Yet, its NAFTA obligations and its dismal environmental record in combatting climate change illustrate the difficulties in achieving desired ends with less than robust means. Indeed, as Baldwin and Dalby in Chapter 7 and Laxer in Chapter 8 demonstrate, the federal government and the producer provinces, at least to date, appear to have decided that the ability to secure the energy supply (for the US!) through tapping oil from the tar sands—i.e., the issue of energy security—should take precedence over a reduction in greenhouse gas emissions—i.e., the issue of environmental security. In addition, one must position the country's policies vis-à-vis those of other states, most notably the US, in order to assess the prospects of multilateral co-operation aiming at the implementation of a more sustainable future and, therefore, a more sustainable foreign and security policy. In this instance, Canada's increasingly decentralized federal system has meant that strong federal action, which might in the short term have a negative effect on provincial revenues and corporate profits, not to mention on relations with the US and on the NAFTA regime, involves political risk-taking of the highest order.

A New Role for the Canadian Forces

As the third part of the book—on hard power—shows, co-operation and innovation can indeed be found in more traditional fields of security policy, such as the realm of the armed forces, where the last decade has seen increased pressure to guarantee the interoperability of the Canadian Forces with their US counterparts. These efforts have been driven by changes in military doctrine and technologies commonly referred to as the 'revolution in military affairs'. While the desire for interoperability has always been stated officially, the drastic cuts in Canada's defence budget in the 1990s and the early 2000s did not allow the Canadian Forces to fully satisfy the Americans on this score. Whether pleasing the Americans is necessarily desired remains questionable, given that the threat perception between Canada and its closest ally has varied, sometimes significantly (e.g., in the case of ballistic missile defence and in involvement— or lack thereof—in Iraq). What can be observed, though, is that the Canadian Forces have been increasingly trained for and are being engaged in asymmetric combat and counter-insurgency missions, changes that reflect nothing less than a qualitative shift from the former and more benign role of the Cold War peacekeeper. This development has not come out of nowhere, and the robust peacekeeping and peace enforcement missions of the 1990s—mainly in the Balkans—represented the first step towards a transformed raison d'être for the Canadian Forces. As Zyla and Sokolsky show in Chapter 12, regardless of cuts in the Defence portfolio, the Canadian Forces have not been 'killed', nor have they refused to share the military burden within NATO. On the contrary, it seems that, counter to the laments of the declinist school, Canada has been one of the key players within the North Atlantic alliance. It is therefore important to revisit the argument that Canada's military capabilities have decreased over the last decade. While this is certainly true in the framework of UN peacekeeping missions and perhaps even in absolute numbers, it is not the case for so-called stabilization missions by NATO and in a comparative perspective, as Zyla and Sokolsky demonstrate.

National and Societal Security

Since September 2001 the involvement of the Canadian Forces in the global War on Terror is a reflection of the idea that national security can be increased by fighting one's enemies abroad in order to stop them coming inside of one's country. Inextricably linked with the military engagement in the War on Terror, however, are a set of domestic and hemisphere measures. These have begun to dominate contemporary discussions because of repeated criticism of a purely military response to terrorism, including the highly problematic aspects of this endeavour in Guantánamo and Abu Ghraib. With a terrorist threat that now has less political salience and generally seems less important than some five years ago (National Intelligence Council, 2008: ix), it is important to be reminded that the 9/11 attacks have resulted in a number of domestic anti-terrorist measures and restrictions of civil liberties in Canada. What is more, as Haglund and Roach demonstrate in Chapters 10 and 11, respectively, these measures aimed at increasing border security and harmonization of Canadian and US policies have had a detrimental effect on human rights policies and, moreover, on societal cohesion in general. The fear of vernacular insecurity due to the influx of Hispanics into the US and the questioning of previously esteemed principles of multiculturalism due to anti-terrorist legislation have had a more far-reaching impact on the domestic polities than on Canadian or US foreign policy (see Robin, 2004).

Future Issues in Canadian Foreign and Security Policy

Decreased attention to terrorist threats has been contrasted with increased interest in other issues that are destined to stay on the CanFSP agenda for the years to come. Out of these, energy and environmental policies will certainly become more important even if there are currently signs of their relative neglect due to the global credit crunch and financial meltdown. Economic security will certainly become one of the most important issues and will stay there for at least several years. But there are also signs of a stronger regional dimension in Canadian foreign and security policy in the coming years. After a renewed interest in the Americas in the 1990s and a stronger orientation towards the states of Latin America and the Pacific Rim, one can expect a stronger emphasis on the relations with Canada's Arctic neighbours. Media sound bites of a 'race to the Arctic' are certainly misleading if not outright false. Yet, the impact of climate change on the livelihood and lifeways of Canada's indigenous people in the three northern territories and the prospects for new sea routes and the exploration of hydrocarbon resources seem to indicate that the attention to Arctic issues will not evaporate as quickly as was the case in the mid-1980s under the Mulroney government. Despite omnipresent changes in CanFSP in terms of issues and practices, one will also see continuity. Canadians will continue to seek comfort in the narratives of the middle power and good international citizen, but they might do so with more caution than in the past.

References

Buzan, Barry. 1991. *People, States and Fear*, 2nd edn. Boulder, Colo.: Lynne Rienner.
Cannon, Lawrence. 2009. 'Notes for an Address by the Honourable Lawrence Cannon, Minister

of Foreign Affairs, on Canada's Arctic Foreign Policy', Whitehorse, Yukon, 11 Mar. At: <w01.international.gc.ca/minpub/Publication.aspx?isRedirect=True&publication_id=386 933&language=E&docnumber=2009/11>. (18 Mar. 2009)

Khanna, Parag. 2009. *The Second World: How Emerging Powers are Redefining Global Competition in the Twenty-first Century*. London: Penguin.

Krause, Keith, and Michael C. Williams. 1996. 'Broadening the Agenda of Security Studies? Politics and Methods', *Mershon International Studies Review* 40: 229–54.

Latham, Andrew A. 2001. 'Theorizing the Landmine Campaign: Ethics, Global Cultural Scripts, and the Laws of War', in Rosalind Irwin, ed., *Ethics and Security in Canadian Foreign Policy*. Vancouver: University of British Columbia Press, 160–78.

National Intelligence Council. 2008. *Global Trends 2025: A Transformed World*. Washington: NIC. At: <www.dni.gov/reports/2025_Global_Trends_Final_Report.pdf>. (20 Mar. 2009)

Robin, Corey. 2004. *Fear: The History of a Political Idea*. New York: Oxford University Press.

Thomsen, Robert C., and Nik Hynek. 2006. 'Keeping the Peace and National Unity: Canada's National and International Identity Nexus', *International Journal* 61, 4: 845–58.

Index

Abdelrazik, Abousfian, 215–16
AbitibiBowater, 130
Aboriginal people, in Arctic, 260–1; see also First Nations
Abu Ghraib, 284
Accord between the Government and the Voluntary Sector, 71
accountability, 74
Afghanistan, 13, 17; Canada's involvement in, vii, xxvii–xxviii, 49, 83, 90, 92–4, 177, 183, 214, 226, 245, 246; in Canada's national interest, 242–3; Canadian deaths in, 40, 183, 185; Conservatives and, 93–4; exit options, 184, 246–7; extension of Canada's mission in, 91, 93, 94, 232, 245; as failed state, 93; humanitarian aid to, 92; Provincial Reconstruction Teams in, 84, 88, 93, 96n7; public opinion of war in, 182–3, 184–5; US involvement in, 45, 245
Agamben, Giorgio, 130, 136n2
Agenda for Peace, 13, 174
Aggestam, Lisbeth, 50n3
aircraft, spending on, 181
Air India bombings (1985), 212, 219, 222, 223, 227; public inquiry into, 225
Aitken, Hugh, 143
Alberta, oil production, 132, 147, 149; see also tar sands
Allied Command Europe (ACE): Mobile Land Force, 241; Rapid Reaction Corps, 241
Al Qaeda, 215, 226
Ambrose, Rona, 134
Americanization, 195, 196
Andrew, Arthur, 10
Angus Reid poll, June 2008, 176
Anholt-GfK Roper, Nations Brand Index (2008), 48
anti-Americanism, 192, 203–4
Anti-Terrorism Act (ATA), 212, 214, 215; criminalizing financial support for terrorism, 215; designating groups and persons as terrorists, 215–16; human security and, 220; increased police powers, 219–20, 226
anti-terrorism laws, xxvii

Appathurai, James, 232
Aquinas, Thomas, 24
Arar, Maher, xxvii, 217, 227; Commission of Inquiry, 218, 224
Arau, Sergio, *Un día sin Mexicanos*, 206
Arctic: Canadian geopolitics and, 254–5; Canadian identity and, 266–7, 280; changing concepts of security in, 263, 265–6; competition in, 192, 255–6; delineation of continental shelf, 253, 256, 263; Inuit representatives, 260; media attention, 266; melting ice in, 254, 255; military presence in, 257, 260–1, 268; resource potential in, 253, 254, 255, 260; security threats in, 260; sovereignty, 134, 206n2, 259, 260, 266–7, 270; surveillance capabilities in, 268; territorial claims in, 255–6; threats to security in, 265; US policy in, 259–60
Arctic Cooperation Agreement, 258
Arctic Council, 251, 261, 265, 269
Arctic foreign policy, vii, xxviii, 252–3; Canada's bilateral relationship with US, 253; changing bureaucracy and, 262–3; diplomatic response to, 269–70; under Harper, 270–1; indigenous agency and, 260–1; legal response to, 267; middle-power model, 251–4, 271; military response to, 267–8; shift in Canada's, 253–4; soft and hard power and, 266; unilateralism and, 264; US–Canada relations and, 256–8, 260
Arctic Front, 134
Arctic Rangers, 261, 266, 268
Arctic Security Working Group, 265
Arctic Waters Pollution Prevention Act (AWPPA), 258, 263
armed forces. See Canadian Forces (CF).
asbestos, 128–9
Asia: oil market, 149, 150; rise of dragons, vi
Aspe, Pedro, 189
Athabasca River basin, 147
Athabasca tar sands. See tar sands.
Atlantic alliance, xxviii, 13
Axworthy, Lloyd, 23, 31n2, 64, 76n2, 154, 243; on Canada as a guide, 109; middle-power diplomacy, 62, 64, 67

Baldwin, Andrew, xxv, 283
Balkans, the, xxviii, 179, 226; crisis in, 234, 238–41; peace-enforcement missions, 246
'bare life', 124, 125, 136n2
Bátora, Jozef, xxiv–xxv, 46, 281, 283
Baudrillard, Jean, 69
Benatta, Benamar, 217
Berlin Wall, fall of, vi, 236, 237
Betz, David, 181
bin Laden, Osama, 215
biopower, 124; as concern for life, 124–5; Foucault on, 123–5
Bland, Douglas, 177, 235
Bombardier, 45
Bosnia, 13, 240, 241
Bosold, David, xxiii, 20, 281
Botero, Giovanni, 24
Bothwell, Robert, 22
Bouldin, Matthew, 179
Boutros-Ghali, Boutros, 13, 174
Brand Canada, 41
Brazil, 12, 251
Brem, Stefan, 65
brinkmanship, 30–1
Britain: Canada's independence from, 5, 102; oil and gas companies in, 144; relationship with US, 203
Buchanan, Patrick, 194, 198
Burchill, R., 102
Bush, George W.: administration of, 32n5, 183, 192, 199, 243; 'coalition of the willing', 85, 178, 185n6, 244
Byers, Michael, 39–40; Intent for a Nation, xx

Cameron, Maxwell A., 65
Canada: dependence on US security decisions, 179–80; environmental record, 127–33; as 'good international citizen', 214–16, 280; improving attractiveness abroad, 108–9; marginalization of, 12–13, 17
Canada Among Nations, 49, 235
Canada and the Circumpolar World, 269
Canada Command, 181
'Canada–Cool–Connected' initiative, 108–9, 281
Canada Corps, 90
Canada First Defence Strategy, 180, 181, 268
Canada in the World, 47, 85–6, 87, 107–8
Canada's International Policy Statement (2005), 86–7, 88, 90, 91, 93
Canada's World Poll (2008), 51n9
Canada25, xxiii, 41–2, 43, 45
Canada 21 Council, xxiii, 41, 42, 43, 45
Canada–US border: Mexicanization, 194, 199; migration across, 196–7

Canada–US Free Trade Agreement: natural gas and, 148; proportionality clause, 150–1
Canada–US relations, vi, xvi, 13, 199–204; after 9/11, 213; Arctic foreign policy and, 256–8, 258–9; energy resources and, 132–3; foreign policy objectives and, 10; immigration policies and, 203–4; possibility of armed conflict, 192; as threat to American security, 199–200; war in Afghanistan and, 183
Canadian Airborne Regiment, in Somalia, 170
Canadian Air-Sea Transportable Brigade Group (CAST), 236
Canadian Centre for Foreign Policy Development, 51n4
Canadian Council of Chief Executives, 189
Canadian Expeditionary Force Command, 181
Canadian Forces (CF), xviii, xxvi, 88, 89, 180; Arctic sovereignty and, 268; command structure, 181; critics of, 177–8; cuts to, 177; development institutions and, 87–8; interoperability with US military, 284; information technology and, 172; NATO operations and, 13–14; new missions of, 172–5; new security environment and, 89–90; overseas deployments, 233; as peacekeepers, 40, 170; transformation of, 172, 176, 177, 180–4; underfunding of, 177
Canadian International Development Agency (CIDA), 70, 88, 103; Business Process Road Map Overview, 74; organizational changes to, 89; Performance Report 2003, 87; Policy Statement of 1996, 73; risk assessment and, 76
Canadianization, of US–Mexico border, 195, 196, 197–8
Canadian Operational Support Command, 181
Canadian school of human security, 67
Canadian Security Intelligence Service (CSIS), 216, 217, 218
Canadian Special Operations Forces Command, 181
Cannon, Lawrence, 280
capitalism, growth and, 126
carbon markets, 131–2
Carter, Jimmy, 142, 145
Cellucci, Paul, 244
Central and Eastern Europe (CEE), 238; 'hand of friendship', 237
Champlain, Samuel de, 207n10
Chapnick, Adam, 20, 22, 24, 25, 26, 28
Chapter IV missions, 170, 239
Charter of Rights and Freedoms, 212, 219; deportation of non-citizens to torture, 216; safe third country agreement and, 218

Chastelain, Gen. A.J.G.D. de, 238
child soldiers, 67, 86
Chile, 244
China, 12, 251
Chirac, Jacques, visit to Nunavut, xxix n2
Chrétien, Jean, vi, vii, 11, 21, 94, 202, 243;
    decision not to join US in Iraq, 244;
    proportionality clause and, 151; War on
    Terror and, 92
circumpolar organizations, 261–2
civilian power, xxiii, 35, 43, 44
civil-military relations, evolution of, 175–6
civil wars, 173
Clark, Joe, 1985–6 Foreign Policy Review, 42
climate change, xxv, 131; Arctic and, 253, 254;
    Canada's performance, 283; Conservatives
    on, 132, 134; energy-related CO_2, 154
Climate Change Performance Index (2009),
    155, 158n21
'coalition of the willing', 85, 178, 185n6, 244
Coast Guard, 262, 268
Cohen, Andrew, xviii, 234, 235
Cold War, v, xvi, 7, 237; Canada's
    middlepowerhood during, 4, 22; end of, 4,
    176
collateral damage, 181
Collenette, David, 64
combat resources, spending on, 181
compromise, as middle-power behaviour, 26,
    28, 38
Conference Board of Canada, 235
Conference of Defence Associations, 235
Conference of the Parties, 11th (COP 11), 121
Conference on Security and Cooperation in
    Europe (CSCE), 265
Connolly, William, xiii
conscription, abolition of universal, 175
Consejo Mexicano de Asuntos Internacionales,
    189
Constitution Act, 102
consumption, urban, 126
contractualism, 72
Cooper, Andrew, 4–5, 38–9, 45, 104, 105, 110;
    on niche diplomacy, 66–7
Cooper, Barry, 177
Copeland, D., 106
Copenhagen School, 96n4, 195
Cotler, Irwin, 220
Council for Canadian Security in the 21st
    Century, 177
Council on Foreign Relations, 21, 189
Cox, Robert, 6, 142–3
crisis response missions, 174
Croatia, UN Protected Areas in, 239
Cross-Cultural Roundtable on National

Security, 214, 225, 228n16
Cyprus, 15, 178

Dalby, Simon, xxv, 283
Dallaire, Roméo, 170
Darfur, 17, 39–40
David, Charles Philippe, 26
Dayton peace agreement, 240
declinist school, xviii, 49, 232–3, 234, 266,
    247n2
defence budget (Canada), 180, 184; see also
    Canadian Forces (CF)
defence policy, vs security policy, xiv–xv
democratization: interventionism and, 15, 16;
    violence and, 173
Denmark, interests in Arctic region, 255, 259
Department of External Affairs, 102, 103; see
    also Department of Foreign Affairs and
    International Trade (DFAIT)
Department of Fisheries and Oceans, Arctic
    policy and, 263
Department of Foreign Affairs and
    International Trade (DFAIT), xvii, 88, 244;
    Arctic policy and, 262, 263; budget cuts to,
    234; international campaign on terrorism
    and, 86; International Campaign to Ban
    Landmines and, 107; International Security
    Research and Outreach Program (ISROP),
    51n4; Northern Dimension of Canada's
    Foreign Policy, 269; organizational culture,
    104–5; organizational structure of, 89, 102–
    4, 114; public diplomacy and, 108; relations
    with domestic environment, 105–6; roles
    of, 105; transformation of, 42–3; use of
    information technology, 109–11, 115;
    website, 109, 110–11
Department of Indian Affairs and Northern
    Development (DIAND) (now Indian and
    Northern Affairs Canada), 262
Department of National Defence (DND), xvii,
    88, 180; budget cuts, 234, 235; Chief of the
    Defence Staff, 181; organizational changes
    to, 89
Department of Public Safety and Emergency
    Preparedness, 221
desecuritization, 76
Deutsch, Karl, 194
development assistance, 7, 82; to Afghanistan,
    93; Liberals and, 91, 94; militarization
    of, 84; moral vision of, 82; policies,
    xxiv, 11, 81, 82–3, 87; securitization of,
    84; used for national security and anti-
    terrorist activities, 87; weakening of moral
    motivation for, 95; see also international
    assistance; international development;

official development assistance

Dewitt, David B., xv, 141

Dialogue on Foreign Policy, 108

diamonds: blood, 126; conflict, 86, 126

Dion, Stéphane, 121, 131; green tax shift, 132, 133

'la diplomatie ouverte' (open diplomacy), 109

'dirty oil' debate, 148–50; *see also* tar sands

Disaster Assistance Response Team (DART), 90

Dolata-Kreutzkamp, Petra, xxviii, 280

Dorn, Walter, 178

Downing, Brian M.: *Military Revolution and Political Change*, 171

Duchêne, François, 43

Dulles, John Foster, 30

earth-imaging satellite, 181–2

Earth Summit, 126

Eayrs, James, 141

economic crisis, 133, 149, 185; Russia and, 144; US and, 45, 135

Economist, xii

e-Discussions, 109, 111, 115

Eisenhower, Dwight D., 30

emergency preparedness, 221, 226

energy: Canada as supplier to US, 132, 151; Canada's production, 138, 146; conservation, 142, 154, 156–7; policies, 140, 153, 156

energy crisis, triple, 139–40, 142

energy independence, 152, 156

energy middle power, 151–3

energy satellites, 143, 155

energy security, xiv–xv, xxv–xxvi, 156, 283; Arctic foreign policy and, 263; Canada's lack of policy for, 139–40; tar sands and, 131–3

energy superpower, 49, 141–2, 143–7

environment: as external to humanity, 126; policies and, vii, 51n9, 125, 127–33

environmental security, xiv–xv, xxv, 134, 283; Arctic foreign policy and, 263–4

Europe: societal security and, 195; zone of peace, 205

European Community Monitoring Mission (ECMM), 239

European Security Strategy, 113

European Union (EU), 84, 116; and Arctic foreign policy, 259, 262; civilian power and, 43; climate and energy policies, 51n6; Common Foreign and Security Policy, 35; foreign affairs administration, 113–14; human security doctrine and, 113; public diplomacy and, 114; soft power and, xxv

Evans, Gareth, 27

exclusive economic zone (EEZ), 256

External Affairs and International Trade, 103

failed states, xiv, 83, 88, 95; Western response to, 174

Fenianism, 201; *see also* New Fenianism

Finland, on Arctic Council, 261

Finlandization, 150–1

First Nations: forest sector and, 130–1; jurisdiction over, 130; state biopower and, 124; water quality on reserves, 122; *see also* Aboriginal people

Florini, Ann, 272n2

Foreign Affairs Canada, 103; *see also* Department of Foreign Affairs and International Trade (DFAIT)

foreign aid: under Conservatives, 91, 81; *see also* development assistance

foreign and security policy, Canada's (CANFSP), xii–xiii; concepts in analysis, xix–xxi; definition of, xiii–xiv; decision-making and, 105–6; democratization, 63–9, 75; domestic influences on, 4; evaluation of, 46–7; factors influencing, xiii–xiv; internationalism and, xv, 6; interventionism, 14; lack of leadership and direction, 12; neglected issues, 44–5

Foreign Policy Centre, 112

Foreign Policy Dialogue: Report to Canadians, 108

Foreign Policy for Canadians, 21

foreign policy review, 21, 42, 47, 86

foreign policy statement, 41; *see also* *International Policy Statement*

foremost power, Canada as, xx, 141

forest sector, Canada's, 122, 129–31

Foucault, Michel, 123; on life and biopower, 123–5; notion of security, 123; *Security, Territory, Population*, 123; *Society Must Be Defended*, 123

Fourth Generation Warfare (4GW), 181

France, 244; defence spending, 236–7

Franklin, Benjamin, 189, 192

freedom-from-fear doctrine, 73, 85, 94–5

freedom of expression, terrorism speech and, 225

Free Trade Agreement, Canada–US (FTA), 10, 148, 153

Freeze, Colin, 202

French Canadians, migration to US, 197

Future Brand, Country Brand Index (2008), 48

Gallie, Walter, xiii

'Gas Exporting Countries Forum', 144

G8, 12; Global Partnership Programs, 85

Gelber, Lionel, 5

Germany, 35, 43, 233, 244; Canada's withdrawal from, 236; civilian power and, 43; contribution to UN peacekeeping, 242; as middle power, 191

global civil society, 66, 68, 75

globalization, vi, 135, 195; international order and, 172–3

Global Peace and Security Fund (GPSF), 90

Golan Heights, 178

good international citizenship, 37, 122; as middle-power behaviour, 27, 28–9; mythology of, 280

Goose, Stephen, 65

Gorbachev, Mikhail, 265

Gotlieb, Allan, 22

Government On-Line Initiative, 106

Granatstein, J.L., 22, 177, 178, 234, 235

Grassy Narrows First Nation, 130–1

Greenhill, Robert, 11, 48

greenhouse gas (GHG) emissions, 142, 283; Canada's, 121, 156; Canada's commitments to reducing, 154–5; tar sands and, 148, 150

Greenspan, Alan, 154

Griffiths, Franklyn, 192

G20, 12

Guantanamo Bay, 217–18, 284

guerrilla warfare, 173

Haglund, David, xxvi–xxvii

Haiti, 13, 83

Hammarskjöld, Dag, xviii

Hampson, Fen Osler, xvii, 23

Hans Island, 255

hard power, 44, 45, 46, 169; difference from soft power, 62, 221; see also soft power

Harper, Stephen, vi, vii, 12, 93, 132, 183, 192, 231, 245; Afghanistan and, 93–4, 246; aid programming under, 91; Arctic foreign policy under, 270–1; on Canada as energy superpower, xxv, 49, 134, 138, 151, 255; on Canada–US security co-operation, 200; International Policy Statement, 21; on middle-power diplomacy, 28; on national security, 94; official development assistance and, 82; 'Security and Prosperity Partnership' and, 151; security–development approach, 95

Hay, Robin, 11

Hayter, Sir William, 102

Heinberg, Richard, 151

helicopters, 182

Hercules tactical transport aircraft, 182

Heritage Foundation, 9

hierarchical model, geography and, 50n1

Higgott, Richard A., 38–9

Hillier, Gen. Rick, 97n12, 245

Hillmer, Norman, xvii, 235

HMCS Winnipeg, 241

Holbraad, Carsten, 24

Holloway, Steven Kendall, xx

Holmes, John W., vi, 6, 26, 155; on middlepowermanship, xxii, 30–1

homeland security, 180

Homer-Dixon, Thomas, 147

horizontal competition, 195

Huebert, Robert, 14

humane internationalism, 82

humanitarian interventions, 174–5; militarization of, 13–14

human rights: deportation of terrorists, 216; international law, 67; restraints to security policies, 218–19

human security, xiv–xv, 44, 66–9, 74, 75, 123, 220–2, 243; after 9/11, 226; all-risk approach, 220, 227; Anti-Terrorism Act and, 213, 220; anti-terrorism and, 227; approach, 96n5; Arctic foreign policy and, 263, 264–5; Asian countries and, 73; biopower and, 124, 125; Conservatives and, 69; development assistance and, 95; as foreign policy objective, 71–2; freedom-from-fear doctrine, 67–8, 85; institutional consolidation of, 68; neo-liberalism and, 125; war on terrorism and, xxvii

human security/development nexus (HSDN), xxiii, 62, 63; democratization, 69; see also security–development nexus

Human Security Network, 67, 68, 113

Human Security Program, 90

Humble Oil, 257

Huntington, Samuel, 196, 198

Hurricane Katrina, 221

Hurtig, Mel, 235

Hussein, Liban, 215

Hussein, Saddam, 243

Hynek, Nik, xxii, xxiii–xxiv, 22, 29, 44, 46, 282

Ibn Saud, meeting with Franklin Roosevelt, 145

icebreakers, construction of, 268, 269

Iceland, on Arctic Council, 261

identity, Canadian, xxi; Arctic sovereignty discourse and, 267, 280; diplomatic history and, 46–7; national interests and, xv

identity formation, role theory and, 39–40

Ignatieff, Michael, vi, 14

image, xv, 108–9; see also role perception

Immediate and Rapid Reaction Forces (Air), 241

immigration law, as anti-terrorism law, 214, 223, 227

immigration policies (Canada's), 202–3; US perception of, 213, 218, 223

India, 12, 142, 251

Indian Act, 130

Indian and Northern Affairs Canada (INAC), 262

indigenous communities: in Arctic, 260–1; devolution of power to, 269; see also Aboriginal people; First Nations

InfoBank, 110

information revolution. See revolution in military affairs (RMA).

information technology (IT): armed forces and, 172; campaign to ban landmines and, 65; and Canada's soft power, 283; DFAIT and, 106; in support of diplomacy, xxv, 109–11, 115; use by Norwegian foreign ministry, 112–13

Innis, Harold, 141

Innovative Research Group (IRG), 2005 survey, 182

intergovernmental organizations, xiii

international assistance: moral motivation of, 81, 82; reduction of contribution, 17; security issues in, 94–5

international assistance envelope (IAE), 90–1, 97n17

International Campaign to Ban Landmines (ICBL), 23, 31n2, 65, 107; see also Ottawa Convention; Ottawa Process

International Control Commission, 15

International Criminal Court, 67, 86

international development, 17, 87, 88; NGOs and, 63, 70, 75, 76; see also international assistance; security–development nexus

International Energy Agency (IEA), xxvi, 143, 152; main objective, 158n16; projection of Canadian oil production, 146–7

internationalism, 6–7, 7–8, 16; public support for, 9–10, 10–11; reduction in spending on policies, 11; resources needed for, 17

international law, attempts to strengthen, 44, 46

International Monetary Fund, 84

international order, 7, 172

International Polar Year, 261

International Policy Statement, xii, 11, 21, 183, 243; Arctic policy and, 268

international relations (IR), xix; level-of-analysis problem, xix

international role perception, 40, 41, 48; divergence from internal role perception, 49; see also role perception

International Security Assistance Force (ISAF), 85, 97n15, 179, 180–1, 182; Canada's contribution, xviii, 49, 92; deficiencies of, 231–2; see also Afghanistan

international trade: Canada's diminishing influence in, 12; chemicals with known health risks, 129

International Trade Canada, 103

Internet: campaign to ban landmines and, 65; diplomatic efforts and, xxv; see also information technology (IT)

interventionism, 13–15; critics of, 14–15; imposing solutions on failed states, 15–16

Inuit Circumpolar Council, 262, 269

Inuit representatives, in Arctic, 260

Inukshuk, 3, 109

Iran, 144

Iraq: Canada and, xxvii, 214–15, 226, 243–5, 284; US in, 45, 85, 243

Irish nationalists, 201, 203, 207n17

Jabarah, Mohamed, 217, 218

Jackson, Robert, xiv

jihadists. See terrorists.

Kandahar. See Afghanistan; Provincial Reconstruction Team in Kandahar.

Keating, Tom, xxii, 20, 35, 109, 135, 281

Keirstead, B.S., 104

Keohane, Robert, 38

Khadr, Ahmed Said, 202

Khadr, Omar, 218, 227, 228n6; detention at Guantanamo Bay, 217–18

Khanna, Parag, 281

Khawaja, Momin, 224

Kimberley Process, 86

King, William Lyon Mackenzie, 20, 23, 200

Kingston dispensation, 200, 206

Kirton, John, 12, 141

Klare, Michael, 145–6

Korea, 28

Kosovo, xix, 13, 17, 83, 213, 221, 240

Krulak, Gen. Charles, 245

Kyoto Accord, vii, xxv, 154

Kyoto Protocol, 121, 126, 131; inability to meet commitments, 133–4

Labrador, oil production, 149

landmines, campaign to ban, 23, 31n2, 38, 64–6, 75; see also Ottawa Convention; Ottawa Process

Lapierre, Jean, 201, 202

Latin America, resource extraction industries and, 128

Laurier, Sir Wilfrid, 102

Lawler, Peter, 9, 15

Lawson, Robert J., 65

Laxer, Gordon, xxv–xxvi
League of Nations, 5
Lewis, Stephen, 8–9
Liberal Party: *Canada in the World*, 85–6; CanFSP review (1994), 63–4; *Foreign Policy Handbook*, 64; 'Red Book', 42, 63; tar sands and, 132
liquefied natural gas (LNG), 144
Lis, John, 236
Locke, Wade, 158n13
Lomonosov Ridge, 256
Lonsdale, David, 172
Lougheed, Peter, 147
Lyon, Peyton, 10, 25
Lysøen Declaration, 68

MacKay, Peter, 246–7
Mackenzie Valley pipeline proposals, 148
'making live and letting die', 124, 125, 128, 129, 131
Maloney, Sean, 235
Manley, John, 92, 94, 189, 231
Manley report, 93, 231–2
Martin, Paul, vii, 12, 21, 29, 94, 204, 245; Canada's climate record and, 121; Canada's mission in Afghanistan and, 92–3, 245; creation of DFAIT, 103; and National Missile Defense, 183; 'Security and Prosperity Partnership' and, 151; third sector review, 70; victory speech, 29
Matthew, Richard A., 65
Maull, Hanns, 43
Mearsheimer, John, 191
mediation, as middle-power behaviour, 7, 26
Mexicanization, of Canada–US border, 194, 199
Mexico, 244; drug-related violence, 198; immigration into US, 190, 198, 206, 207n14; military action with US, 193, 194; NAFTA proportionality clause and, 151; in security community, 189, 190
middle-power concept, 5–6, 81; behavioural model of, xxiii, 27–8, 38–9; critique of previous, 39–40; cycles of popularity, 20–1; elusive nature of, 22–3; emergence of, 5; hierarchical model of, xxiii, 24, 36–7; methodological problems of, 36–9; normative model of, xxiii, 37–8; popularity of, 16, 21–2
middlepowerhood, vii, xxi, 23, 24–6, 29–30, 251; climate change policies and, 133–4; criticism of Canada's, 35; determining, 24–5; limits to, 37; tautology, 28, 38
middlepowermanship, xxi, 23, 26–9, 30–1, 251; Arctic foreign policy and, 271; soft power and, 266; tautology, 28, 38; utility of, 31
middle power ranking, vi, xxii, 9, 26–7, 43, 64, 281; Canada as, xx, 3–4, 36, 42; energy-enviro, 140, 142–3, 151–3; followers or leaders, 66; more countries emerging as, 12, 17; neglected issues, 44–5
migration: from Canada to US, 196–7; between countries in security community, 190; from Mexico to US, 190, 198, 206, 207n14; as threat to societal security, 195
military expenditures, 182, 235; Canada's reduction in, 177; *see also* Canadian Forces (CF)
military revolution. *See* revolution in military affairs (RMA).
military-technical revolution. *See* revolution in military affairs (RMA).
millennium bomber, 202
Miller, Lyman, 141
Mingst, Karen, 65
mining companies, 122; *see also* resource extraction sector
missile defence in Canada, 183
Mitzen, Jennifer, 40
model power, 35, 41, 49–50, 281, 282; Canada as, 42–3; difference from middle power, 44
modernity, as humanity separated from nature, 126
Molot, Maureen A., 235
Montreal Protocol, 44, 126
morality: foreign aid and, 81–2; good international citizenship and, 27
moral power, 29, 43; middle, 12, 29, 85, 86
Mulroney, Brian, vi, 8, 21, 69, 222; cuts to military spending, 235, 236
multiculturalism, 16, 213–14; human rights and, 220; as security asset, 224–6, 227; as security threat, 222–4, 226–7
multilateral institutions, 28
multilateralism, xxi, 28, 44, 142; Canada and, 8–9; as middle-power behaviour, vi, 27, 38
multinational corporations (MNCs), xiii
Munton, Don, 7
Muslim population, in Canada, 214, 220, 223, 224

NAFTA, xxvii; Mexico and, 151; proportionality clause, 140, 150–1, 153, 155, 156, 283
Napolitano, Janet, 199
National Energy Board, 152, 153
National Energy Policy (NEP), 155
National Energy Program, 152, 153
National Forum on International Relations, 63, 108
national interest, study of, xix–xx

National Missile Defense, 183
national security, 81; Arctic foreign policy and, 263
NATO, xiii, 7, 13; budget, 242; Canada's contribution to, v, vii, xxvii–xxviii, 7, 13, 232, 242, 284; Manley report and, 231–2; UN's interest in, 13; and Canada in 1990s, 236–46; Implementation Force (IFOR), 240; London Summit in 1990, 237; military interoperability with, 184; military technologies and, 172; new institutions, 237–8; Prague Summit of 2002, 241; Stabilization Force (SFOR), 240
NATO countries, levels of defence spending, 236–7
NATO-led missions: Canada's participation in, 13, 233; in Kosovo, 241–2; in Yugoslavia, 238–9
NATO Reaction Force (NRF), 241
natural gas: Canada's production, 157n3; Canada's proven supplies, 153–4; exports, 153; in Canada–US Free Trade Agreement, 148; in tar sands production, 147–8
natural resource management, 130
Natural Resources Canada, Arctic policy and, 263
Nayar, Baldev Raj, 142
Neack, Laura, 25
neo-liberal environments, 125–7
network diplomacy, 51 n4
'network node', 42
Neufeld, Mark, 22
Neumann, I.B., 112
New England, French Canadian migration to, 196, 197
New Feniansim, 200, 201, 203, 206
Newfoundland, oil production, 149
new missions, 175
New Public Management (NPM), xvii, 105
new wars, 173, 174
niche diplomacy, 66–7
Niebuhr, Reinhold, 18
non-governmental organizations (NGOs), vii, xiii, xxiv, 282; accountability and, 74; campaign to ban landmines and, 65; Canada's soft power and, 64; contractualism and, 72; funding of, 72; human security/international development agenda and, 63; relationship with Canadian government, 75; risk assessment and, 74–5; service-delivery model, 72–3, 76; soft power and, 65; 'Southern' partners, 75; third sector transformation and, 70, 76
non-profit and voluntary sector, 69–71; see also third sector

nonstate realm, 65
NORAD, 7, 257
NORDREG, 262
norm entrepreneurship, 28, 252, 255, 272n2
North America: societal security and, 195; security perimeter, 205; zone of peace, 189
North American Free Trade Agreement. See NAFTA.
North American security community, xxvi–xxvii, 189–90, 204, 205; 'good neighbours', 193; possible end to, 194, 201; power standing and, 191
North Atlantic Cooperation Council, 237
North Atlantic Treaty Organization. See NATO.
Northern Dimension of Canada's Foreign Policy, 269, 270
Northern Gateway pipeline (Enbridge), 149
Northern Strategy, 269, 270
North–South Institute, 45
Northwest Passage, 134, 206n2, 253; Canada's claims to, 192, 255, 257–8, 258–9, 270; environmental security and, 263–4; melting ice and, 254; US encroachment on, 256, 267
Norway, xxv, 116; interests in Arctic region, 255, 259; non-governmental organizations in, 112; public diplomacy and, 111–13; relationship with Sweden, 193
Nossal, Kim Richard, xvii, xxii–xxiii, 8, 9, 38–9, 44, 109, 281; on power, 51n5
nuclear energy, use in tar sands production, 148
Nunavut, 269
Nye, Joseph S., 61–2, 266

Obama, Barack, 192; 'dirty oil' debate and, 148–50; visit to Canada, 200
Obregón, Alvaro, 193
October Crisis, 212, 217, 219
Off, Carol, 239
Office for Democratic Governance (formerly Canada Corps), 90
official development assistance (ODA), 82, 83, 85–6; see also development assistance
Ogdensburg Agreement, 201
oil: Canada's consumption, 157; Canada's exports to US, 150; Canada's production, 146–7, 157, 150, 157n3; government-owned companies, 144; 'peak', 139; power ranking and, 140–1; prices, 133, 135; spills, 263; supply crises, 139, 152
Okalik, Paul, 261
Oliver, Dean F., 23
Olympic Winter Games, Vancouver (2010), 3, 109
One Year Later: Progress Report on the

Implementation of Canada's National Security Policy (2005), 87–8
Ontario Provincial Police, 194
ontological security, 40, 46
Operation Deliberate Force, 240
Operation Desert Storm, 236
Operation Enduring Freedom, xviii, 92, 242
Operation Palladium, 240
Organization of Petroleum Producing Countries (OPEC), 141
Organizations for Economic Co-operation and Development (OECD), 84; Donor Assistance Committee (DAC), 84
Osbaldeston, Gordon, 103
Ottawa Convention, 44, 47, 64–6, 72, 75, 107
Ottawa Process, 38, 48, 68, 75, 86, 107, 111, 282; human security agenda and, 67; soft power and, 66

Page, Don, 7
Painter, David, 144
pandemics, human security and, 220, 221
Panel on Accountability and Governance for the Voluntary Sector (PAGVS), 70, 71
Paquin, Stéphane, xvii
Paris, Roland, 66
Parmar, Talwinder Singh, 222
Partnership for Peace program, 237, 238
Paul, T.V., 142
peace-building missions, xviii, 83
peace-enforcement missions, xviii, 46, 239
peacekeeping, xvii–xviii, 178; Canada's tradition of, xviii, 18, 39–40, 170, 176, 177, 242, 280; Canadian self-perception as, 170, 184; first-generation, 178, 185n5; fourth-generation, 185n5; role perception and, 47; second-generation, xviii, 185n5; third-generation, xviii, 185n5
peacekeeping operations, 7, 8, 12, 13, 27, 241–2
peacemaking, 178
peace missions, 174; new form of, 178; United Nations and, 174; *see also* crisis response missions
'peak oil' theory, 139
Pearson, Lester, v, xviii, 6, 20, 24, 117n7, 235; Canadian military and, 178; diplomacy of, 23; as Secretary of State, 234
Pearson, Mike, 64
Pembina Institute: on greenhouse gas emissions, 154–5; of tar sands, 147
Permanent Joint Board of Defence, 201
Pershing, Gen. John, 193
Ping, Jonathan H., 25
pipeline infrastructure, 140, 152; tar sands

and, 149–50
Polar Sea (US icebreaker), 258, 268, 269
policy-making processes, xvi–xvii; middle power label, 8; objectives, 6; public opinion and, 9–10, 48–9
Pope, Sir Joseph, 102
Potter, Evan, 41
poverty, security–development nexus and, 83, 84, 95
power, 45, 51n5; analysis of Canada's, xx–xxi; measuring capabilities, 45; *see also* hard power; soft power
power ranking, 25; hard power and, 169; measures, 36–7; oil resources and, 140–1
Pratt, Cranford, 10–11, 82
Price, Robert, 65
primary power, 157n7
Prime Minister's Office (PMO), 244; Arctic policy-making and, 262
principal power, xx, 36, 141
Privy Council Office (PCO), 244; Arctic policy-making and, 262
Provincial Reconstruction Teams, 84, 96n7; in Kandahar, 88, 93, 97n15
public diplomacy, Canadian, 107–9; European Union, 114; information technology and, 106–11
public opinion, 11, 47–8; of Canada's peacekeeping role, 176; of Canada's security policy, 182; relevance in policy-making, 48–9
Putin, Vladimir, 143, 144

Qatar, 144
Quebec, 195; DFAIT and, 114; immigration to US, 196; public diplomacy strategies, 109

'race to the Arctic', 255, 285
'RAINBOW' plans, 193
Rand Corporation, fossil-fuel study, 148
Ravenhill, John, 20, 21
re-branding, xxiii, 35, 40, 281–2; fallacy of, 41–2
reconstruction process, 178, 179
'RED' plans, 193
refugee policy, Canada's, 202–3, 218
Rempel, Roy, xvii; *Chatter Box*, xvii; *Dreamland*, xvii, xx
Report of the International Commission on Intervention and State Sovereignty, 174
Report of the Panel on UN Peace Operations (Brahimi Report), 174
Report of the Somalia Commission of Inquiry, 170
resource extraction sector, xxv, 128, 135

'responsibility to protect' (UN), 122, 123, 124, 129
Ressam, Ahmed, 202, 203, 216
Reston, James, on brinkmanship, 30–1
results-based management (RBM), xvii, 63, 69, 73–5, 76
retail economy, 132
revolution in military affairs (RMA), 170–1, 171–2, 284
Rice, Condoleeza, 40
Richter, Andrew, 183
Ringmar, Eric, xv
Rioux, Jean Francois, 11
risk assessment, 74, 76
Roach, Kent, xxvii
Robertson, Norman, 234
Robertson, Scot, 177
role conception, 39, 41, 47; divergence from role perception, 49, 50
role expectation, 39, 40; see also international role perception
role perception, 40, 47; Canadians' own, 47–8; divergence of internal and external, 48–9
role performance, 47, 50n2
role theory, 47, 50; identity formation and, 39–40
Roman Catholic Church (Quebec), 197
Roosevelt, Franklin: administration of, 193; Kingston dispensation, 200; meeting with Ibn Saud, 145
Rosberg, Carl, xiv
Rosenau, James N., Turbulence in World Politics, 65
Rotterdam Convention, 129, 136n4
Roussel, Stéphane, xvii, 26
Royal Canadian Mounted Police (RCMP), 89, 268; in Arctic region, 262; co-operation with US after 9/11, 216–17
Russia: cutting natural gas exports to Ukraine, 144; economic crisis and, 144; as energy superpower, 138, 143–4; interests in Arctic region, 255, 259; oil and gas production, 157n1, 157n2; underwater planting of flag at North Pole, 255, 256
Rutherford, Kenneth R., 65
Rwanda, genocide in, 170

Saami Council, 261
'safe third country' agreement, 212–13, 218, 223, 227
St Laurent, Louis, Gray Lecture, 7, 8
Sapolsky, Harvey, 199–200
SARS outbreak, 221
satellite: Canada as, xx, 36; energy-enviro, 140, 143, 155

Saudi Arabia: CO_2 emissions and, 155; as energy superpower, 143, 144–5; oil production, 157n4; proven reserves, 157n5; as swing producer, 145, 157n4
Schlesinger, Arthur, Jr, 198
Scott, Katherine, 70
seabed mapping, 268, 269
Securing an Open Society: Canada's National Security Policy (2004), 87–8, 91, 183, 221
'Security and Prosperity Partnership' (SPP), 151, 272n7
security certificates, 223, 227
security community, North American, xxvi–xxvii, 189–90, 204, 205; 'good neighbours', 193; possible end to, 194, 201; power standing and, 191
security–development approach, 84–9, 96n2; case in Afghanistan, 92–4; institutional and organizational consequences, 89–91
security–development nexus, 81, 82, 83–4, 96n2, 282–3; Conservatives and, 91
security policy, xii–xiii, xiv–xv; vs defence policy, xiv–xv
Selden, Zachary, 236
self-image, national, xv, 135, 184
Senate Committee on National Security and Defence, Wounded, 183
September 11 terrorist attacks, xxiv, 81, 92, 179, 201, 203, 212, 285; Canadian response to, xxvii, 216, 221; effect on development policies, 82–3
service-delivery model, 76
'Seven Sisters' of oil, 144
Seven Years War, 207n10
Shakikh, Mubin, 224
shariah law, 224
Sharp, Mitchell, 1970 Foreign Policy Review, 42
Simmons, Matt, 152
Skelton, O.D., 117n7
Skilling, H.G., 104
Sloan, Elinor, 172
Slovenian independence, 238
'Smart Border' security agreement, 213, 218
Smith, Rupert, 174
societal security, 194, 206; Mexican immigration to US, 197–8
society-building process, 179
Söderbergh, Bengt, 147–8
soft power, xxiv–xxv, 11, 44, 45, 46, 69, 107, 169; alternative interpretation of, 69; Arctic foreign policy and, 266; Axworthy's, 62; Canada's, 62–3; difference from hard power, 62; NGOs and, 65; Nye's definition, 61–2; public opinion and, 47–8; see also

hard power

Sokolosky, Joel, 178, 284

Solana, Javier, 113, 247n5

Somalia, 13, 170, 179

sovereign power, 124

sovereignty, xiv, 134

specialized operations forces (SOF), 181

Special Joint Committee of the Senate and House of Commons, 63–4

Special Joint Committee on Canada's International Relations, 269

Speech from the Throne: 2007, 268; 2008, 246

SS *Manhattan*, 257, 263

Stabilization and Reconstruction Task Force (START), 90

Stairs, Denis, 9, 23, 28, 29

Standing Committee on Foreign Affairs and International Trade, *Canada and the Circumpolar World*, 269

Standing NATO Maritime Group 1, 241

Standing Naval Forces Atlantic (SNFL), 241

'staples approach' (Aitken), 141, 143, 155

staple trap, 141

state-building, 179

Statute of Westminster, 102

Stephenson, Mercedes, 177

Stern Review of 2006, 133

Stewart, Christine, 64, 76n2

Strait of Malacca, 259

strategic petroleum reserves (SPRs), 153; Canada's, 152; exemption, 152–3

Sudetenland crisis, 200

Suez crisis, xviii, 15, 20, 46

superpower, energy-enviro, 140, 141–2

Supreme Court, 218, 219; security certificates and, 223

surveillance equipment, 181–2

Sweden, 140; on Arctic Council, 261; relationships with Norway, 193

Szeto, Ray, 177

tacit power, 46

Taliban, 215

Tamil Tigers, 215

Tardivel, Jules-Paul, 197

tar sands, 121, 131–3, 157, 283; CO_2 emissions, 148; collapse of oil prices and, 135; ecological impact of, 147; energy return, 147; limits to, 140, 147–50; oil export to US, 148–50; use of natural gas, 154

Task Force on Community Investment, *Report of the Joint Tables*, 71

territorial defence, 175

terrorism, xiv–xv, 173, 220, 284–5; in Canada, 222, 223–4, 227; Canada's reactions to, vii, xxvii; defined in Anti-Terrorism Act, 224; financing, 215; modern, 201; public opinion, 182; speech, 225, 227

terrorism, war on: Canada's contribution to, 86, 284; role perception and, 47; security–development nexus and, 84

terrorists, 201–2; Canada as point of entry, 202, 216; Canadian lists of, 215–16; living in US legally, 203

third sector: funding of, 70; government-initiated transformations of, 69–71, 76

'three-block war' model, 84, 88, 96n6, 245–6

3D (defence, diplomacy, and development) approach, 88, 89, 92, 283; to Arctic sovereignty, 270

Tomlin, Brian, xvii, 25, 65

torture, 216, 217

To Walk Without Fear (Cameron, Lawson, Tomlin), 65

Trailbreaker pipeline (Enbridge), 149

transformation, military, 172, 177, 180–4

Transport Canada, 262

Trudeau, Pierre Elliott, 20–1, 22, 108; creation of Department of External Affairs, 103; criticism of postwar internationalism, 8; foreign policy review, 21

turbot war, 264

underdevelopment, security–development nexus, 83, 84, 95

Underhill, Frank, 199

Union of Myanmar (Burma), 28

Union of Soviet Socialist Republics (USSR), collapse of, vi, 13, 237; *see also* Russia

United Kingdom: contribution to UN peacekeeping, 242; defence spending, 237; *see also* Britain

United Nations Act (Canada), 215

United Nations Assistance Mission in Rwanda (UNAMIR), 170

United Nations Convention on the Law of the Sea (UNCLOS), 251, 252, 256, 258, 263, 264, 267

United Nations' Protection Force (UNPROFOR), 179, 239

United Nations Security Council, 12, 13, 174; Resolution 1088, 240; Resolution 1373, 213, 215; Resolution 1624, 225; veto power on, 25–6

United Nations (UN), xiii, 8; anti-terrorism efforts, 227; Canada's contribution to, v, 4, 7, 8–9, 13, 39; Committee against Torture, 216; CIDA and, 74; crisis response missions, 174; Declaration on the Rights of Indigenous Peoples, 261; Framework

Convention on Climate, 121; High Commission for Refugees, 202; interest in NATO, 13; peacekeeping missions, xviii, 12, 13, 15, 242; 'responsibility to protect', 37; Special Session on Africa, 9

United States (US): 2008 presidential election, 133; in Afghanistan, 245; armed forces, 172; border security, 199, 205; Congressional Committee on Energy and Commerce, 149; contribution to UN peacekeeping, 242; defence spending, 236; effect on Canadian efforts, 36; Energy Independence and Security Act (2007), 148; as energy superpower, 143, 145–6; interoperability with Canadian military, 184; Joint Forces Command, 194; Mexico and, 193, 197; military in Arctic, 257; oil exports, 151; oil production, 157n9; Patriot Act, 213, 216; policy in Arctic, 255, 259–60; position on international straits, 259; possibility of armed conflict with Canada, 192; in security community, 189, 190; societal security and, 194–5, 197; as superpower, 45; see also Canada–US relations

unmanned aerial vehicles, 181–2, 232

UNOSOM, 170, 179

UN Protected Areas (UNPAS), in Croatia, 239

urban consumption, 125–6

US–Mexico border: Canadianization of, 195; militarization of, 193–4; violence and, 194

values, Canadian, 14, 47, 107–8, 169

vertical competition, 195

Vietnam, 15

Vietnam War, Canada's involvement in, vi

Villa, Poncho, 193

Voluntary Sector Initiative, 70–1

Voluntary Sector Roundtable, 70

von Bredow, Wilfried, xxvi

Waisová, Šárka, xxiv

Waldner, Benita Ferrero, 113

Wapner, Paul, 66

war and warfare: asymmetric, 179, 284; civil, 173; democratization and, 173; fighting among the people, 181; internal, 173; new, 173, 174

Warkentin, Craig, 65

War Measures Act, 212

War of the League of Augsburg, 207n10

War on Terror, xxiv, 83, 85, 95, 125; Canada's contribution to, 86, 284; role perception and, 47; security–development nexus and, 84

Washington Consensus, 11

Waxman, Harry, 148, 149, 158n12

Weld, William, 189

Welsh, Jennifer, 17, 22, 35, 44–5

Wendt, Alexander, 272n1

Western Accord, 153

Western societies, 195–6; civil-military relations in, 175–6

Westphalian state system, xiv, 113

Weyerhaeuser, 130

White Paper: 1993, 11; 1994, 242; 1995, 71; 1999, 71

Wight, Martin, 7

Williams, Jody, 23, 31n2, 65

Woerner, Manfred, 247n6

women, in armed forces, 175

World Bank, 84; arrangement with CIDA, 74

World Trade Organization (WTO), vi, 12

World War II, v, 20

Wounded, 183

Wrong, Hume, 234

Yugoslavia, NATO in, 238–9

Yugoslav National Army (JNA), 238

zone of peace: Arctic, 265; European, 205; North American, xxvi–xxvii, 189–90, 191, 193, 194, 201, 204, 205

Zyla, Ben, xxvii, 284